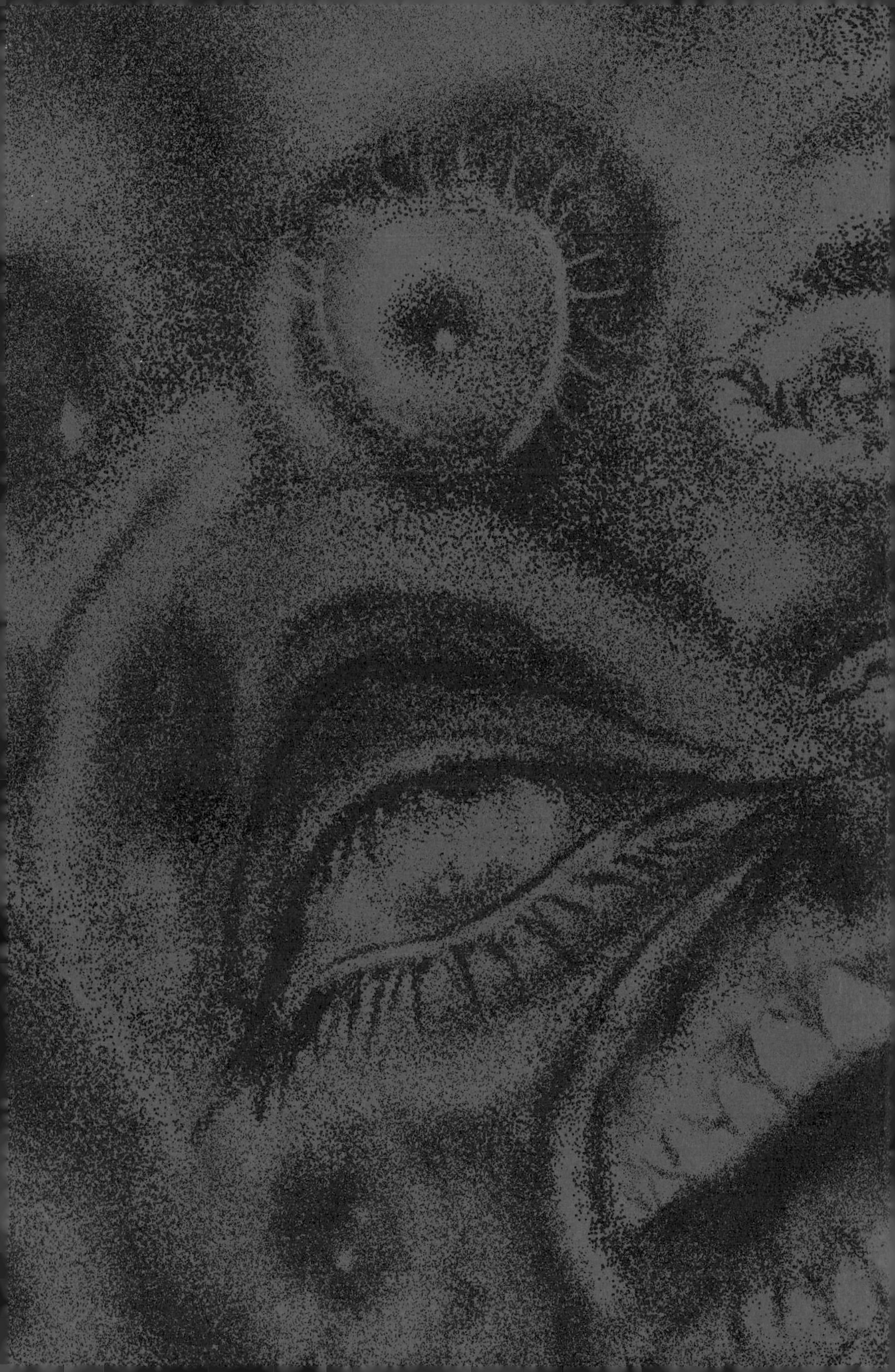

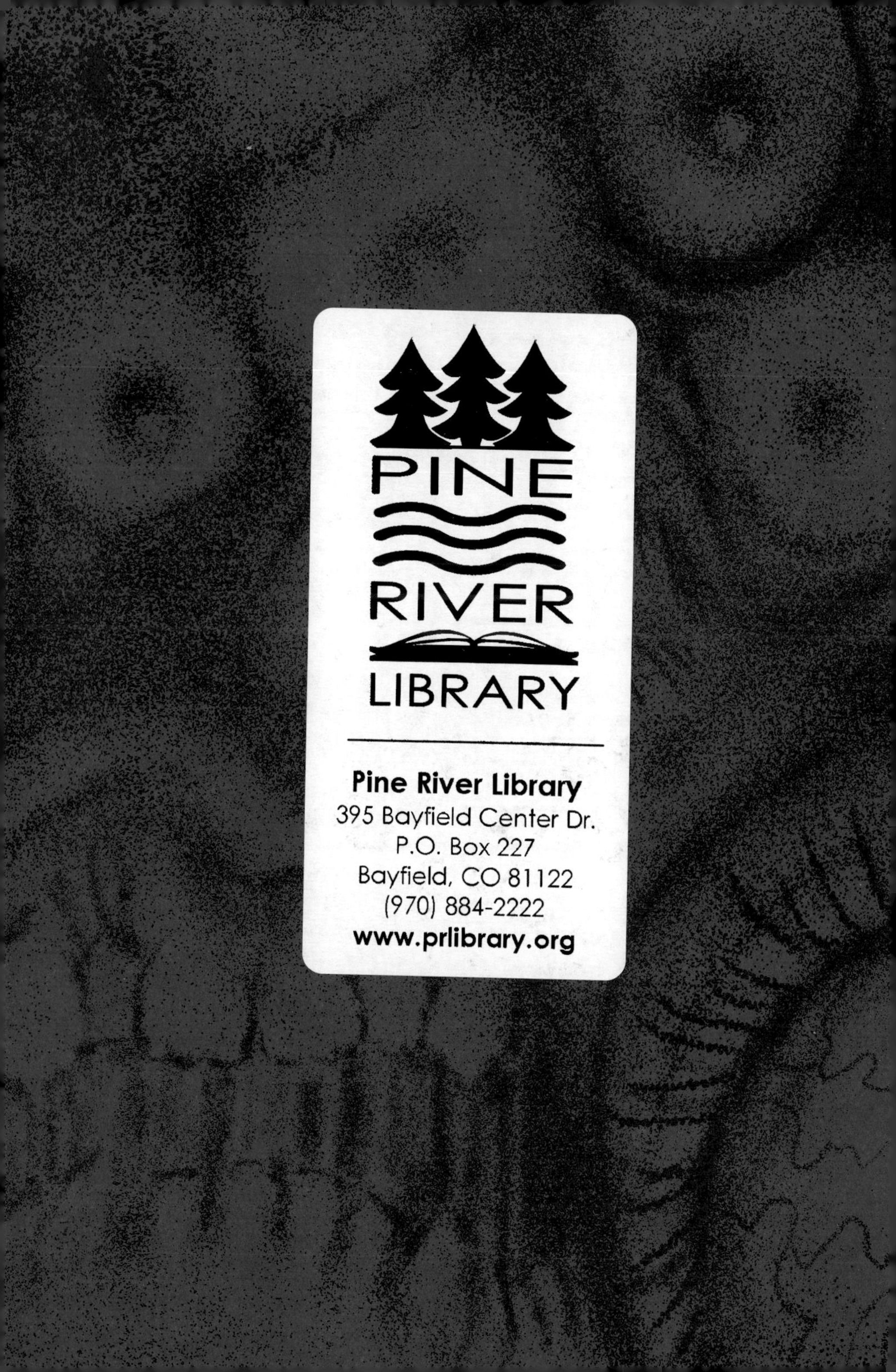

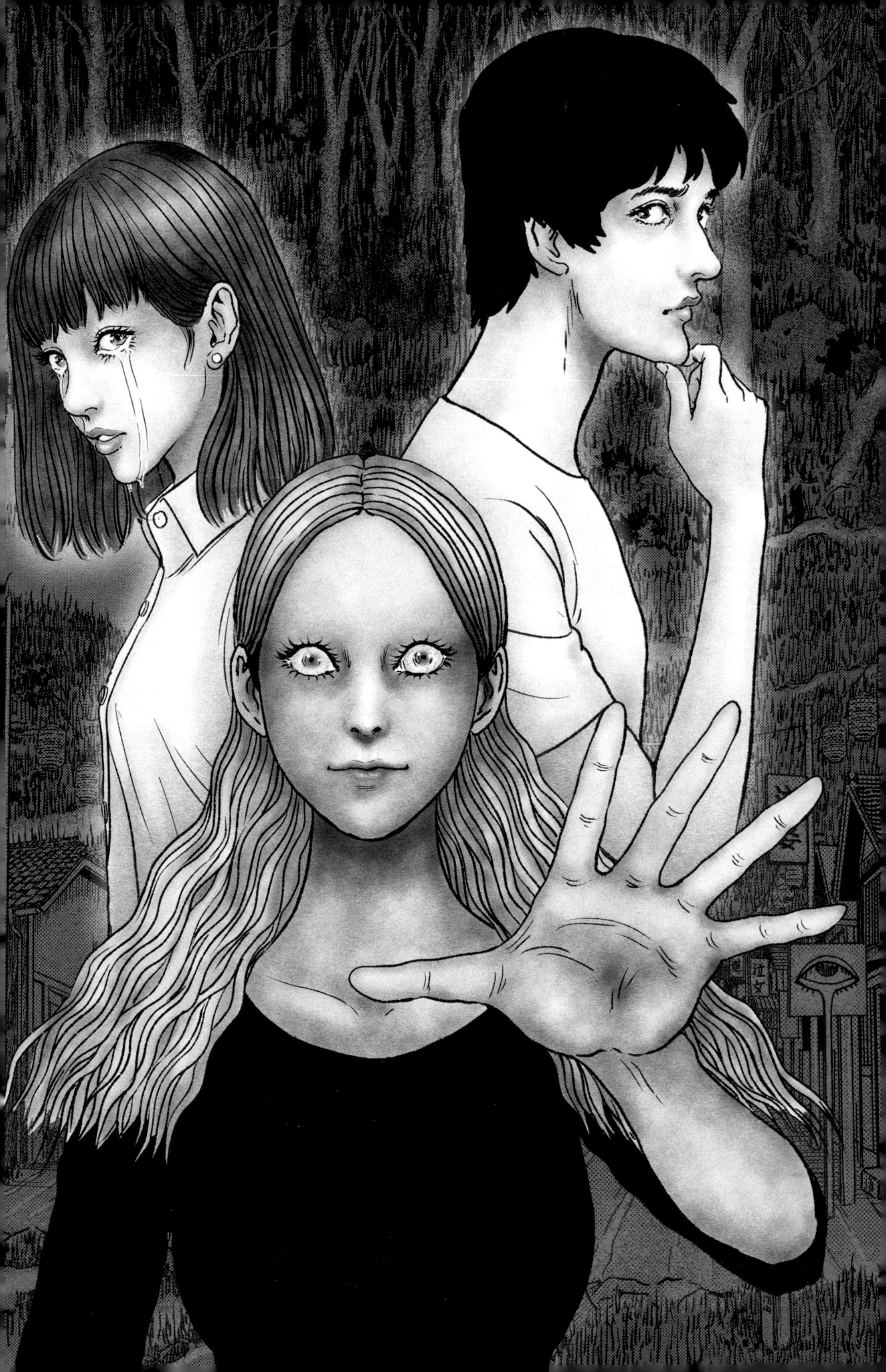
泣女

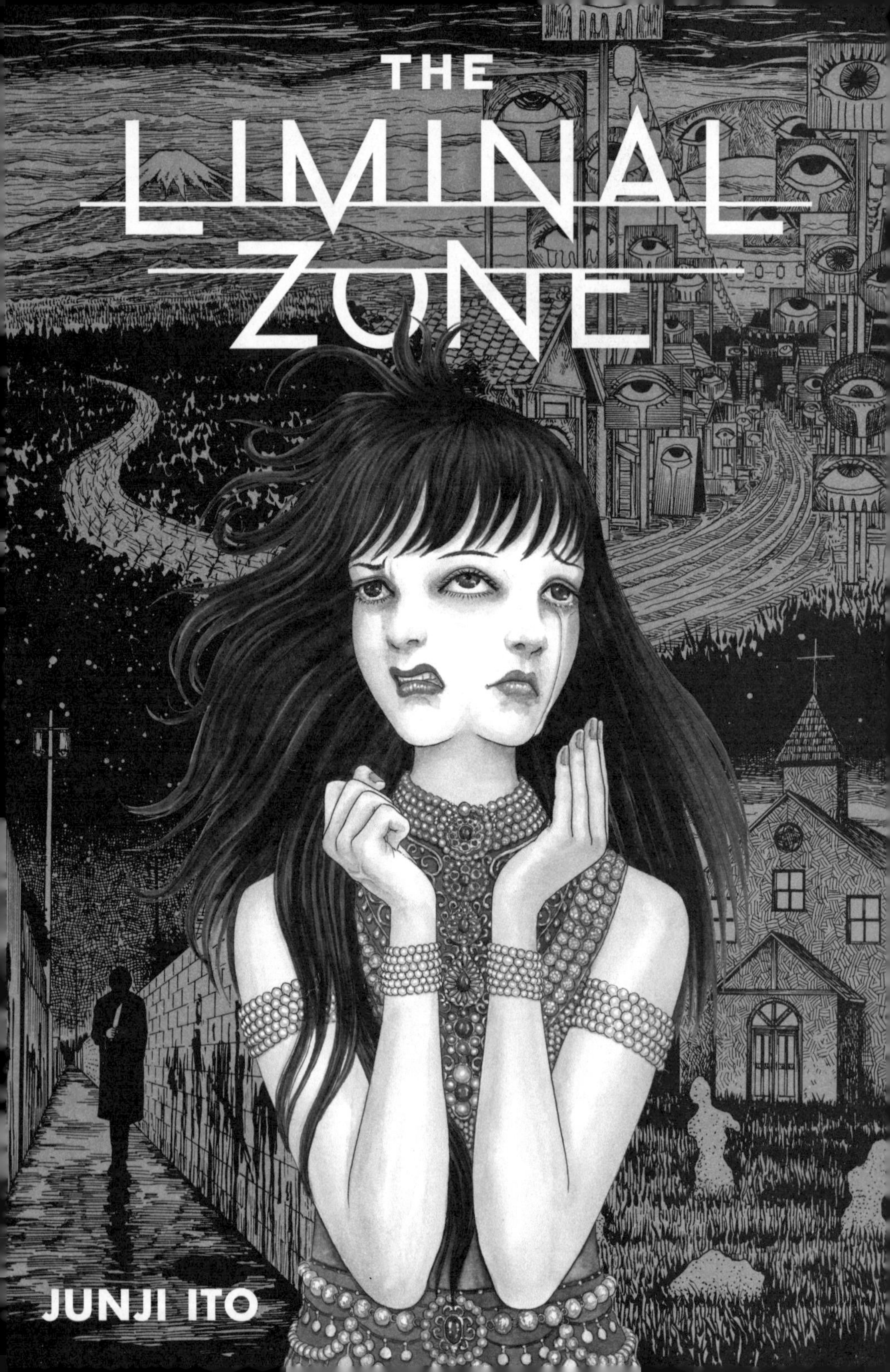
THE
LIMINAL
ZONE
JUNJI ITO

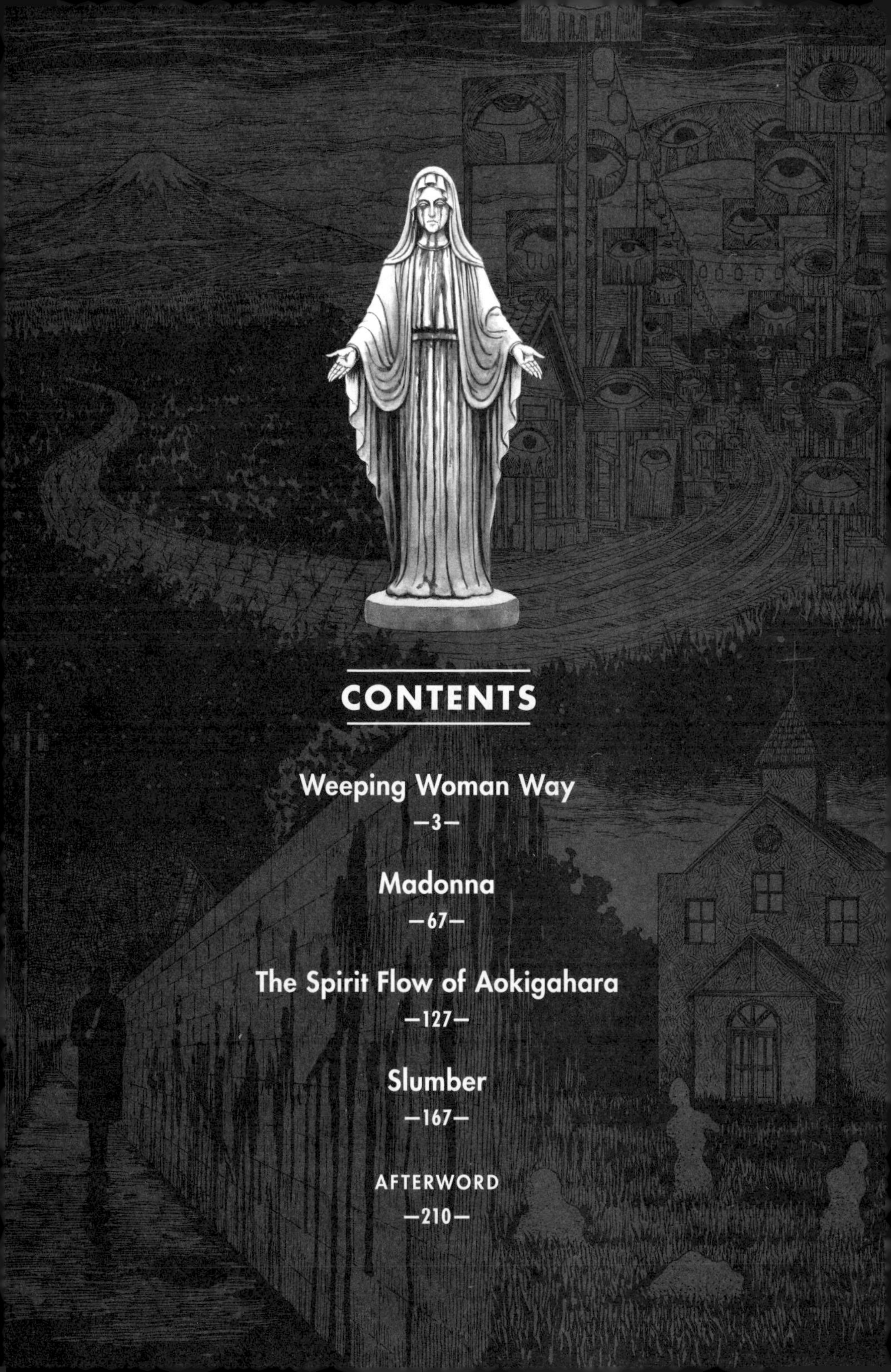

CONTENTS

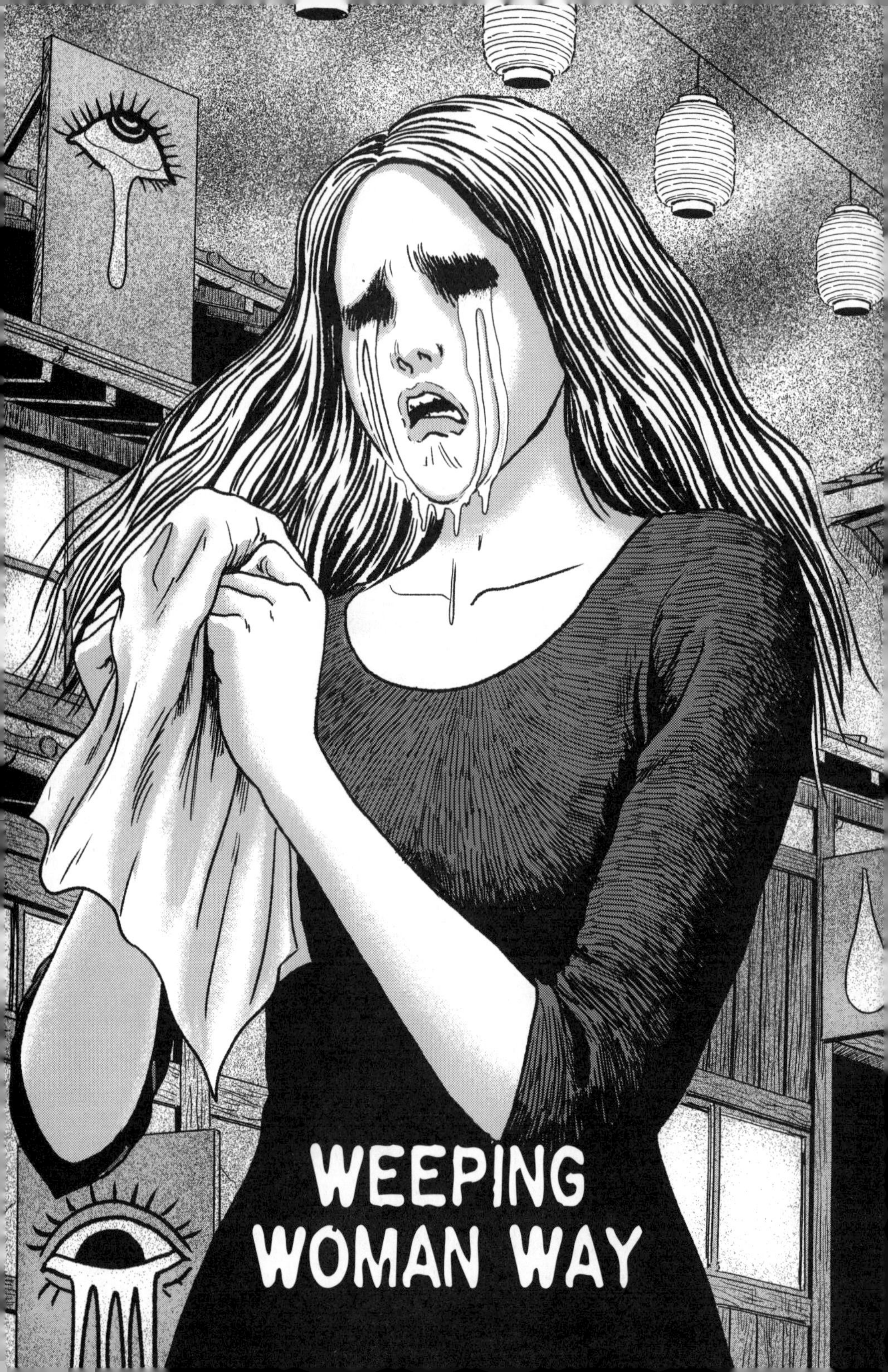
WEEPING
WOMAN WAY

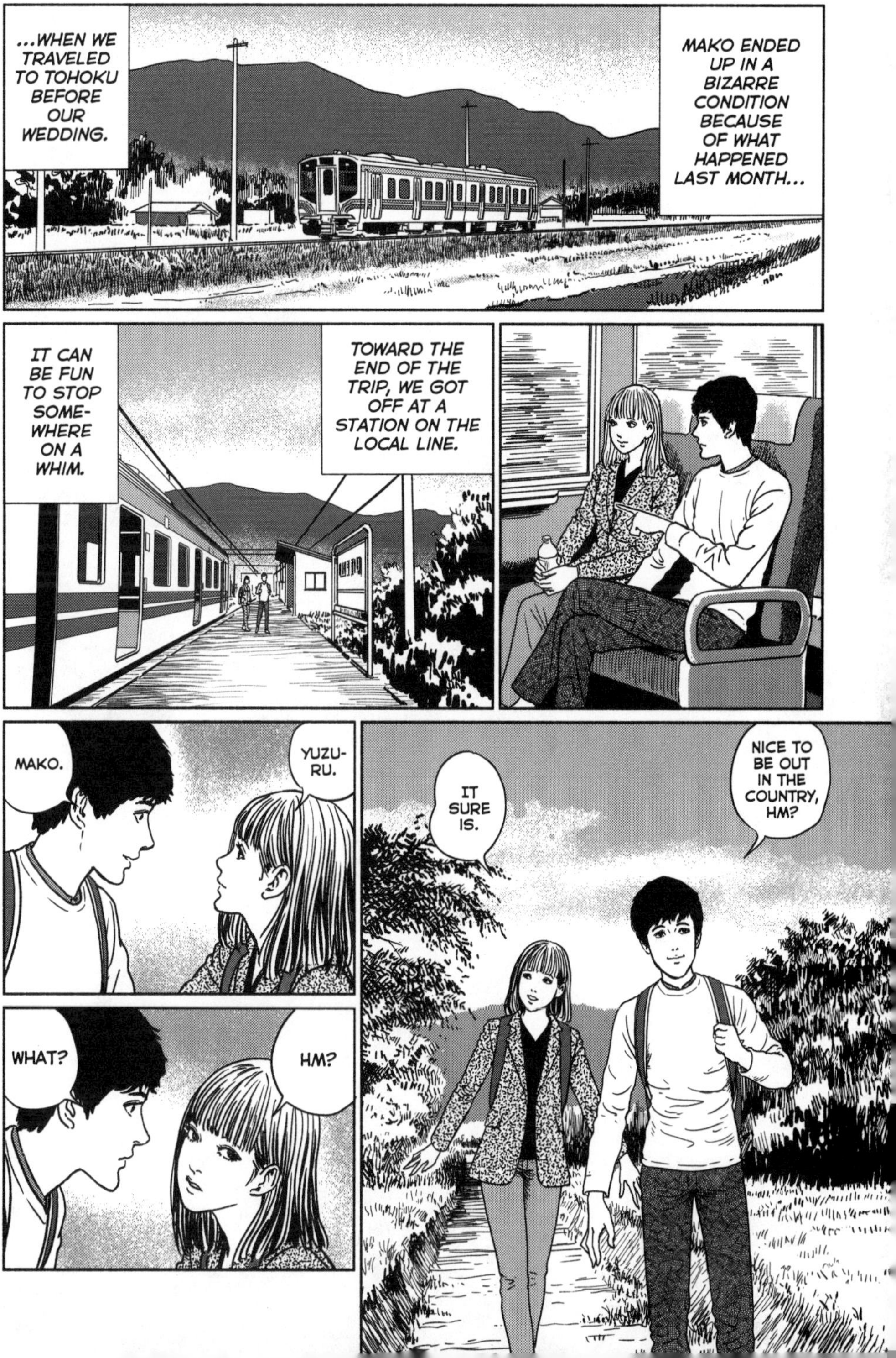
MAKO ENDED UP IN A BIZARRE CONDITION BECAUSE OF WHAT HAPPENED LAST MONTH...
...WHEN WE TRAVELED TO TOHOKU BEFORE OUR WEDDING.
TOWARD THE END OF THE TRIP, WE GOT OFF AT A STATION ON THE LOCAL LINE.
IT CAN BE FUN TO STOP SOME-WHERE ON A WHIM.
NICE TO BE OUT IN THE COUNTRY, HM?
IT SURE IS.
YUZU-RU.
MAKO.
HM?
WHAT?

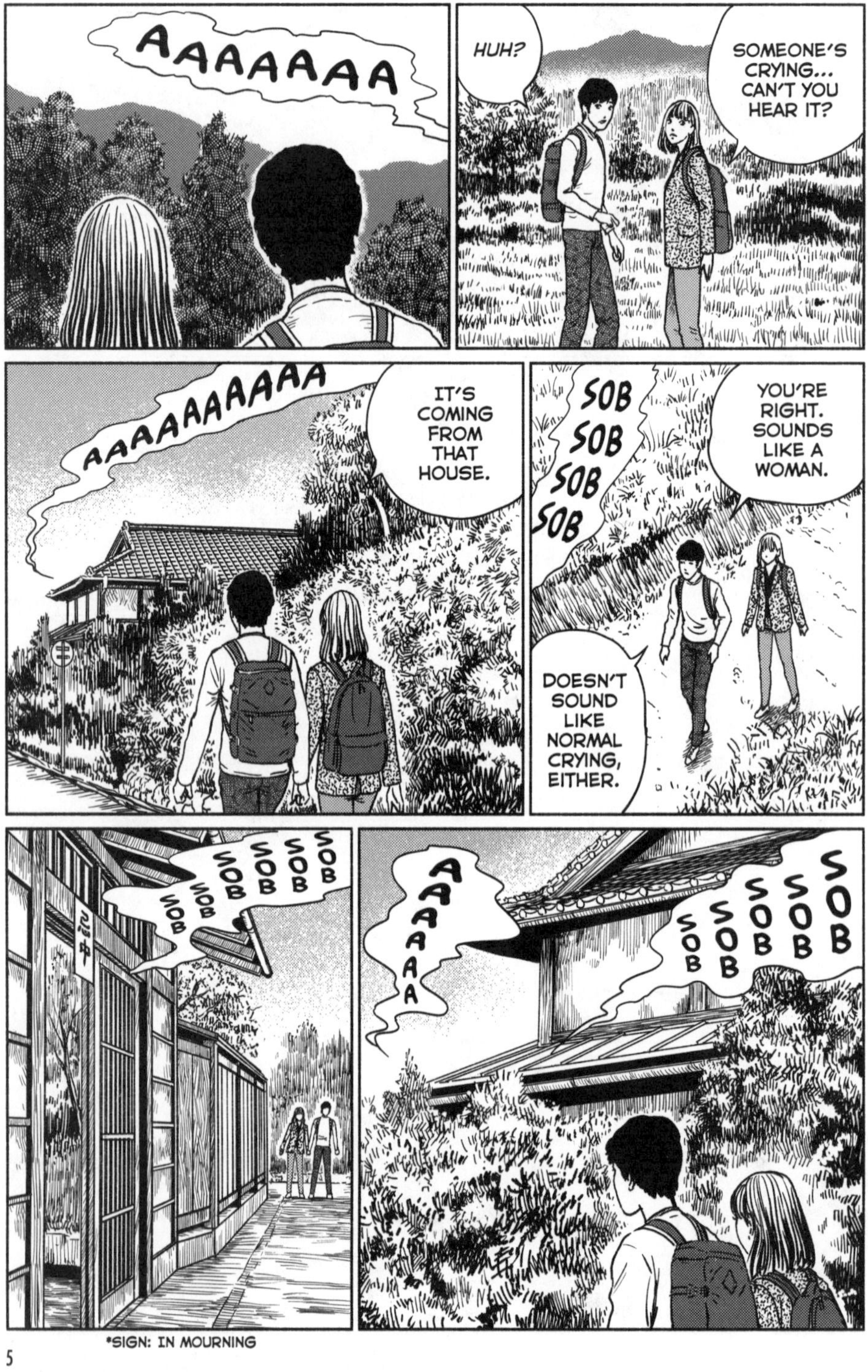
SOMEONE'S CRYING... CAN'T YOU HEAR IT?
HUH?
AAAAAAA
YOU'RE RIGHT. SOUNDS LIKE A WOMAN.
SOB SOB SOB SOB
DOESN'T SOUND LIKE NORMAL CRYING, EITHER.
IT'S COMING FROM THAT HOUSE.
AAAAAAAAAAA
SOB SOB SOB SOB SOB
AAAAAA
SOB SOB SOB SOB SOB SOB

*SIGN: IN MOURNING

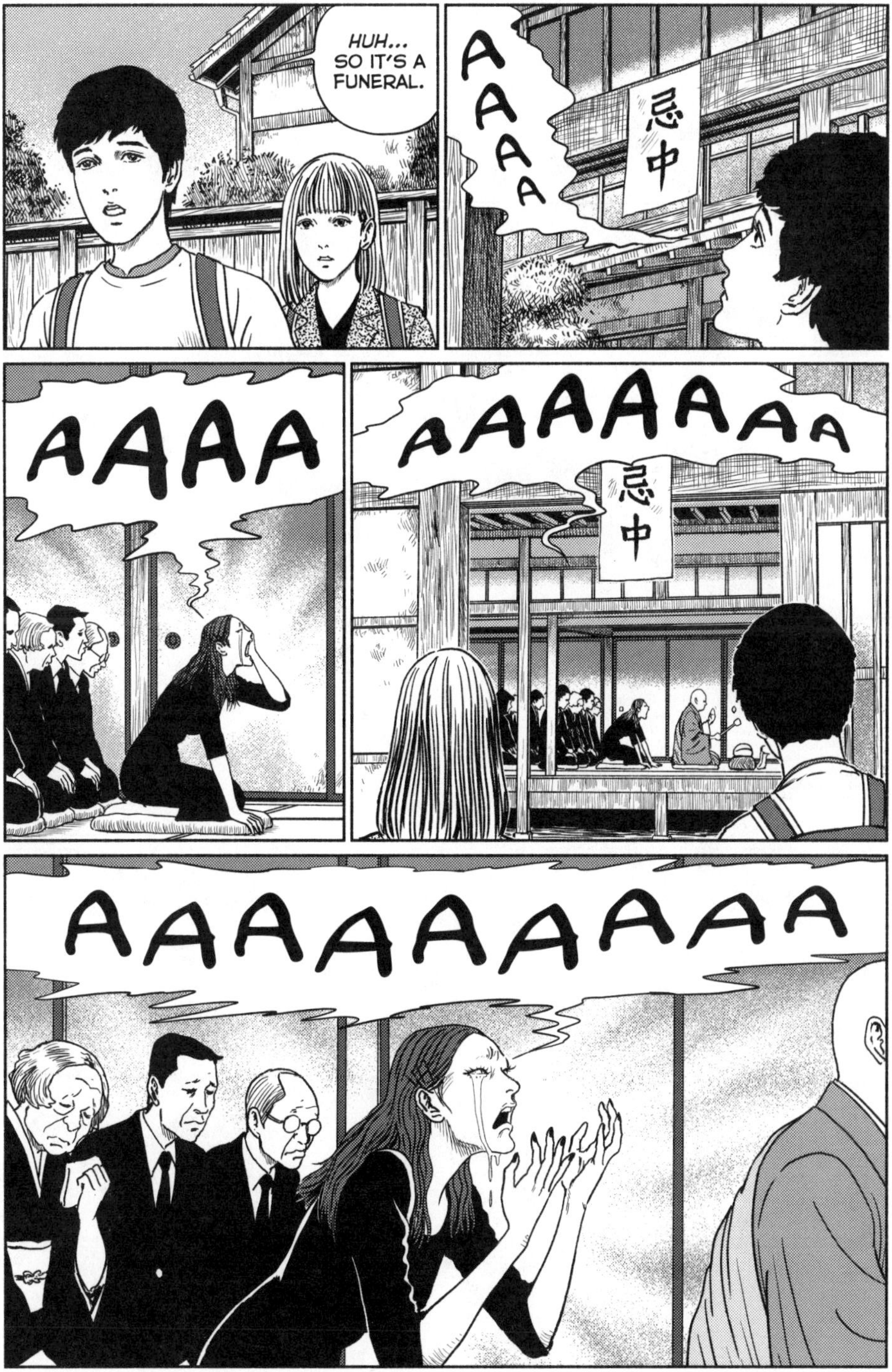
AAAA
忌中
HUH... SO IT'S A FUNERAL.
AAAAAAAA
忌中
AAAA
AAAAAAAAA

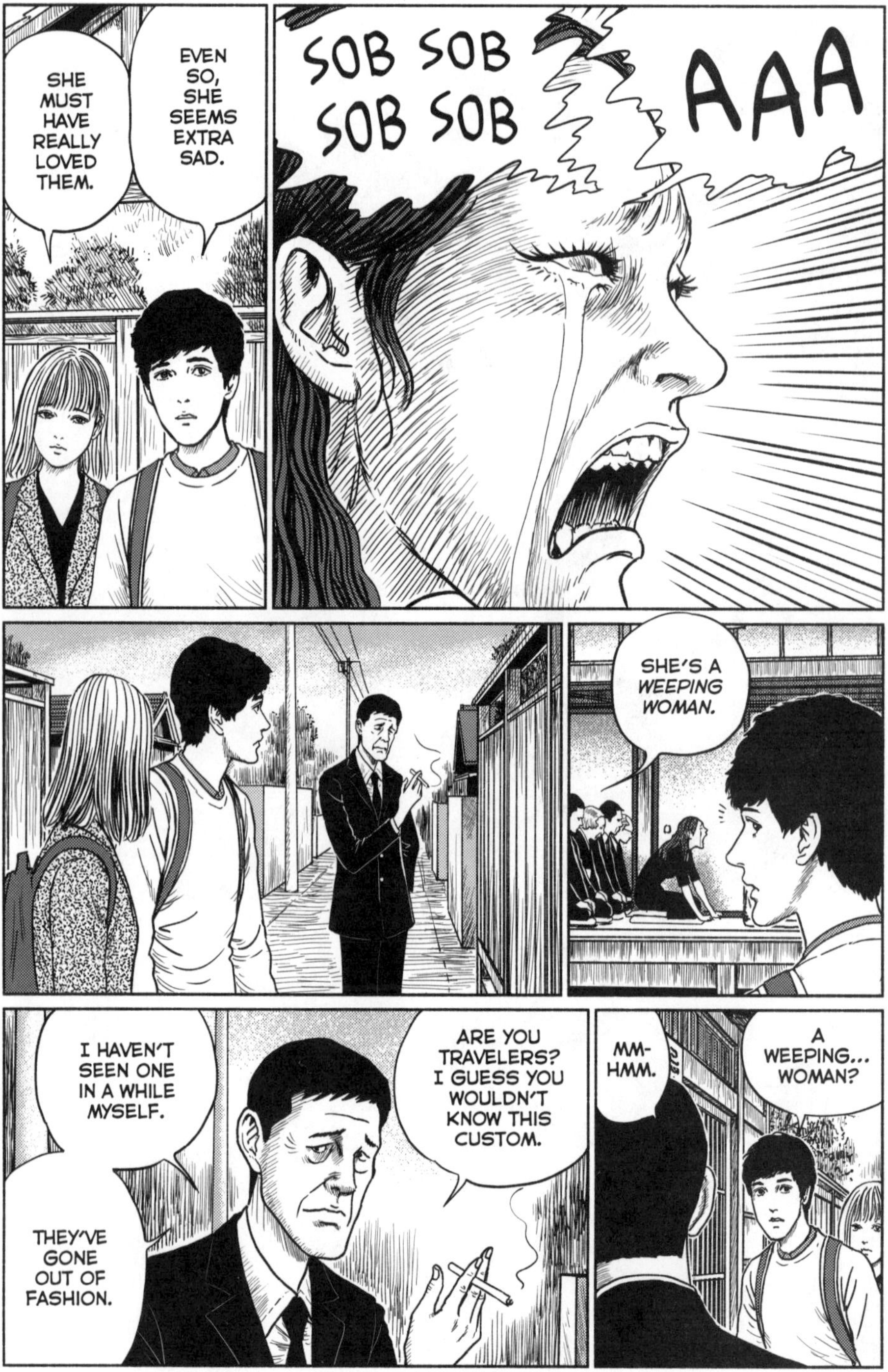
AAA
SOB SOB SOB SOB
EVEN SO, SHE SEEMS EXTRA SAD.
SHE MUST HAVE REALLY LOVED THEM.
SHE'S A WEEPING WOMAN.
A WEEPING... WOMAN?
MM-HMM.
ARE YOU TRAVELERS? I GUESS YOU WOULDN'T KNOW THIS CUSTOM.
I HAVEN'T SEEN ONE IN A WHILE MYSELF.
THEY'VE GONE OUT OF FASHION.

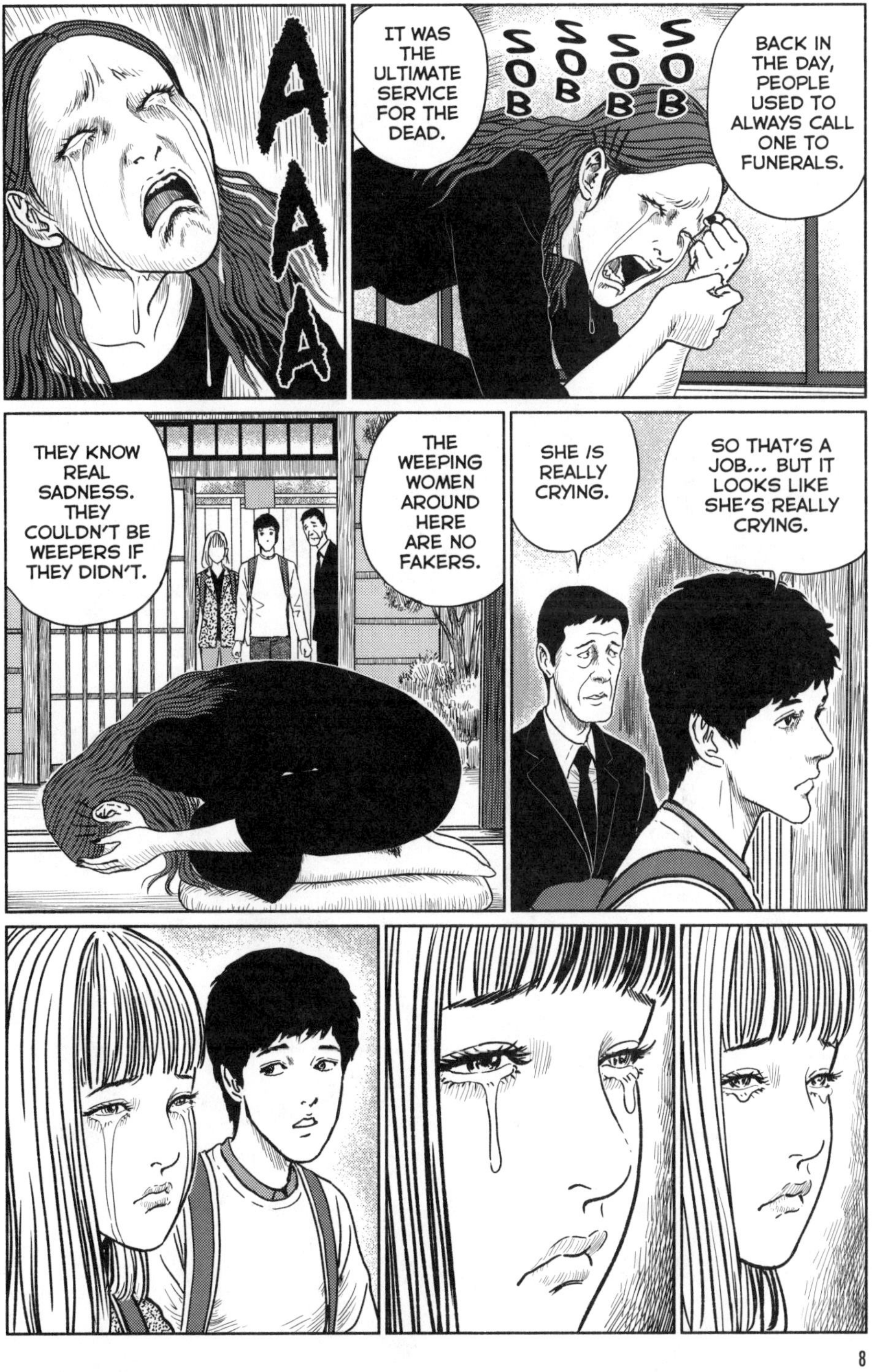
BACK IN THE DAY, PEOPLE USED TO ALWAYS CALL ONE TO FUNERALS.
SOB SOB SOB SOB
IT WAS THE ULTIMATE SERVICE FOR THE DEAD.
AAA
SO THAT'S A JOB... BUT IT LOOKS LIKE SHE'S REALLY CRYING.
SHE *IS* REALLY CRYING.
THE WEEPING WOMEN AROUND HERE ARE NO FAKERS.
THEY KNOW REAL SADNESS. THEY COULDN'T BE WEEPERS IF THEY DIDN'T.

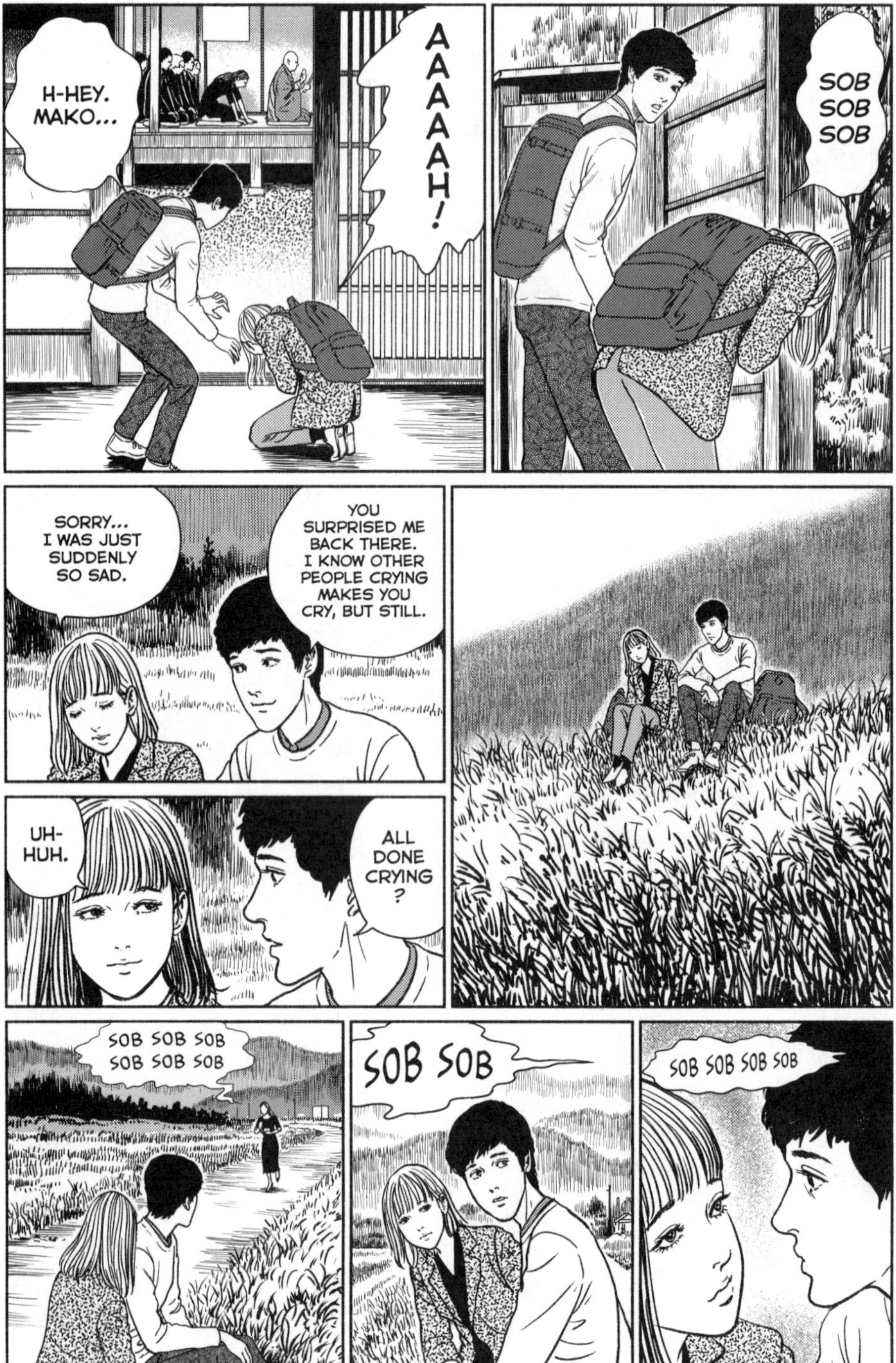
SOB SOB SOB
AAAAAH!
H-HEY. MAKO...
YOU SURPRISED ME BACK THERE. I KNOW OTHER PEOPLE CRYING MAKES YOU CRY, BUT STILL.
SORRY... I WAS JUST SUDDENLY SO SAD.
ALL DONE CRYING?
UH-HUH.
SOB SOB SOB SOB
SOB SOB
SOB SOB SOB SOB SOB SOB

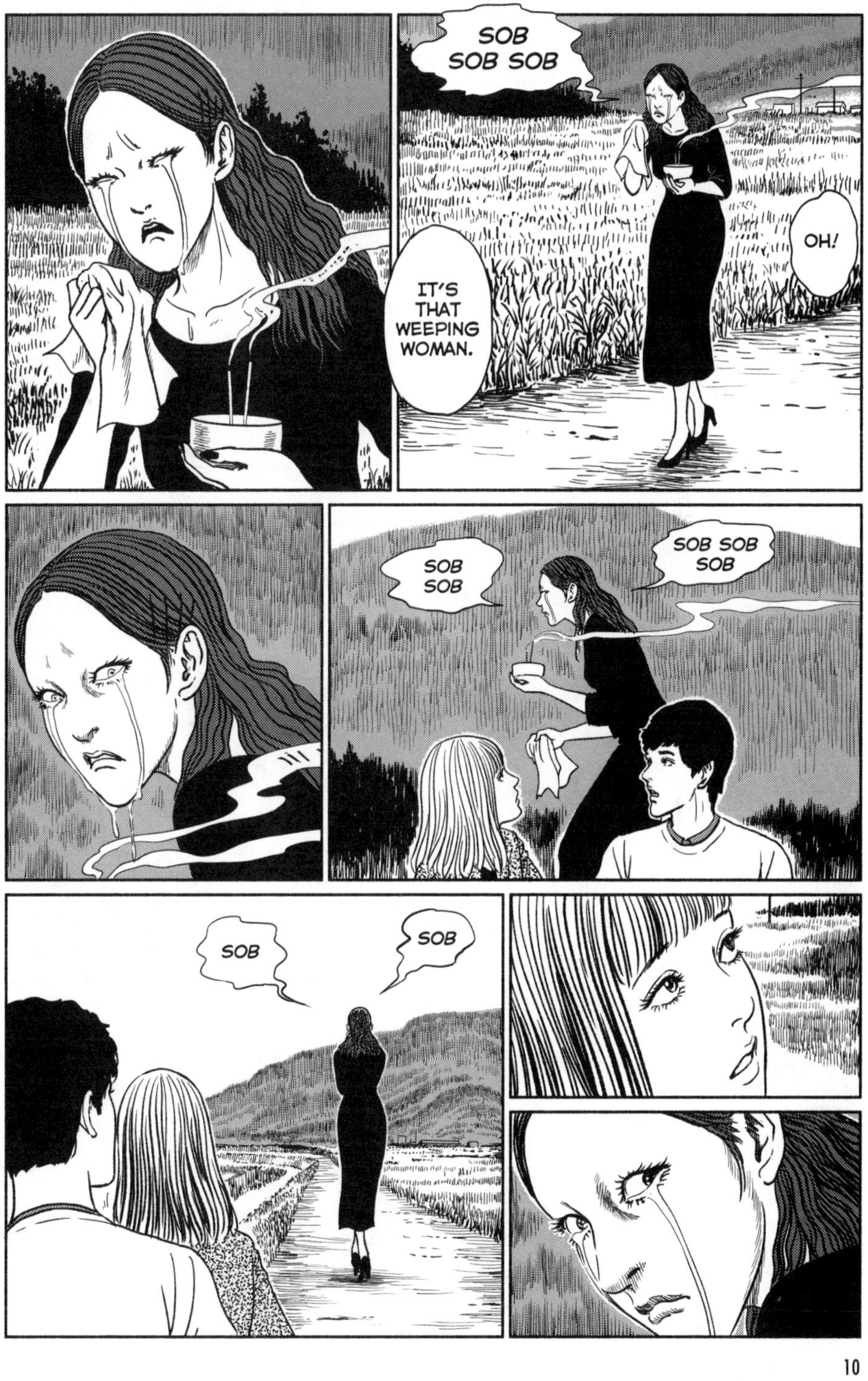
SOB
SOB SOB
OH!
IT'S THAT WEEPING WOMAN.
SOB SOB SOB
SOB SOB
SOB
SOB

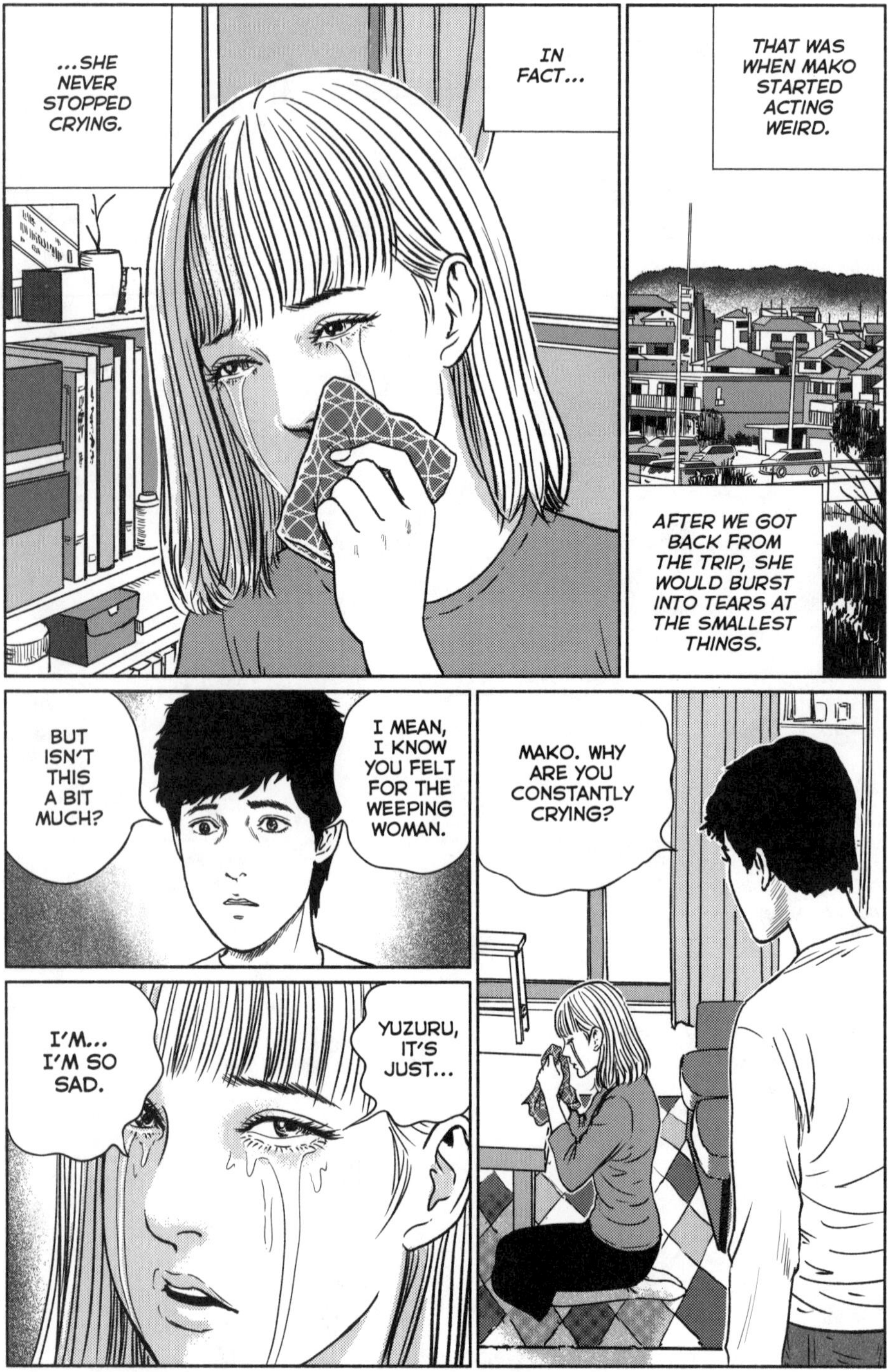
THAT WAS WHEN MAKO STARTED ACTING WEIRD.
AFTER WE GOT BACK FROM THE TRIP, SHE WOULD BURST INTO TEARS AT THE SMALLEST THINGS.
IN FACT...
...SHE NEVER STOPPED CRYING.
MAKO. WHY ARE YOU CONSTANTLY CRYING?
I MEAN, I KNOW YOU FELT FOR THE WEEPING WOMAN.
BUT ISN'T THIS A BIT MUCH?
YUZURU, IT'S JUST...
I'M... I'M SO SAD.

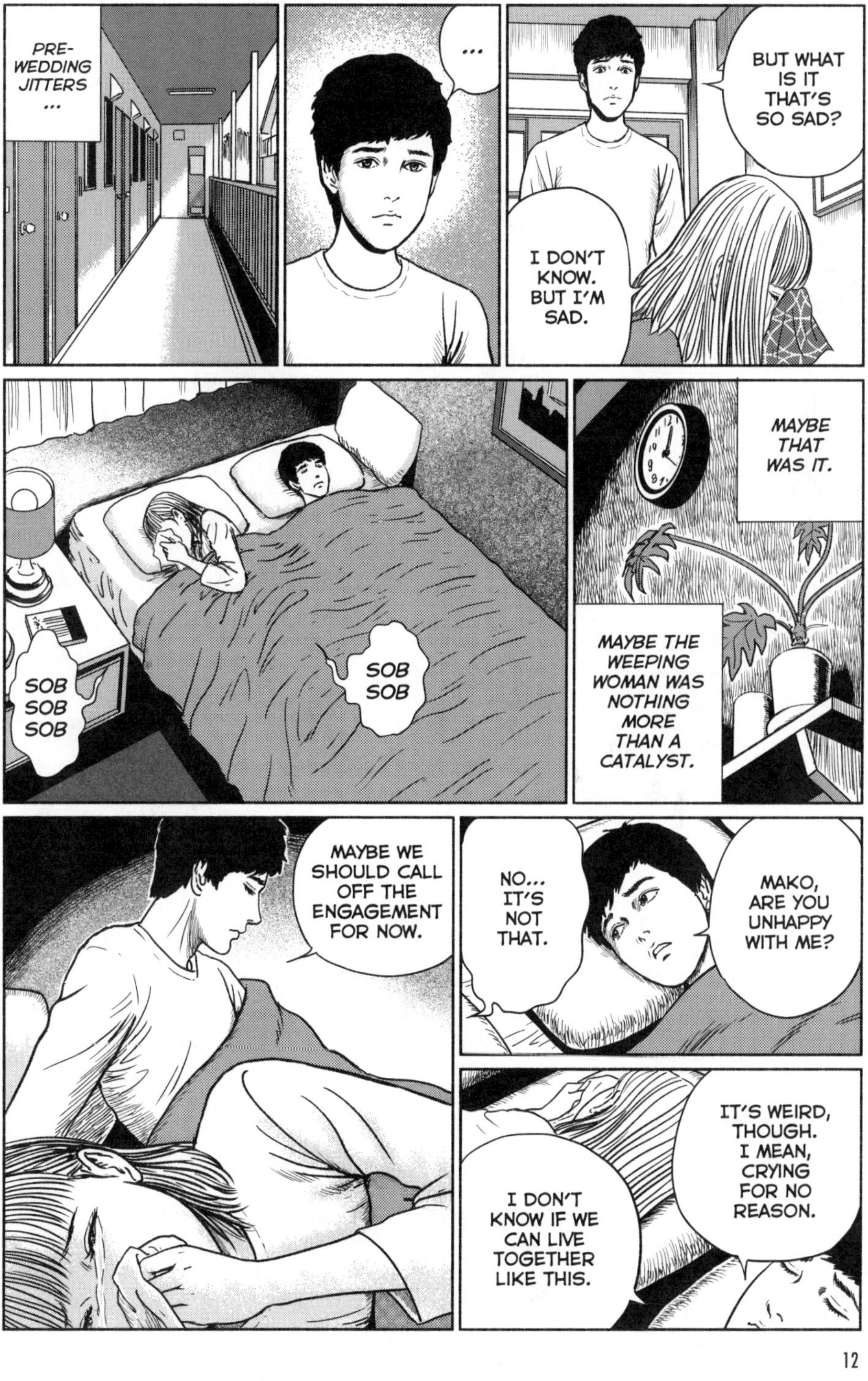
BUT WHAT IS IT THAT'S SO SAD?
I DON'T KNOW. BUT I'M SAD.
...
PRE-WEDDING JITTERS ...
MAYBE THAT WAS IT.
MAYBE THE WEEPING WOMAN WAS NOTHING MORE THAN A CATALYST.
SOB SOB
SOB SOB SOB
MAKO, ARE YOU UNHAPPY WITH ME?
NO... IT'S NOT THAT.
IT'S WEIRD, THOUGH. I MEAN, CRYING FOR NO REASON.
I DON'T KNOW IF WE CAN LIVE TOGETHER LIKE THIS.
MAYBE WE SHOULD CALL OFF THE ENGAGEMENT FOR NOW.

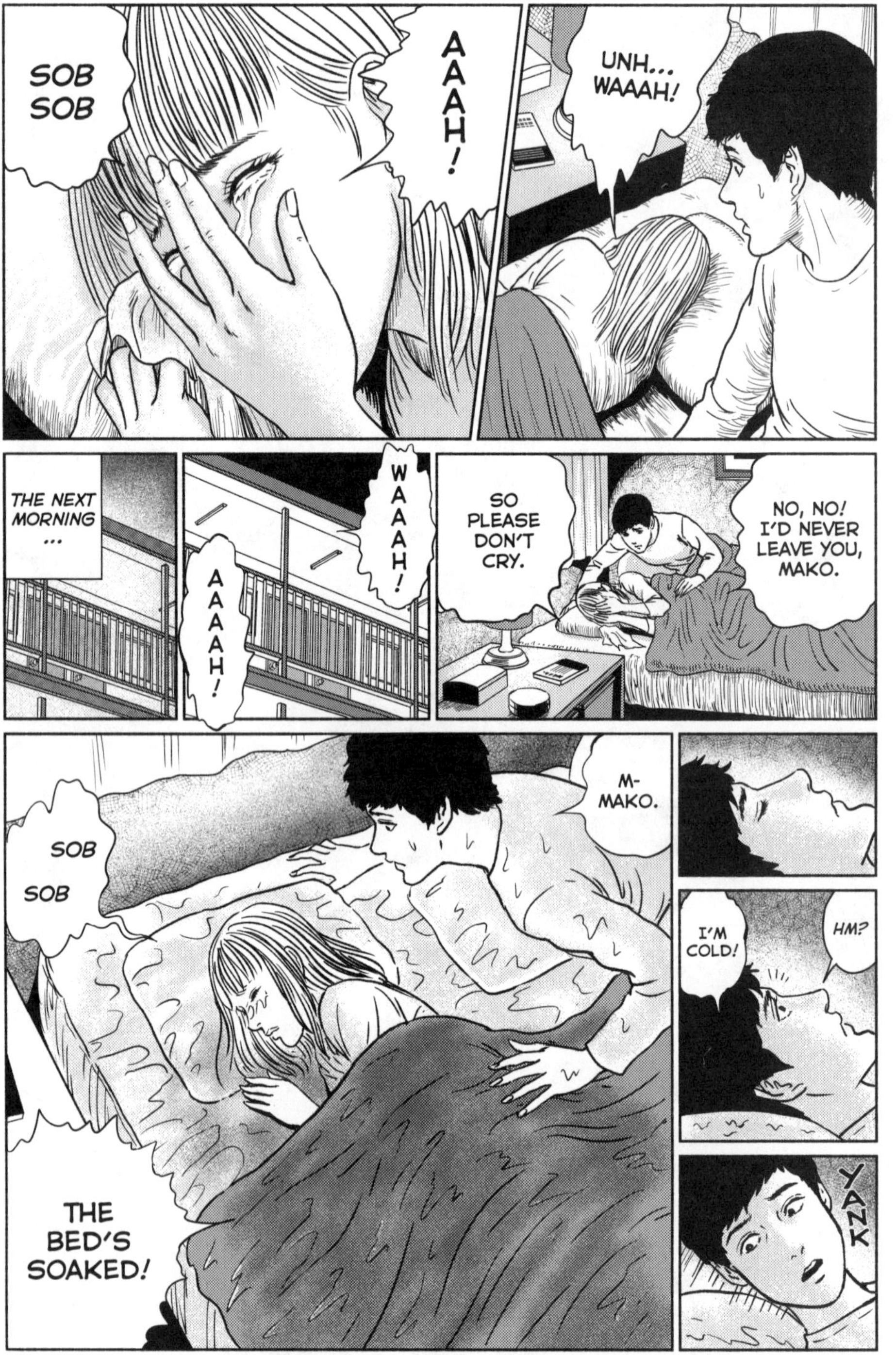
UNH... WAAAH!
AAAH!
SOB SOB
NO, NO! I'D NEVER LEAVE YOU, MAKO.
SO PLEASE DON'T CRY.
WAAAH!
AAAAH!
THE NEXT MORNING ...
HM?
I'M COLD!
YANK
M-MAKO.
SOB SOB
THE BED'S SOAKED!

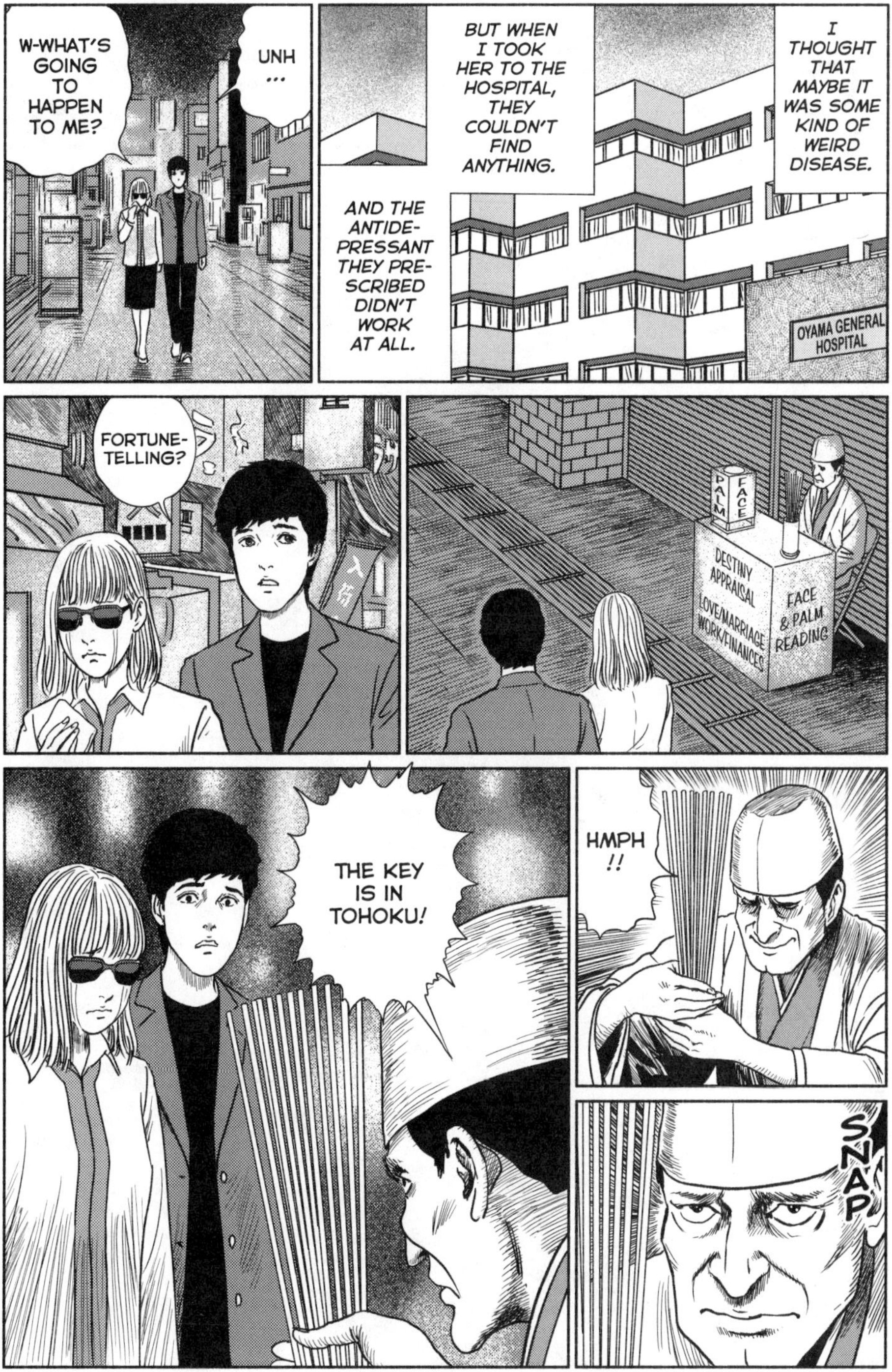
I THOUGHT THAT MAYBE IT WAS SOME KIND OF WEIRD DISEASE.
BUT WHEN I TOOK HER TO THE HOSPITAL, THEY COULDN'T FIND ANYTHING.
AND THE ANTIDE-PRESSANT THEY PRE-SCRIBED DIDN'T WORK AT ALL.
OYAMA GENERAL HOSPITAL
UNH ...
W-WHAT'S GOING TO HAPPEN TO ME?
PALM
FACE
DESTINY APPRAISAL
LOVE/MARRIAGE WORK/FINANCES
FACE & PALM READING
FORTUNE-TELLING?
HMPH !!
SNAP
THE KEY IS IN TOHOKU!

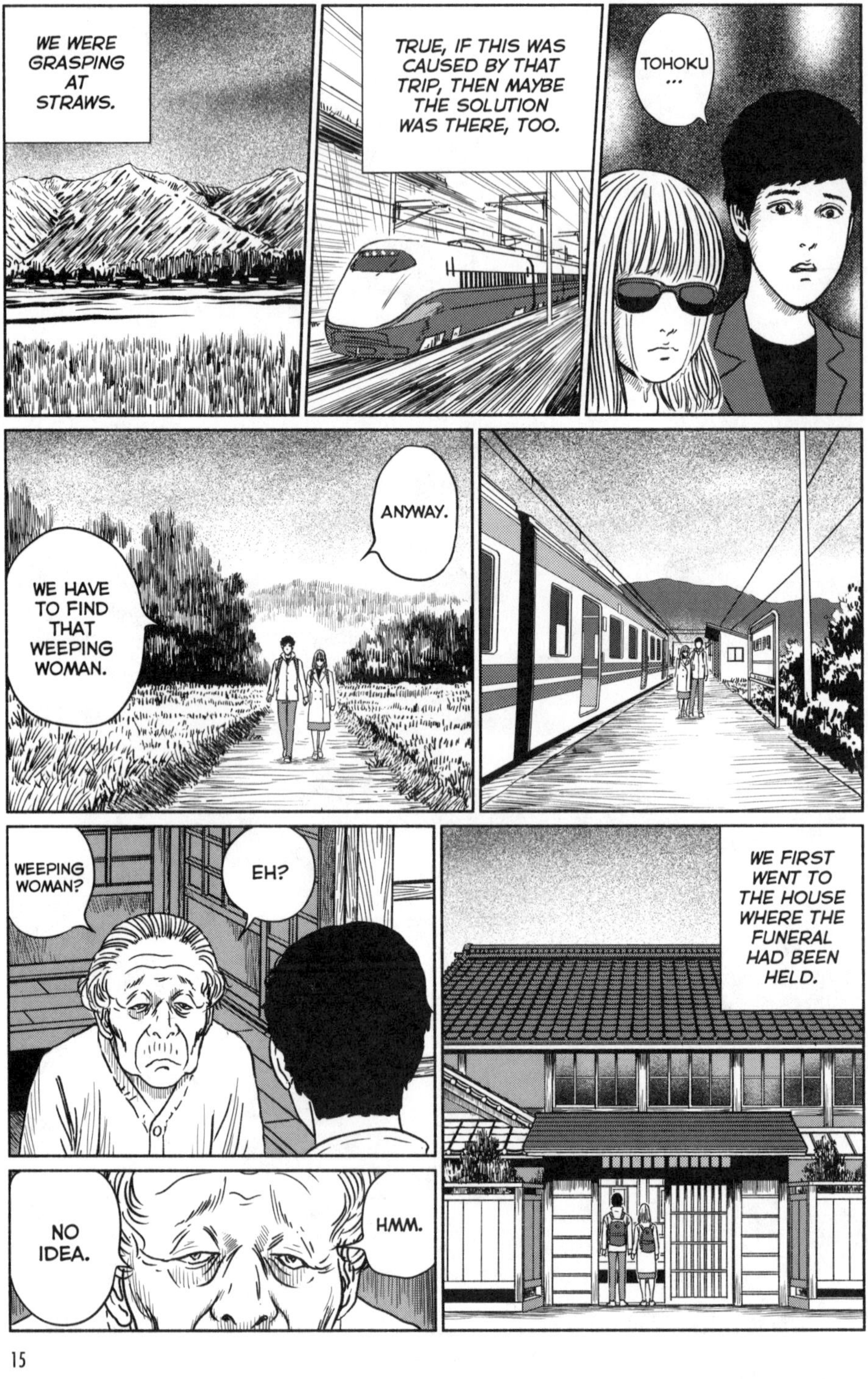
TOHOKU ...
TRUE, IF THIS WAS CAUSED BY THAT TRIP, THEN MAYBE THE SOLUTION WAS THERE, TOO.
WE WERE GRASPING AT STRAWS.
ANYWAY.
WE HAVE TO FIND THAT WEEPING WOMAN.
WE FIRST WENT TO THE HOUSE WHERE THE FUNERAL HAD BEEN HELD.
EH?
WEEPING WOMAN?
HMM.
NO IDEA.

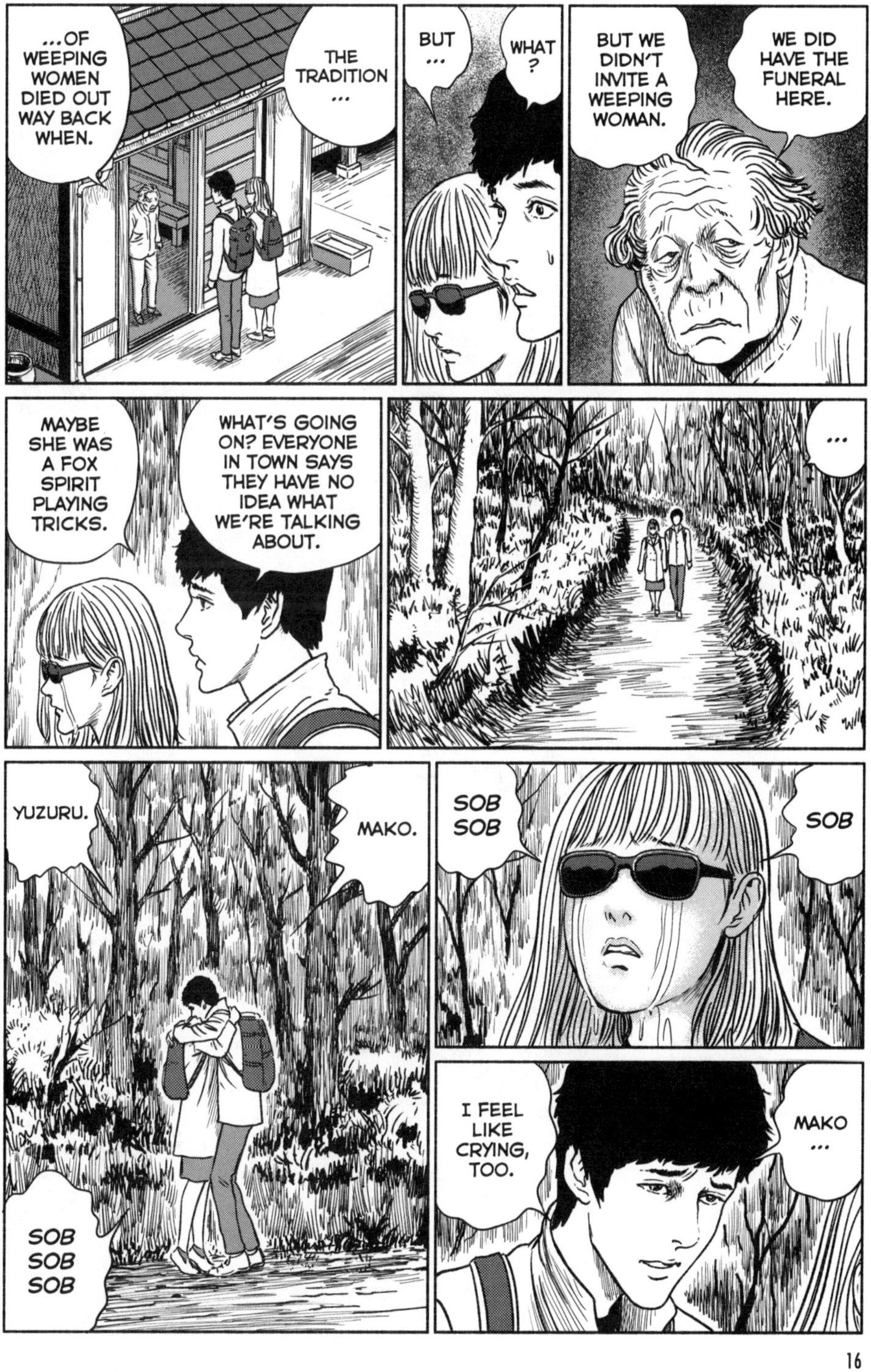
WE DID HAVE THE FUNERAL HERE.
BUT WE DIDN'T INVITE A WEEPING WOMAN.
WHAT?
BUT ...
THE TRADITION ...
...OF WEEPING WOMEN DIED OUT WAY BACK WHEN.
...
WHAT'S GOING ON? EVERYONE IN TOWN SAYS THEY HAVE NO IDEA WHAT WE'RE TALKING ABOUT.
MAYBE SHE WAS A FOX SPIRIT PLAYING TRICKS.
SOB
SOB SOB
MAKO ...
I FEEL LIKE CRYING, TOO.
MAKO.
YUZURU.
SOB SOB SOB

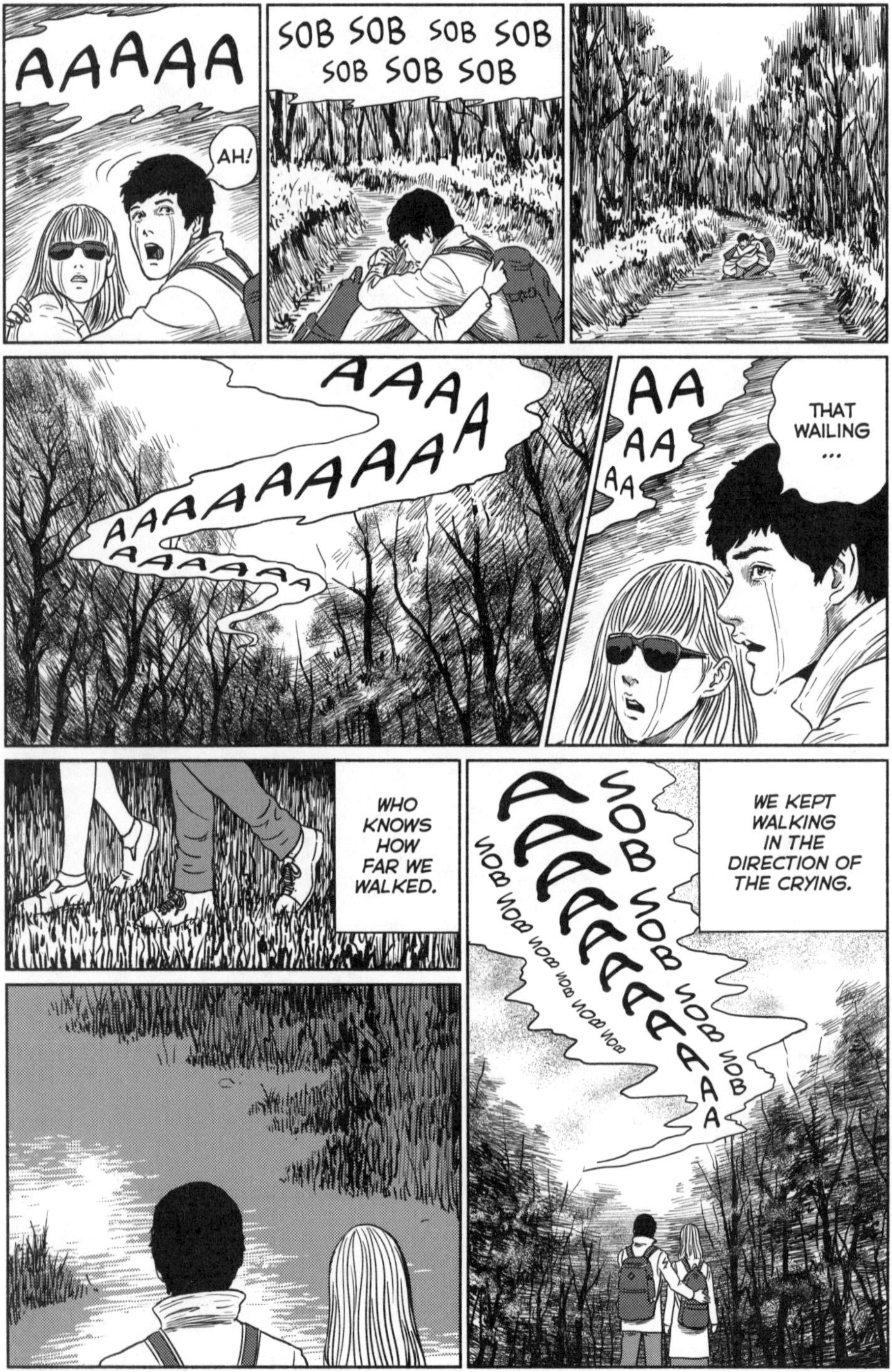
SOB SOB SOB SOB
SOB SOB SOB
AAAAA
AH!
AA
AA
AA
THAT WAILING ...
AAAAAAAAAAAAA
AAAAAAA
SOB SOB SOB SOB SOB
AAAAAAAAAAAAA
WE KEPT WALKING IN THE DIRECTION OF THE CRYING.
WHO KNOWS HOW FAR WE WALKED.

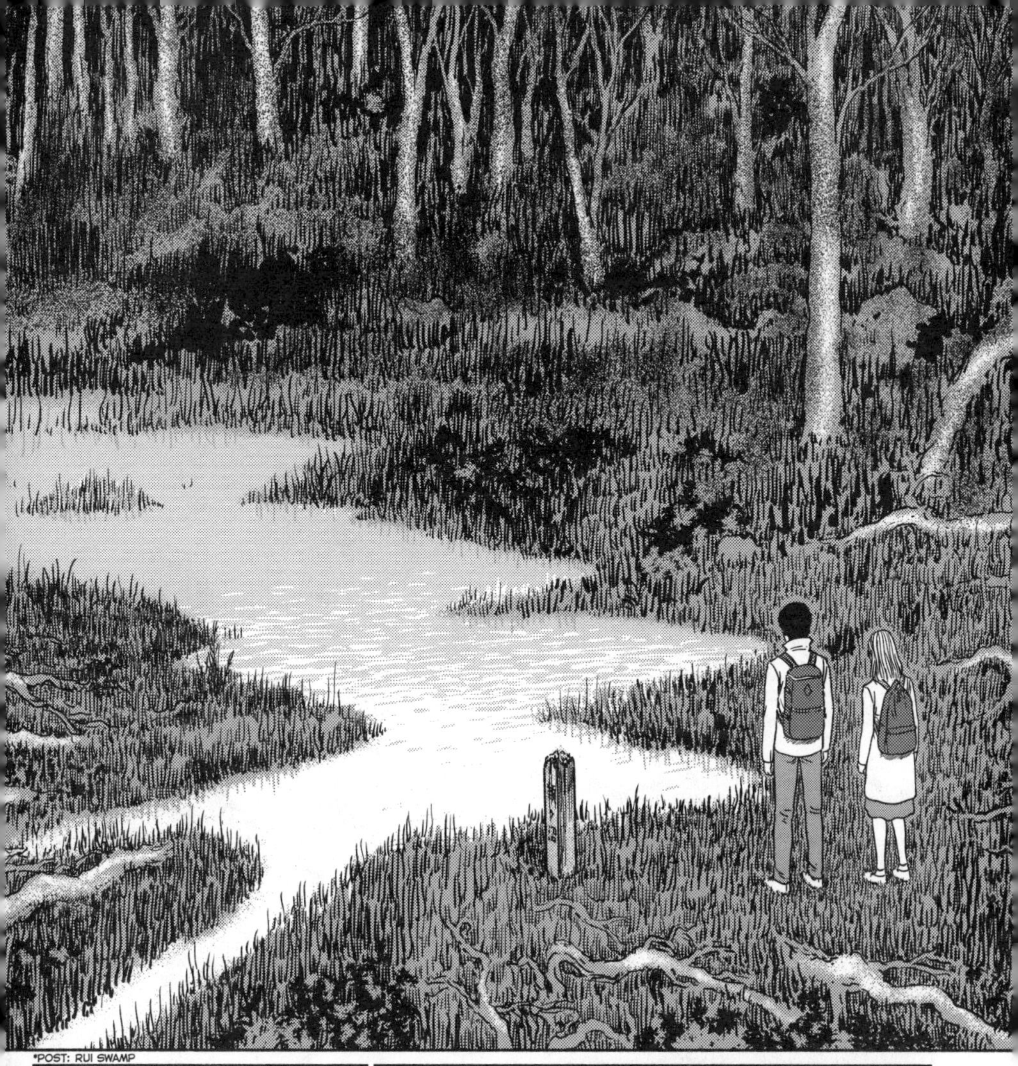

*POST: RUI SWAMP

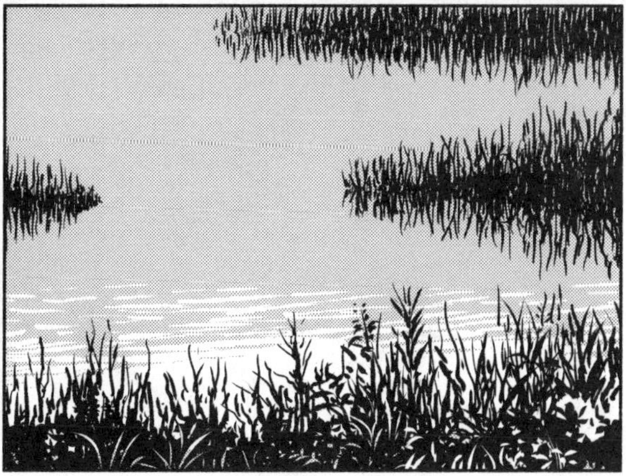

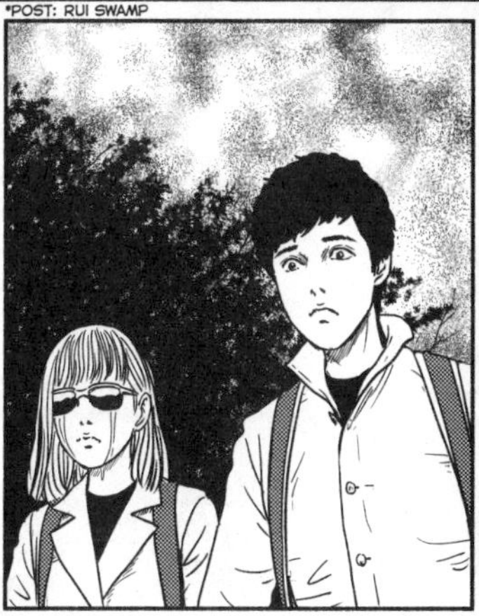

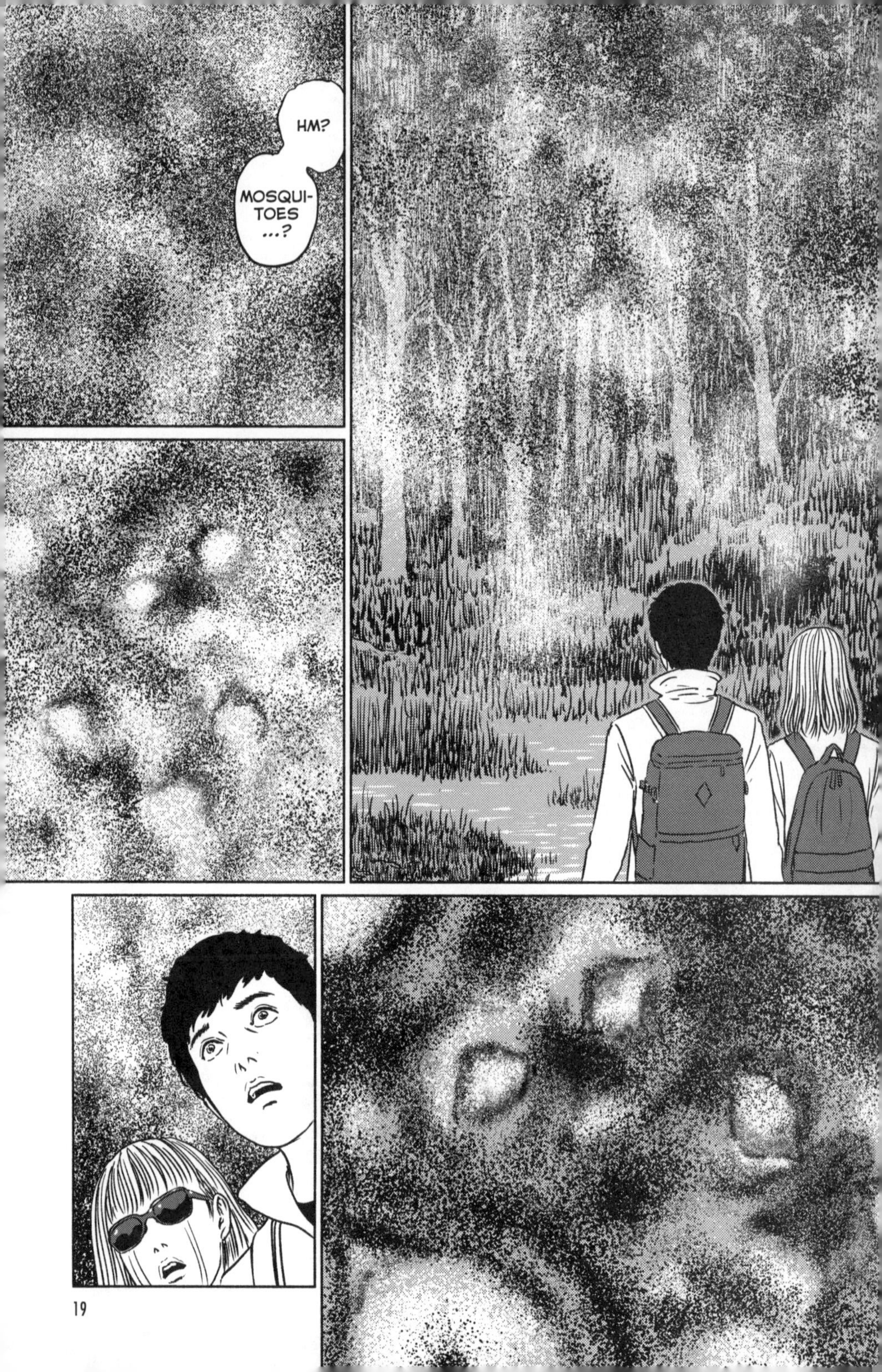
HM?
MOSQUI-TOES ...?

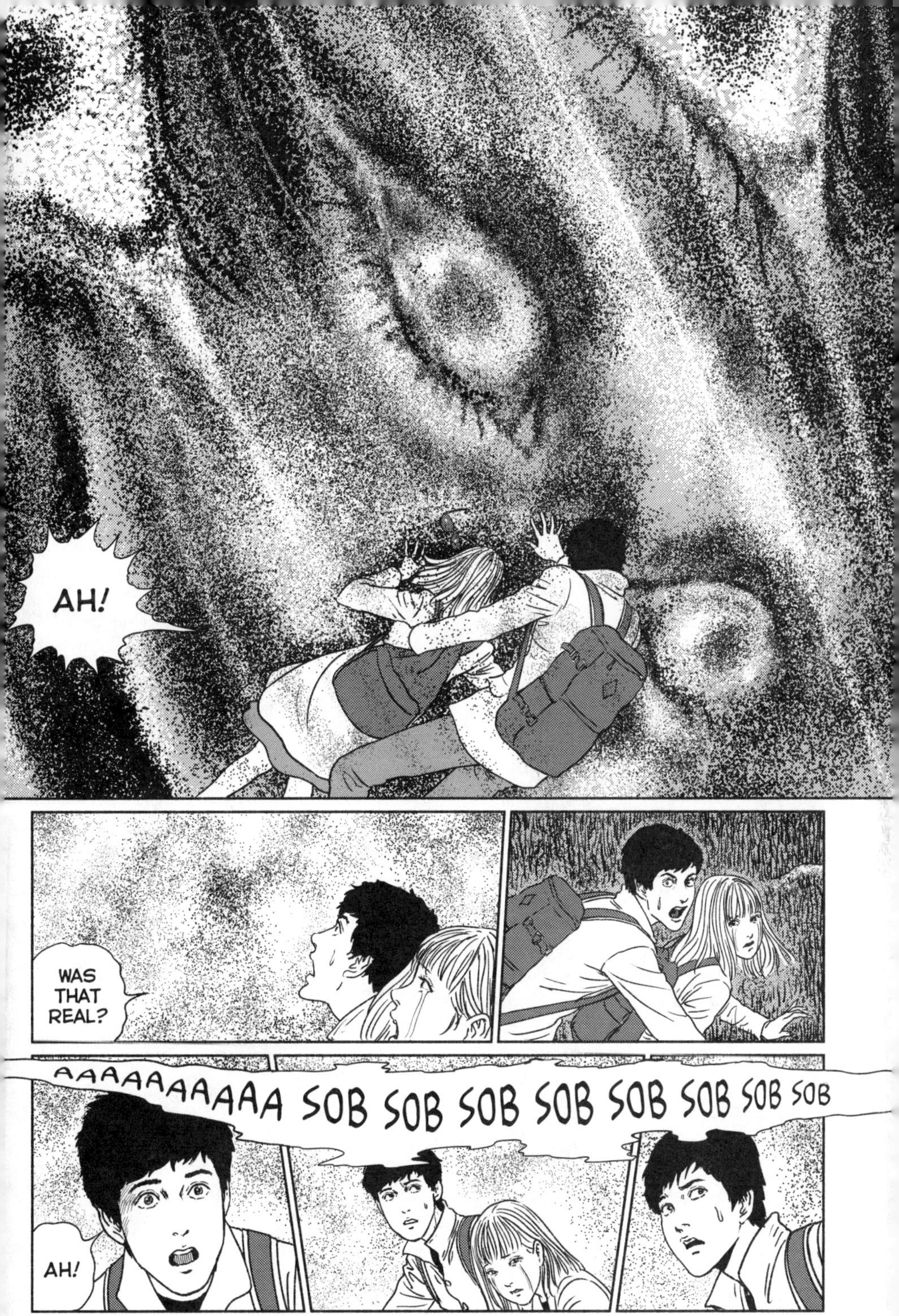
AH!
WAS THAT REAL?
AAAAAAAAAA SOB SOB SOB SOB SOB SOB SOB SOB
AH!

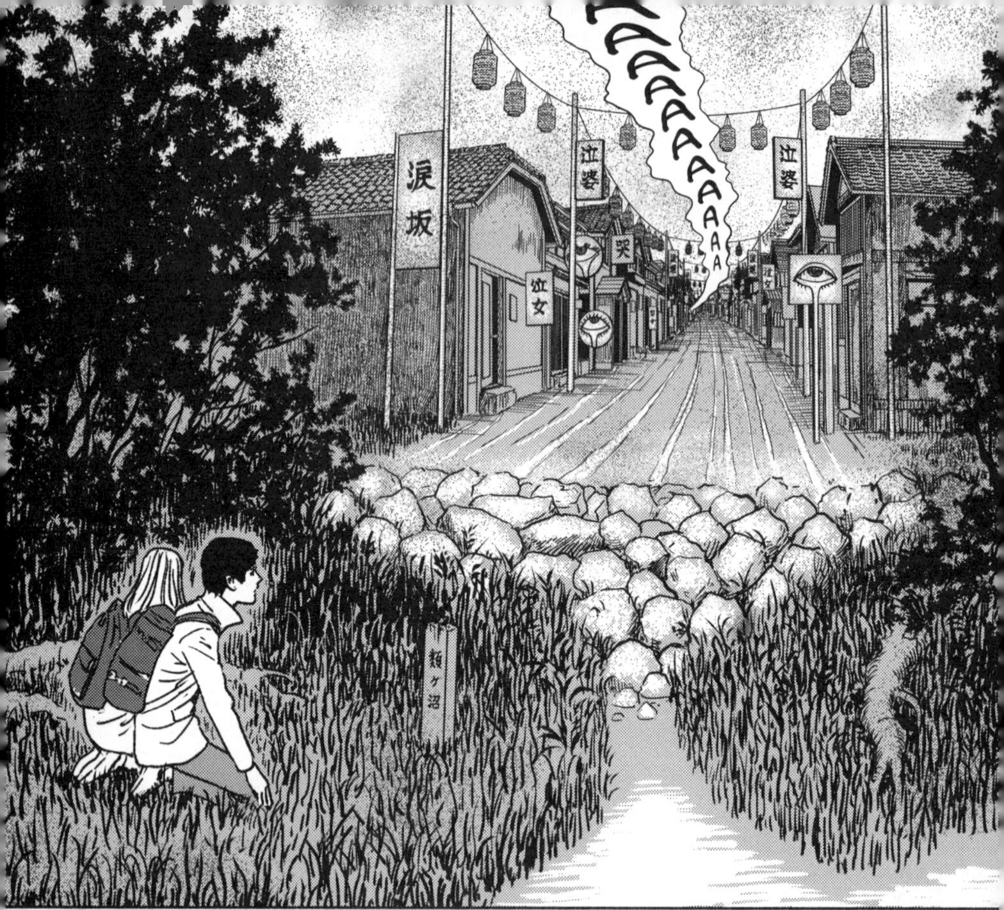
AAAAAAAAAAAA
涙坂
泣婆
泣婆
泣女
哭

*SIGNS: WEEPING WOMAN, WEEPING OLD WOMAN, WEEPING WAY, SOBBING ROAD, TEARS, WAILING, ETC.

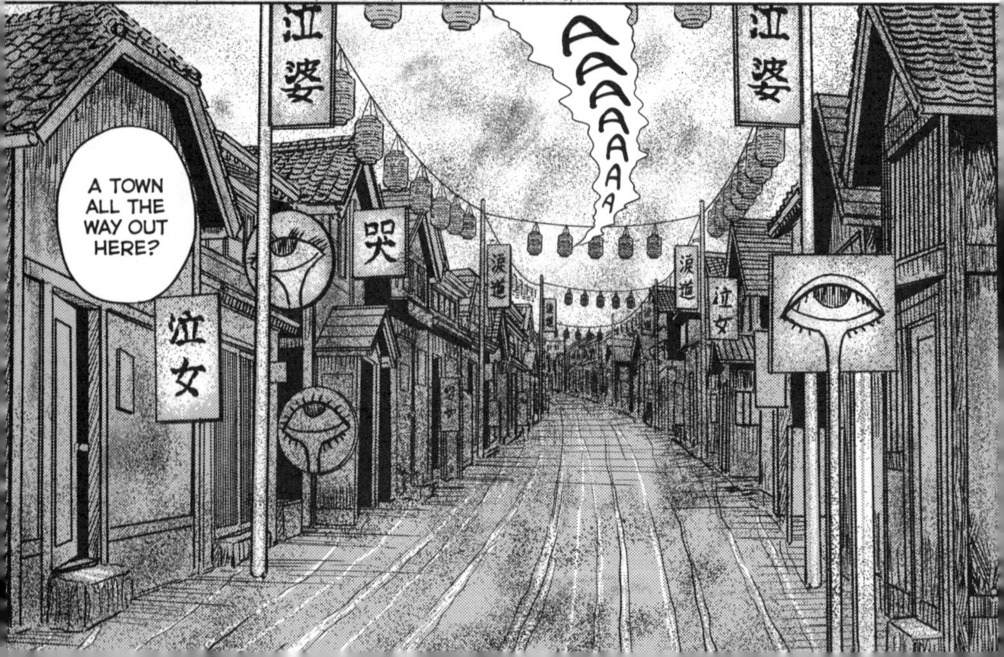
AAAAAAA
泣婆
泣婆
A TOWN ALL THE WAY OUT HERE?
哭
泣女
涙道
涙道
泣女

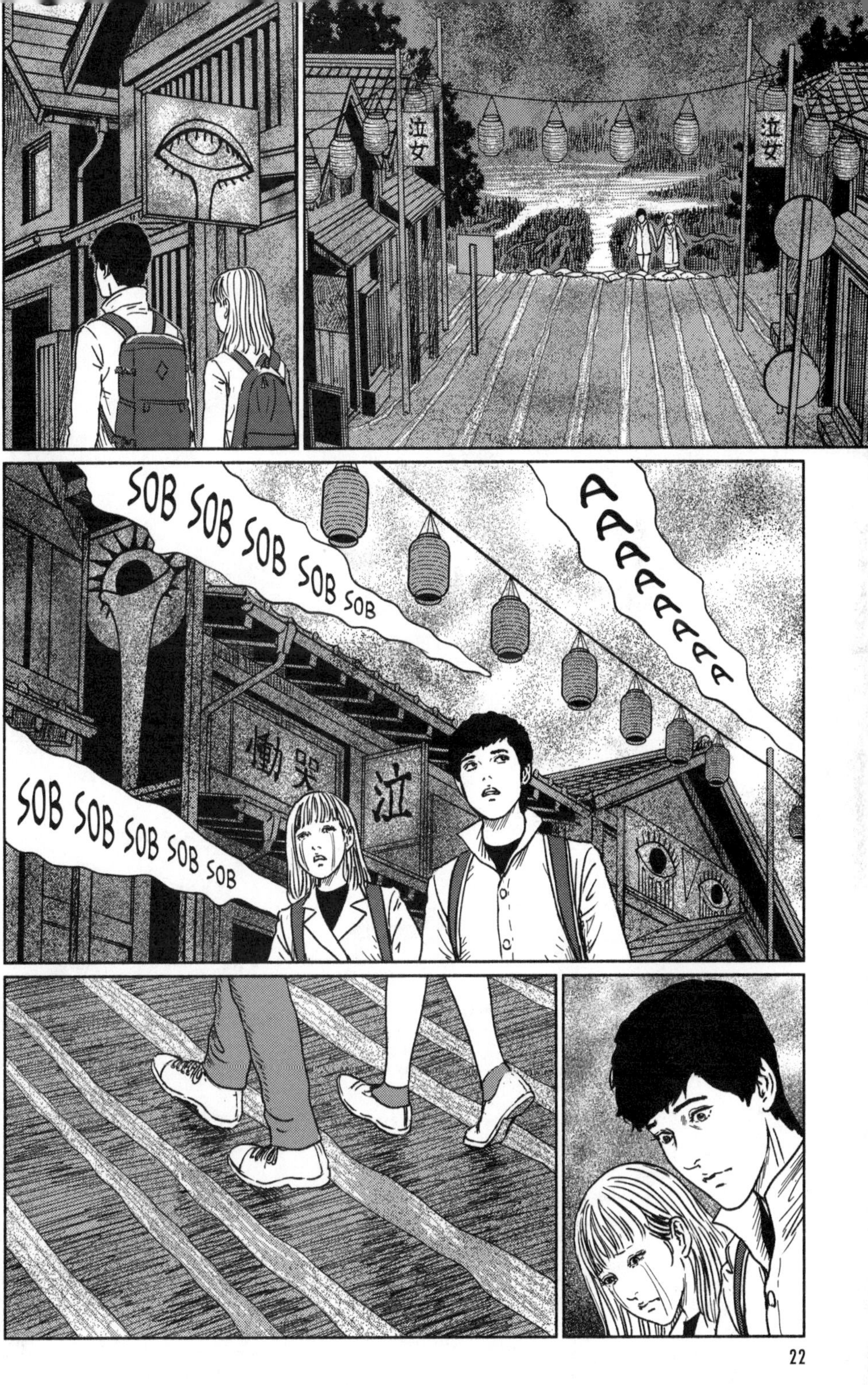
泣女
泣女
AAAAAAA
SOB SOB SOB SOB SOB
泣
慟哭
SOB SOB SOB SOB SOB

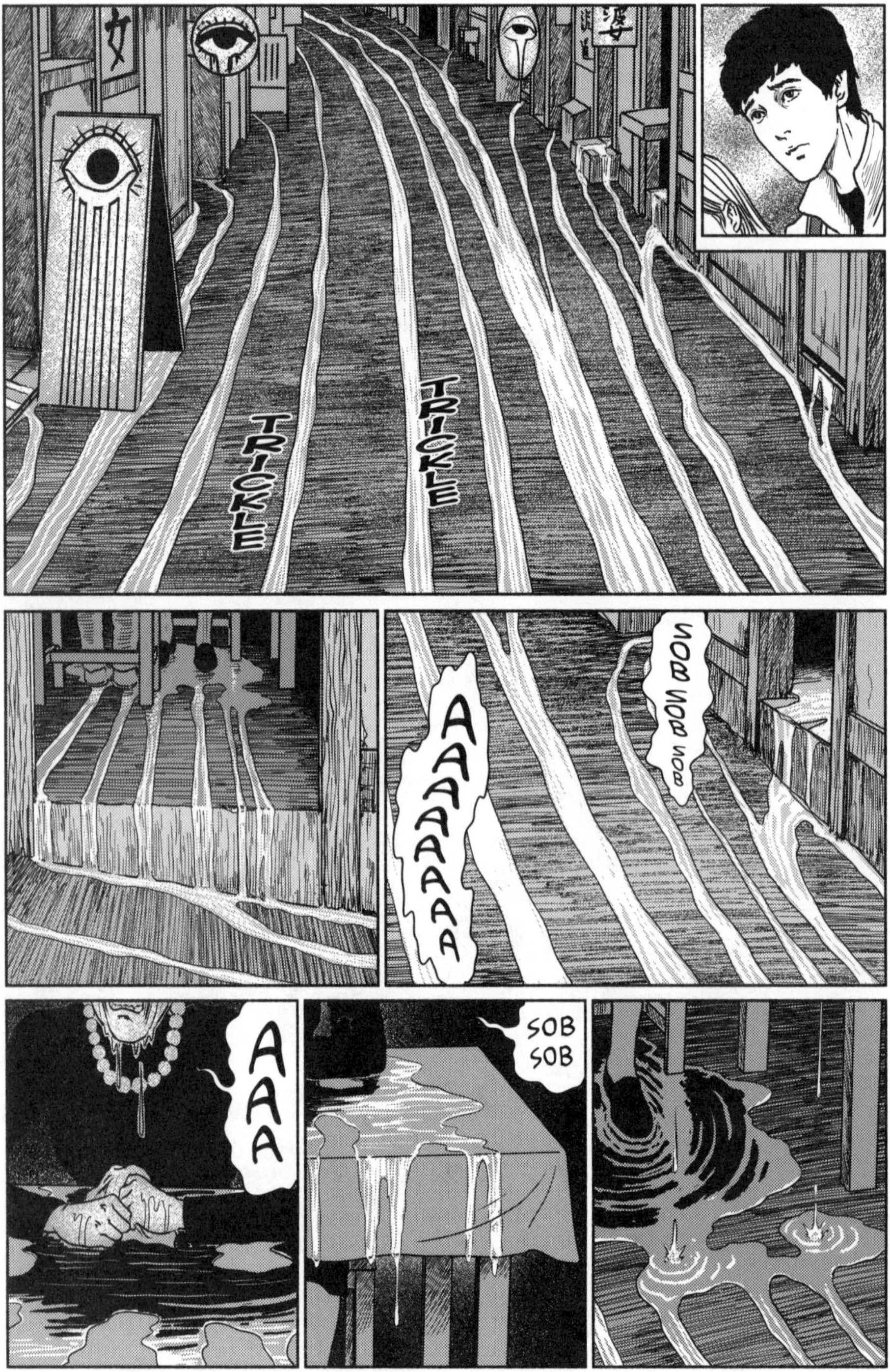

TRICKLE
TRICKLE
SOB SOB SOB
AAAAAAAAA
SOB SOB
AAA

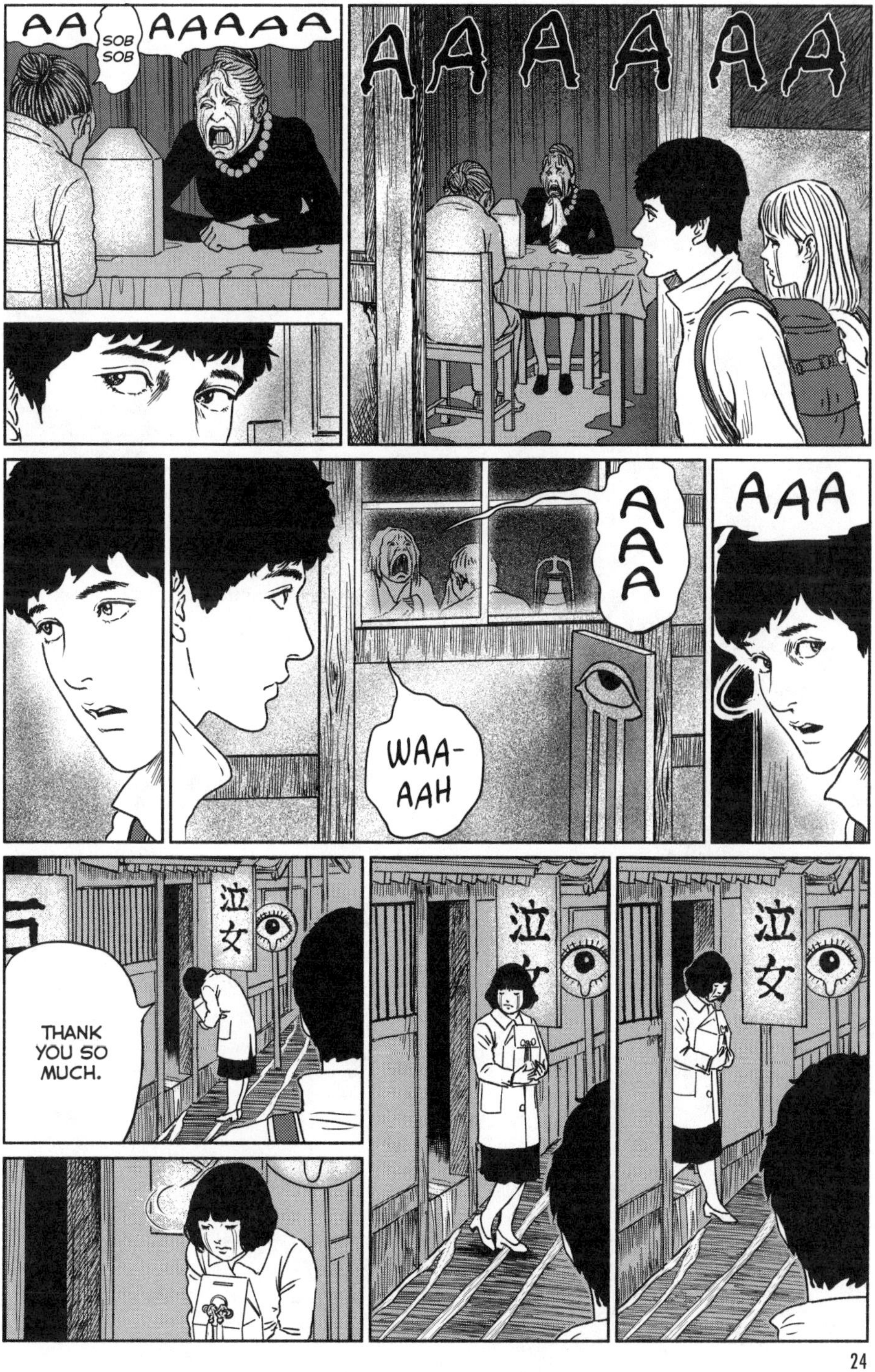
AAAAAA
AA
SOB SOB
AAAAA
AAA
AAA
WAA-AAH
泣女
泣女
泣女
THANK YOU SO MUCH.

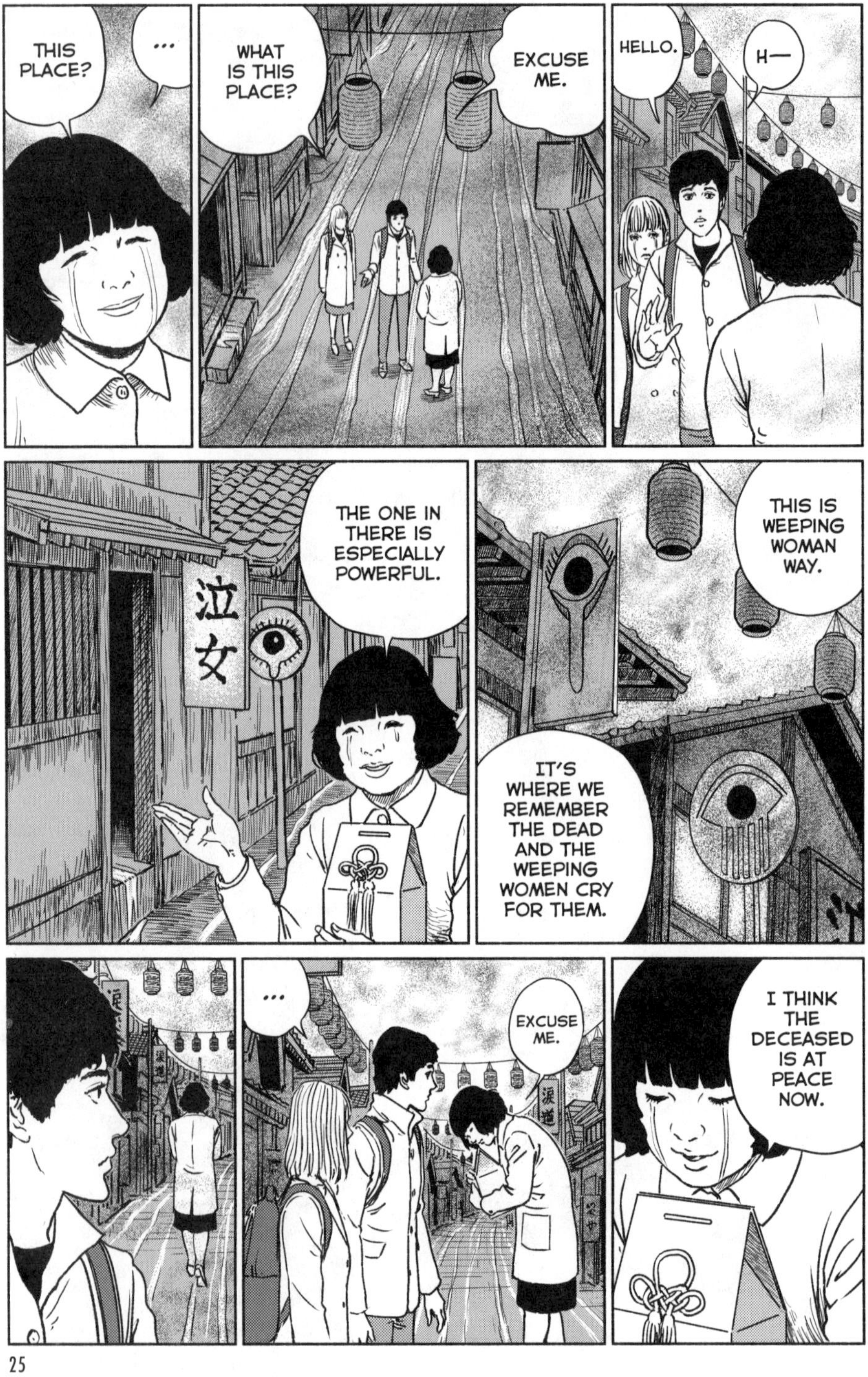
H—
HELLO.
EXCUSE ME.
WHAT IS THIS PLACE?
...
THIS PLACE?
THIS IS WEEPING WOMAN WAY.
IT'S WHERE WE REMEMBER THE DEAD AND THE WEEPING WOMEN CRY FOR THEM.
泣女
THE ONE IN THERE IS ESPECIALLY POWERFUL.
I THINK THE DECEASED IS AT PEACE NOW.
EXCUSE ME.
...

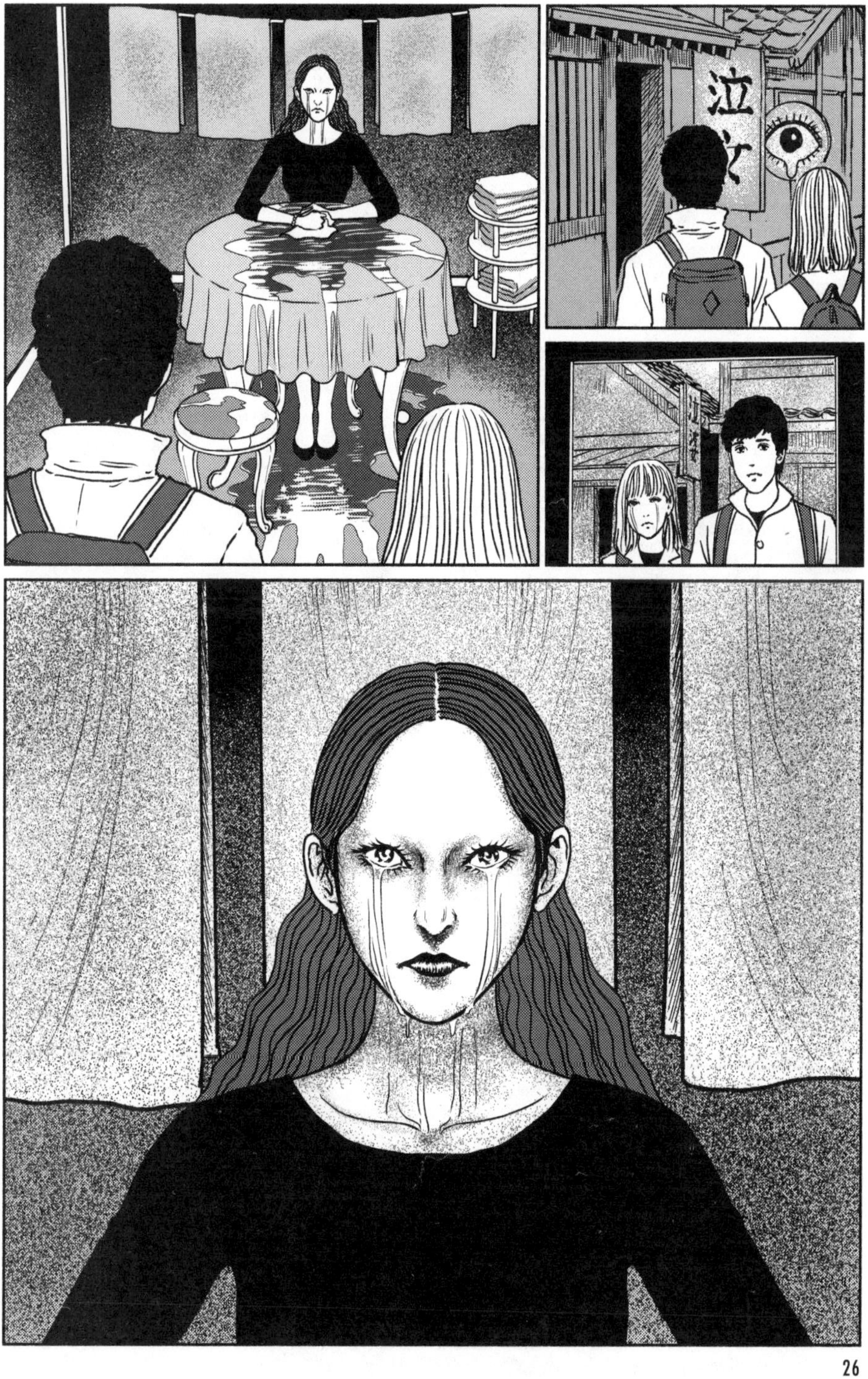
泣

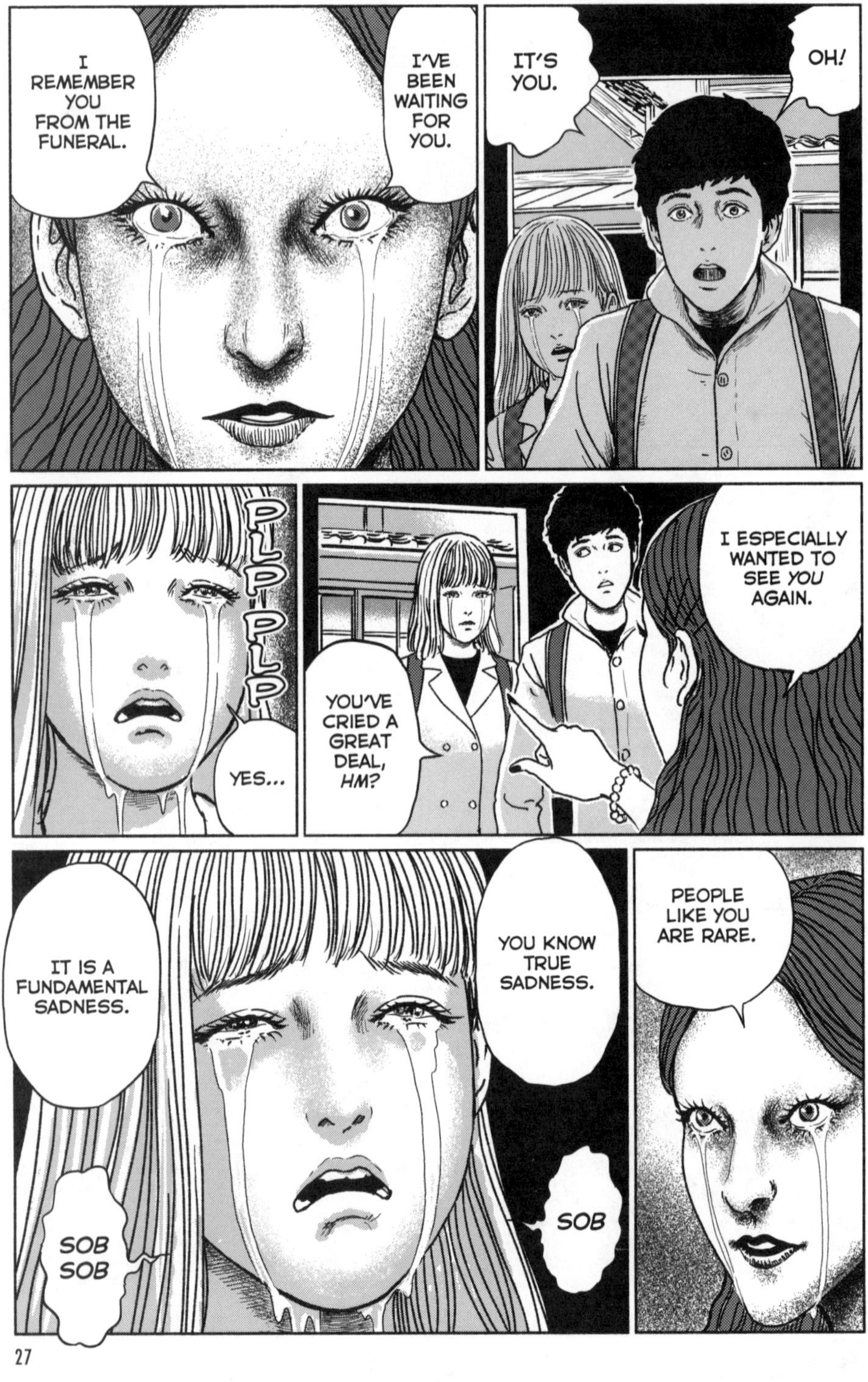
OH!
IT'S YOU.
I'VE BEEN WAITING FOR YOU.
I REMEMBER YOU FROM THE FUNERAL.
I ESPECIALLY WANTED TO SEE *YOU* AGAIN.
YOU'VE CRIED A GREAT DEAL, *HM?*
PLP PLP
YES...
PEOPLE LIKE YOU ARE RARE.
YOU KNOW TRUE SADNESS.
SOB
IT IS A FUNDAMENTAL SADNESS.
SOB SOB

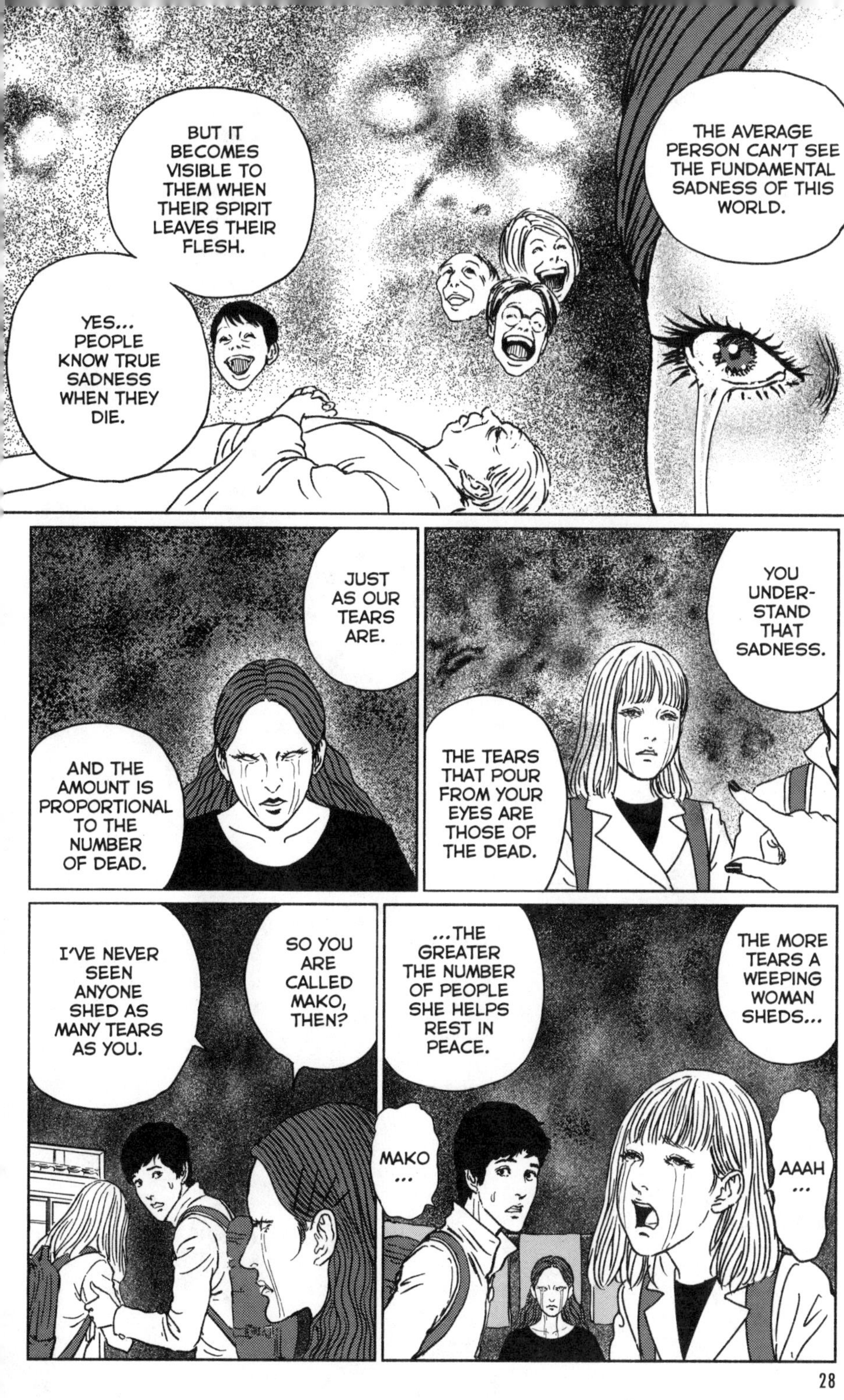
THE AVERAGE PERSON CAN'T SEE THE FUNDAMENTAL SADNESS OF THIS WORLD.
BUT IT BECOMES VISIBLE TO THEM WHEN THEIR SPIRIT LEAVES THEIR FLESH.
YES... PEOPLE KNOW TRUE SADNESS WHEN THEY DIE.
YOU UNDER-STAND THAT SADNESS.
THE TEARS THAT POUR FROM YOUR EYES ARE THOSE OF THE DEAD.
JUST AS OUR TEARS ARE.
AND THE AMOUNT IS PROPORTIONAL TO THE NUMBER OF DEAD.
THE MORE TEARS A WEEPING WOMAN SHEDS...
...THE GREATER THE NUMBER OF PEOPLE SHE HELPS REST IN PEACE.
AAAH...
MAKO...
SO YOU ARE CALLED MAKO, THEN?
I'VE NEVER SEEN ANYONE SHED AS MANY TEARS AS YOU.

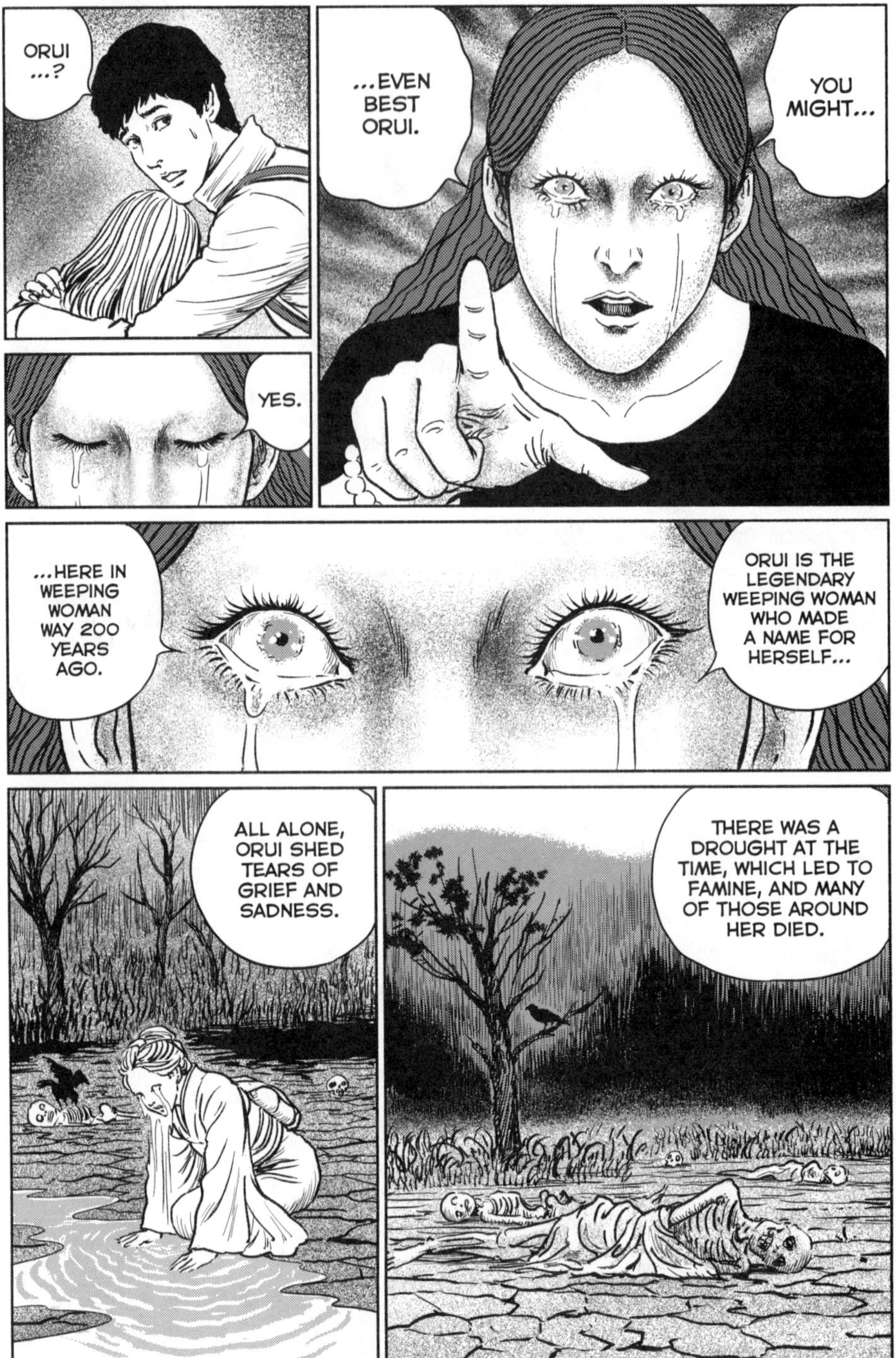
YOU MIGHT...
...EVEN BEST ORUI.
ORUI ...?
YES.
ORUI IS THE LEGENDARY WEEPING WOMAN WHO MADE A NAME FOR HERSELF...
...HERE IN WEEPING WOMAN WAY 200 YEARS AGO.
THERE WAS A DROUGHT AT THE TIME, WHICH LED TO FAMINE, AND MANY OF THOSE AROUND HER DIED.
ALL ALONE, ORUI SHED TEARS OF GRIEF AND SADNESS.

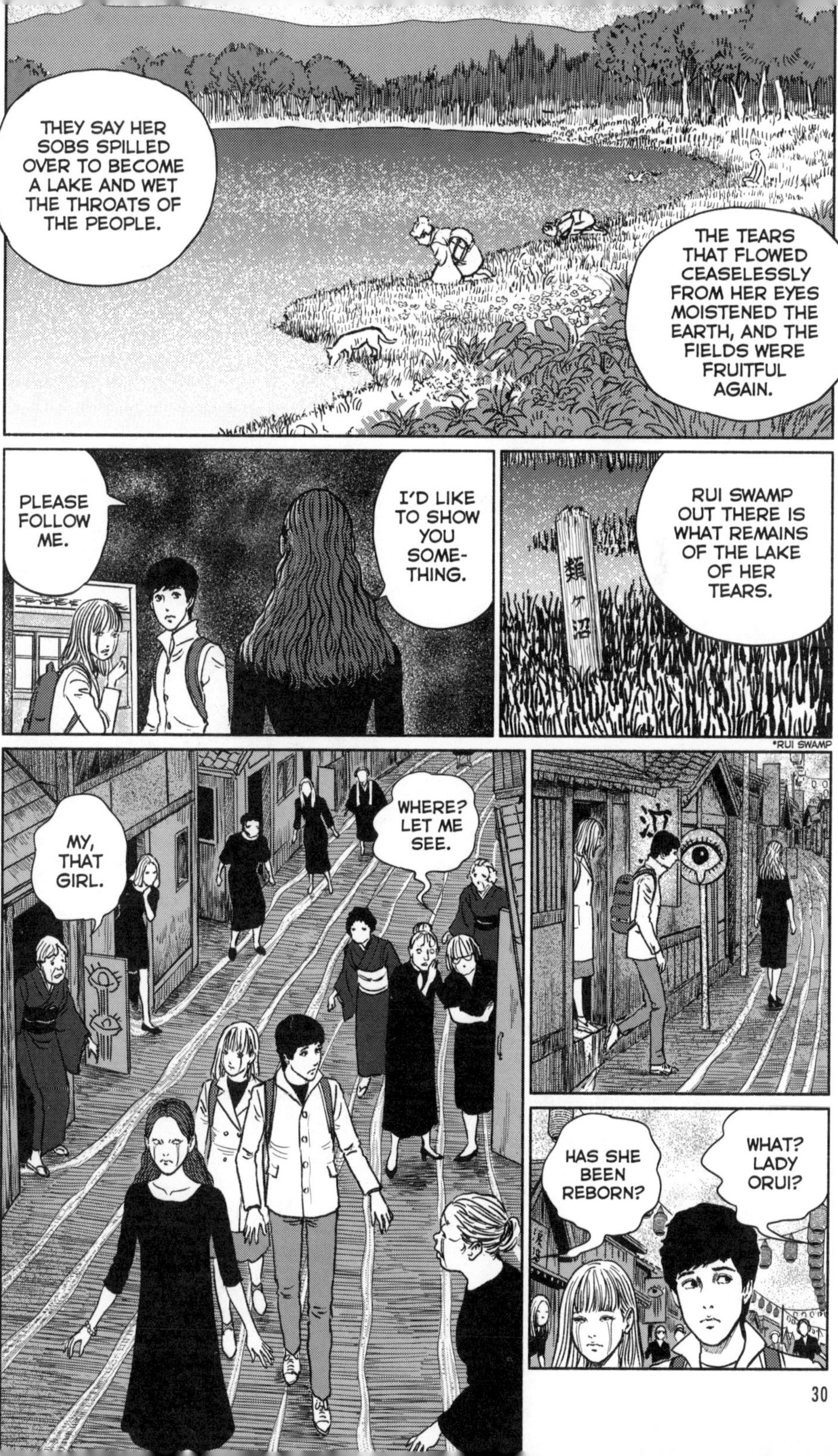
THE TEARS THAT FLOWED CEASELESSLY FROM HER EYES MOISTENED THE EARTH, AND THE FIELDS WERE FRUITFUL AGAIN.
THEY SAY HER SOBS SPILLED OVER TO BECOME A LAKE AND WET THE THROATS OF THE PEOPLE.
RUI SWAMP OUT THERE IS WHAT REMAINS OF THE LAKE OF HER TEARS.
類ヶ沼
*RUI SWAMP
I'D LIKE TO SHOW YOU SOME-THING.
PLEASE FOLLOW ME.
WHAT? LADY ORUI?
HAS SHE BEEN REBORN?
WHERE? LET ME SEE.
MY, THAT GIRL.

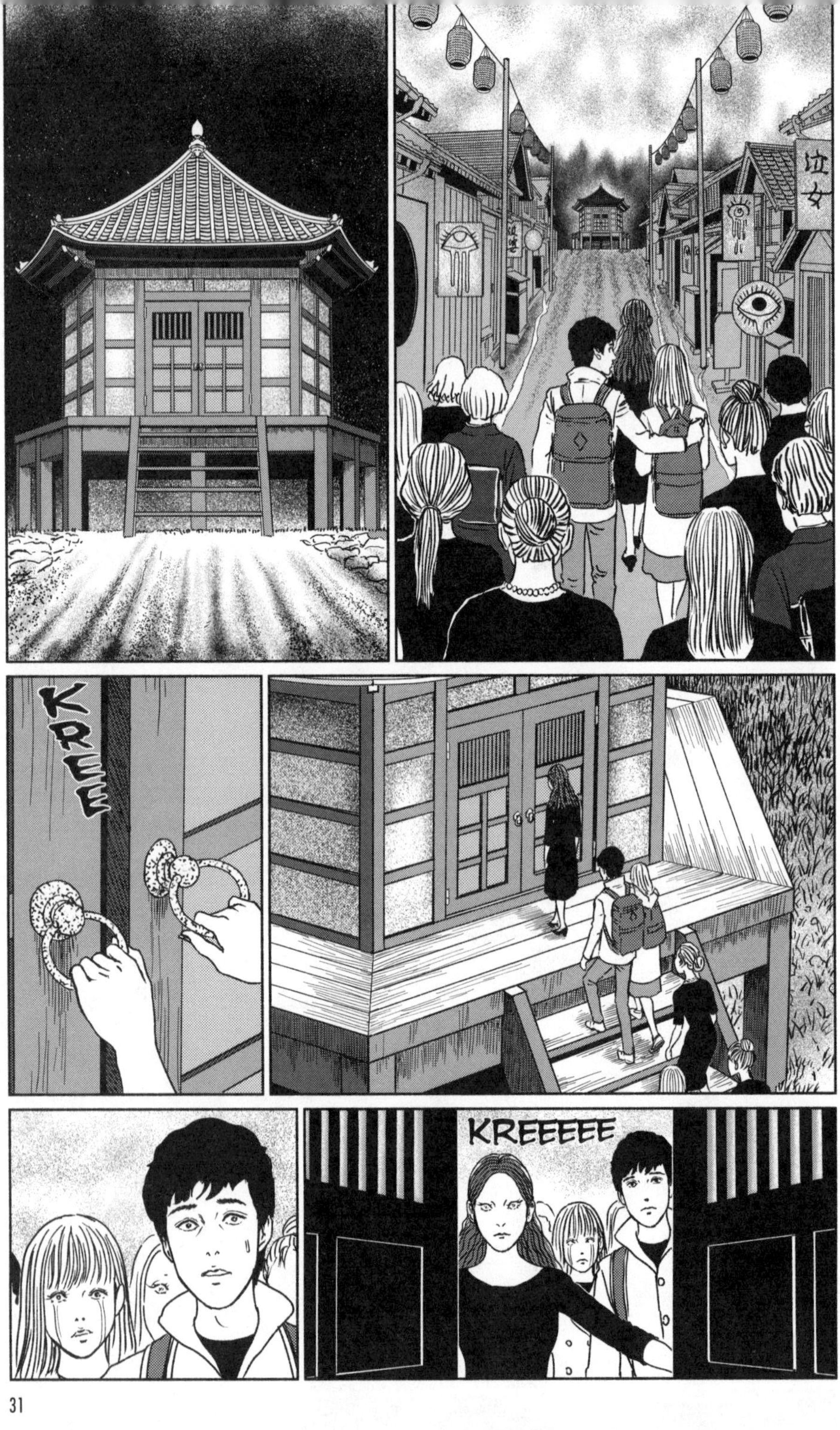
泣女
KREE
KREEEEE

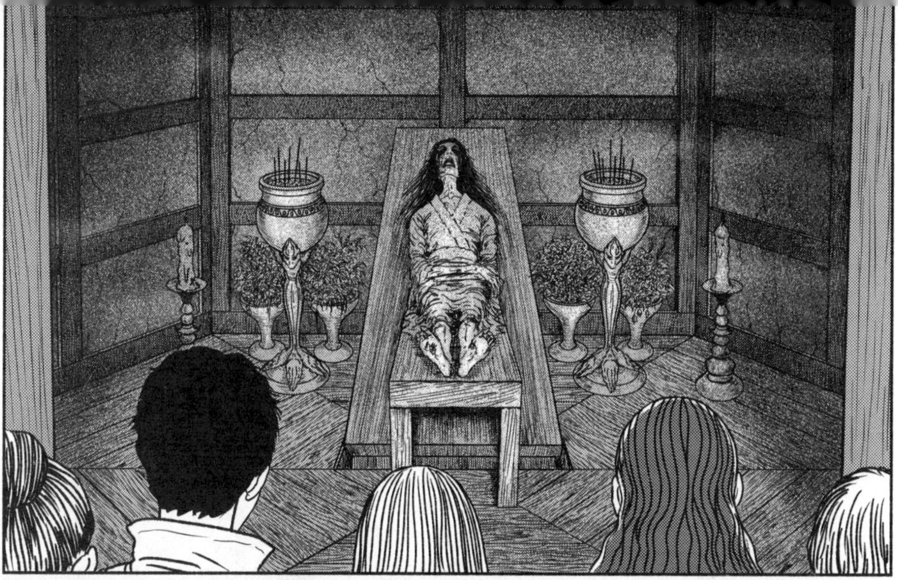
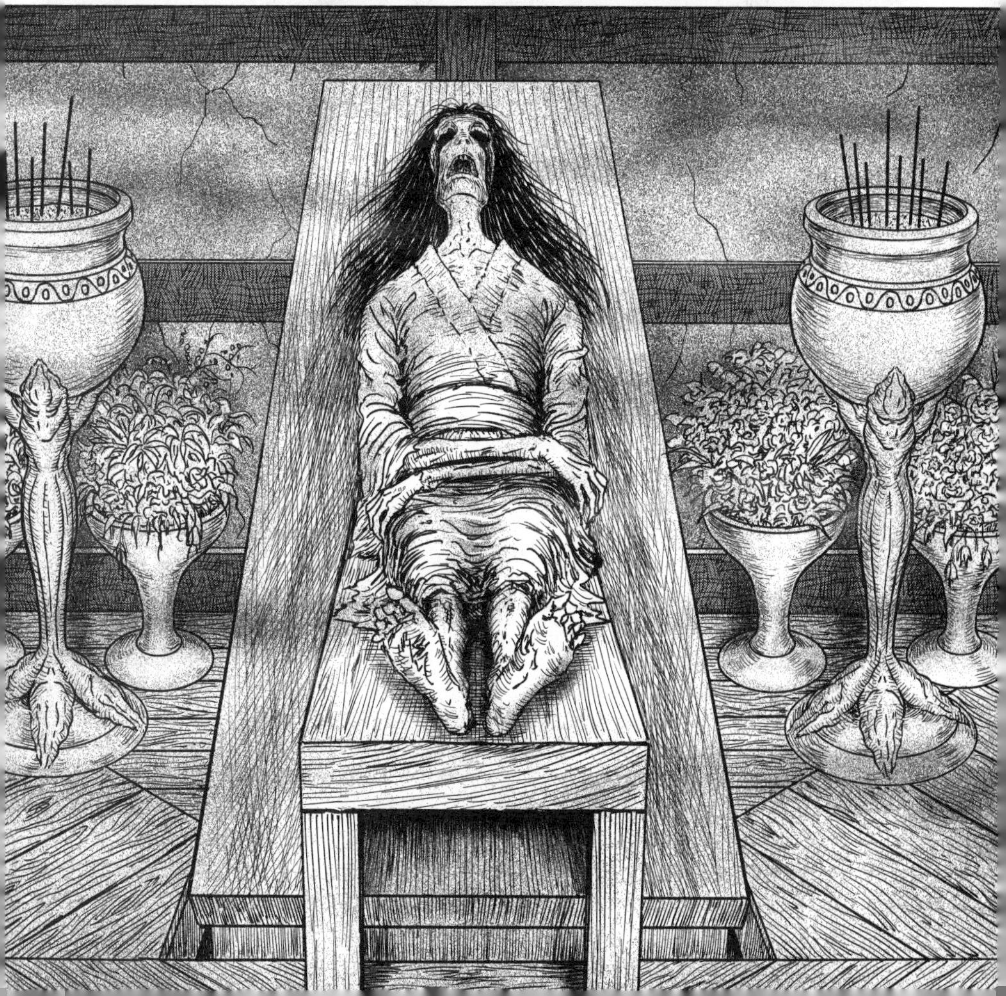

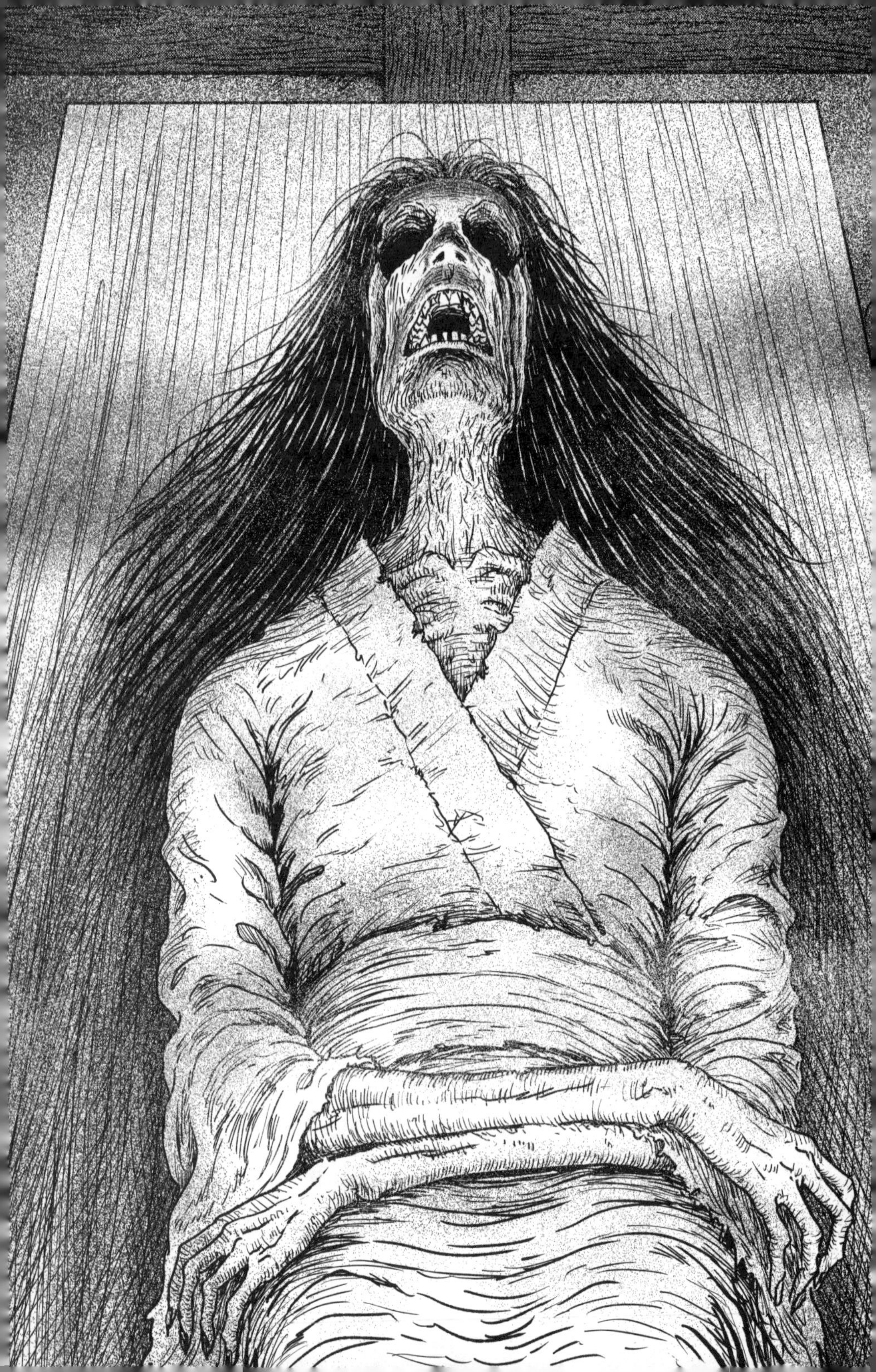

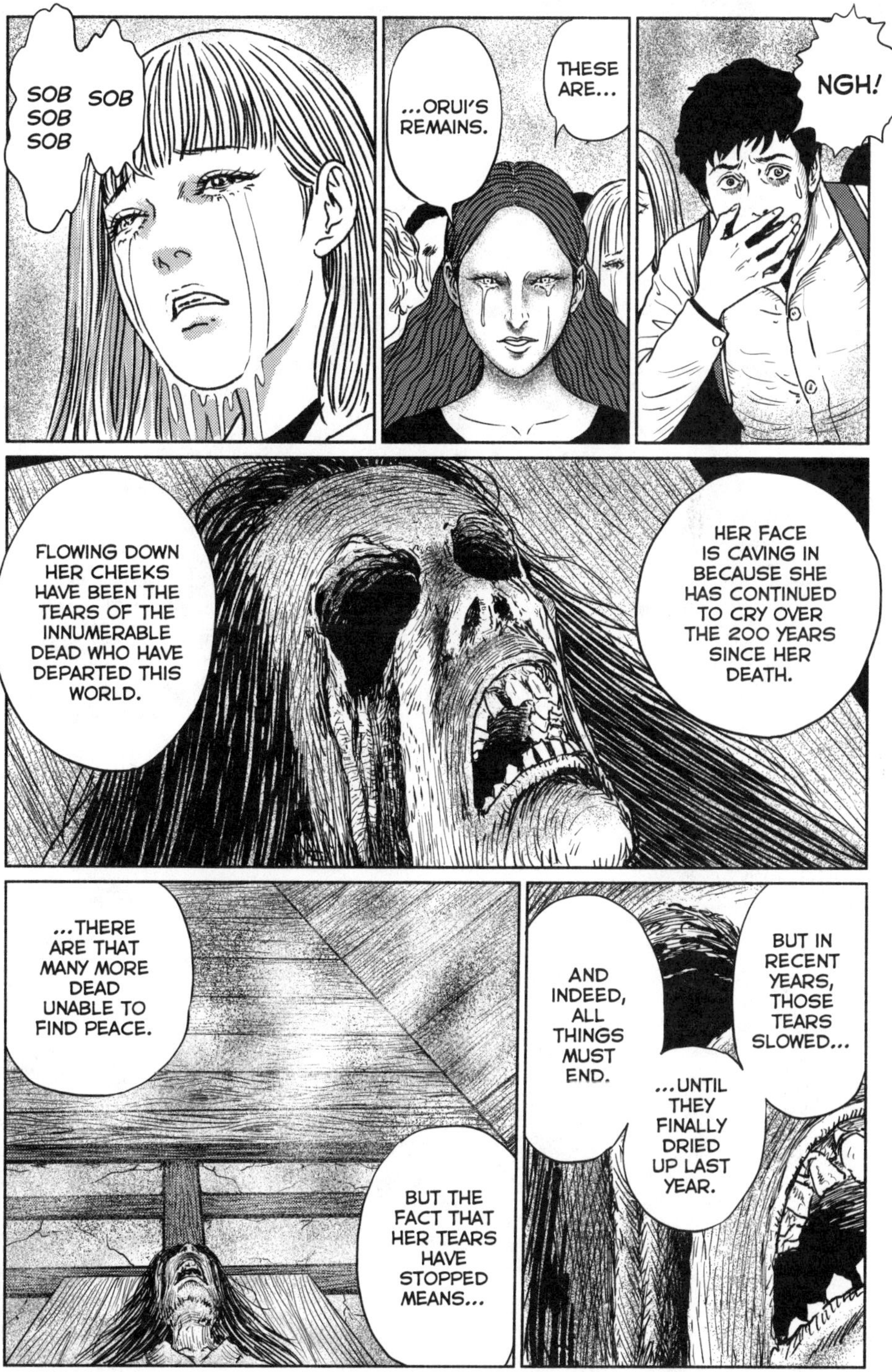
NGH!
THESE ARE...
...ORUI'S REMAINS.
SOB SOB SOB SOB
HER FACE IS CAVING IN BECAUSE SHE HAS CONTINUED TO CRY OVER THE 200 YEARS SINCE HER DEATH.
FLOWING DOWN HER CHEEKS HAVE BEEN THE TEARS OF THE INNUMERABLE DEAD WHO HAVE DEPARTED THIS WORLD.
BUT IN RECENT YEARS, THOSE TEARS SLOWED...
...UNTIL THEY FINALLY DRIED UP LAST YEAR.
AND INDEED, ALL THINGS MUST END.
BUT THE FACT THAT HER TEARS HAVE STOPPED MEANS...
...THERE ARE THAT MANY MORE DEAD UNABLE TO FIND PEACE.

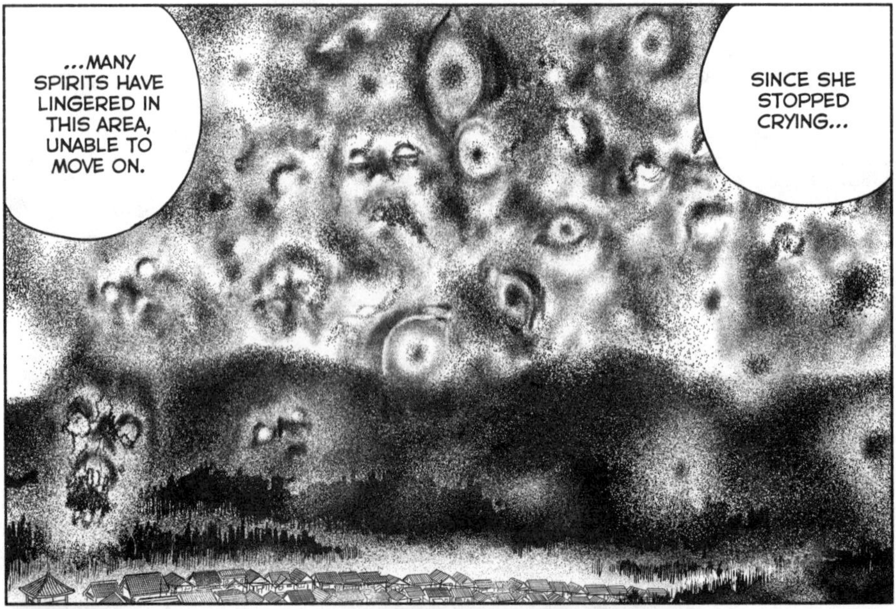
SINCE SHE STOPPED CRYING...
...MANY SPIRITS HAVE LINGERED IN THIS AREA, UNABLE TO MOVE ON.

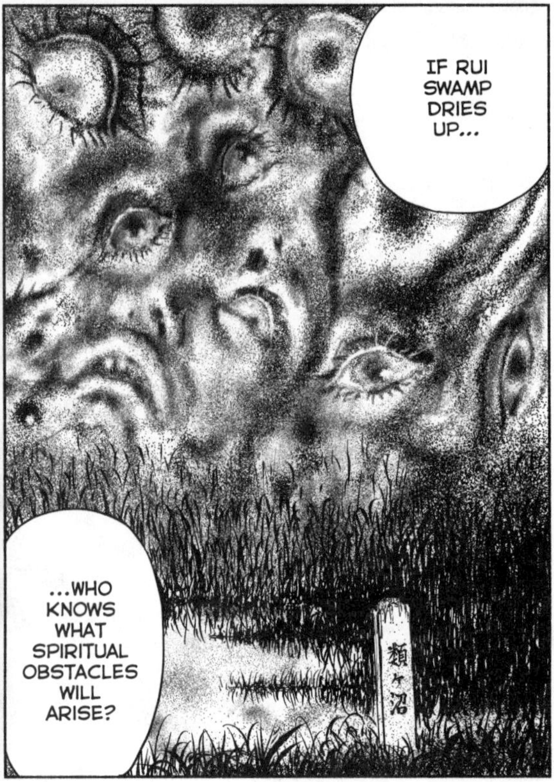
IF RUI SWAMP DRIES UP...
...WHO KNOWS WHAT SPIRITUAL OBSTACLES WILL ARISE?
類ヶ沼

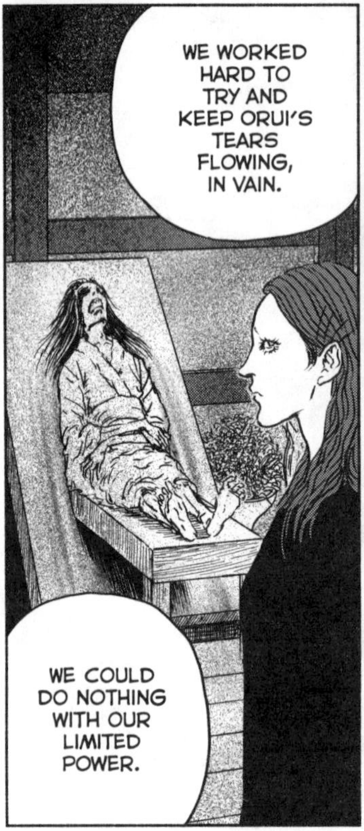
WE WORKED HARD TO TRY AND KEEP ORUI'S TEARS FLOWING, IN VAIN.
WE COULD DO NOTHING WITH OUR LIMITED POWER.

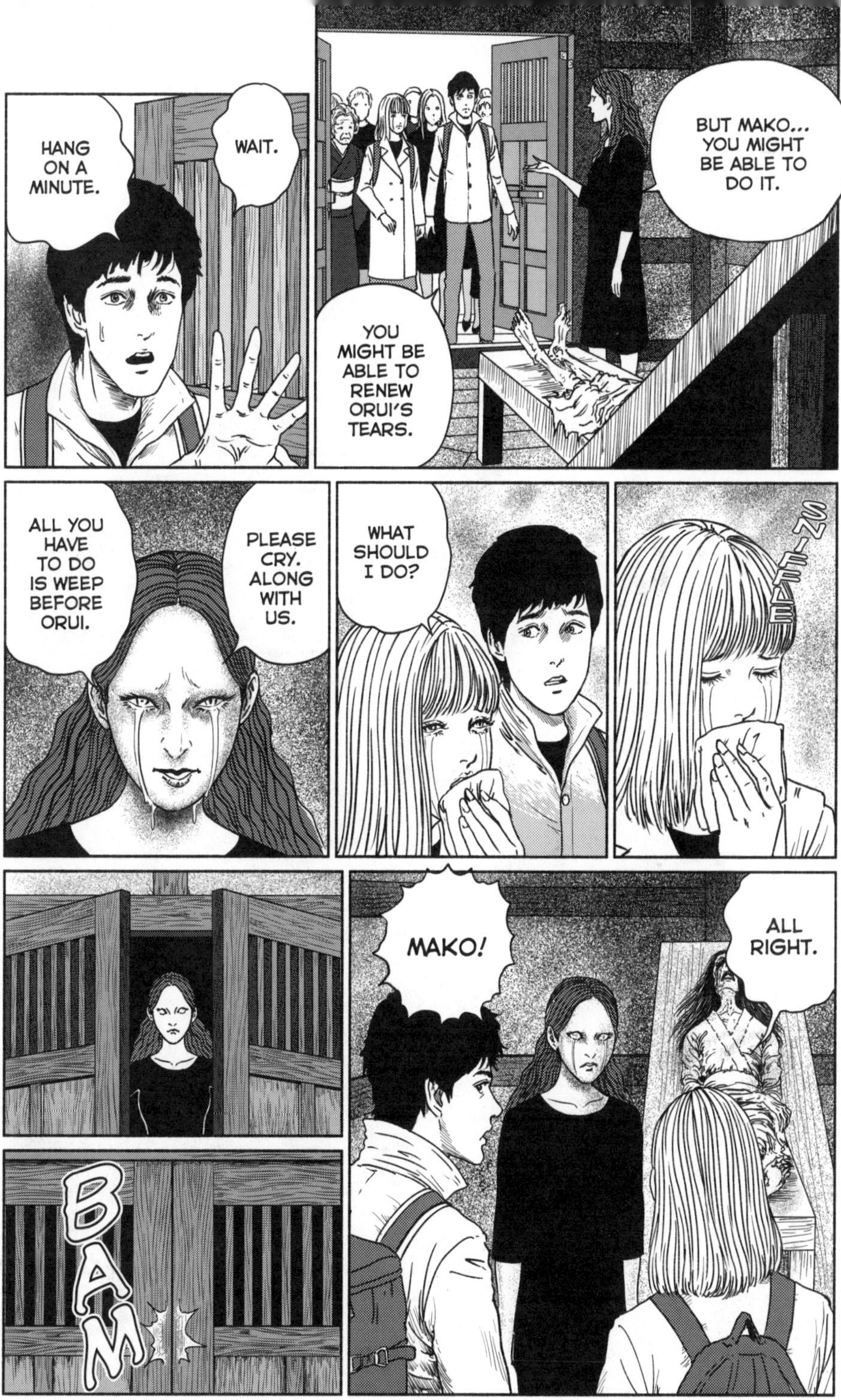
BUT MAKO... YOU MIGHT BE ABLE TO DO IT.
YOU MIGHT BE ABLE TO RENEW ORUI'S TEARS.
WAIT.
HANG ON A MINUTE.
SNIFFLE
WHAT SHOULD I DO?
PLEASE CRY. ALONG WITH US.
ALL YOU HAVE TO DO IS WEEP BEFORE ORUI.
ALL RIGHT.
MAKO!
BAM

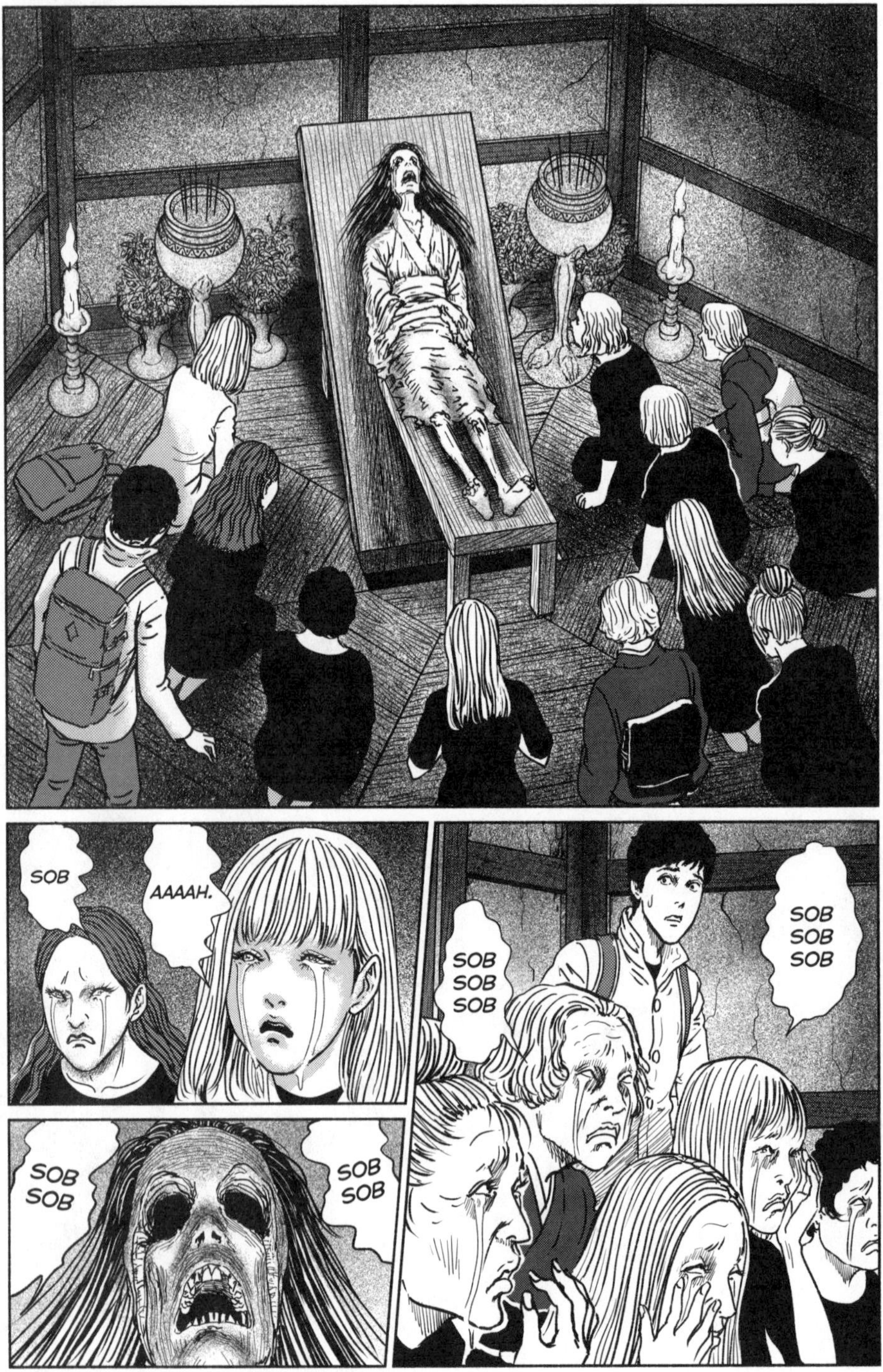
SOB SOB SOB
SOB SOB SOB
AAAAH.
SOB
SOB SOB
SOB SOB

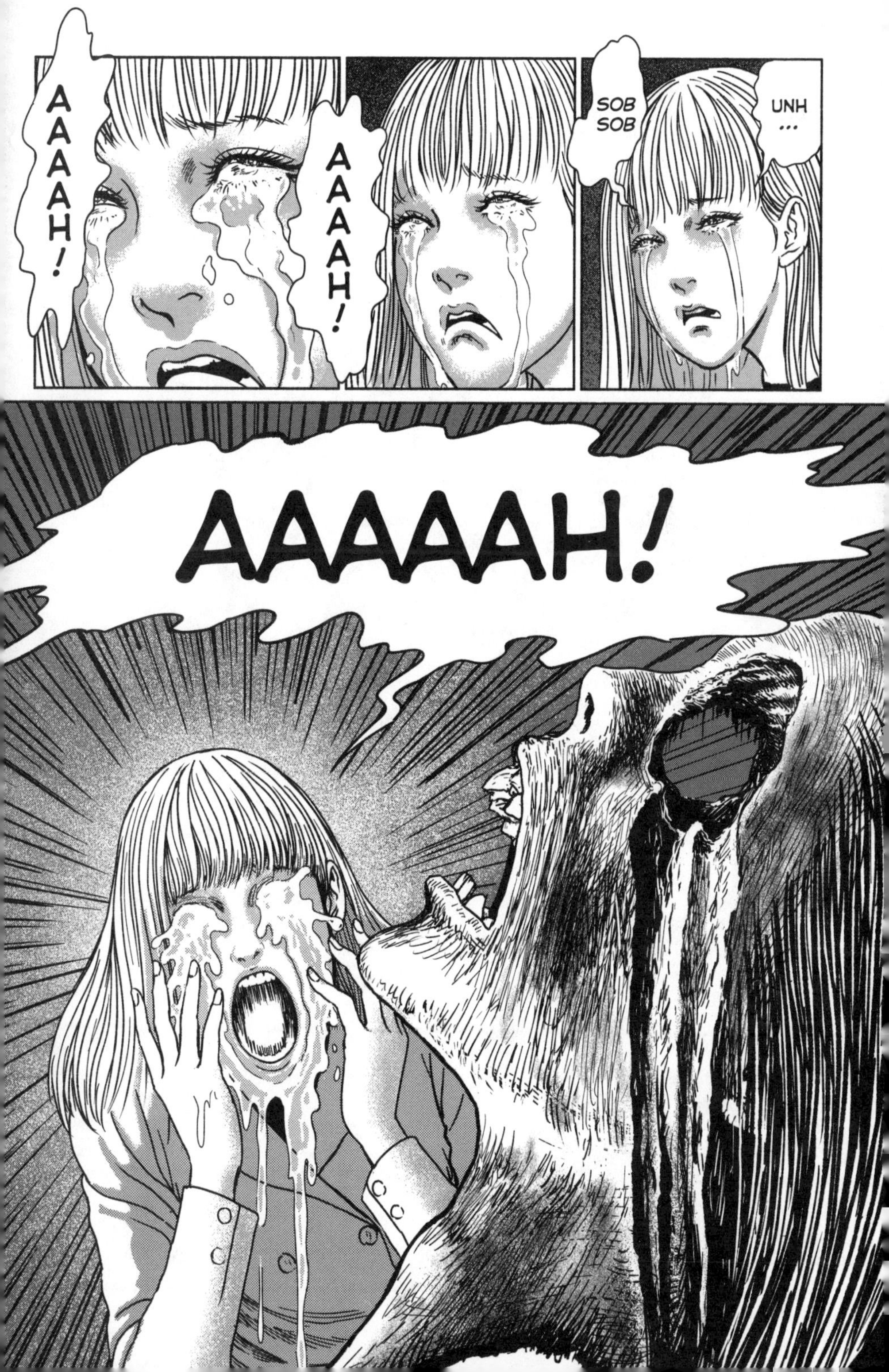
UNH ...
SOB SOB
AAAAAH!
AAAAAH!
AAAAAH!

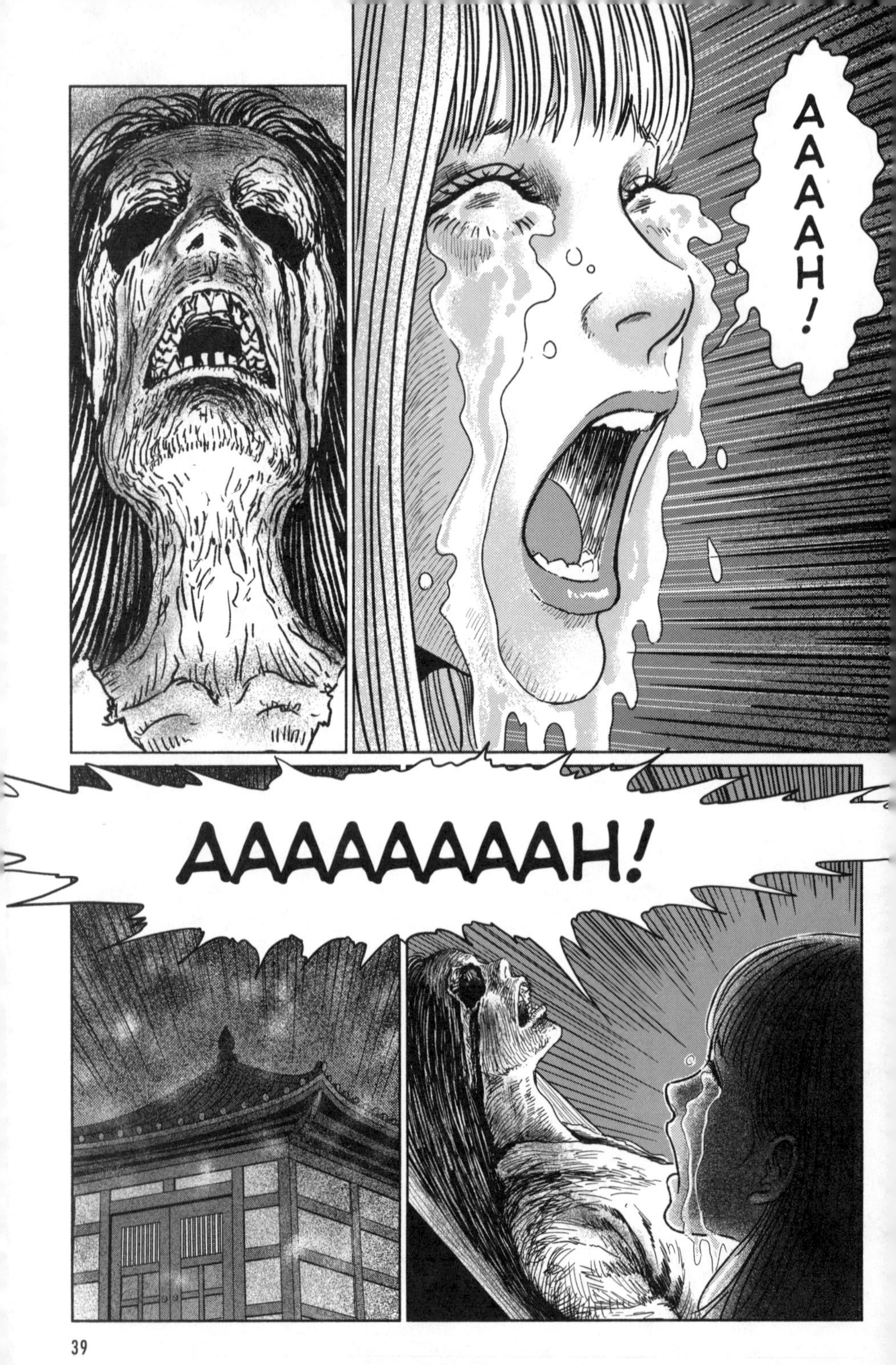
AAAAH!
AAAAAAAAH!

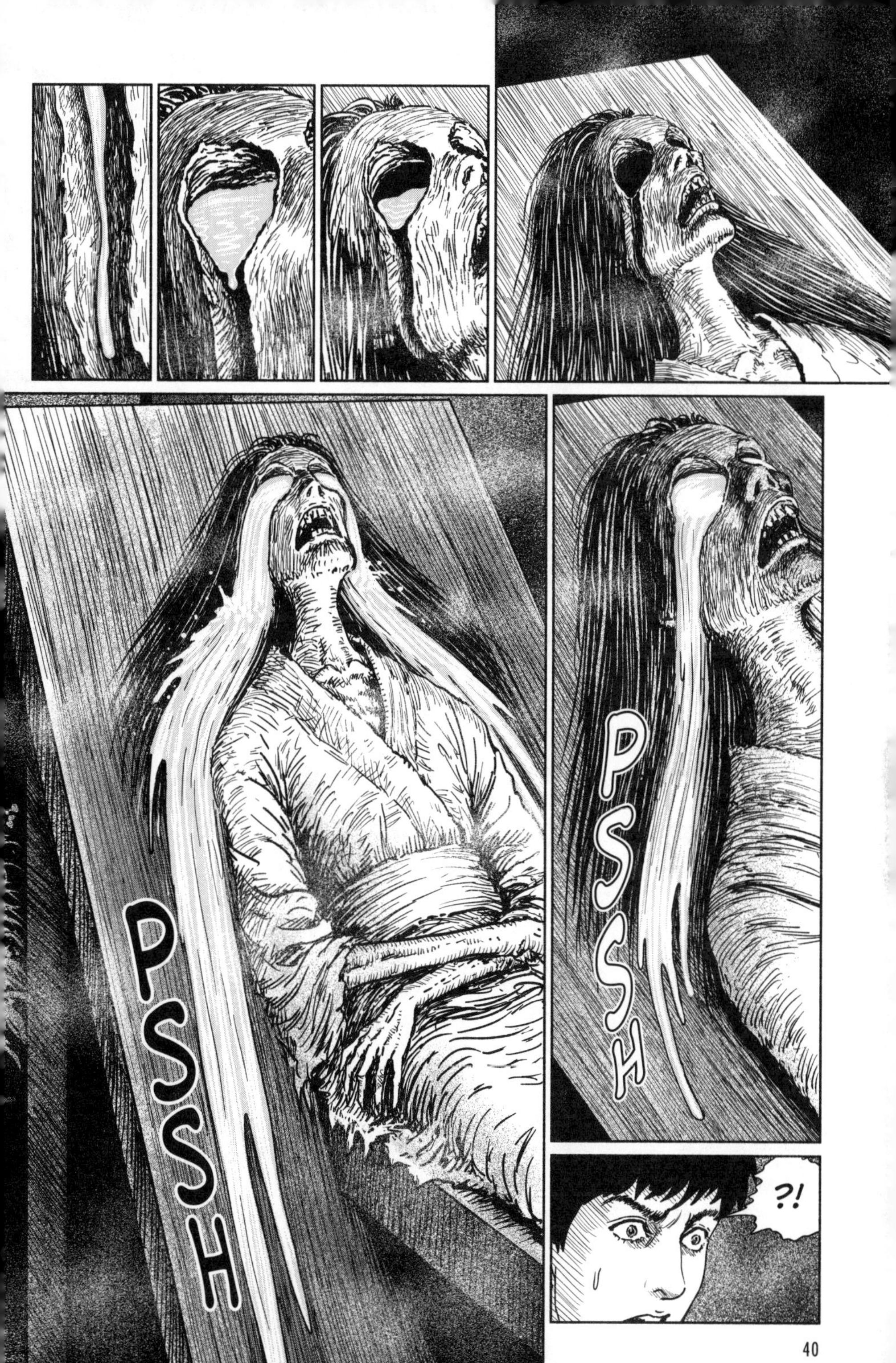
PSSH
?!
PSSH

PSSSH
SPLSSH
AAH!
LADY ORUI'S TEARS!
PSSSH

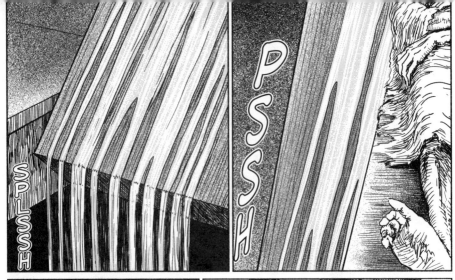

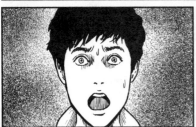

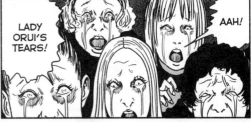

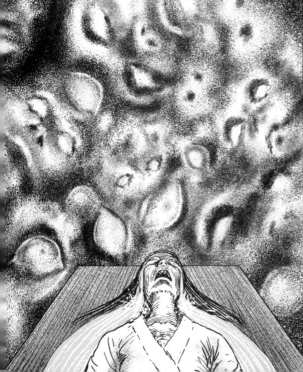

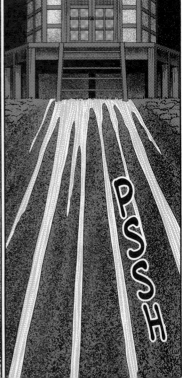

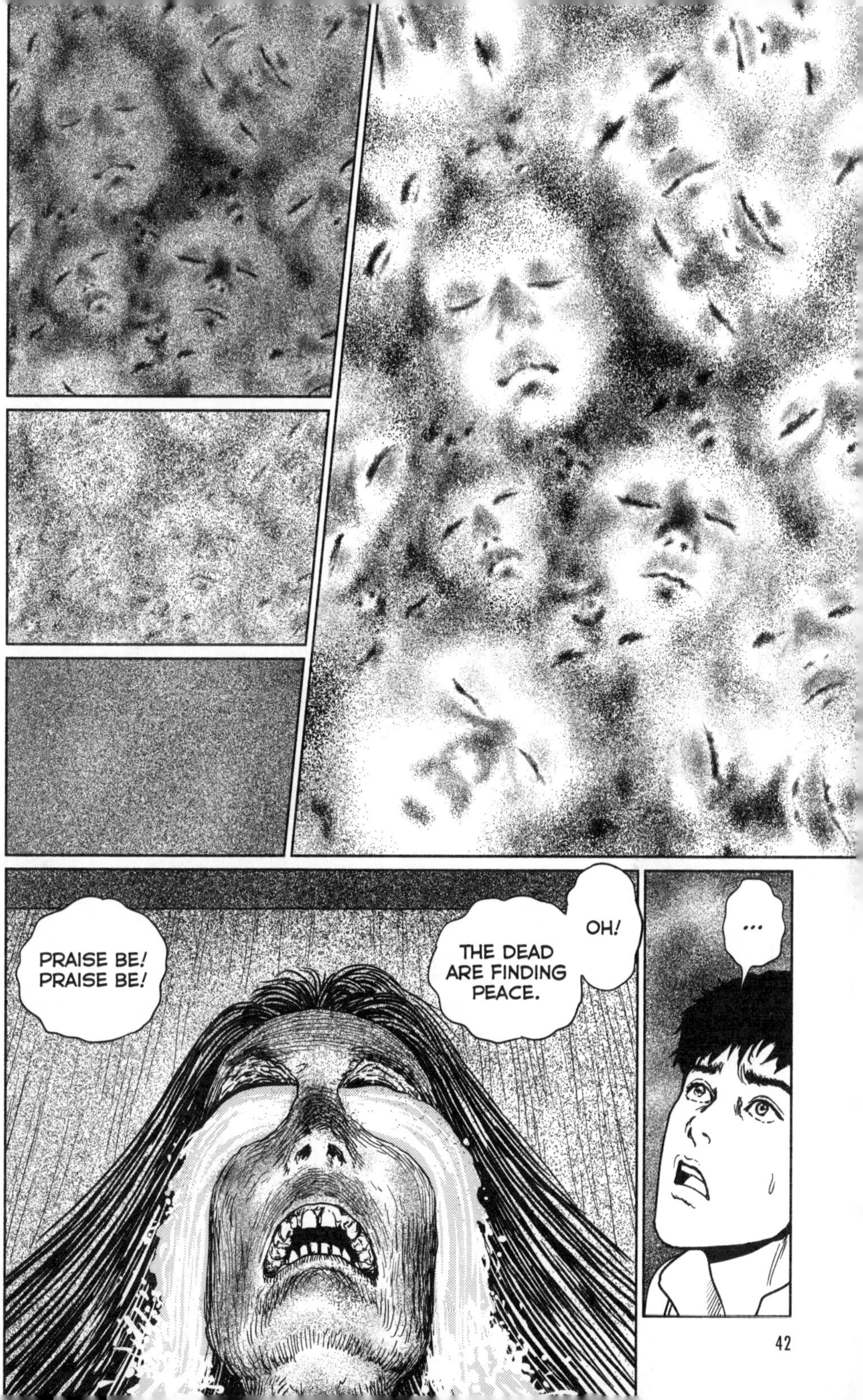
...
OH!
THE DEAD ARE FINDING PEACE.
PRAISE BE! PRAISE BE!

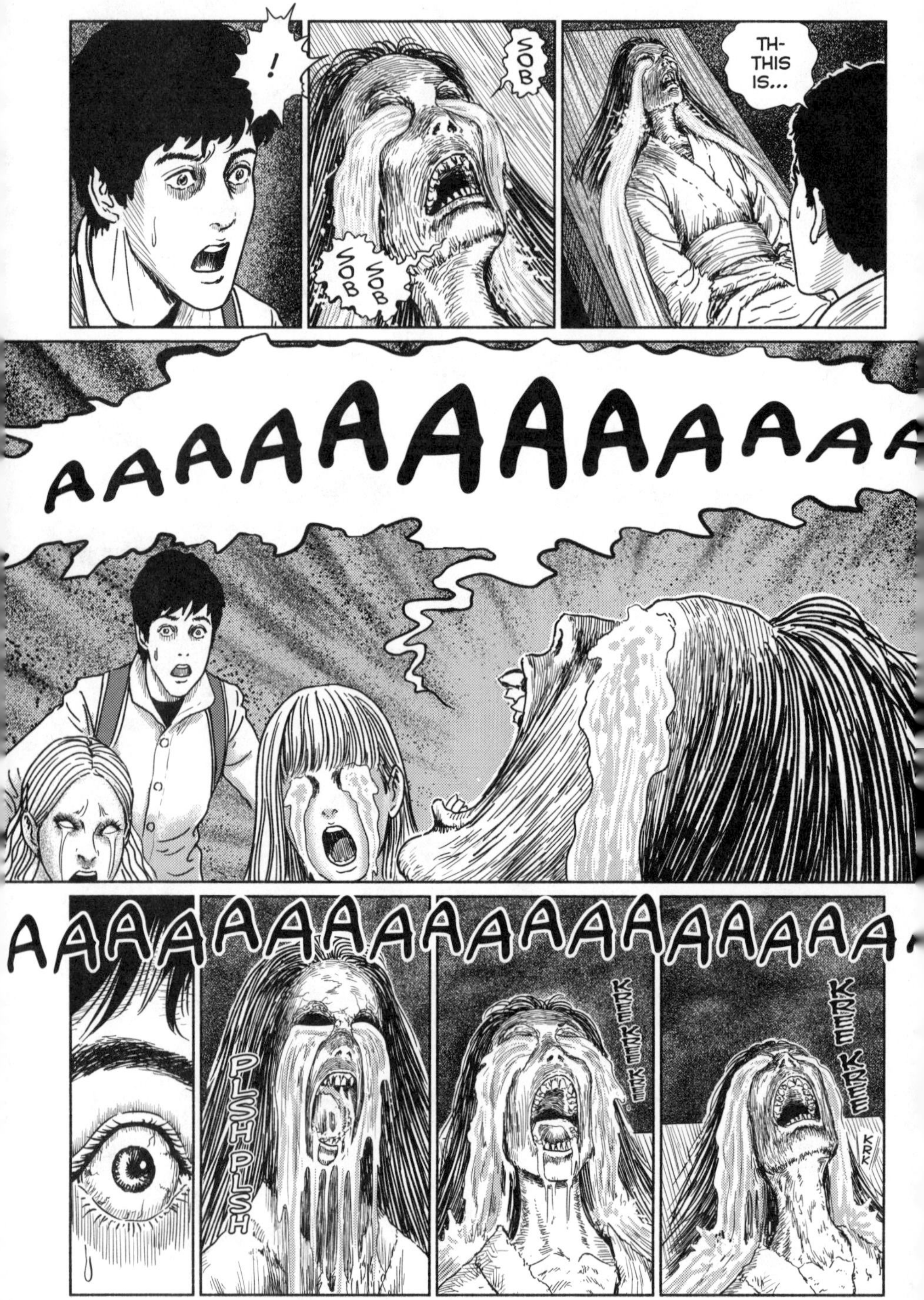
TH- THIS IS...
SOB
SOB SOB
!
AAAAAAAAAAAAA
AAAAAAAAAAAAAAAA.
KREE KREE
KRK
KREE KREE KREE
PLSHPLSH

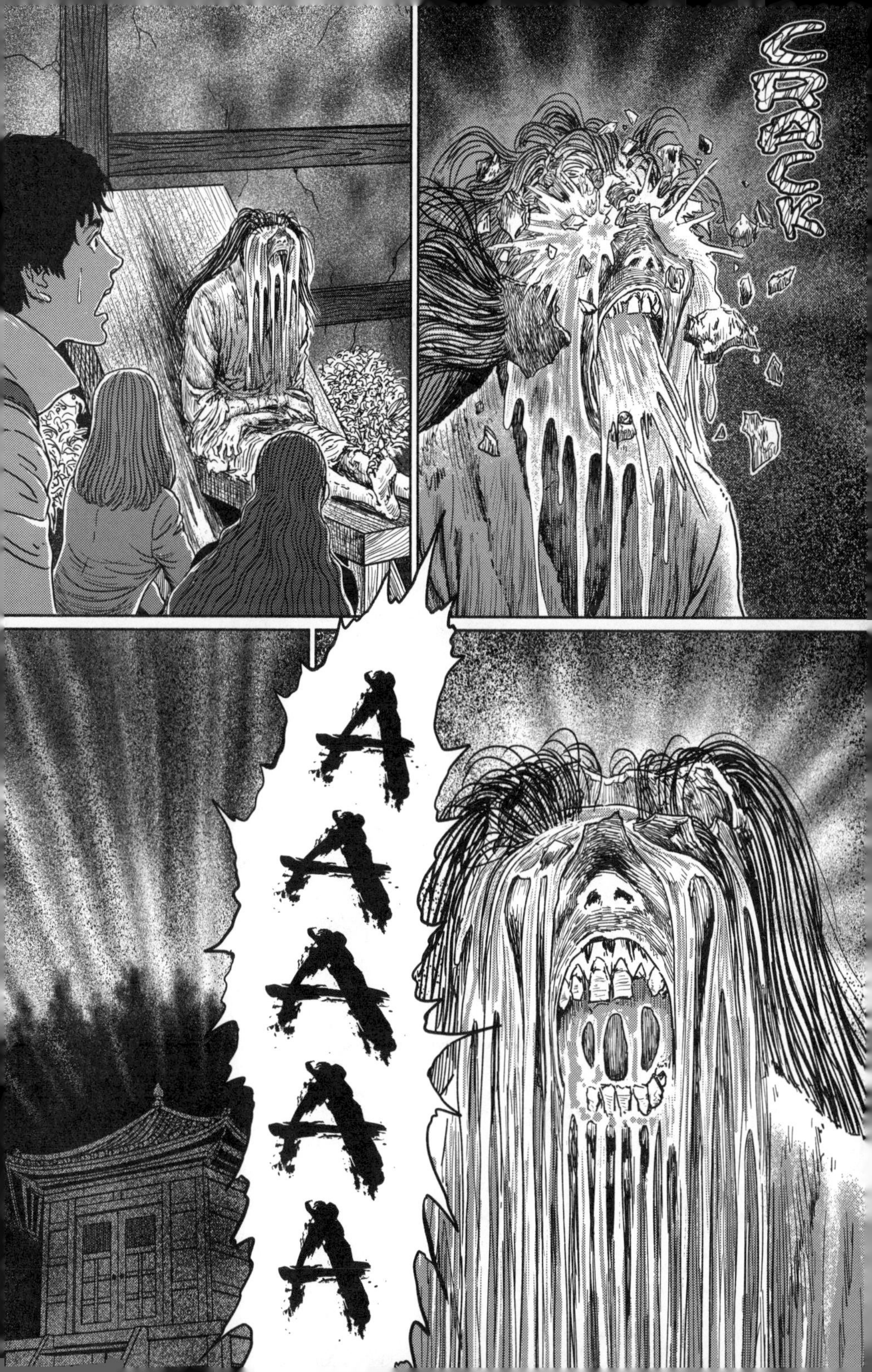
CRACK
AAAAA

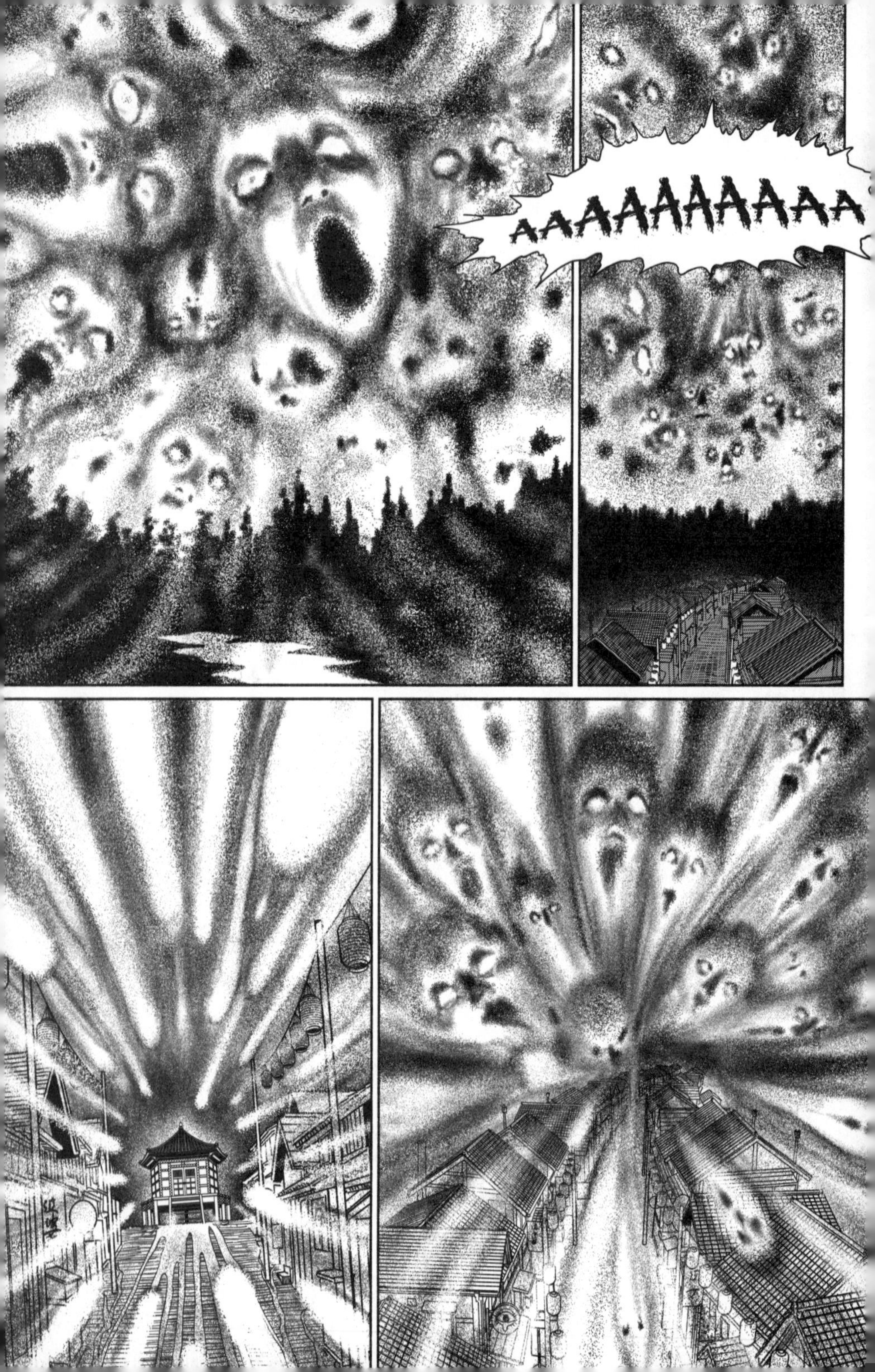
AAAAAAAAAA

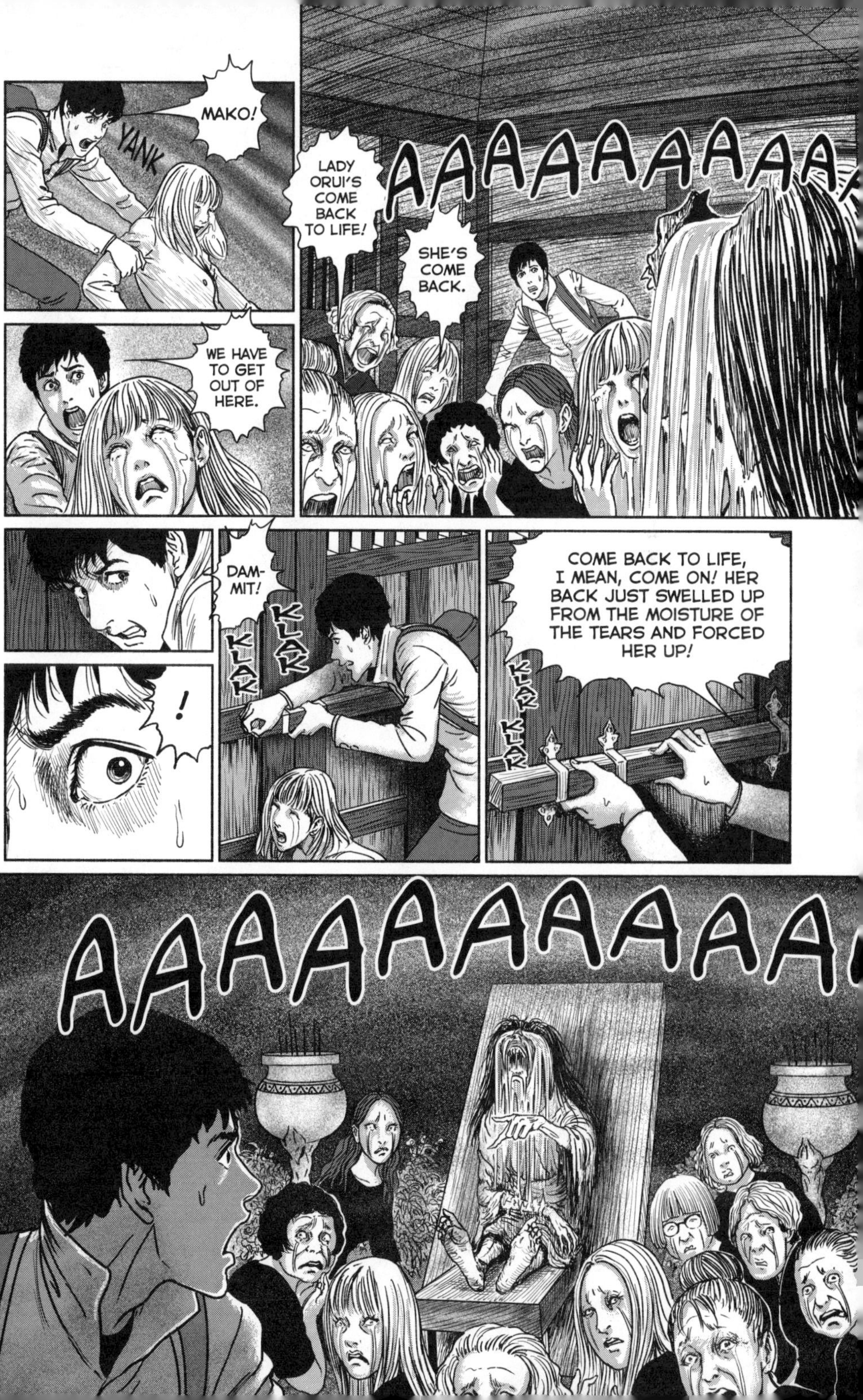
AAAAAAAAAA
LADY ORUI'S COME BACK TO LIFE!
SHE'S COME BACK.
MAKO!
YANK
WE HAVE TO GET OUT OF HERE.
COME BACK TO LIFE, I MEAN, COME ON! HER BACK JUST SWELLED UP FROM THE MOISTURE OF THE TEARS AND FORCED HER UP!
KLAK KLAK
DAM-MIT!
KLAK KLAK
!
AAAAAAAAAA

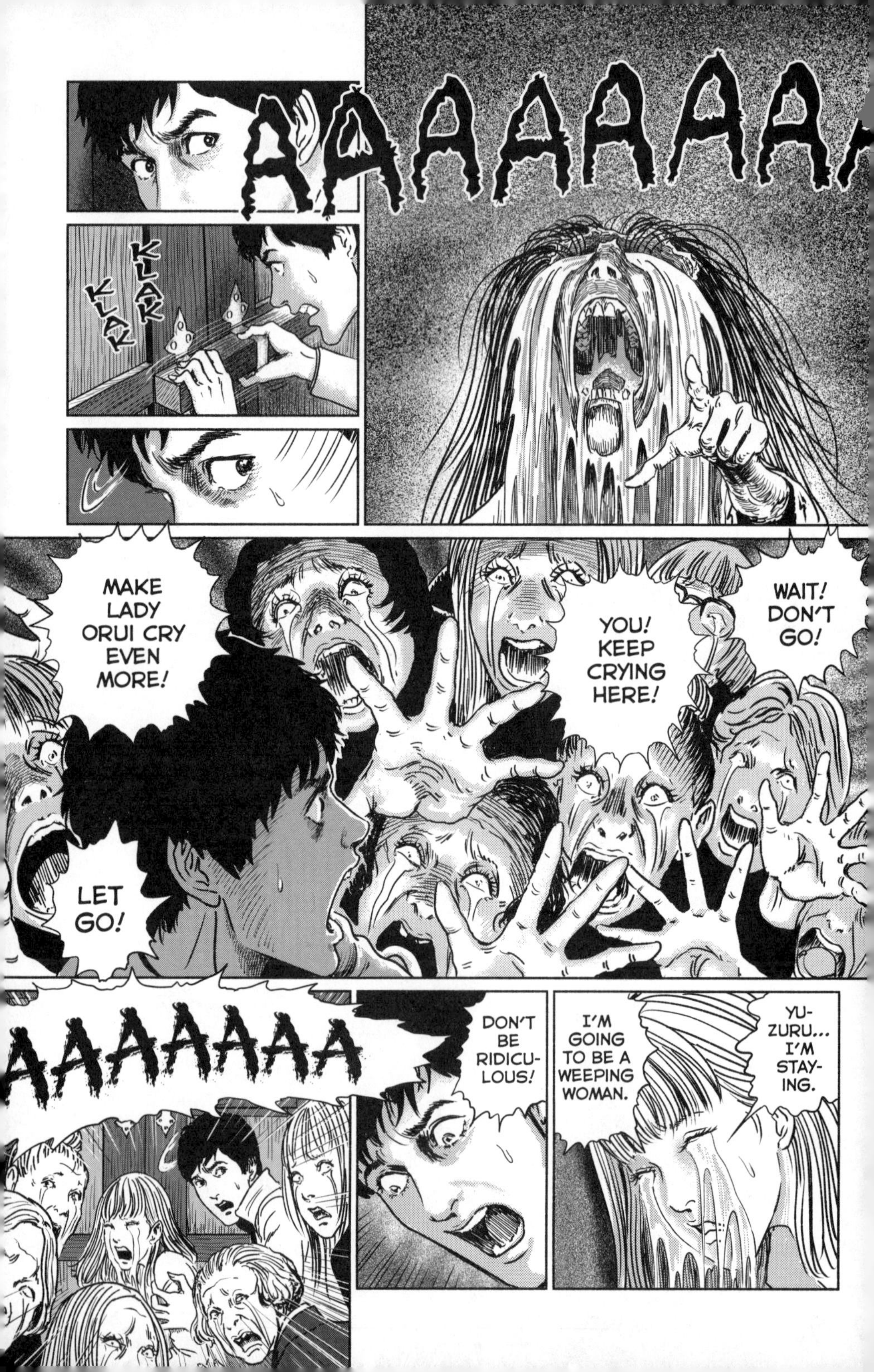

AAAAAAAAA
KLAK KLAK
WAIT! DON'T GO!
YOU! KEEP CRYING HERE!
MAKE LADY ORUI CRY EVEN MORE!
LET GO!
YU-ZURU... I'M STAYING.
I'M GOING TO BE A WEEPING WOMAN.
DON'T BE RIDICULOUS!
AAAAAAA

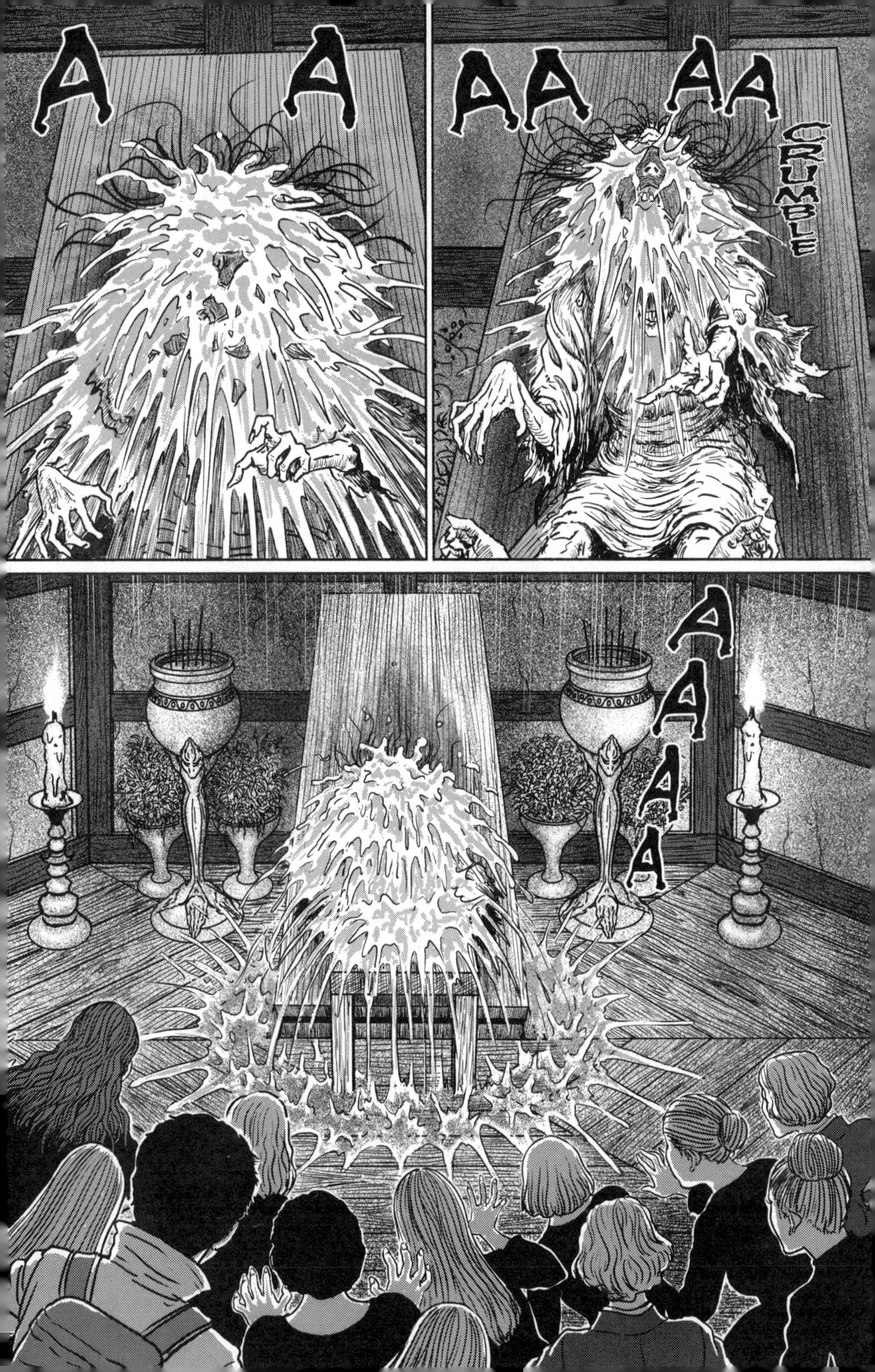
AA AA
CRUMBLE
A A
AAAAA

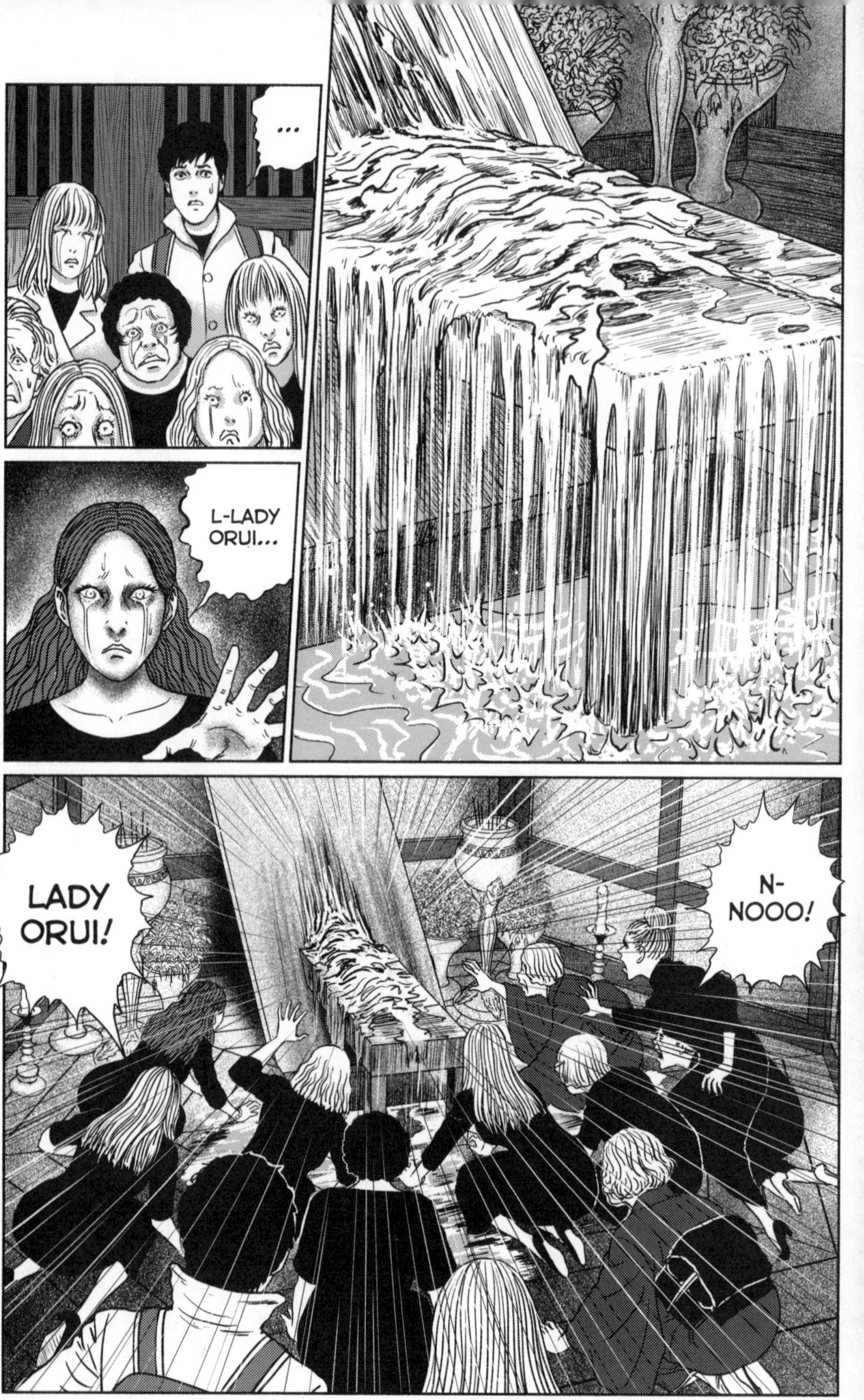
...
L-LADY ORUI...
N-NOOO!
LADY ORUI!

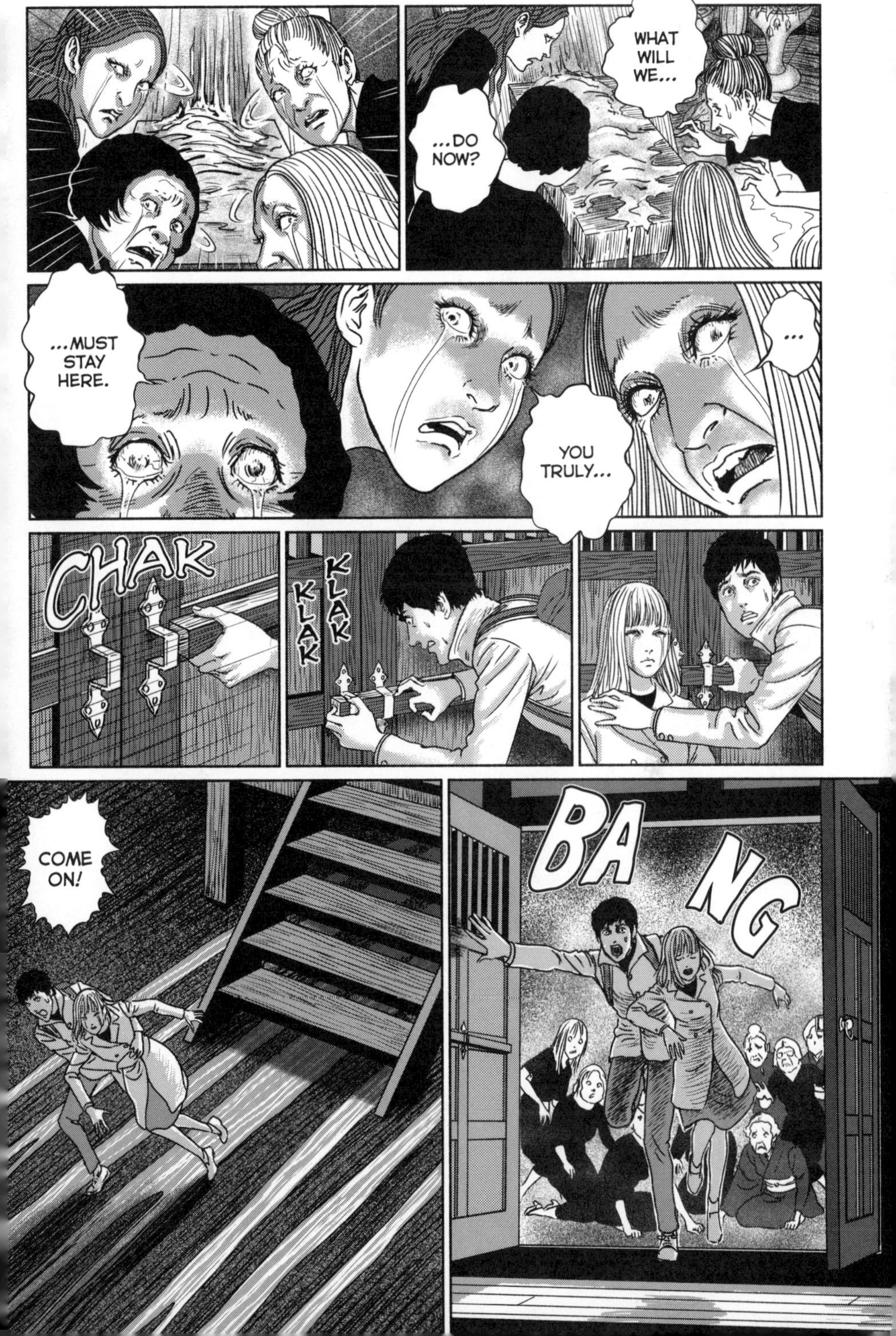
WHAT WILL WE...
...DO NOW?
...
YOU TRULY...
...MUST STAY HERE.
KLAK KLAK
CHAK
BANG
COME ON!

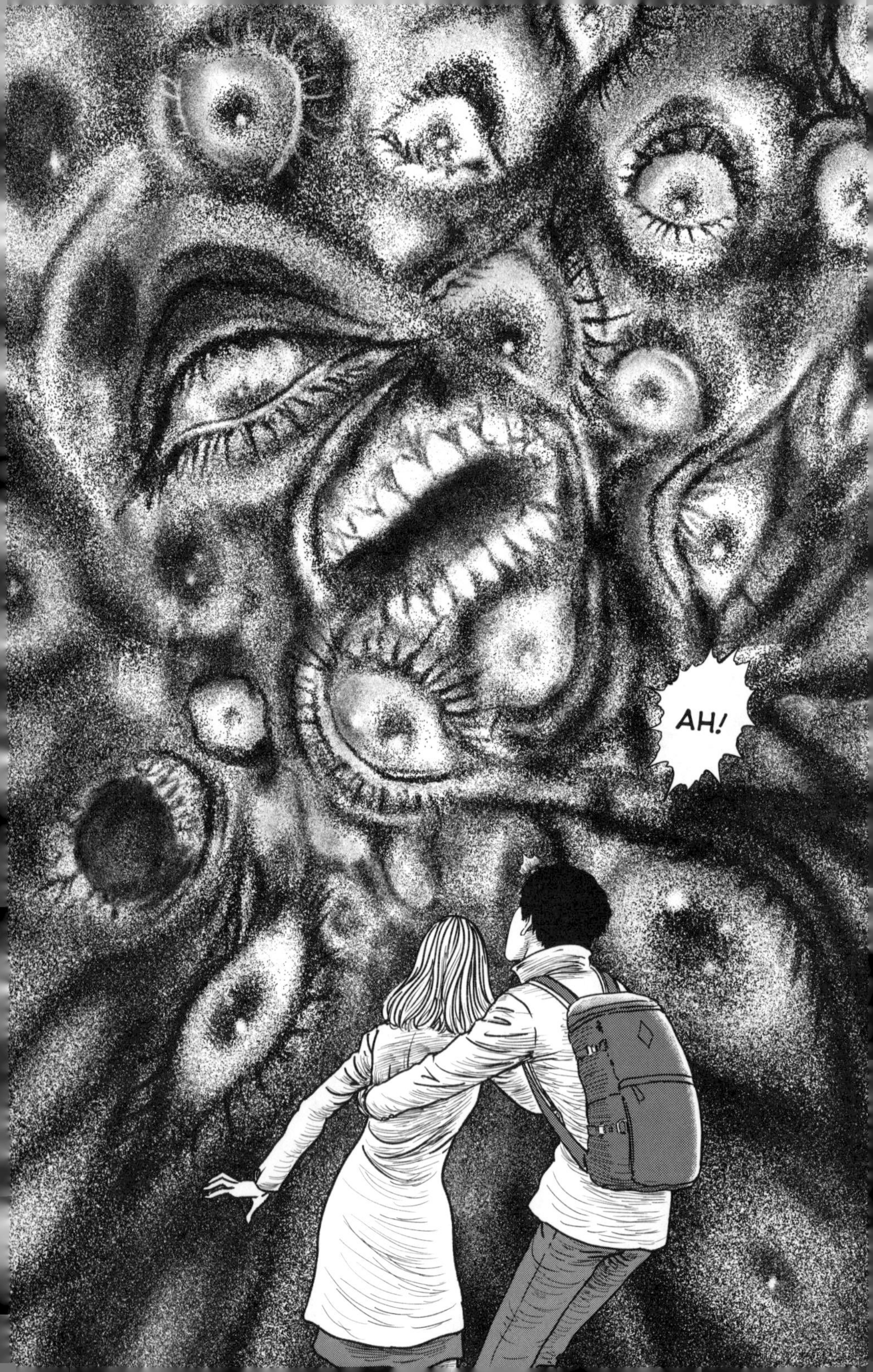
AH!

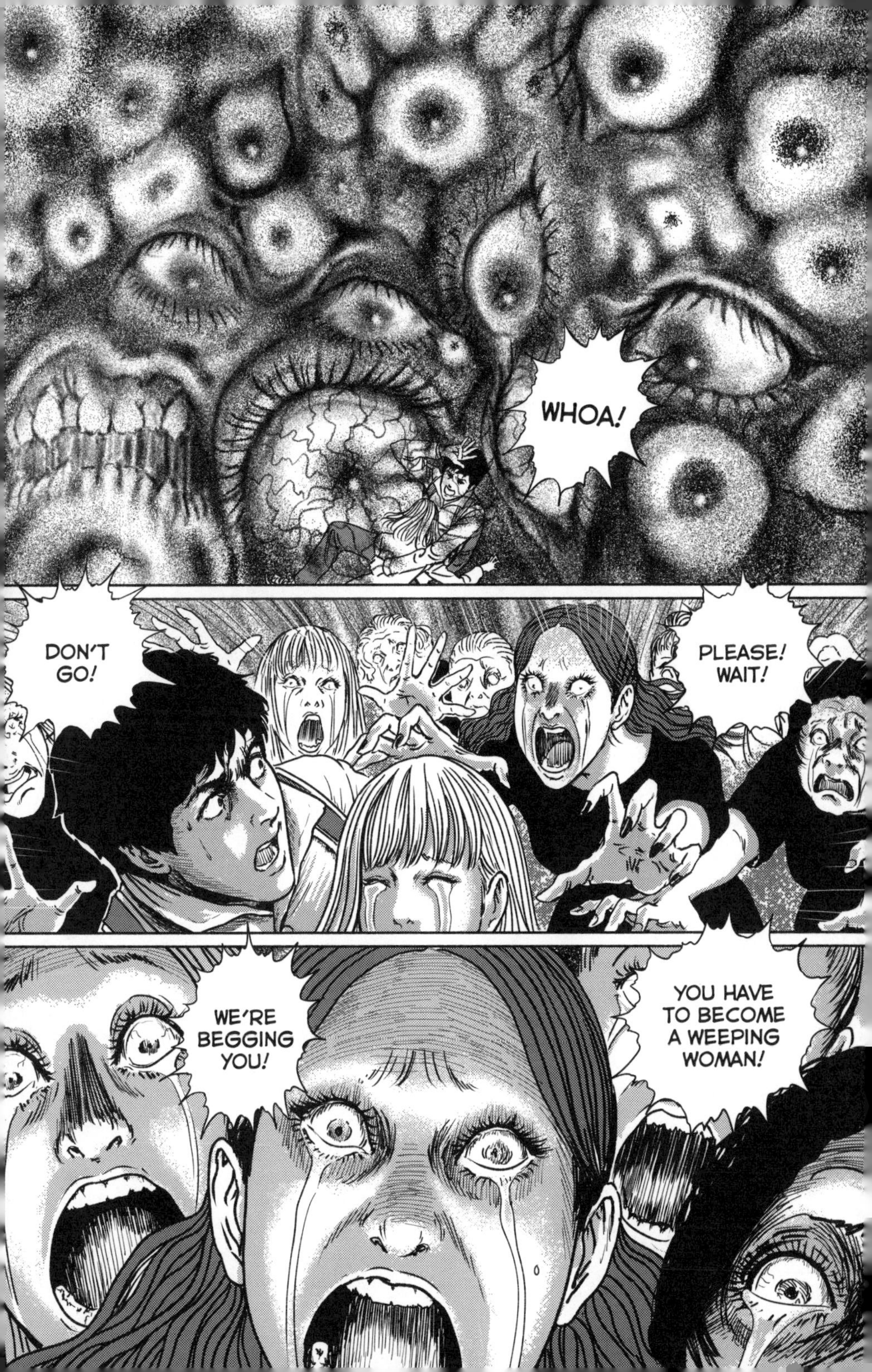
WHOA!
PLEASE! WAIT!
DON'T GO!
YOU HAVE TO BECOME A WEEPING WOMAN!
WE'RE BEGGING YOU!

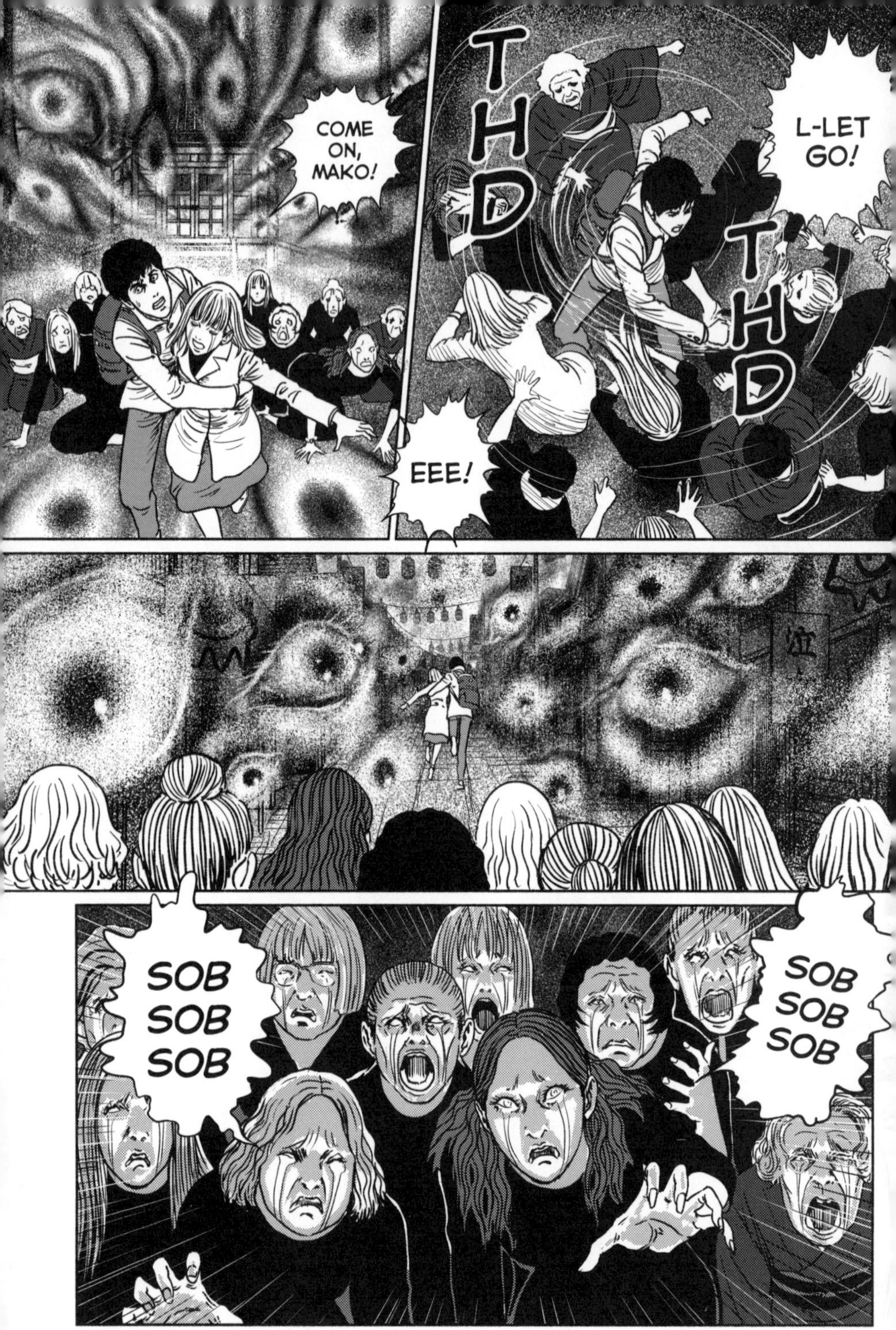
L-LET GO!
THD
THD
EEE!
COME ON, MAKO!
SOB SOB SOB
SOB SOB SOB

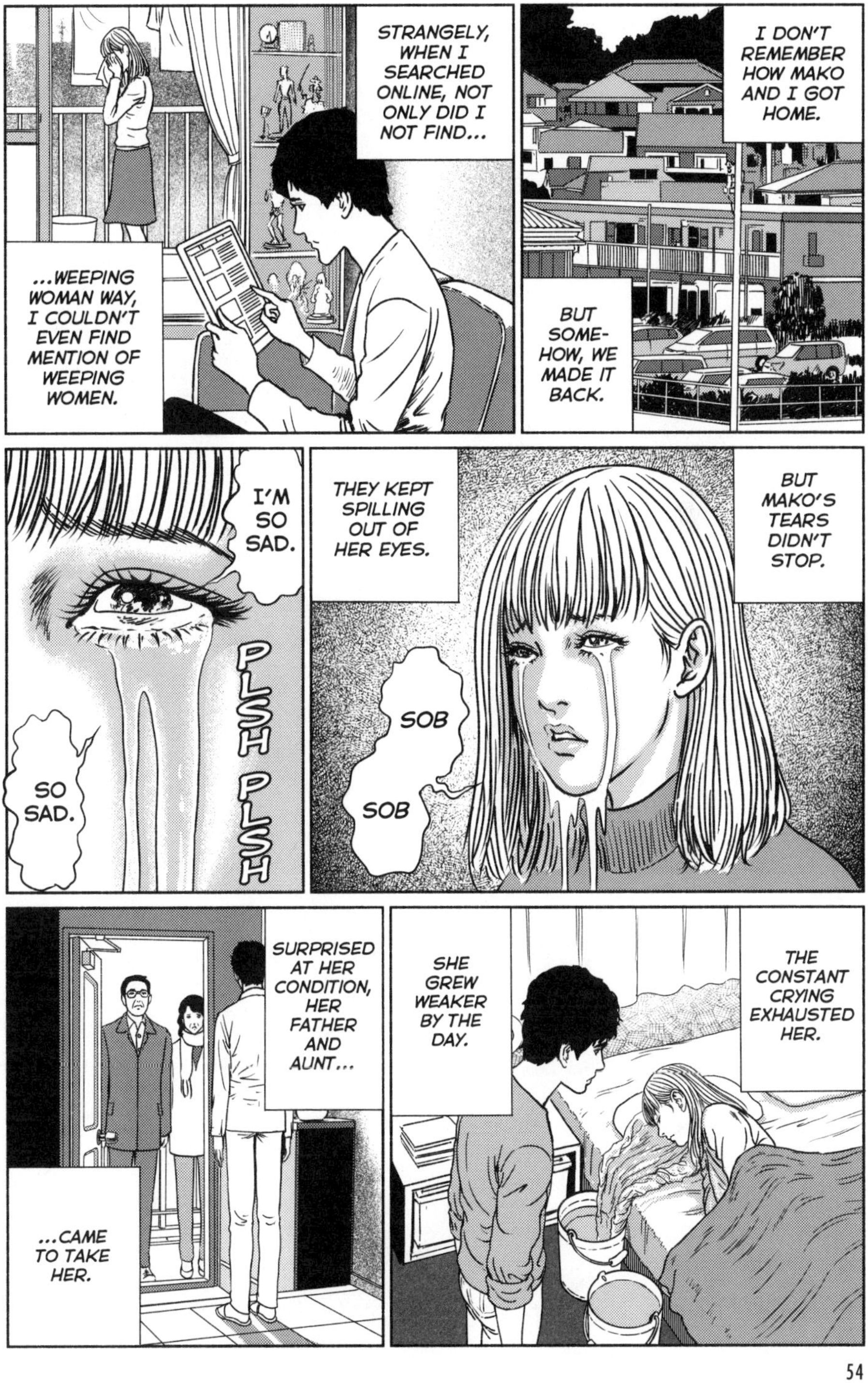
I DON'T REMEMBER HOW MAKO AND I GOT HOME.
BUT SOMEHOW, WE MADE IT BACK.
STRANGELY, WHEN I SEARCHED ONLINE, NOT ONLY DID I NOT FIND...
...WEEPING WOMAN WAY, I COULDN'T EVEN FIND MENTION OF WEEPING WOMEN.
BUT MAKO'S TEARS DIDN'T STOP.
THEY KEPT SPILLING OUT OF HER EYES.
SOB
SOB
I'M SO SAD.
PLSH PLSH
SO SAD.
THE CONSTANT CRYING EXHAUSTED HER.
SHE GREW WEAKER BY THE DAY.
SURPRISED AT HER CONDITION, HER FATHER AND AUNT...
...CAME TO TAKE HER.

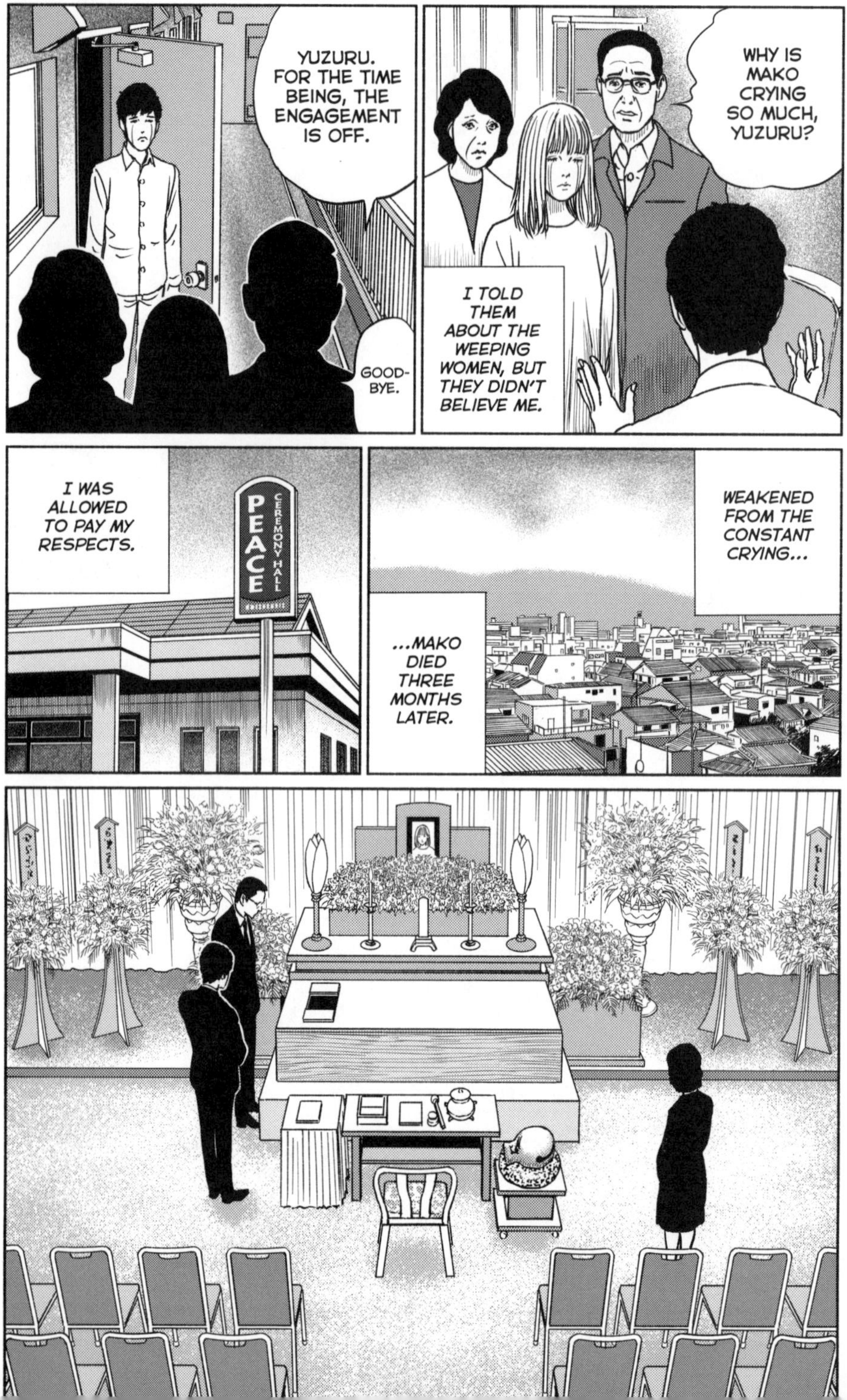
WHY IS MAKO CRYING SO MUCH, YUZURU?
I TOLD THEM ABOUT THE WEEPING WOMEN, BUT THEY DIDN'T BELIEVE ME.
YUZURU. FOR THE TIME BEING, THE ENGAGEMENT IS OFF.
GOOD-BYE.
WEAKENED FROM THE CONSTANT CRYING...
...MAKO DIED THREE MONTHS LATER.
I WAS ALLOWED TO PAY MY RESPECTS.
PEACE
CEREMONY HALL

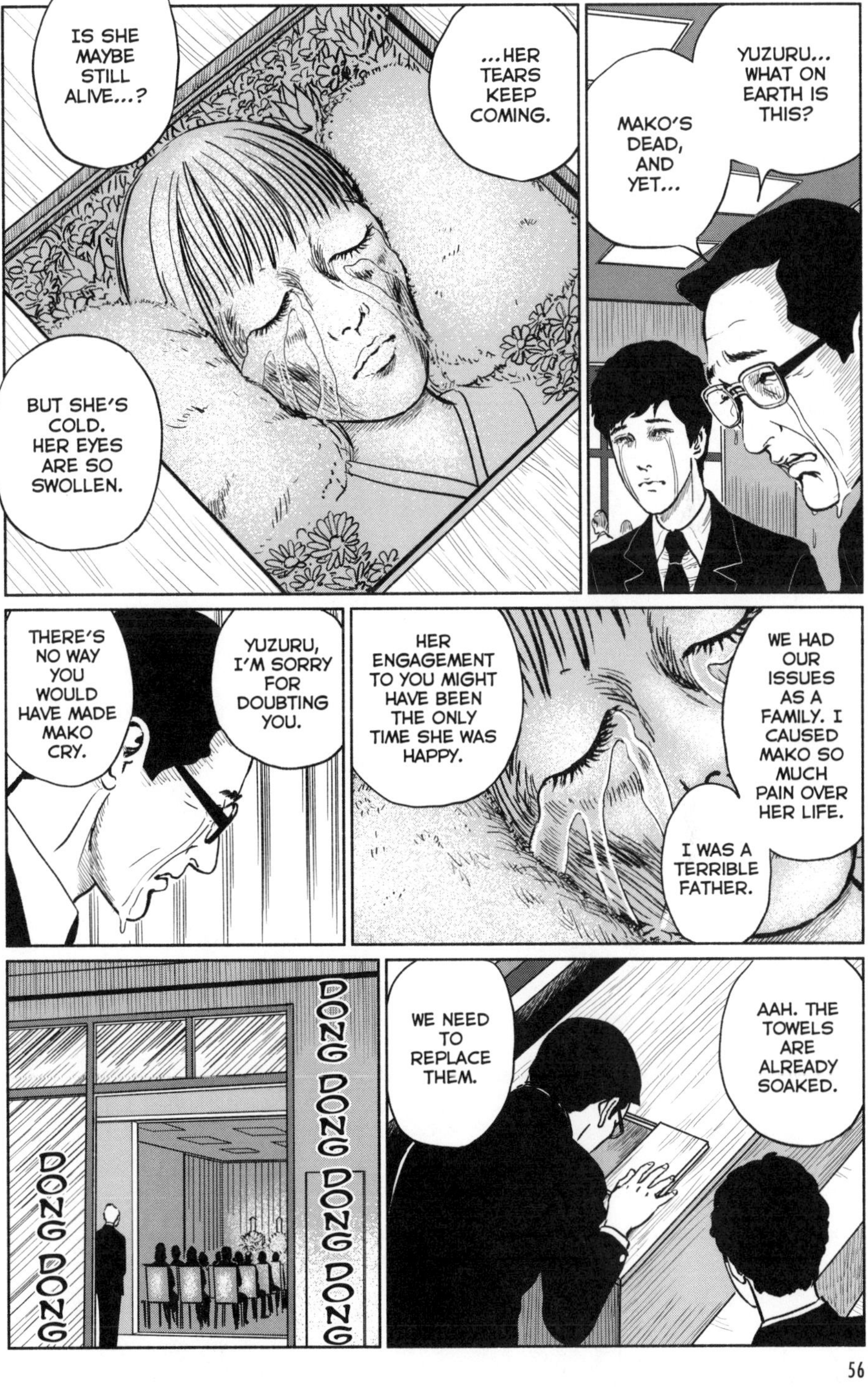
YUZURU... WHAT ON EARTH IS THIS?
MAKO'S DEAD, AND YET...
...HER TEARS KEEP COMING.
IS SHE MAYBE STILL ALIVE...?
BUT SHE'S COLD. HER EYES ARE SO SWOLLEN.
WE HAD OUR ISSUES AS A FAMILY. I CAUSED MAKO SO MUCH PAIN OVER HER LIFE.
I WAS A TERRIBLE FATHER.
HER ENGAGEMENT TO YOU MIGHT HAVE BEEN THE ONLY TIME SHE WAS HAPPY.
YUZURU, I'M SORRY FOR DOUBTING YOU.
THERE'S NO WAY YOU WOULD HAVE MADE MAKO CRY.
AAH. THE TOWELS ARE ALREADY SOAKED.
WE NEED TO REPLACE THEM.
DONG DONG DONG DONG
DONG DONG

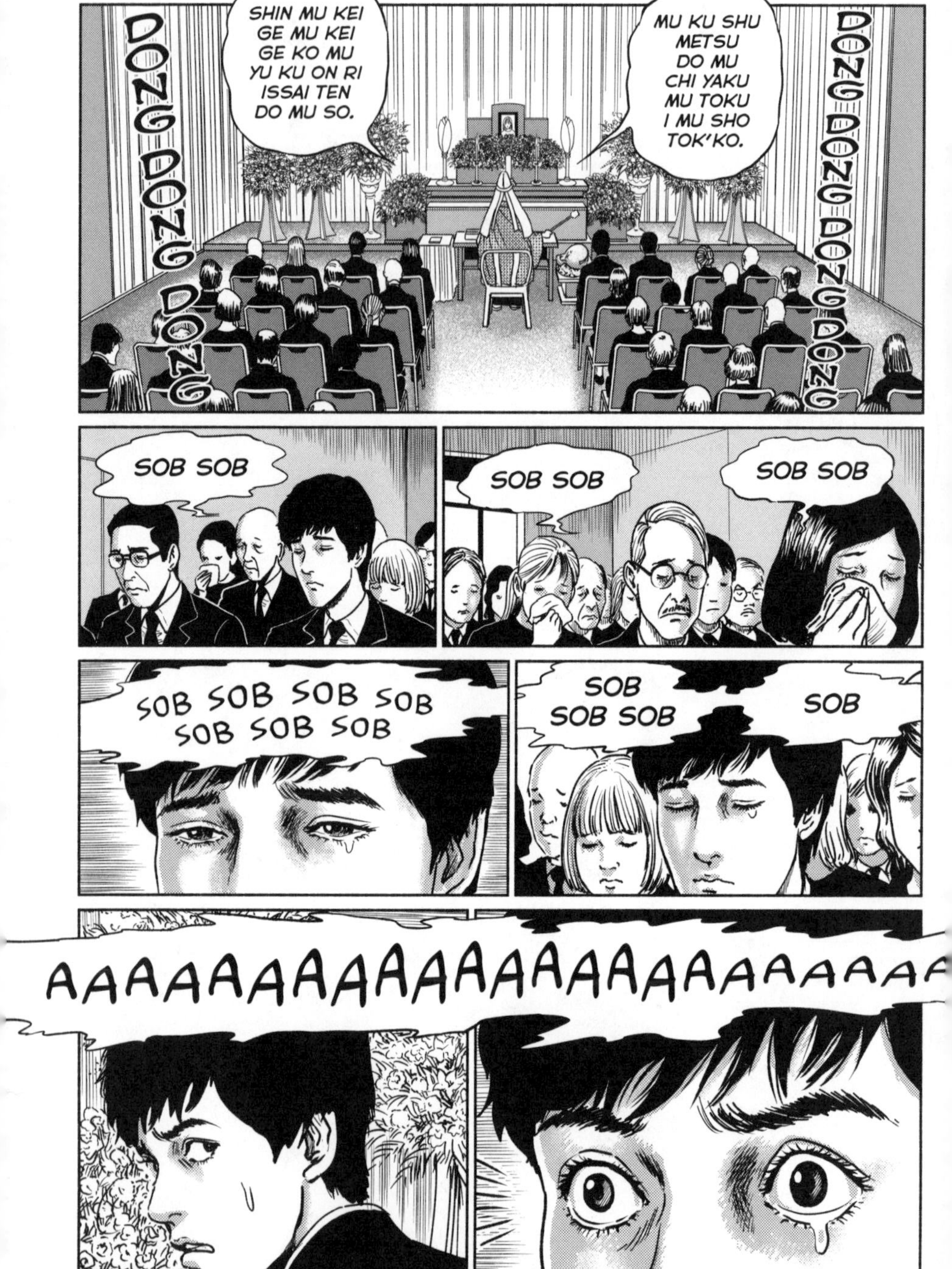
DONG DONG DONG DONG
MU KU SHU METSU DO MU CHI YAKU MU TOKU I MU SHO TOK'KO.
SHIN MU KEI GE MU KEI GE KO MU YU KU ON RI ISSAI TEN DO MU SO.
DONG DONG DONG
SOB SOB
SOB SOB
SOB SOB
SOB
SOB SOB SOB
SOB SOB SOB SOB SOB SOB SOB
AAAAAAAAAAAAAAAAAAAAAA

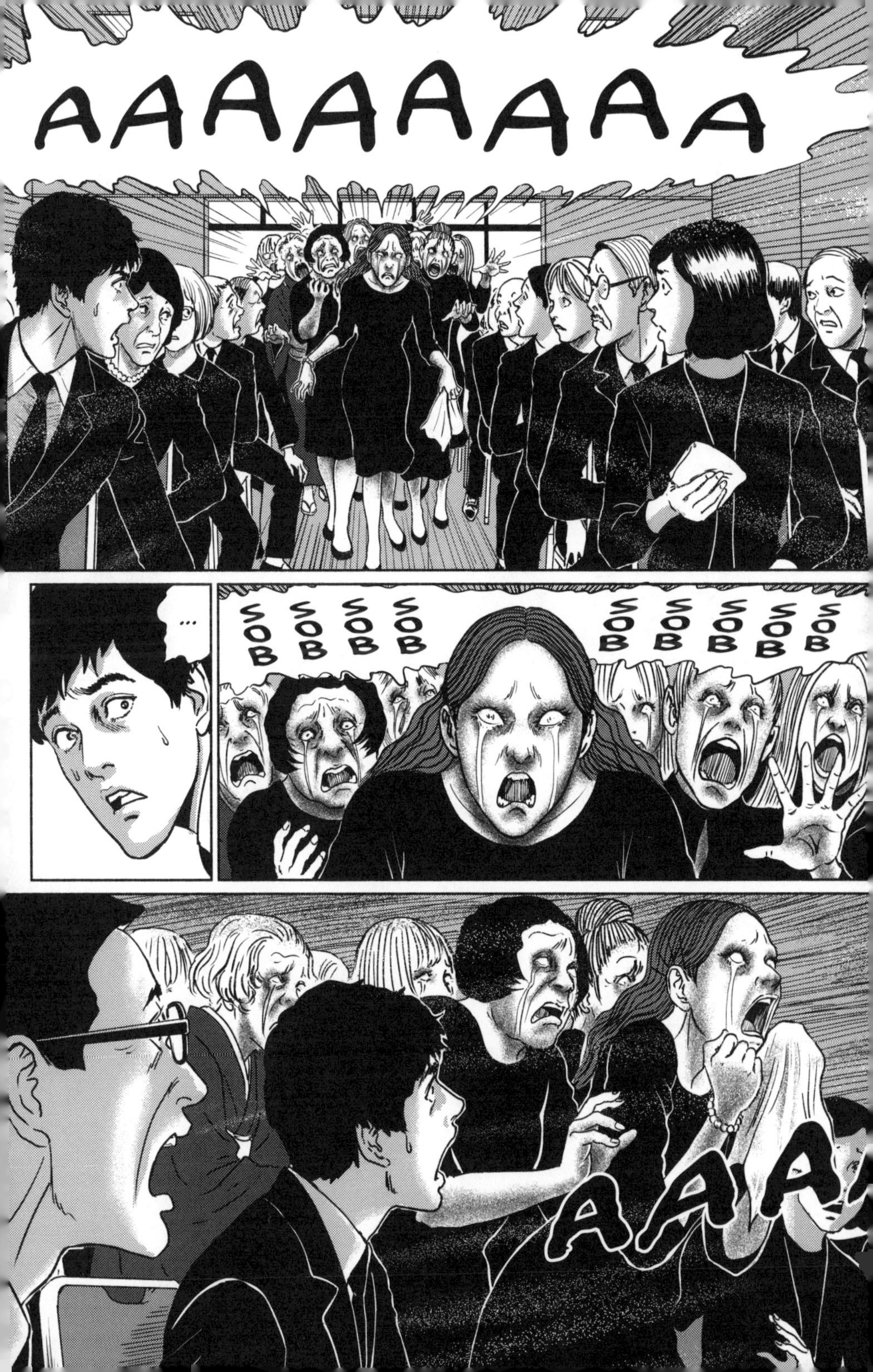
AAAAAAAA
SOB SOB SOB SOB SOB
SOB SOB SOB SOB
...
AAA

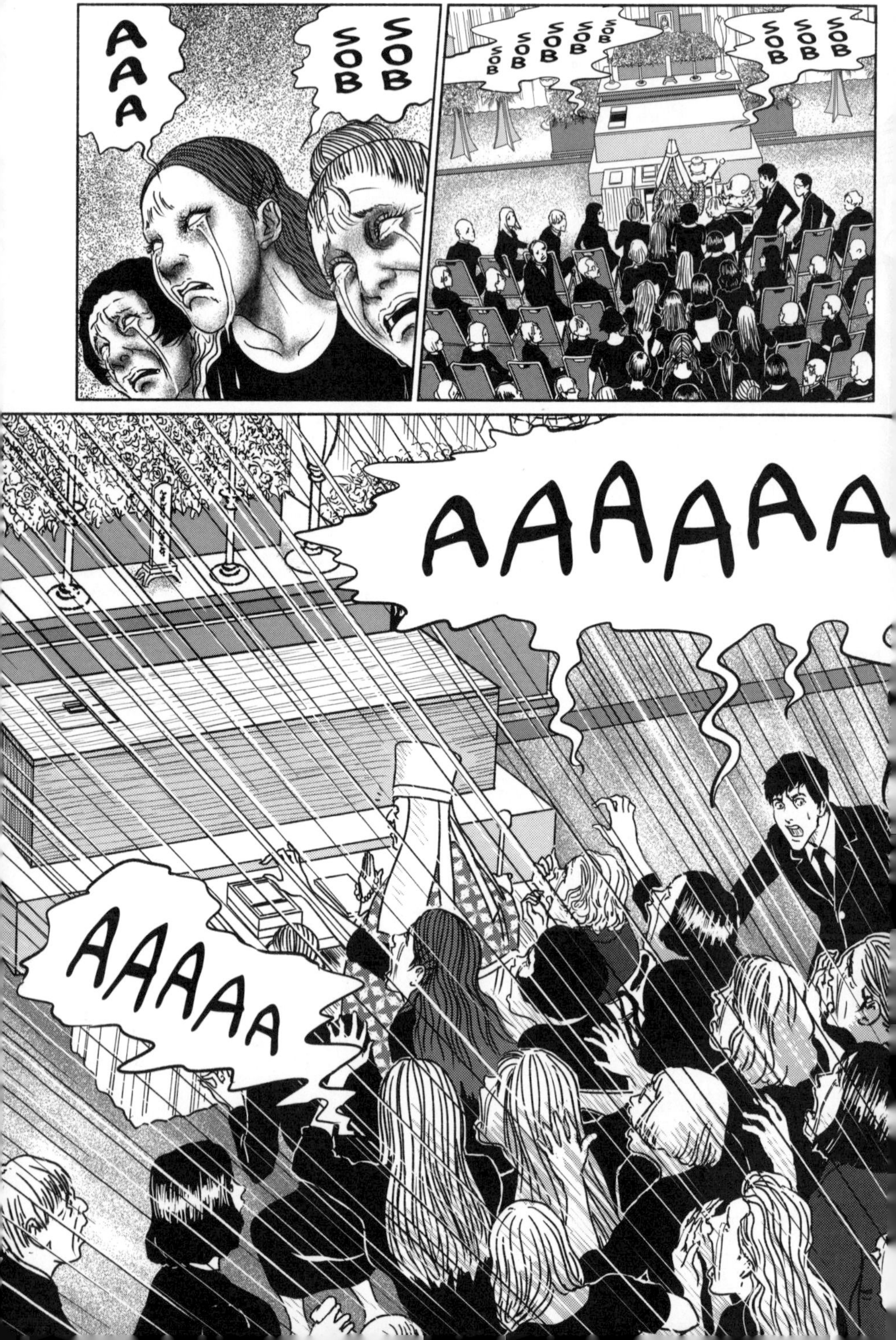
SOB SOB SOB
SOB SOB SOB SOB SOB
SOB SOB
AAA
AAAAAA
AAAAA

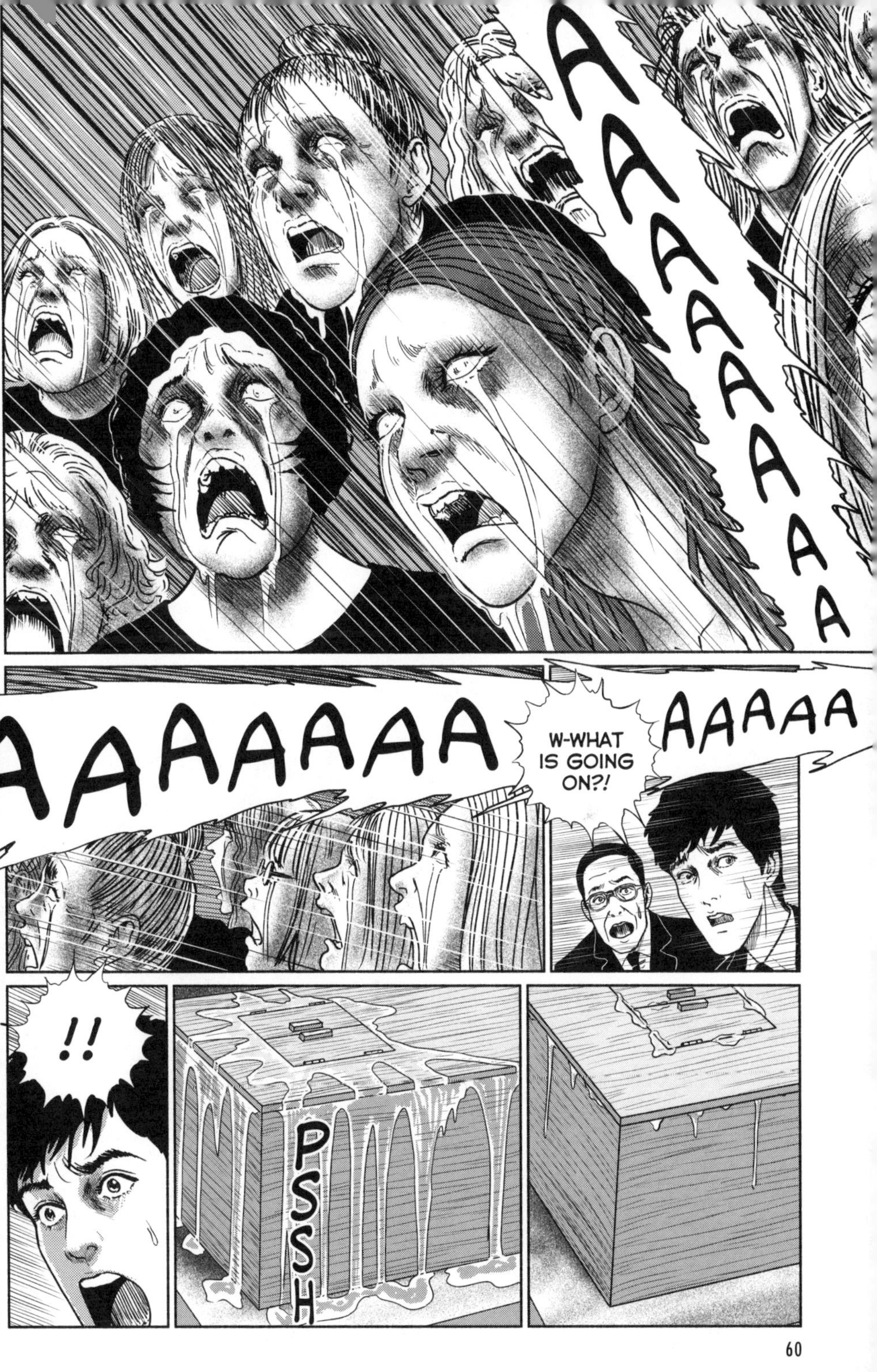
AAAAAAAA
AAAAA
W-WHAT IS GOING ON?!
AAAAAAA
PSSH
!!

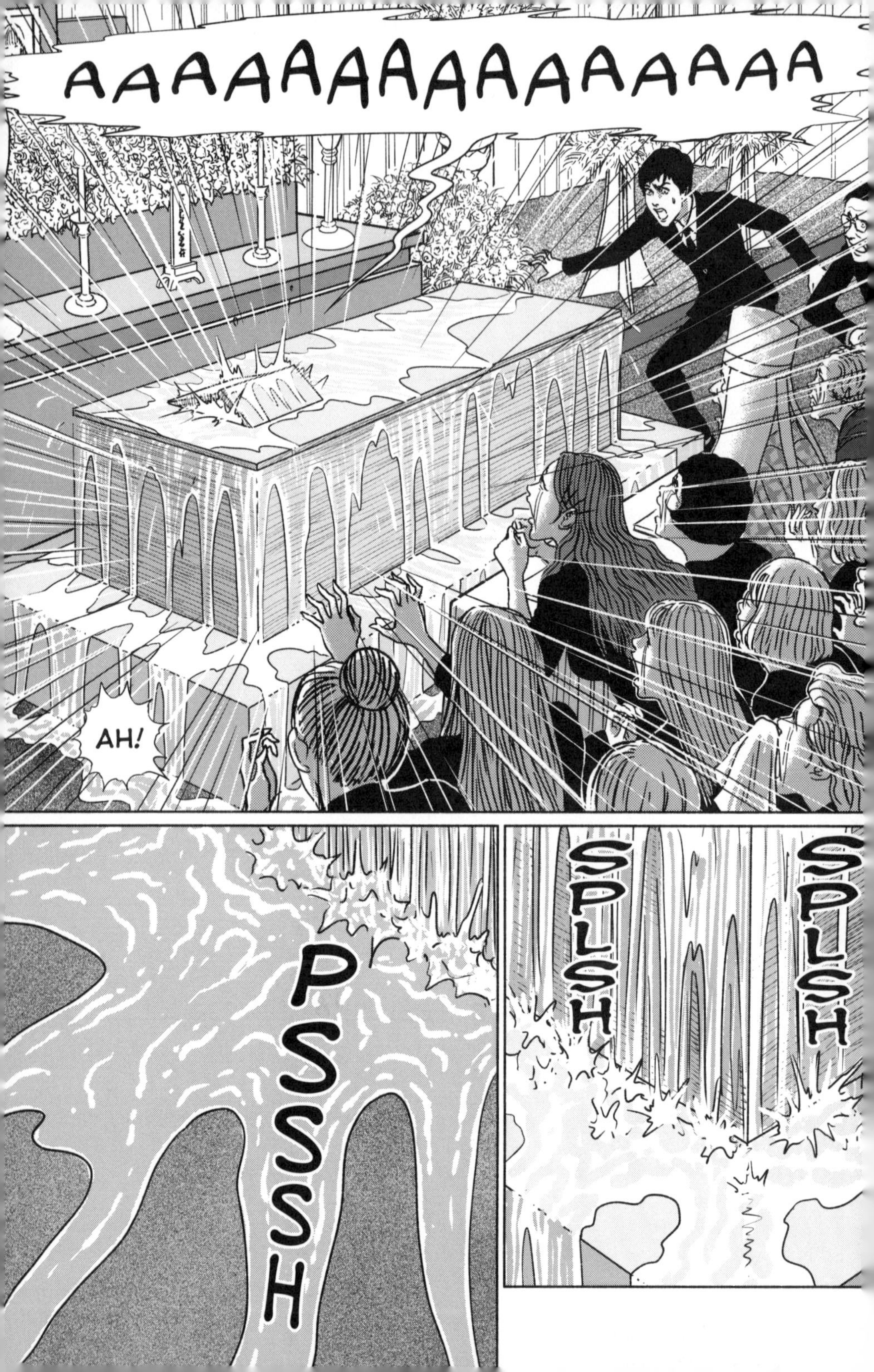
AAAAAAAAAAAAAA
AH!
SPLSH
SPLSH
PSSSH

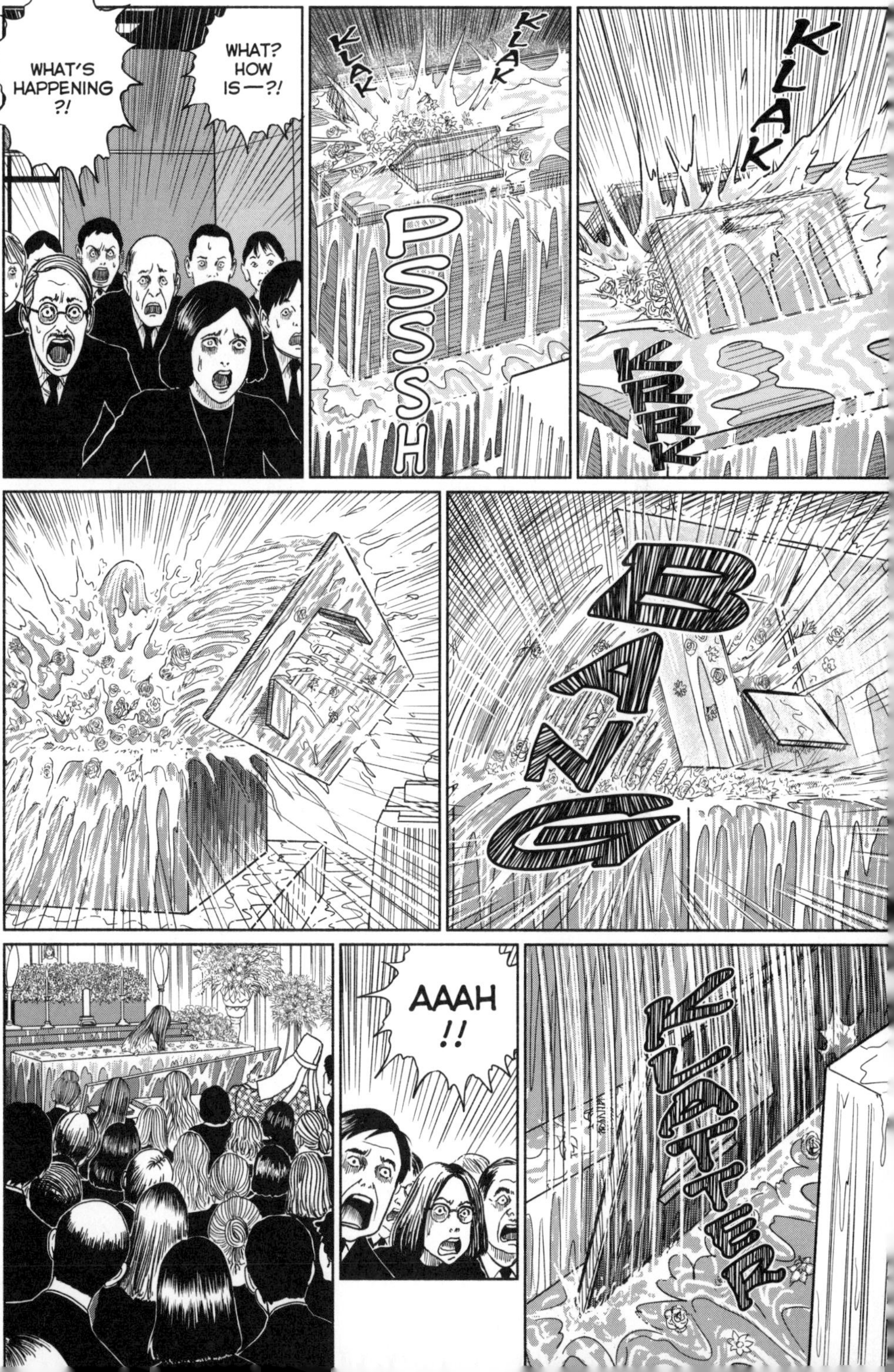
KLAK
KLAK
KLAK
KLAK
PSSSH
WHAT? HOW IS—?!
WHAT'S HAPPENING ?!
BANG
KLATTER
AAAH !!

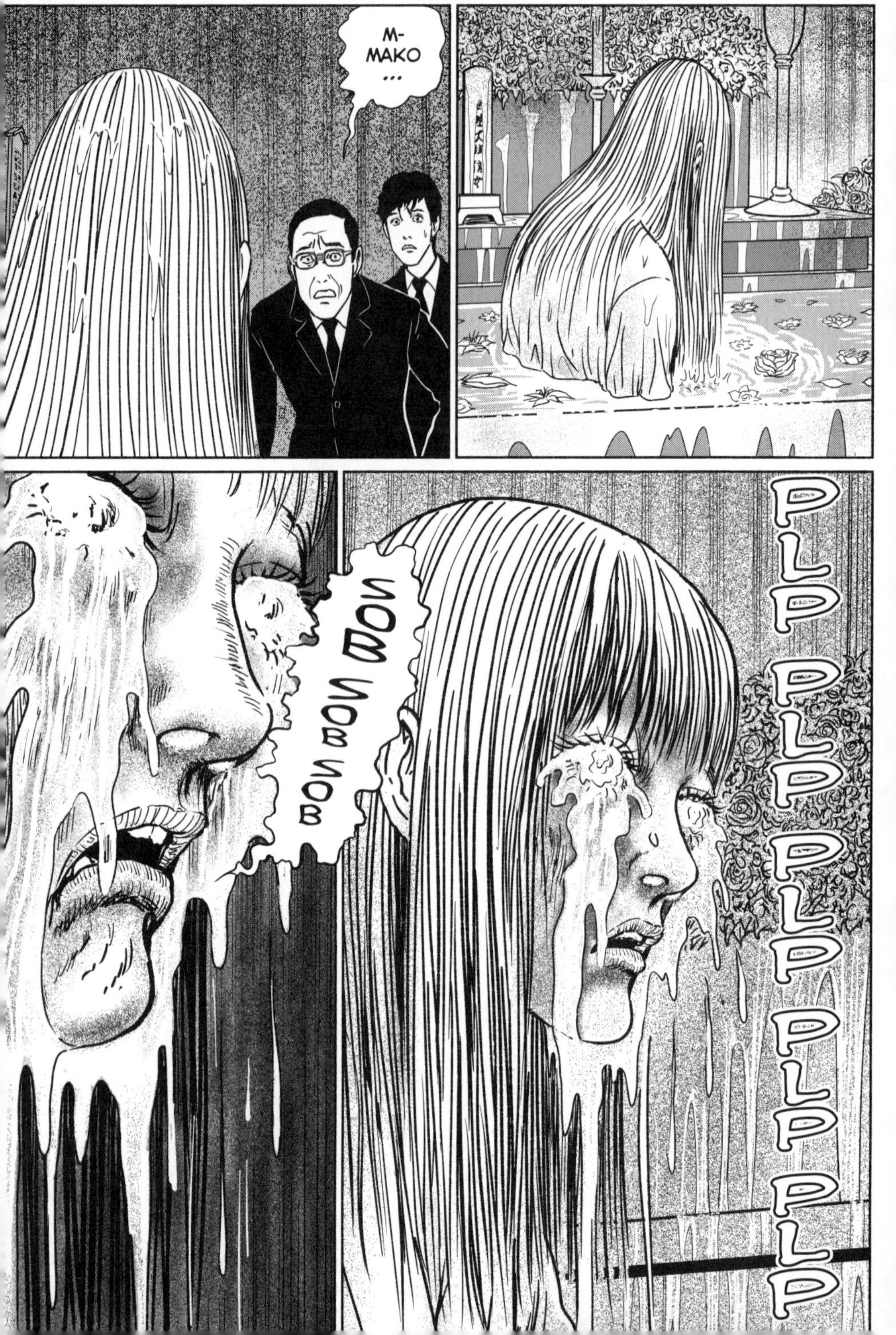
M-MAKO ...
PLP PLP PLP PLP PLP
SOB SOB SOB

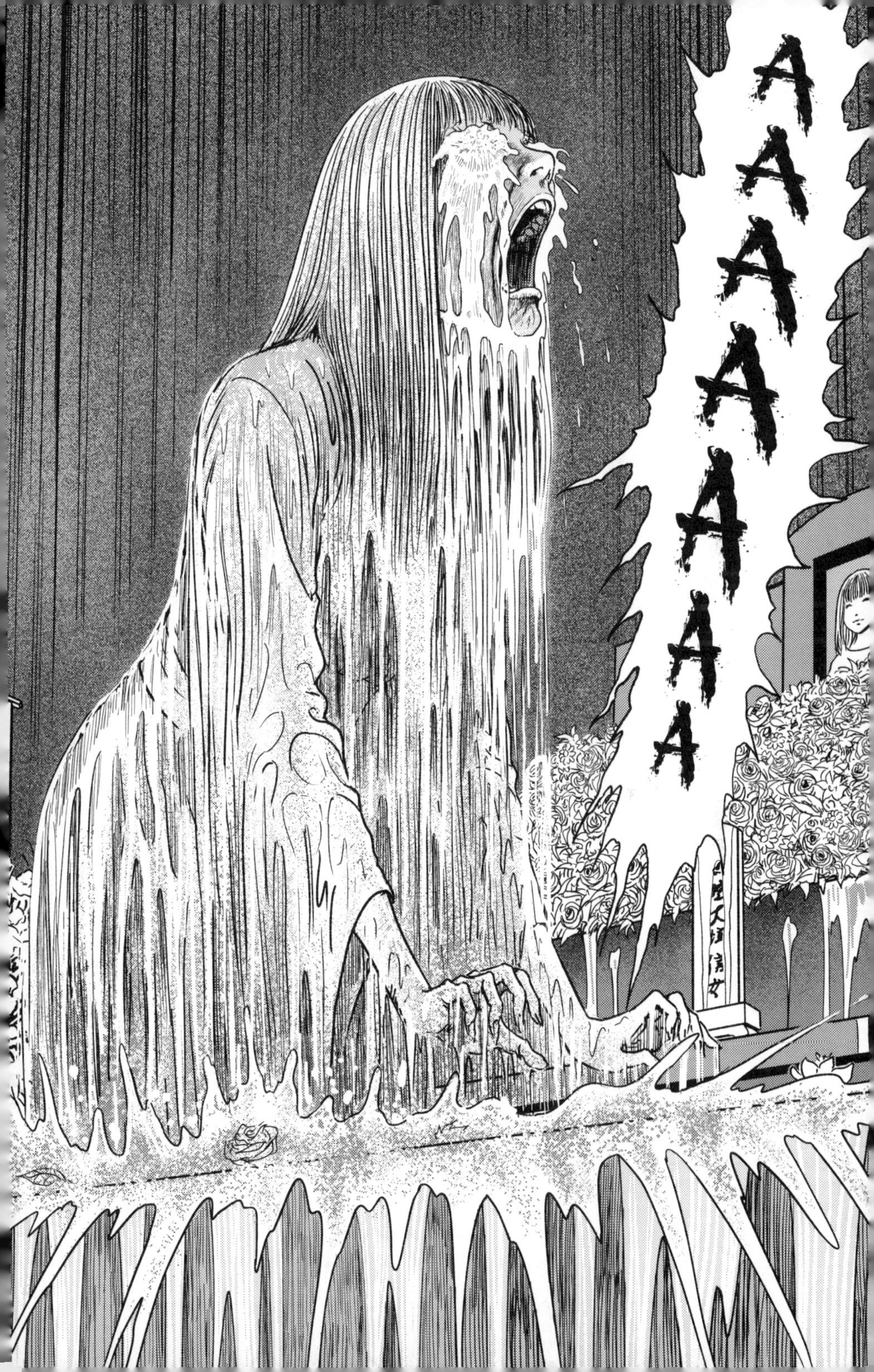
AAAAAAA

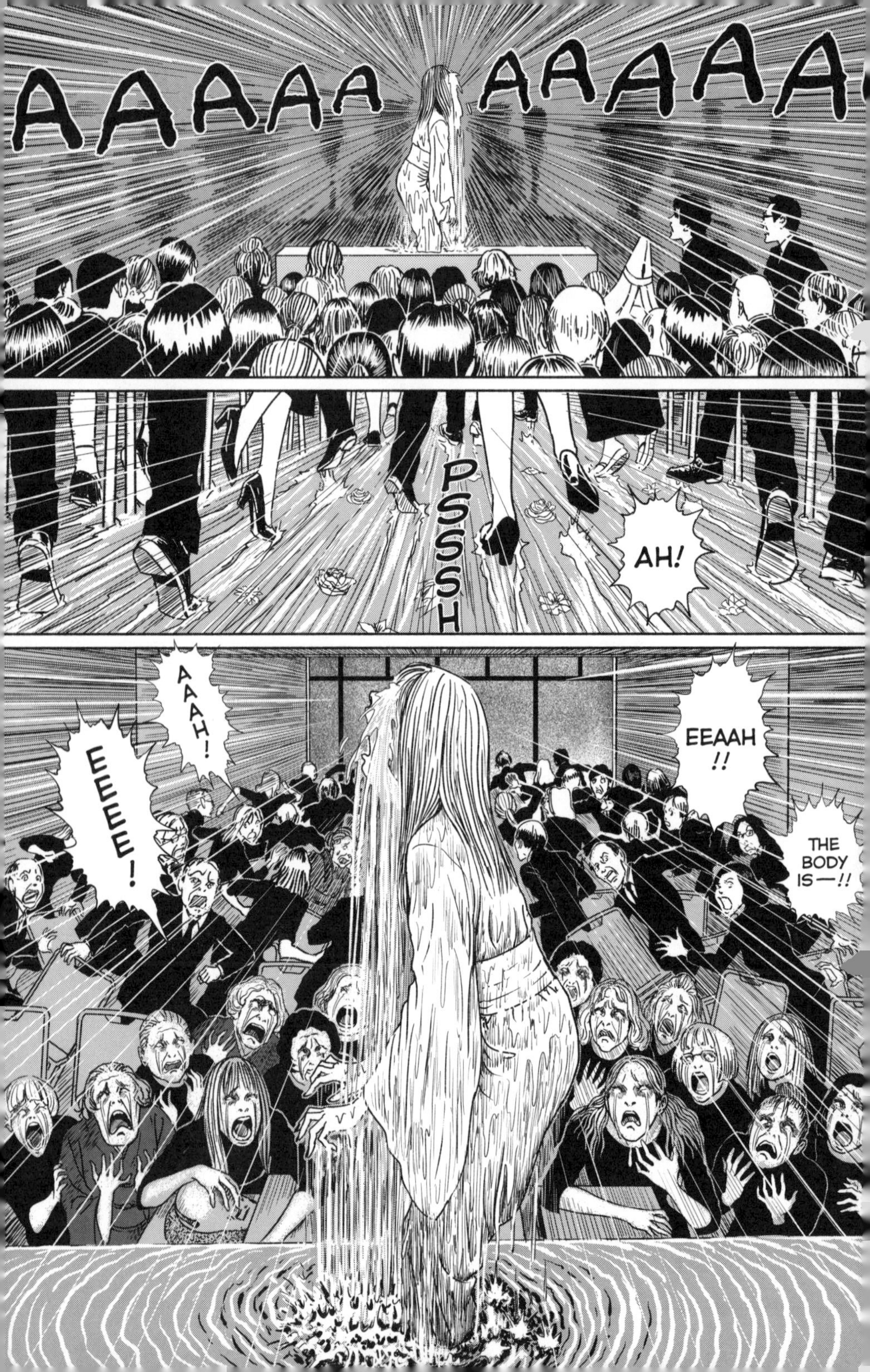
AAAAA AAAAA
AH!
PSSSH
THE BODY IS—!!
EEAAH!!
AAAH!
EEEE!

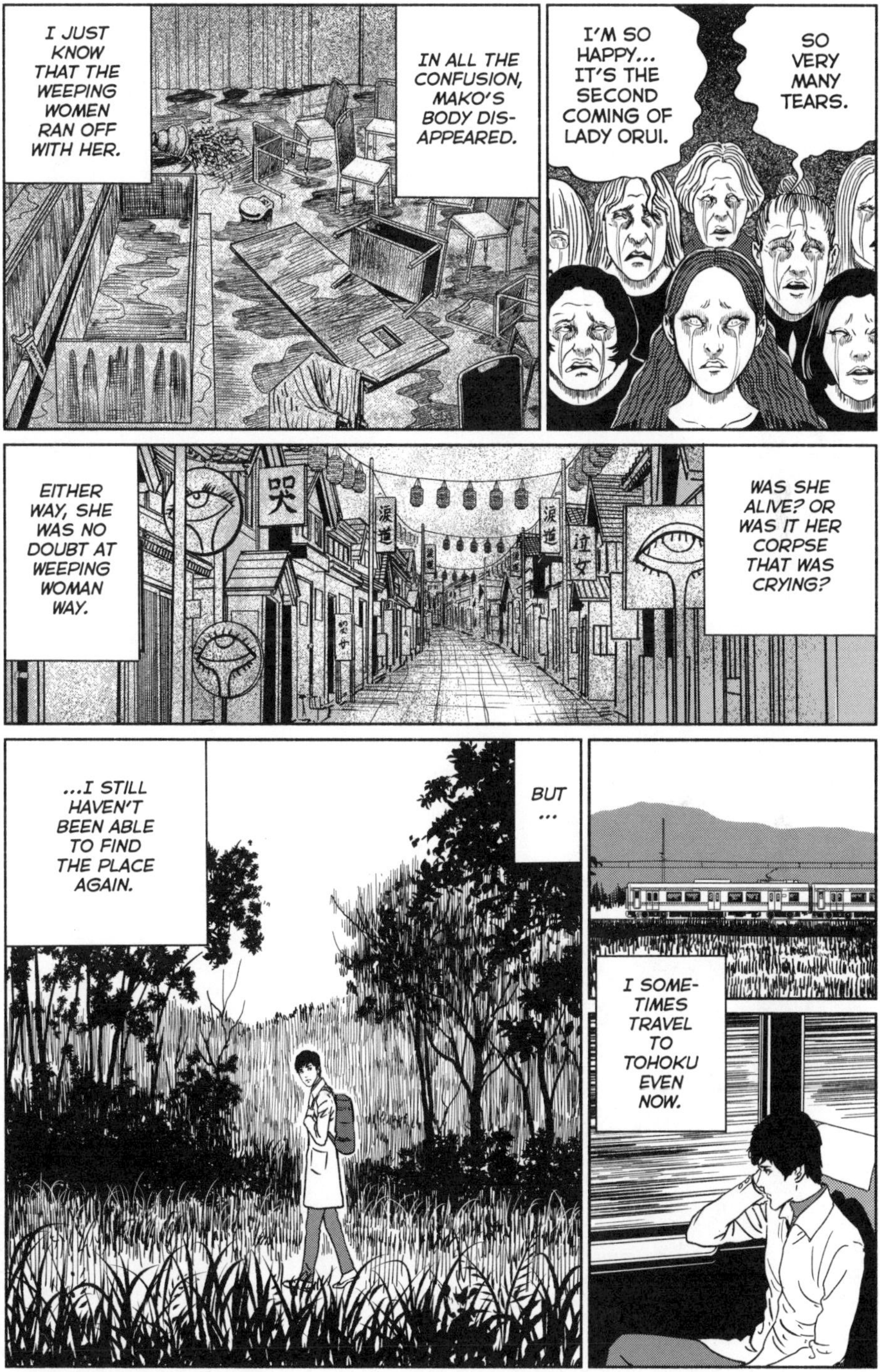
SO VERY MANY TEARS.
I'M SO HAPPY... IT'S THE SECOND COMING OF LADY ORUI.
IN ALL THE CONFUSION, MAKO'S BODY DIS-APPEARED.
I JUST KNOW THAT THE WEEPING WOMEN RAN OFF WITH HER.
WAS SHE ALIVE? OR WAS IT HER CORPSE THAT WAS CRYING?
EITHER WAY, SHE WAS NO DOUBT AT WEEPING WOMAN WAY.
I SOME-TIMES TRAVEL TO TOHOKU EVEN NOW.
BUT ...
...I STILL HAVEN'T BEEN ABLE TO FIND THE PLACE AGAIN.

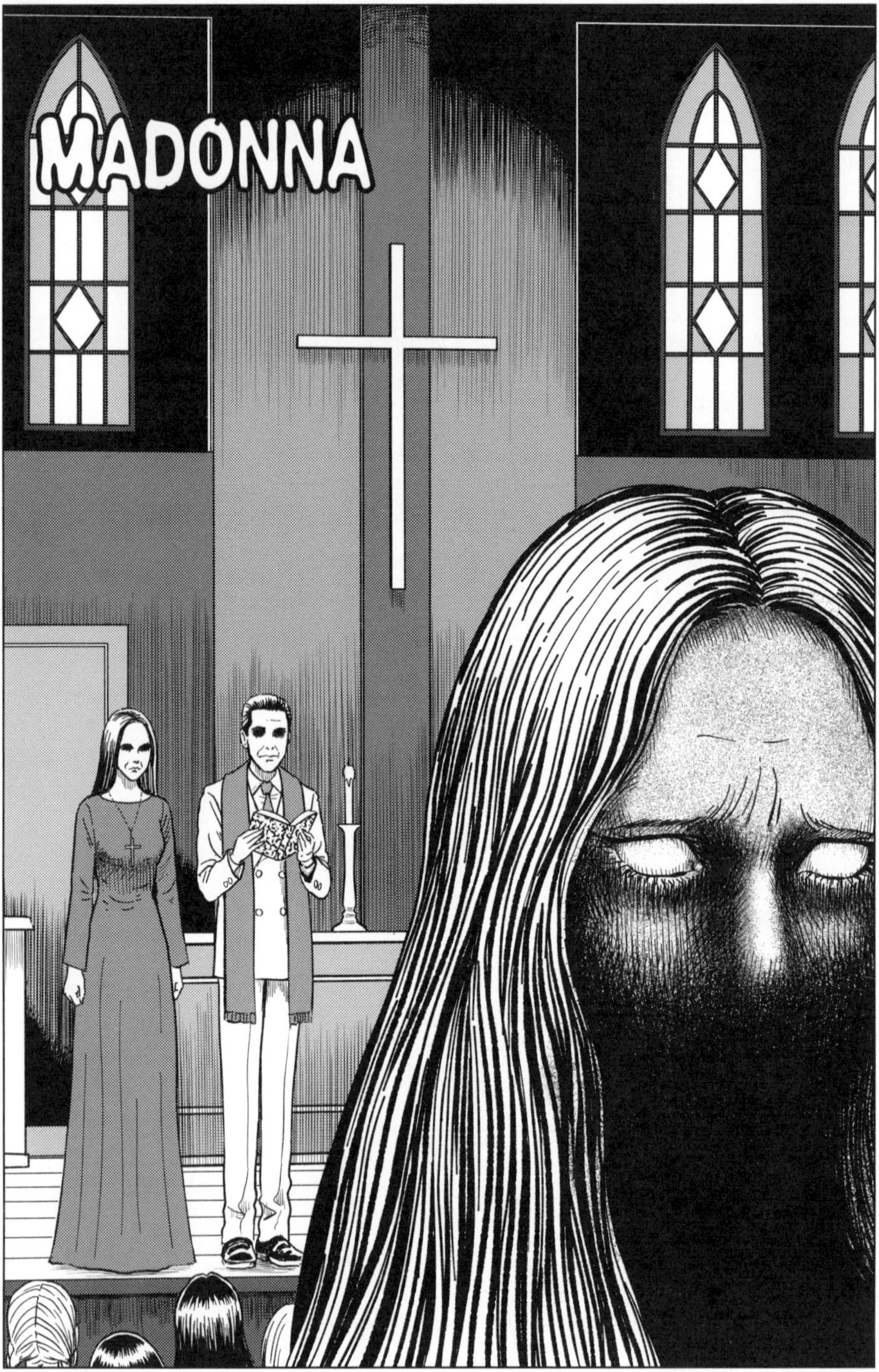
MADONNA

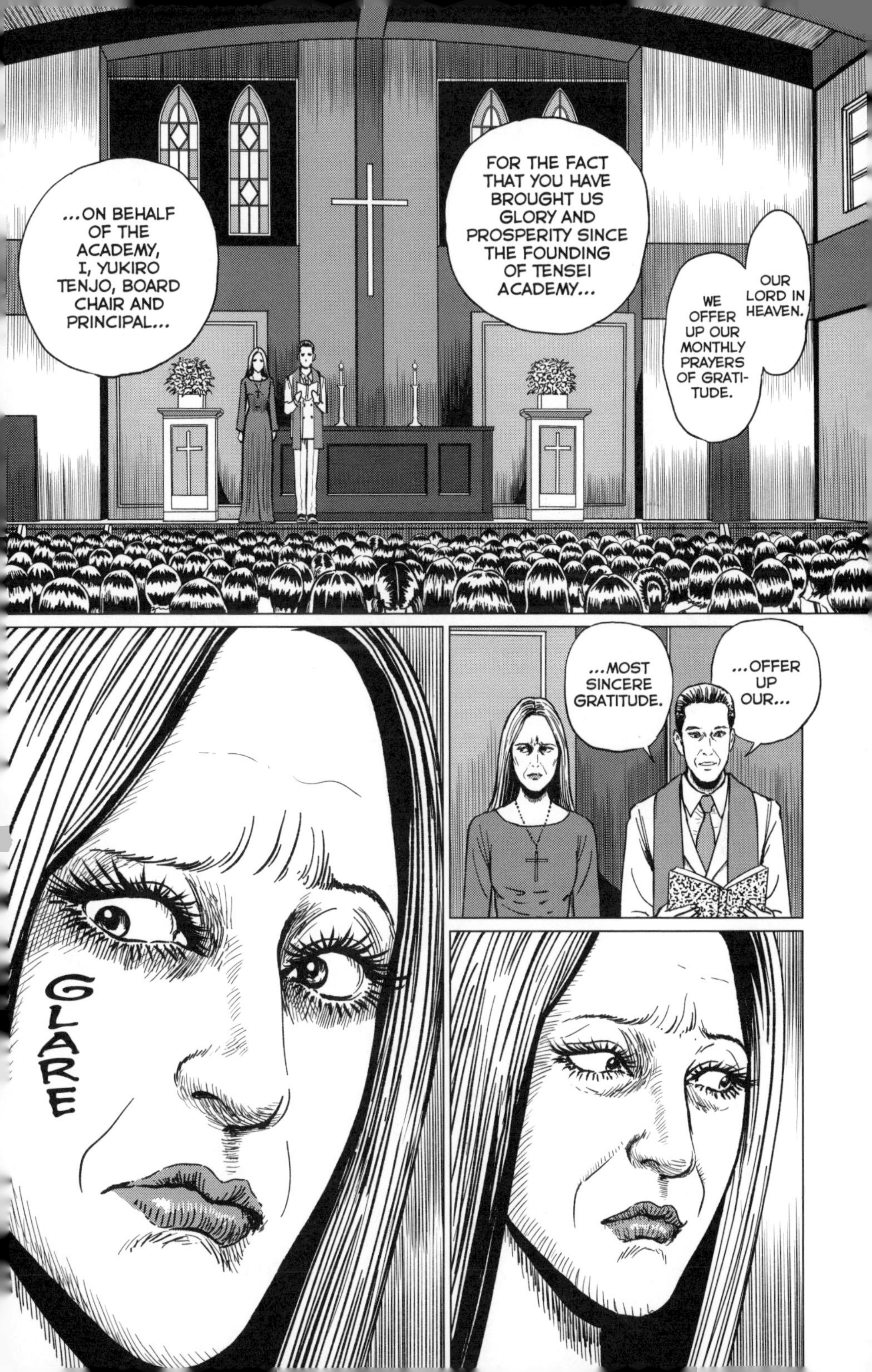
OUR LORD IN HEAVEN.
WE OFFER UP OUR MONTHLY PRAYERS OF GRATI-TUDE.
FOR THE FACT THAT YOU HAVE BROUGHT US GLORY AND PROSPERITY SINCE THE FOUNDING OF TENSEI ACADEMY...
...ON BEHALF OF THE ACADEMY, I, YUKIRO TENJO, BOARD CHAIR AND PRINCIPAL...
...OFFER UP OUR...
...MOST SINCERE GRATITUDE.
GLARE

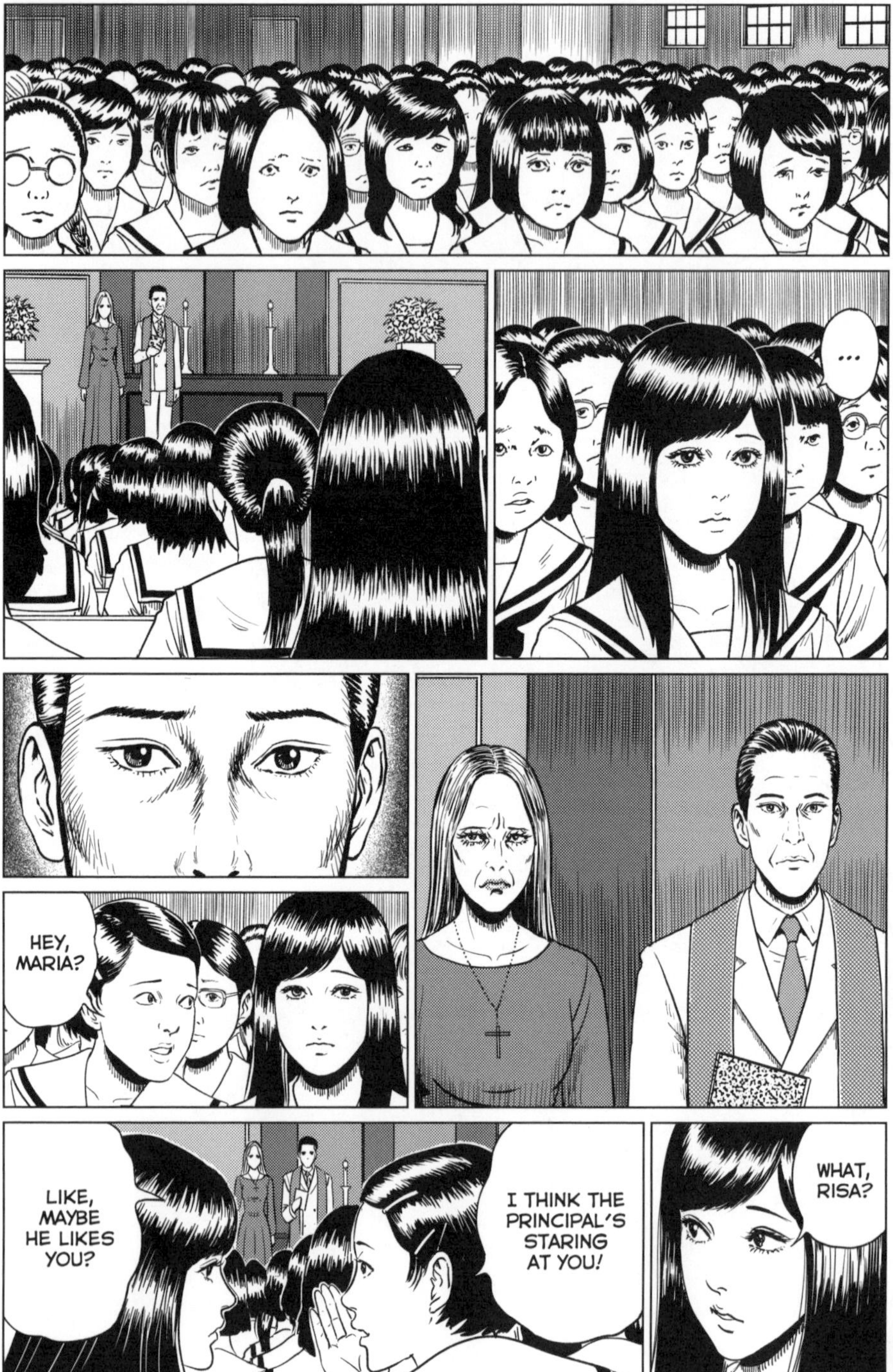
...
HEY, MARIA?
WHAT, RISA?
I THINK THE PRINCIPAL'S STARING AT YOU!
LIKE, MAYBE HE LIKES YOU?

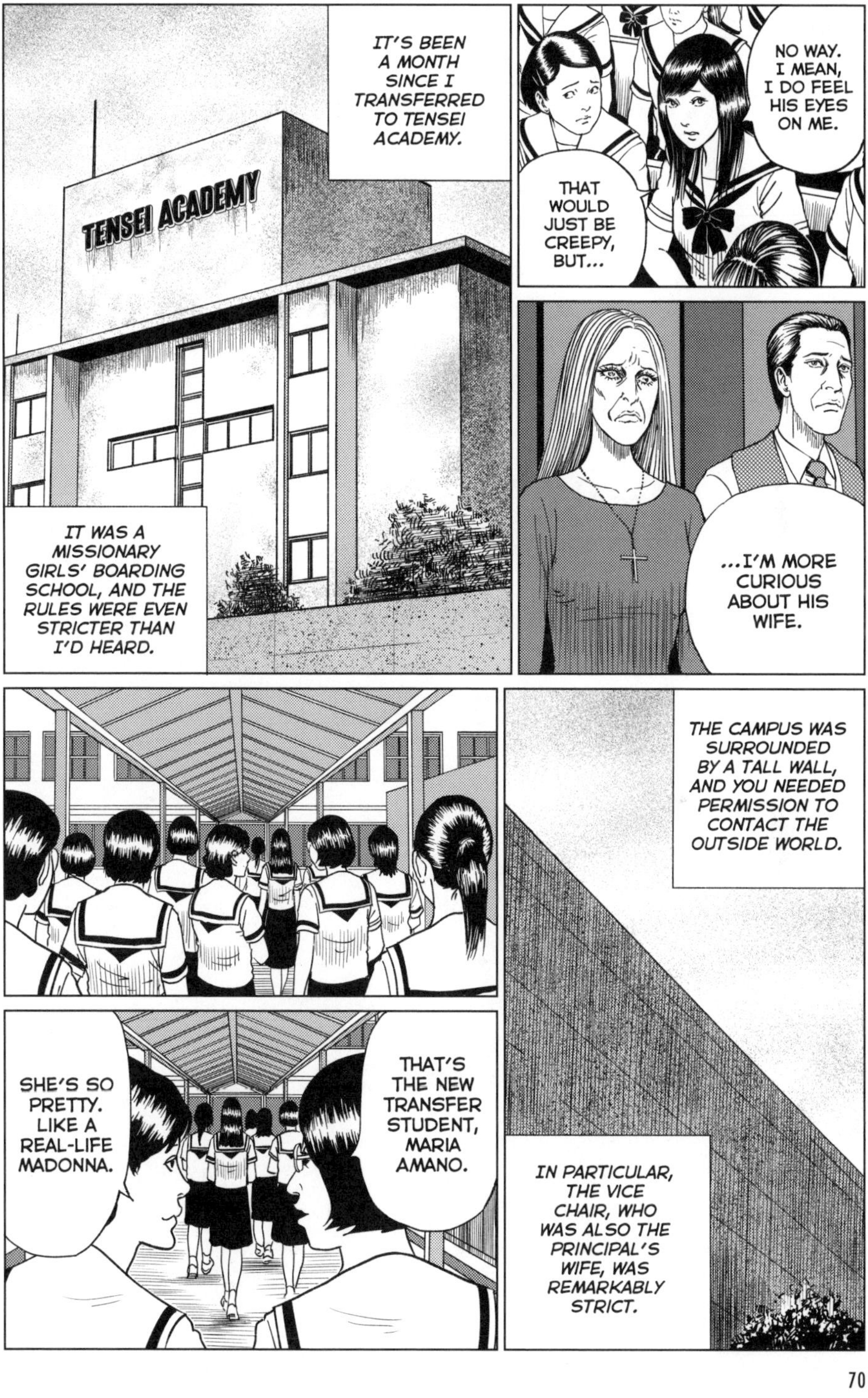
NO WAY. I MEAN, I DO FEEL HIS EYES ON ME.
THAT WOULD JUST BE CREEPY, BUT...
...I'M MORE CURIOUS ABOUT HIS WIFE.
IT'S BEEN A MONTH SINCE I TRANSFERRED TO TENSEI ACADEMY.
TENSEI ACADEMY
IT WAS A MISSIONARY GIRLS' BOARDING SCHOOL, AND THE RULES WERE EVEN STRICTER THAN I'D HEARD.
THE CAMPUS WAS SURROUNDED BY A TALL WALL, AND YOU NEEDED PERMISSION TO CONTACT THE OUTSIDE WORLD.
IN PARTICULAR, THE VICE CHAIR, WHO WAS ALSO THE PRINCIPAL'S WIFE, WAS REMARKABLY STRICT.
THAT'S THE NEW TRANSFER STUDENT, MARIA AMANO.
SHE'S SO PRETTY. LIKE A REAL-LIFE MADONNA.

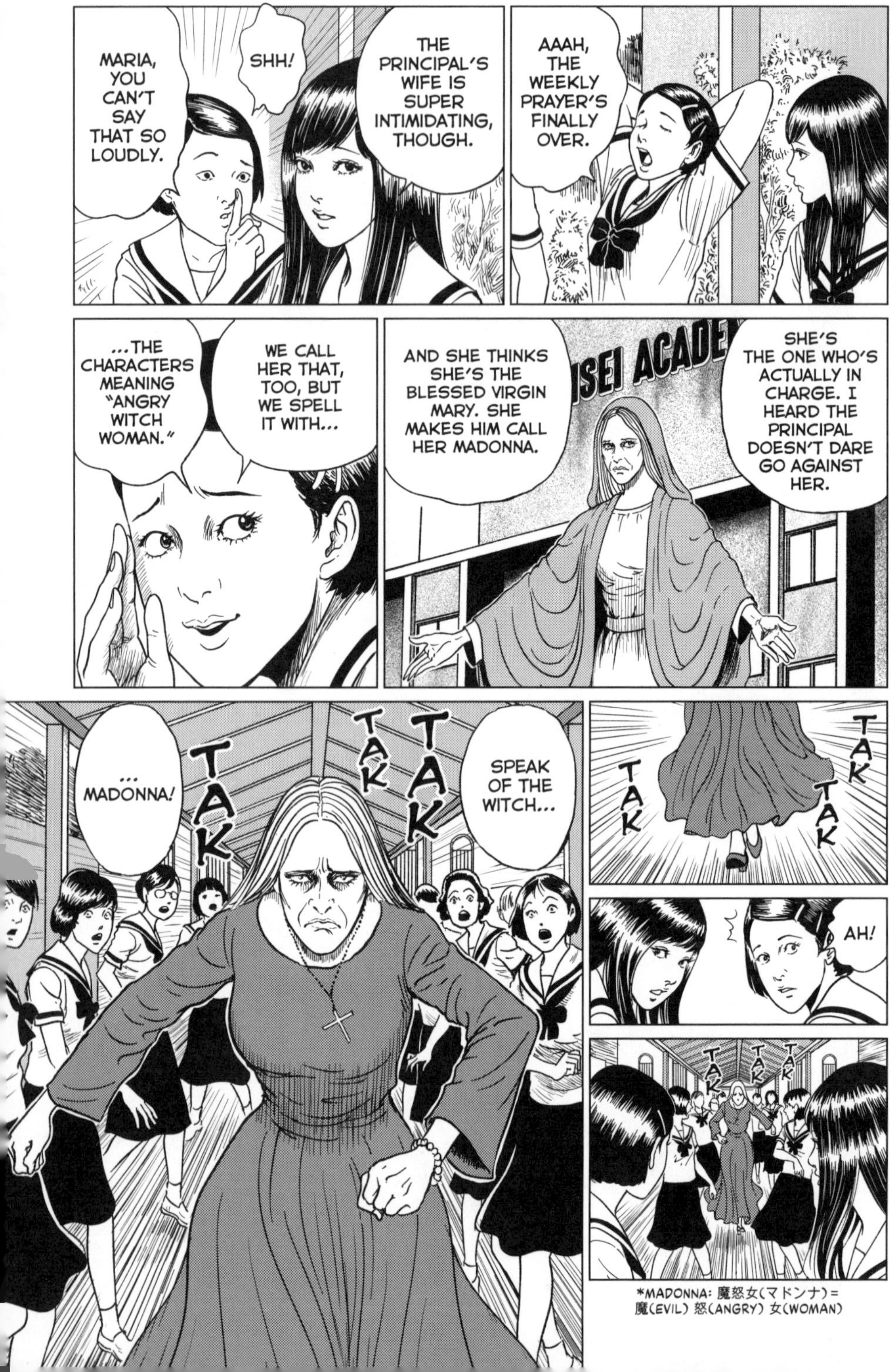
AAAH, THE WEEKLY PRAYER'S FINALLY OVER.
THE PRINCIPAL'S WIFE IS SUPER INTIMIDATING, THOUGH.
SHH!
MARIA, YOU CAN'T SAY THAT SO LOUDLY.
SHE'S THE ONE WHO'S ACTUALLY IN CHARGE. I HEARD THE PRINCIPAL DOESN'T DARE GO AGAINST HER.
ISEI ACADE
AND SHE THINKS SHE'S THE BLESSED VIRGIN MARY. SHE MAKES HIM CALL HER MADONNA.
WE CALL HER THAT, TOO, BUT WE SPELL IT WITH...
...THE CHARACTERS MEANING "ANGRY WITCH WOMAN."
TAK
TAK
TAK
TAK
AH!
TAK
TAK
TAK
TAK
TAK
SPEAK OF THE WITCH...
TAK
... MADONNA!

*MADONNA: 魔怒女(マドンナ) =
魔(EVIL) 怒(ANGRY) 女(WOMAN)

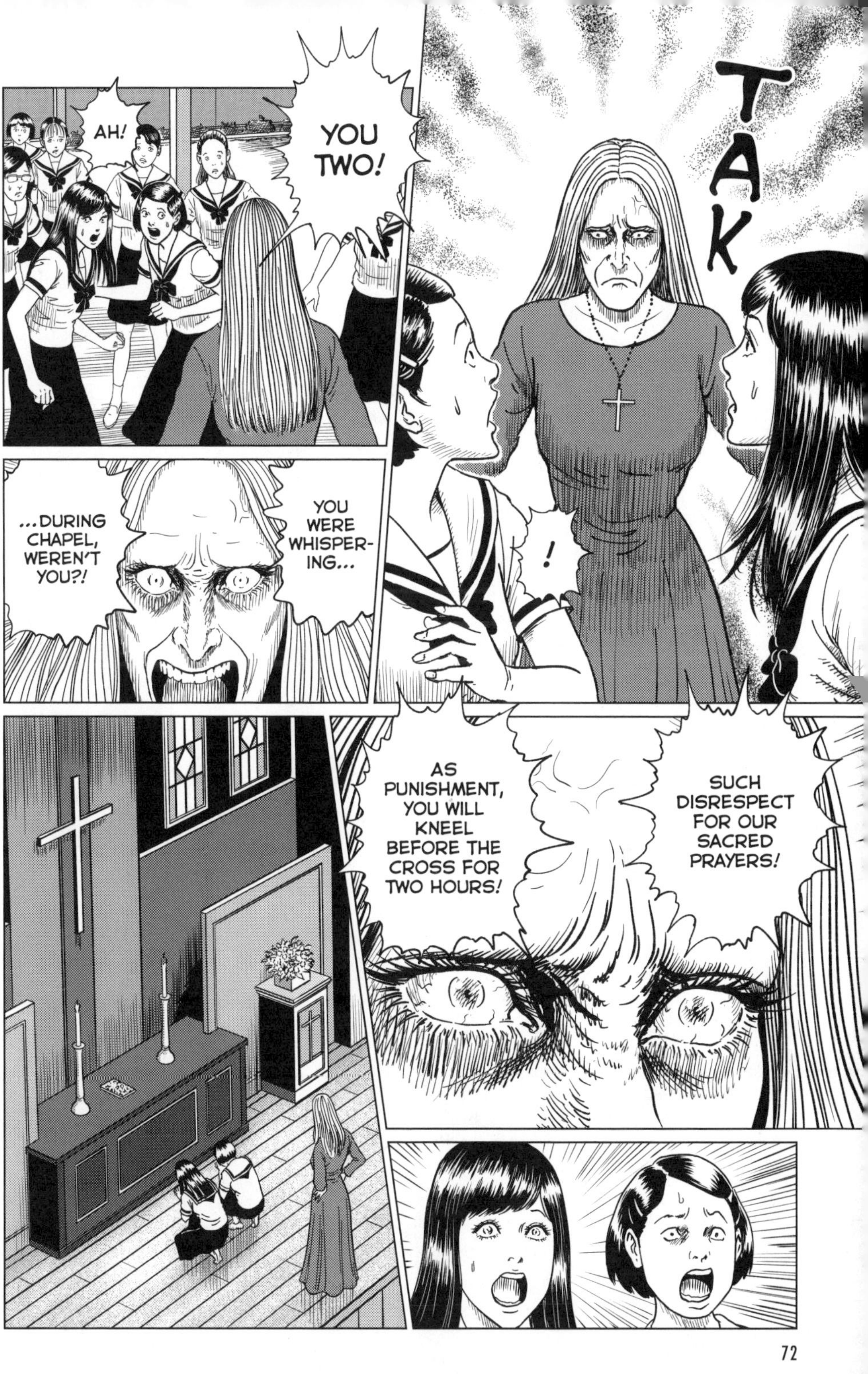
TAK
!
YOU TWO!
AH!
YOU WERE WHISPERING...
...DURING CHAPEL, WEREN'T YOU?!
SUCH DISRESPECT FOR OUR SACRED PRAYERS!
AS PUNISHMENT, YOU WILL KNEEL BEFORE THE CROSS FOR TWO HOURS!

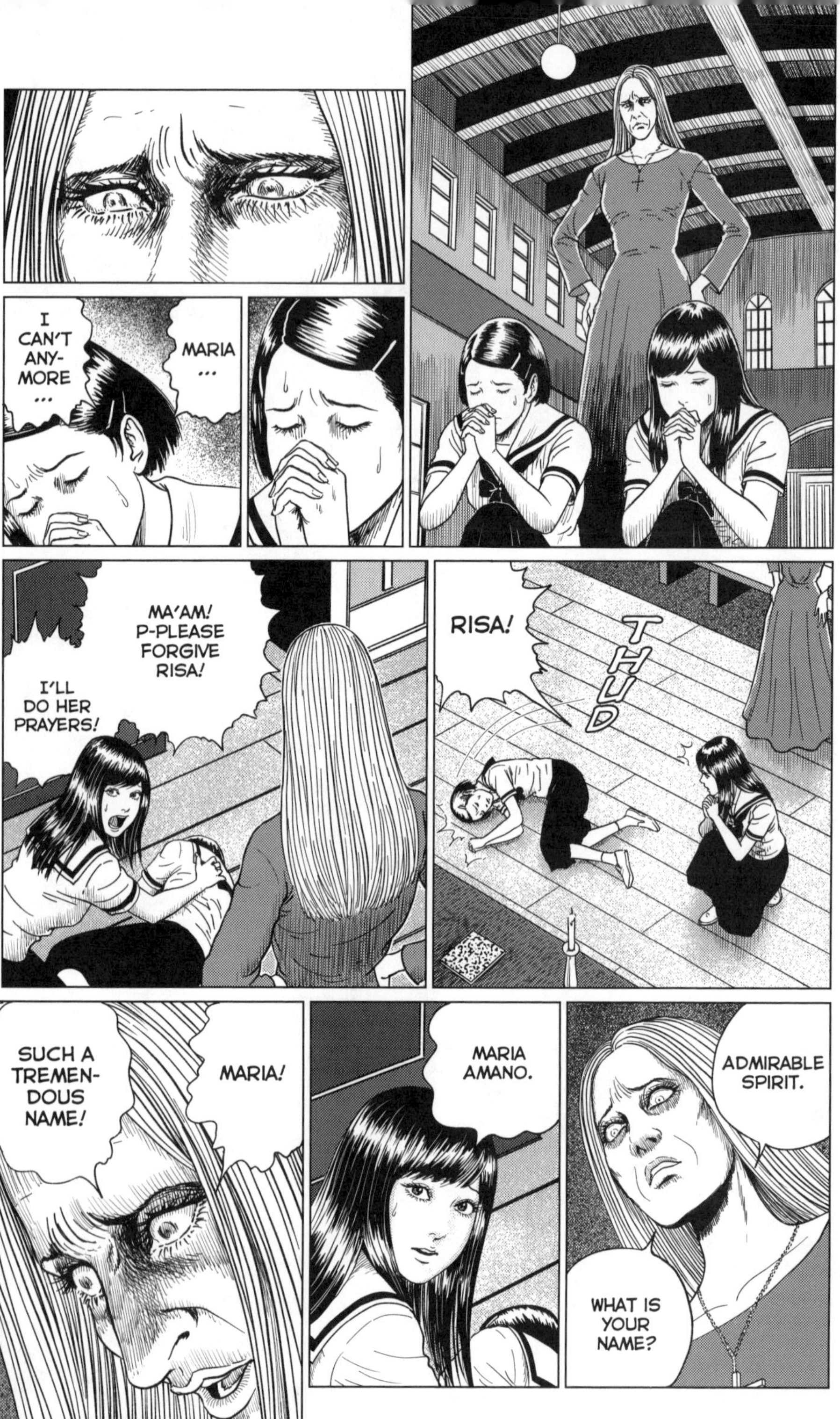
MARIA ...
I CAN'T ANYMORE ...
RISA!
THUD
MA'AM! P-PLEASE FORGIVE RISA!
I'LL DO HER PRAYERS!
ADMIRABLE SPIRIT.
WHAT IS YOUR NAME?
MARIA AMANO.
MARIA!
SUCH A TREMENDOUS NAME!

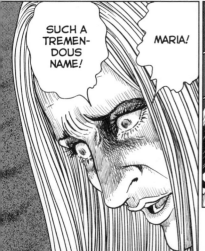

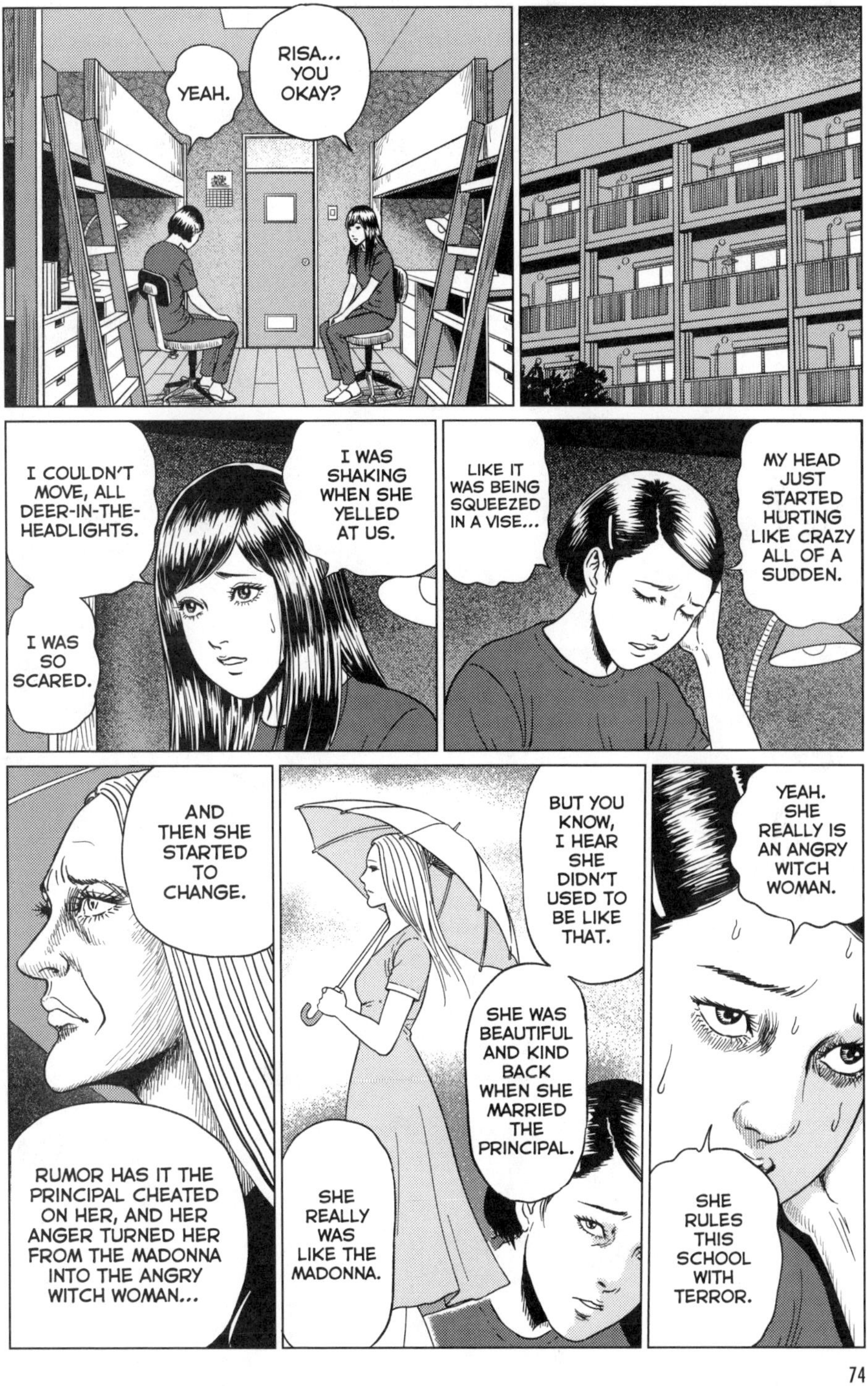
RISA... YOU OKAY?
YEAH.
MY HEAD JUST STARTED HURTING LIKE CRAZY ALL OF A SUDDEN.
LIKE IT WAS BEING SQUEEZED IN A VISE...
I WAS SHAKING WHEN SHE YELLED AT US.
I COULDN'T MOVE, ALL DEER-IN-THE-HEADLIGHTS.
I WAS SO SCARED.
YEAH. SHE REALLY IS AN ANGRY WITCH WOMAN.
SHE RULES THIS SCHOOL WITH TERROR.
BUT YOU KNOW, I HEAR SHE DIDN'T USED TO BE LIKE THAT.
SHE WAS BEAUTIFUL AND KIND BACK WHEN SHE MARRIED THE PRINCIPAL.
SHE REALLY WAS LIKE THE MADONNA.
AND THEN SHE STARTED TO CHANGE.
RUMOR HAS IT THE PRINCIPAL CHEATED ON HER, AND HER ANGER TURNED HER FROM THE MADONNA INTO THE ANGRY WITCH WOMAN...

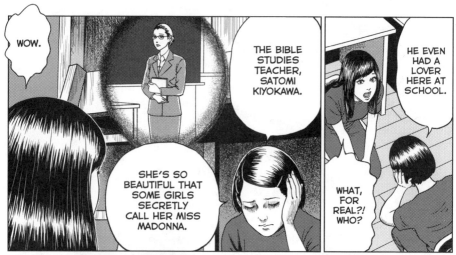

HE EVEN HAD A LOVER HERE AT SCHOOL.
WHAT, FOR REAL?! WHO?
THE BIBLE STUDIES TEACHER, SATOMI KIYOKAWA.
WOW.
SHE'S SO BEAUTIFUL THAT SOME GIRLS SECRETLY CALL HER MISS MADONNA.
BUT, YOU KNOW, THE WITCH WOMAN USED TO BE THE PRINCIPAL'S LOVER, TOO.
WHAT ?!
HIS FIRST WIFE WENT MISSING, AND SHE ENDED UP MARRYING HIM.
AAAH, MARIA... I FEEL SO OUT OF IT.
I'M GOING TO BED.
OH, SORRY. YOU REST, RISA.
HM?

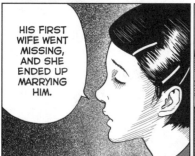

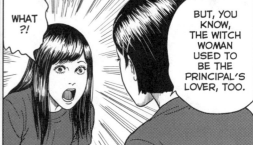

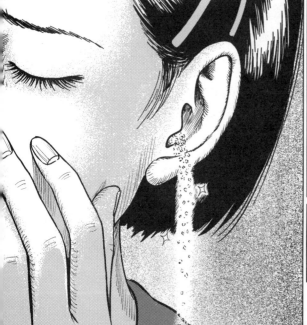

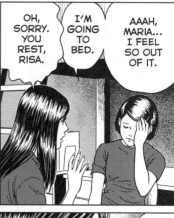

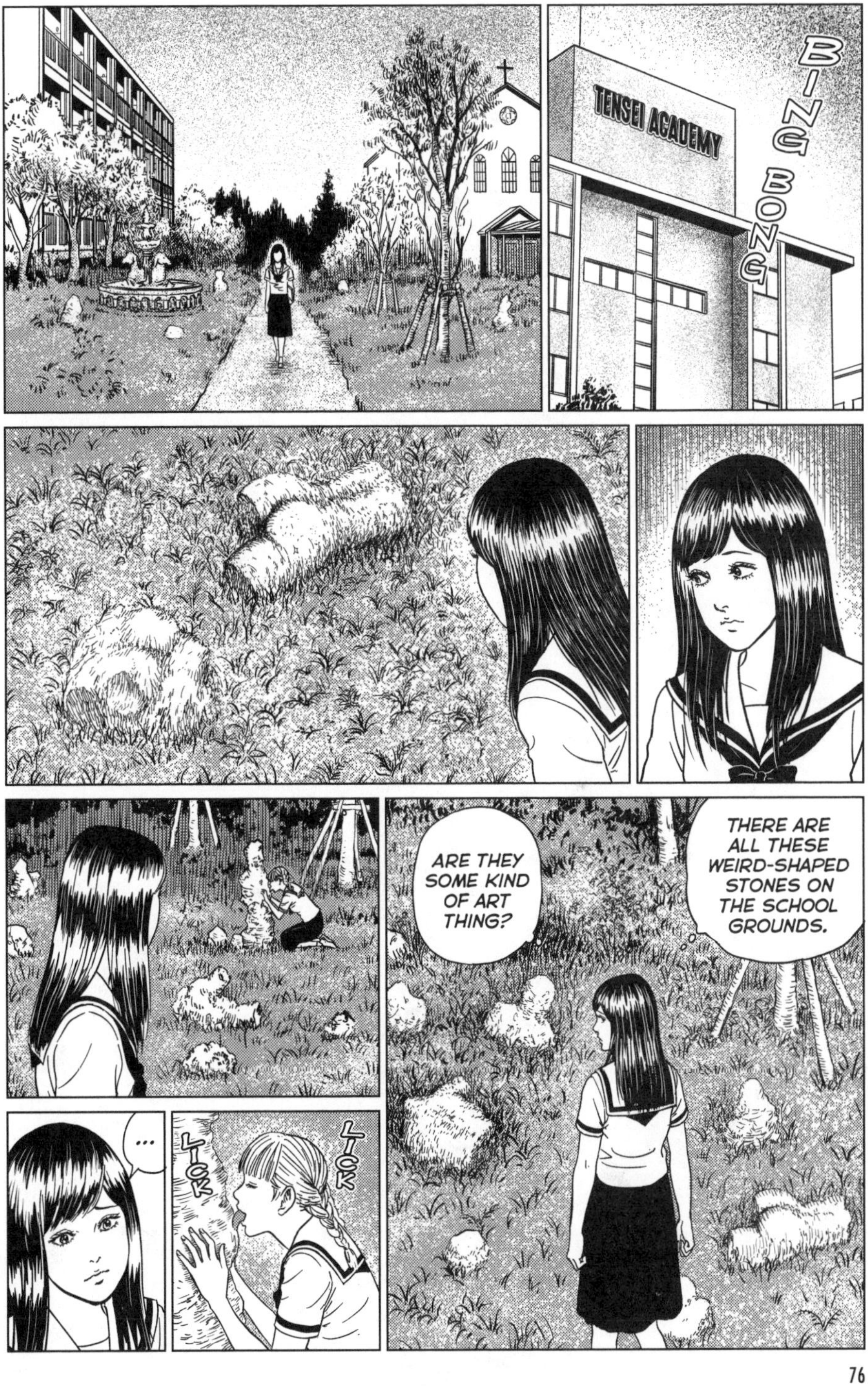
BING BONG
TENSEI ACADEMY
THERE ARE ALL THESE WEIRD-SHAPED STONES ON THE SCHOOL GROUNDS.
ARE THEY SOME KIND OF ART THING?
LICK
LICK
...

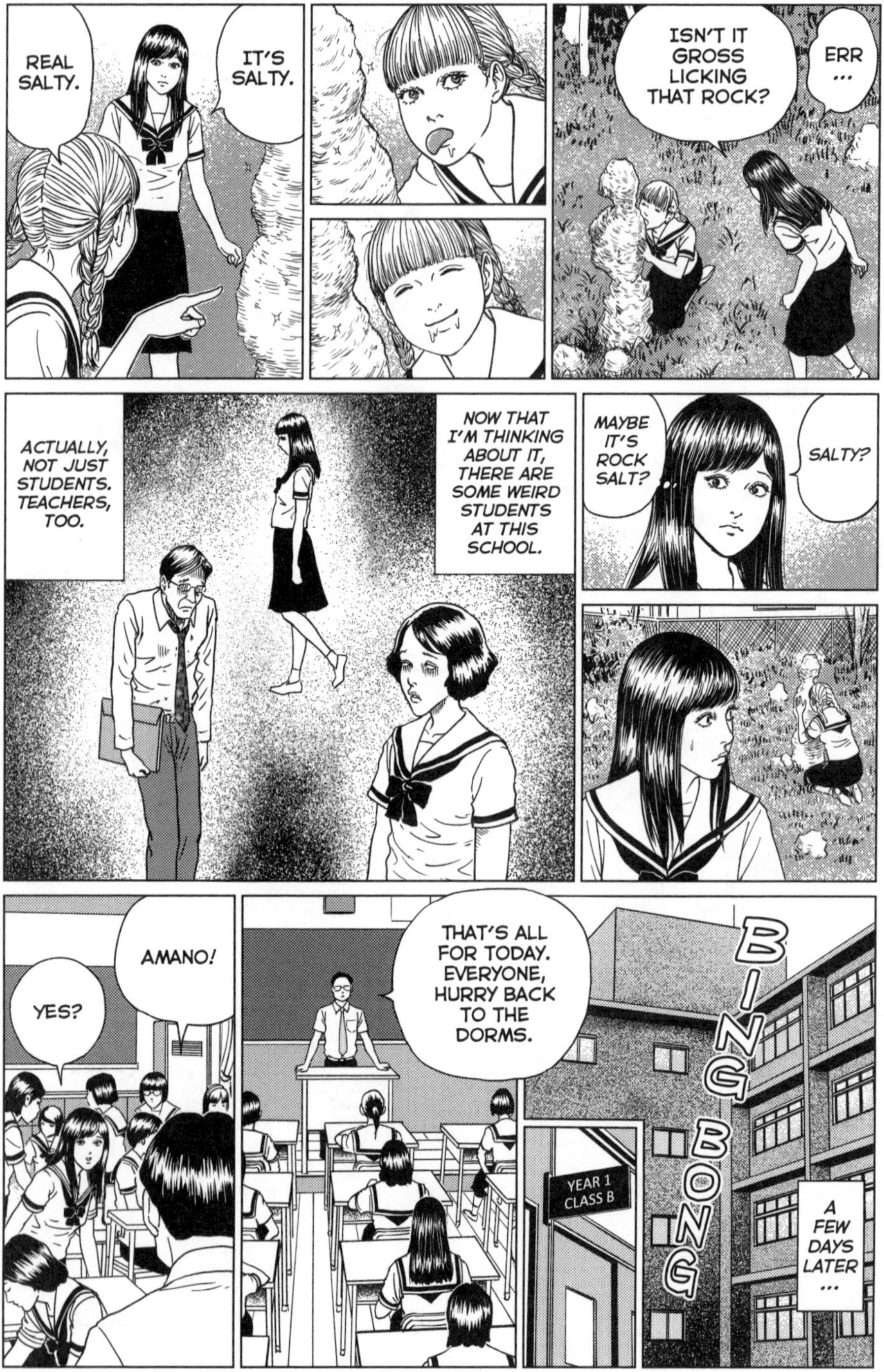
ERR ...
ISN'T IT GROSS LICKING THAT ROCK?
IT'S SALTY.
REAL SALTY.
SALTY?
MAYBE IT'S ROCK SALT?
NOW THAT I'M THINKING ABOUT IT, THERE ARE SOME WEIRD STUDENTS AT THIS SCHOOL.
ACTUALLY, NOT JUST STUDENTS. TEACHERS, TOO.
BING
BONG
YEAR 1 CLASS B
A FEW DAYS LATER ...
THAT'S ALL FOR TODAY. EVERYONE, HURRY BACK TO THE DORMS.
AMANO!
YES?

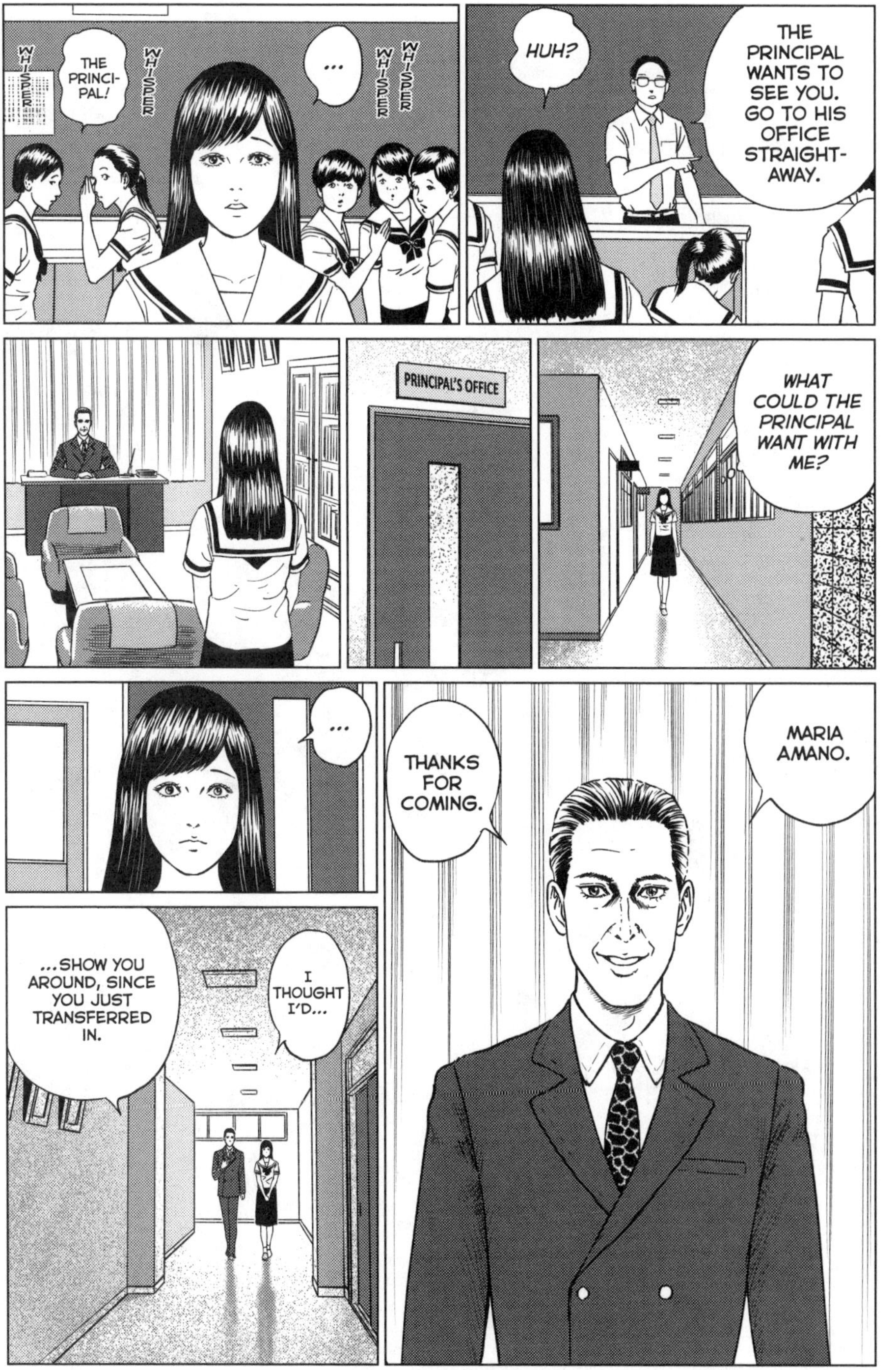
THE PRINCIPAL WANTS TO SEE YOU. GO TO HIS OFFICE STRAIGHT-AWAY.
HUH?
WHISPER
WHISPER
...
WHISPER
THE PRINCI-PAL!
WHISPER
WHAT COULD THE PRINCIPAL WANT WITH ME?
PRINCIPAL'S OFFICE
MARIA AMANO.
THANKS FOR COMING.
...
I THOUGHT I'D...
...SHOW YOU AROUND, SINCE YOU JUST TRANSFERRED IN.

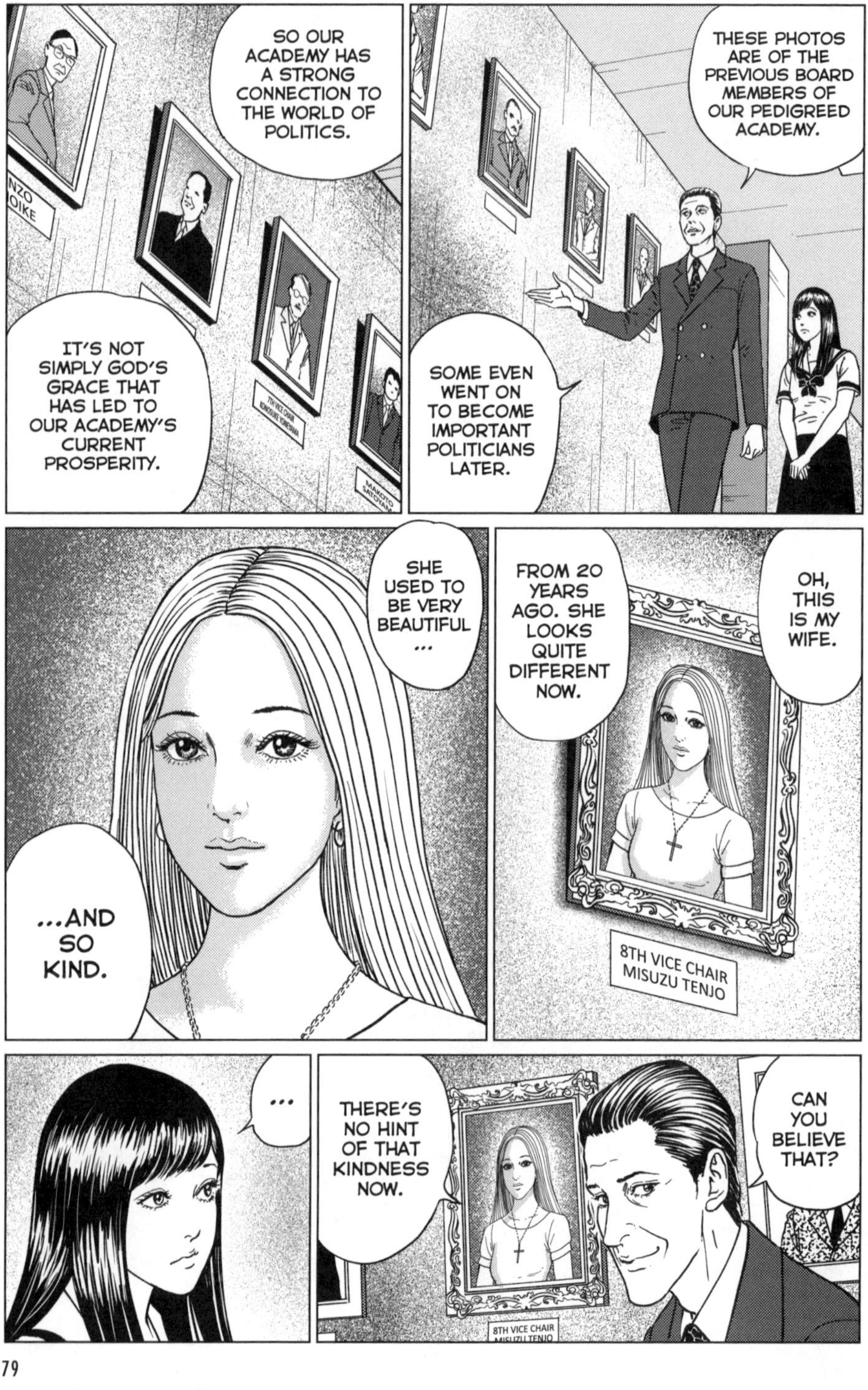
THESE PHOTOS ARE OF THE PREVIOUS BOARD MEMBERS OF OUR PEDIGREED ACADEMY.
SOME EVEN WENT ON TO BECOME IMPORTANT POLITICIANS LATER.
SO OUR ACADEMY HAS A STRONG CONNECTION TO THE WORLD OF POLITICS.
IT'S NOT SIMPLY GOD'S GRACE THAT HAS LED TO OUR ACADEMY'S CURRENT PROSPERITY.
OH, THIS IS MY WIFE.
FROM 20 YEARS AGO. SHE LOOKS QUITE DIFFERENT NOW.
8TH VICE CHAIR MISUZU TENJO
SHE USED TO BE VERY BEAUTIFUL ...
...AND SO KIND.
CAN YOU BELIEVE THAT?
THERE'S NO HINT OF THAT KINDNESS NOW.
8TH VICE CHAIR
...

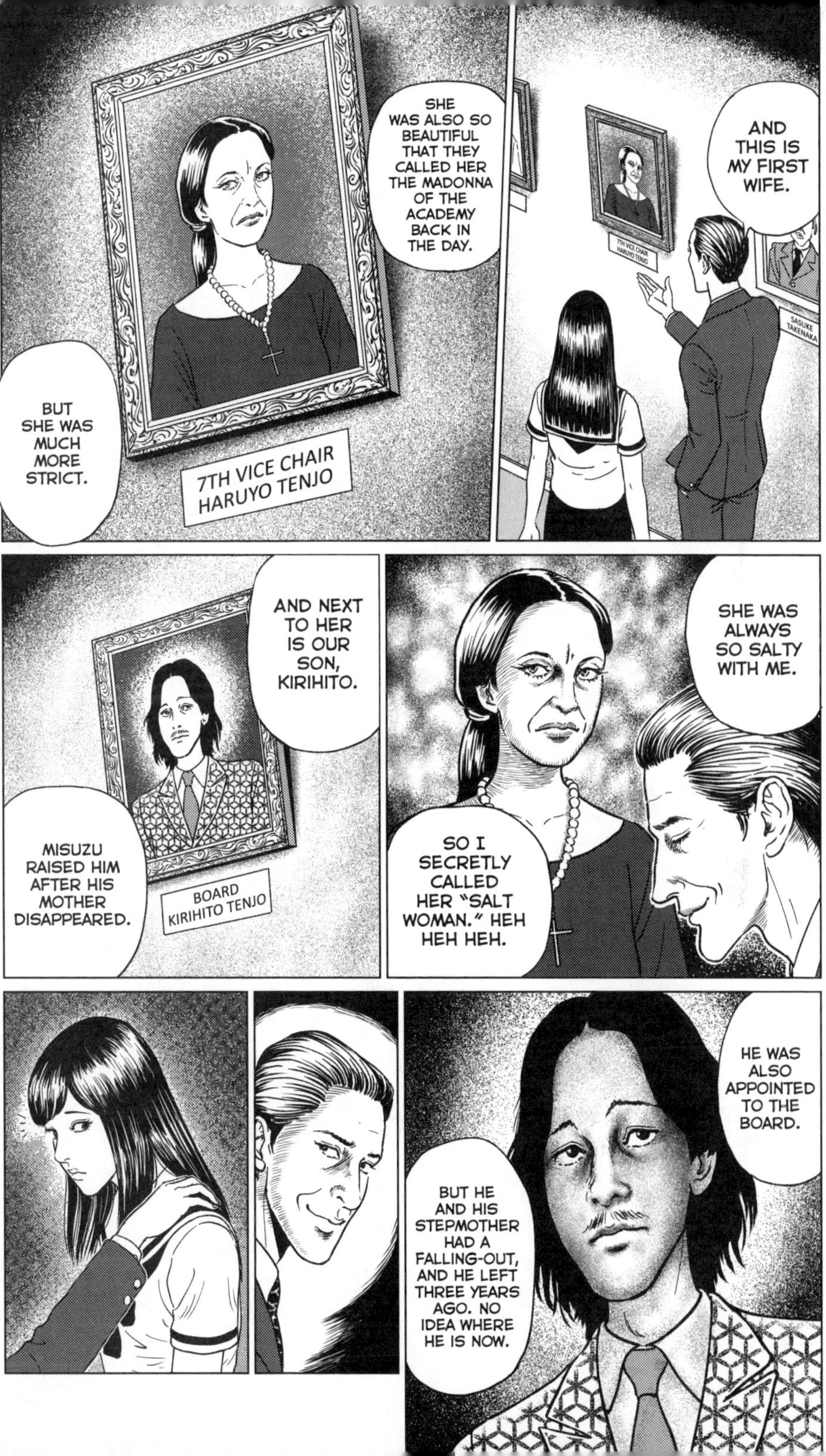
AND THIS IS MY FIRST WIFE.
7TH VICE CHAIR HARUYO TENJO
SASUKE TAKENAKA
SHE WAS ALSO SO BEAUTIFUL THAT THEY CALLED HER THE MADONNA OF THE ACADEMY BACK IN THE DAY.
BUT SHE WAS MUCH MORE STRICT.
7TH VICE CHAIR HARUYO TENJO
SHE WAS ALWAYS SO SALTY WITH ME.
SO I SECRETLY CALLED HER "SALT WOMAN." HEH HEH HEH.
AND NEXT TO HER IS OUR SON, KIRIHITO.
MISUZU RAISED HIM AFTER HIS MOTHER DISAPPEARED.
BOARD KIRIHITO TENJO
HE WAS ALSO APPOINTED TO THE BOARD.
BUT HE AND HIS STEPMOTHER HAD A FALLING-OUT, AND HE LEFT THREE YEARS AGO. NO IDEA WHERE HE IS NOW.

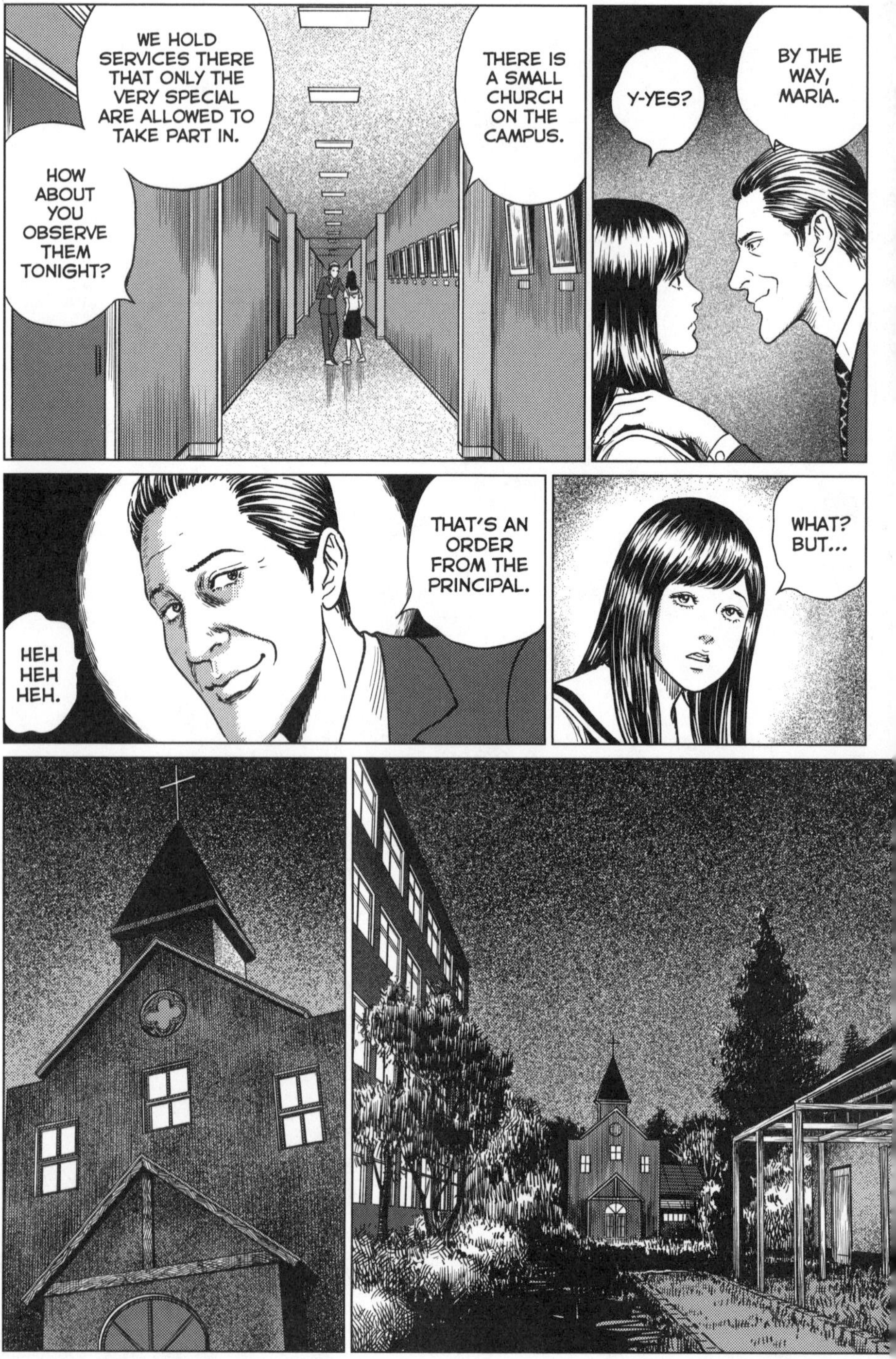
BY THE WAY, MARIA.
Y-YES?
THERE IS A SMALL CHURCH ON THE CAMPUS.
WE HOLD SERVICES THERE THAT ONLY THE VERY SPECIAL ARE ALLOWED TO TAKE PART IN.
HOW ABOUT YOU OBSERVE THEM TONIGHT?
WHAT? BUT...
THAT'S AN ORDER FROM THE PRINCIPAL.
HEH HEH HEH.

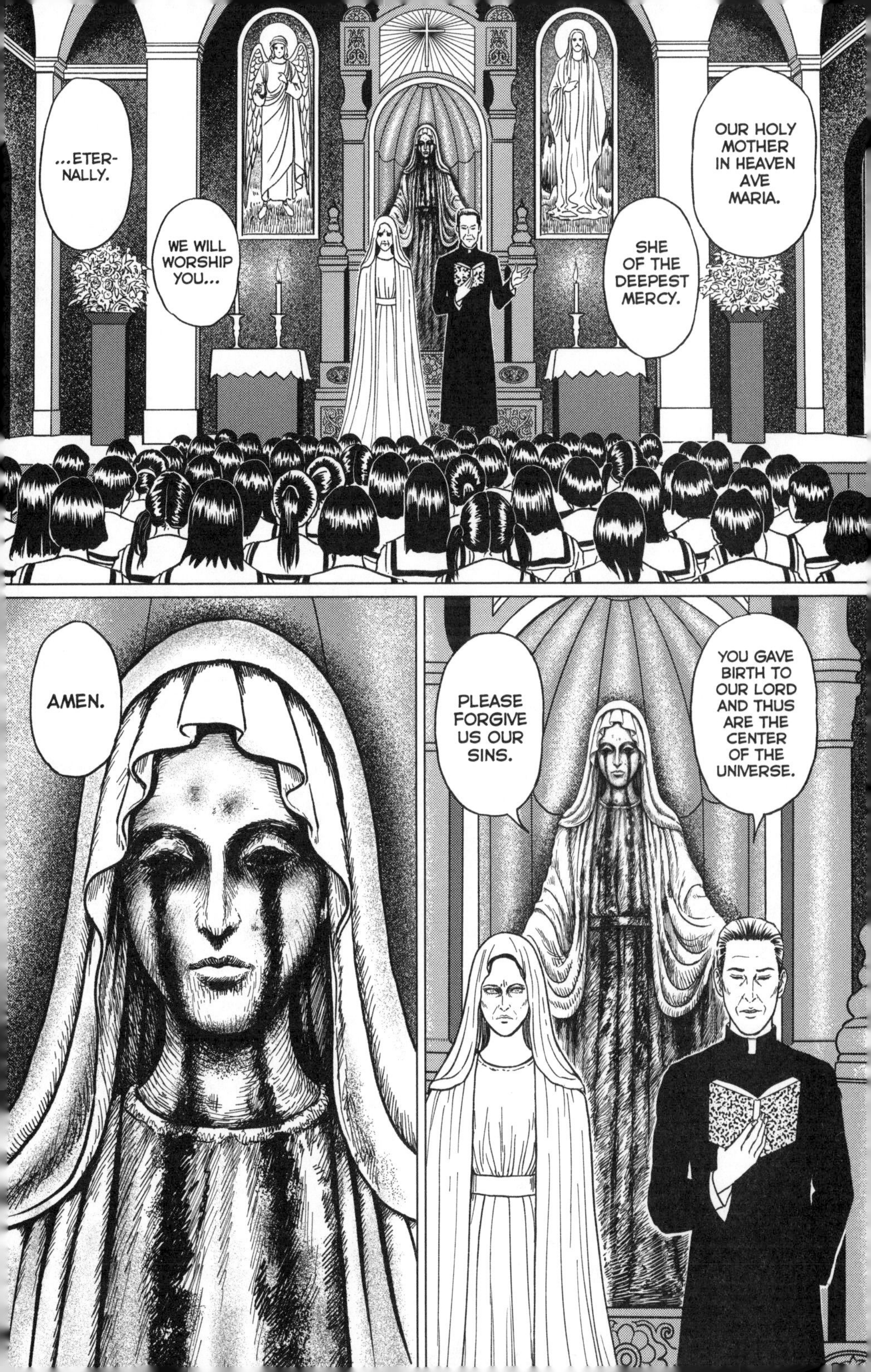
OUR HOLY MOTHER IN HEAVEN AVE MARIA.
SHE OF THE DEEPEST MERCY.
WE WILL WORSHIP YOU...
...ETERNALLY.
YOU GAVE BIRTH TO OUR LORD AND THUS ARE THE CENTER OF THE UNIVERSE.
PLEASE FORGIVE US OUR SINS.
AMEN.

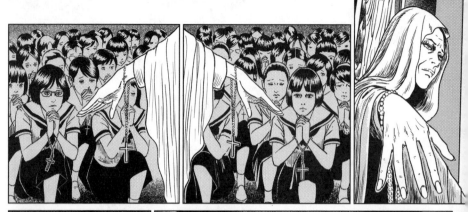

PLEASE
FORGIVE
ME.

BLESSED
MARY...
PLEASE
FORGIVE
MY SINS.

EVERYONE'S
REALLY
AFRAID...

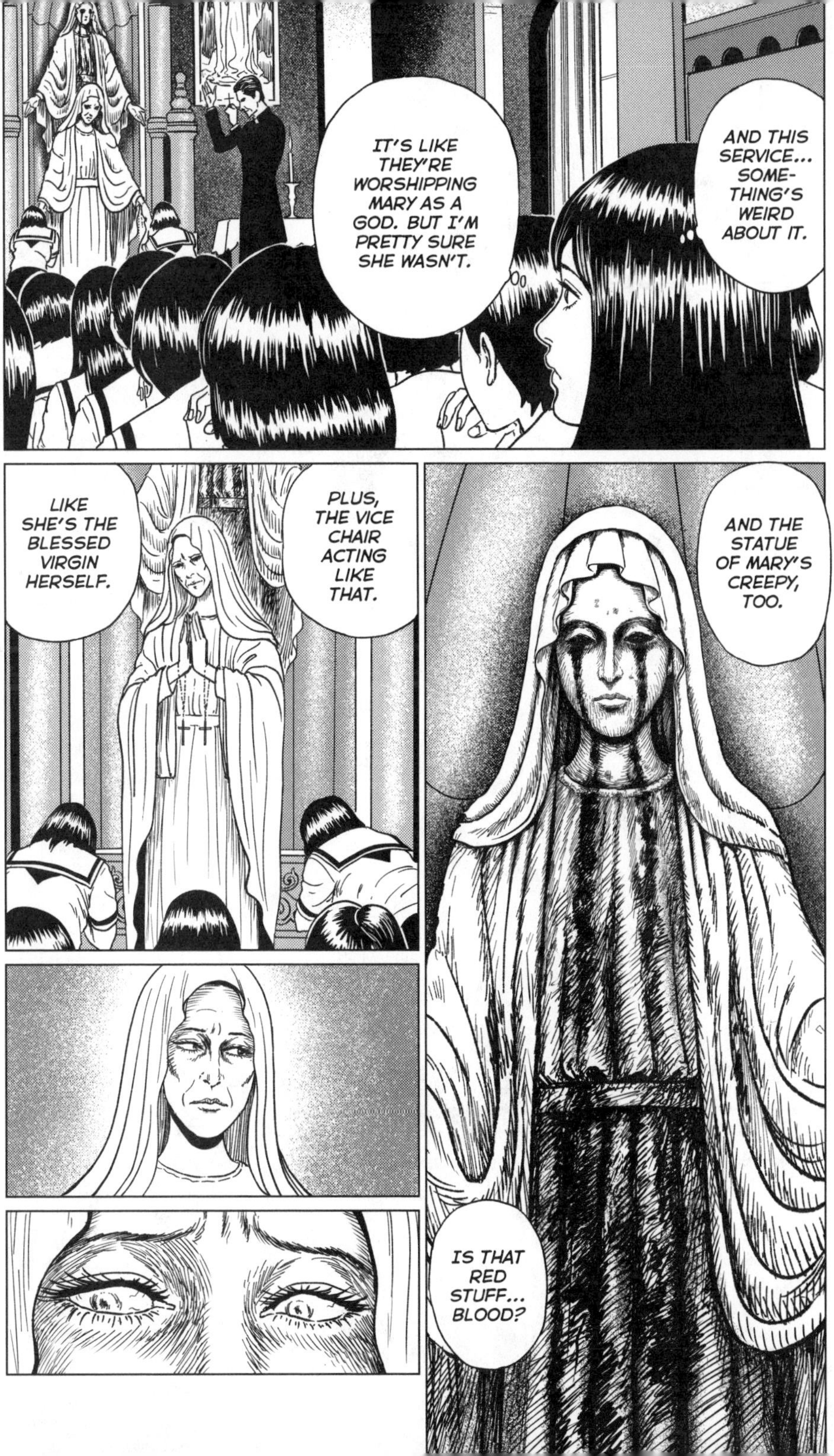
AND THIS SERVICE... SOME-THING'S WEIRD ABOUT IT.
IT'S LIKE THEY'RE WORSHIPPING MARY AS A GOD. BUT I'M PRETTY SURE SHE WASN'T.
AND THE STATUE OF MARY'S CREEPY, TOO.
IS THAT RED STUFF... BLOOD?
PLUS, THE VICE CHAIR ACTING LIKE THAT.
LIKE SHE'S THE BLESSED VIRGIN HERSELF.

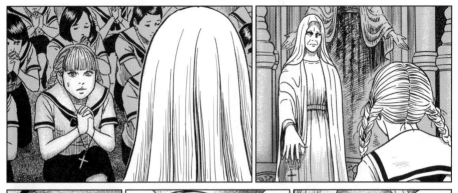

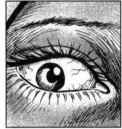

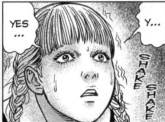

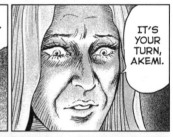

IT'S YOUR TURN, AKEMI.
Y...
SHAKE SHAKE
YES ...
WHY ...
...DO YOU HESITATE?
SHAKE
SHAKE
B- BLESSED MARY...
SHAKE SHAKE
I BEG FORGIVE- NESS!
...

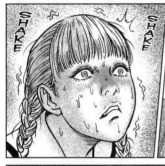

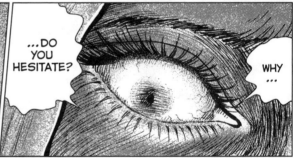

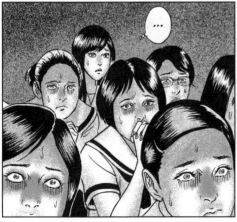

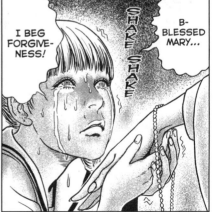

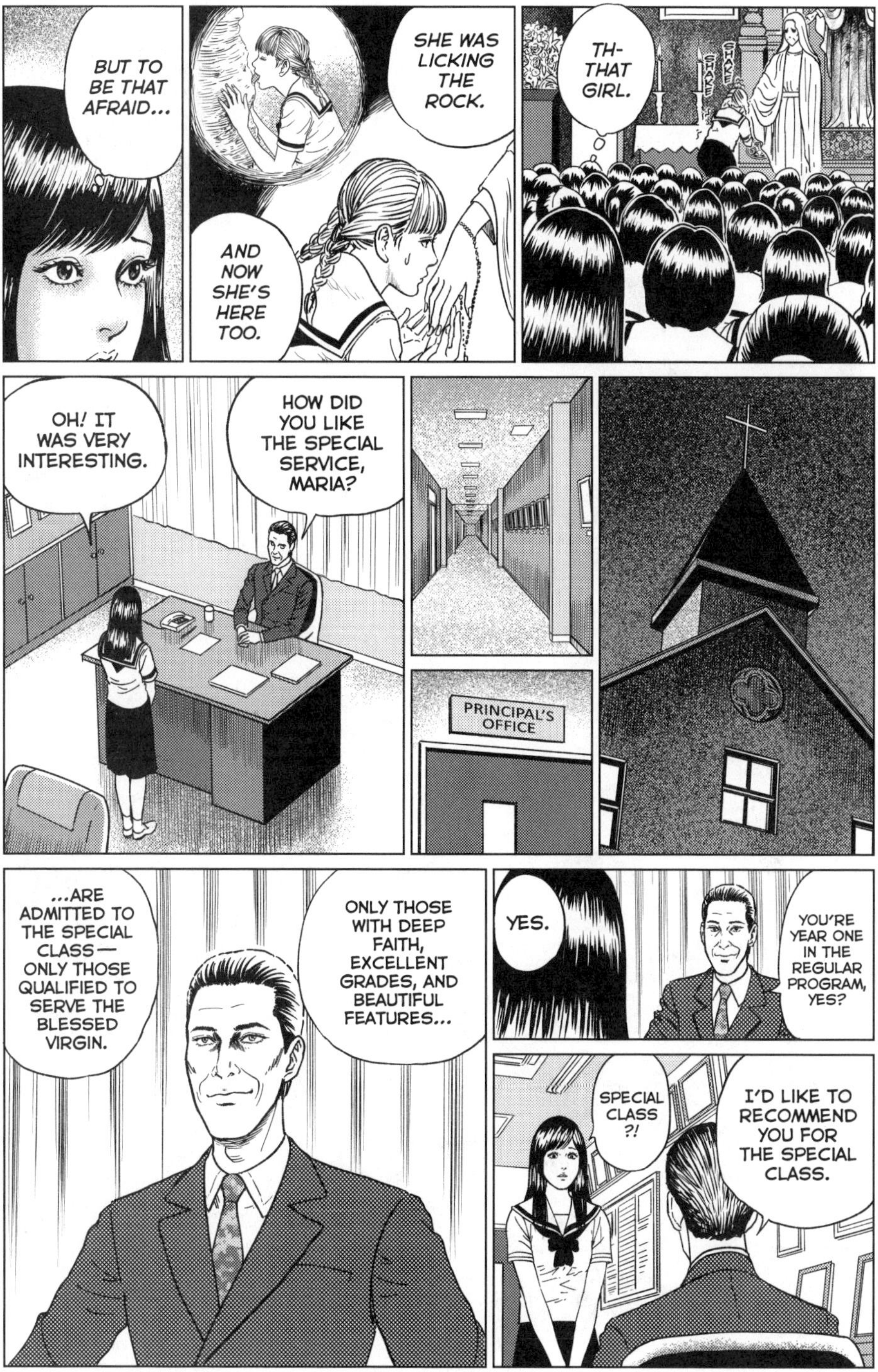
SHAKE
TH- THAT GIRL.
SHE WAS LICKING THE ROCK.
AND NOW SHE'S HERE TOO.
BUT TO BE THAT AFRAID...
PRINCIPAL'S OFFICE
HOW DID YOU LIKE THE SPECIAL SERVICE, MARIA?
OH! IT WAS VERY INTERESTING.
YOU'RE YEAR ONE IN THE REGULAR PROGRAM, YES?
YES.
I'D LIKE TO RECOMMEND YOU FOR THE SPECIAL CLASS.
SPECIAL CLASS ?!
ONLY THOSE WITH DEEP FAITH, EXCELLENT GRADES, AND BEAUTIFUL FEATURES...
...ARE ADMITTED TO THE SPECIAL CLASS— ONLY THOSE QUALIFIED TO SERVE THE BLESSED VIRGIN.

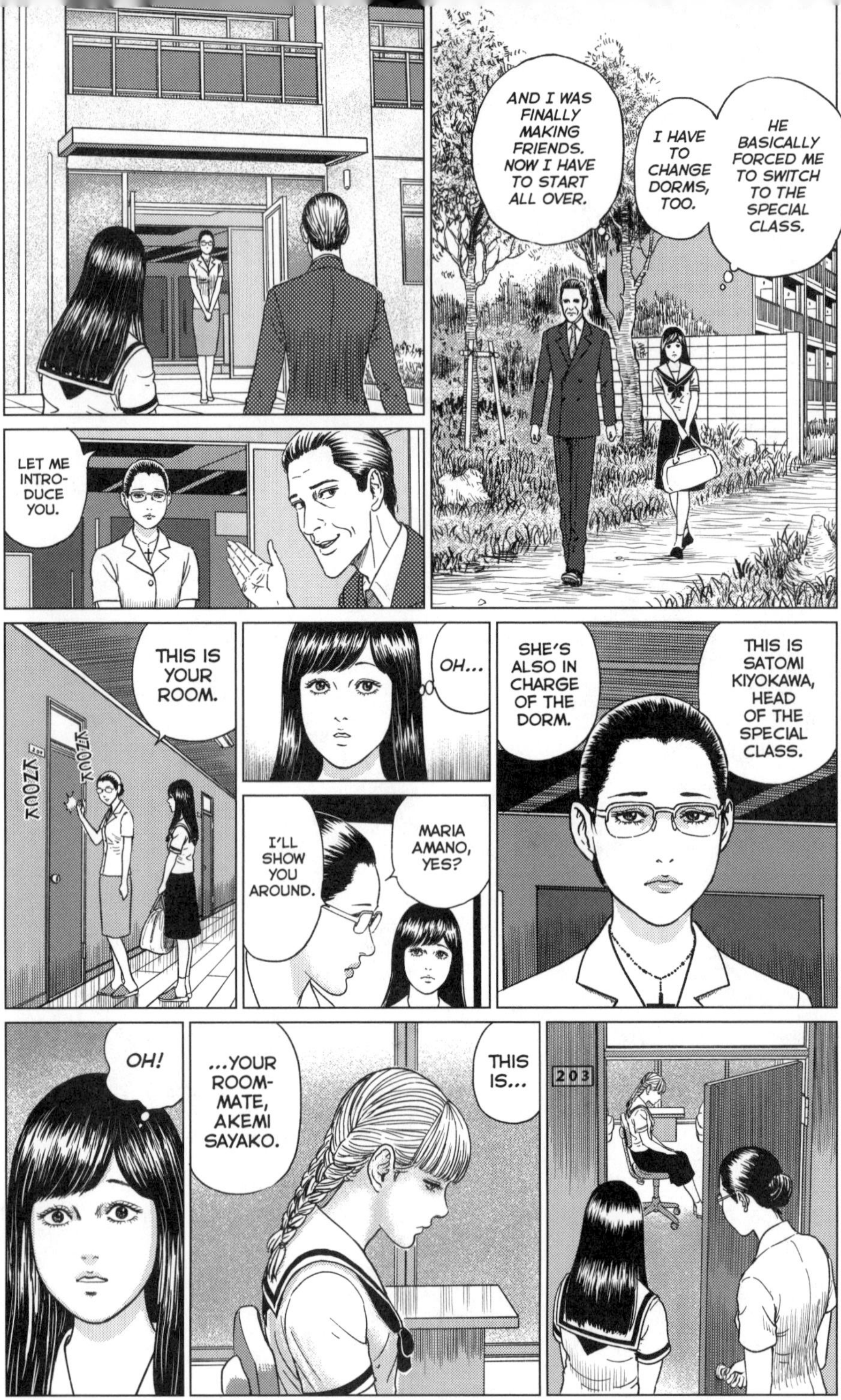
HE BASICALLY FORCED ME TO SWITCH TO THE SPECIAL CLASS.
I HAVE TO CHANGE DORMS, TOO.
AND I WAS FINALLY MAKING FRIENDS. NOW I HAVE TO START ALL OVER.
LET ME INTRODUCE YOU.
THIS IS SATOMI KIYOKAWA, HEAD OF THE SPECIAL CLASS.
SHE'S ALSO IN CHARGE OF THE DORM.
OH...
MARIA AMANO, YES?
I'LL SHOW YOU AROUND.
THIS IS YOUR ROOM.
KNOCK
KNOCK
203
THIS IS...
...YOUR ROOMMATE, AKEMI SAYAKO.
OH!

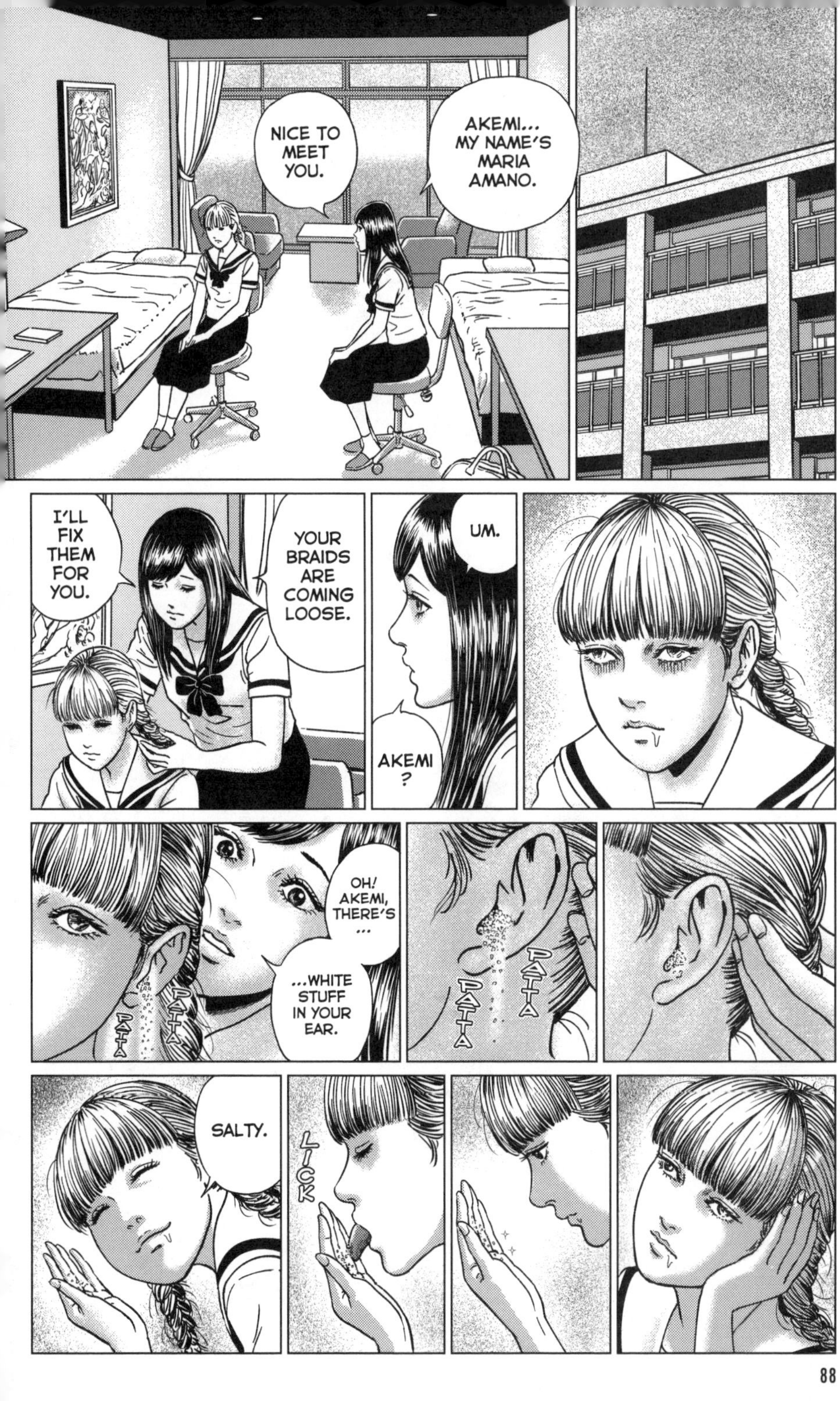
AKEMI... MY NAME'S MARIA AMANO.
NICE TO MEET YOU.
UM.
AKEMI ?
YOUR BRAIDS ARE COMING LOOSE.
I'LL FIX THEM FOR YOU.
PATTA
PATTA
OH! AKEMI, THERE'S ...
...WHITE STUFF IN YOUR EAR.
PATTA
PATTA
LICK
SALTY.

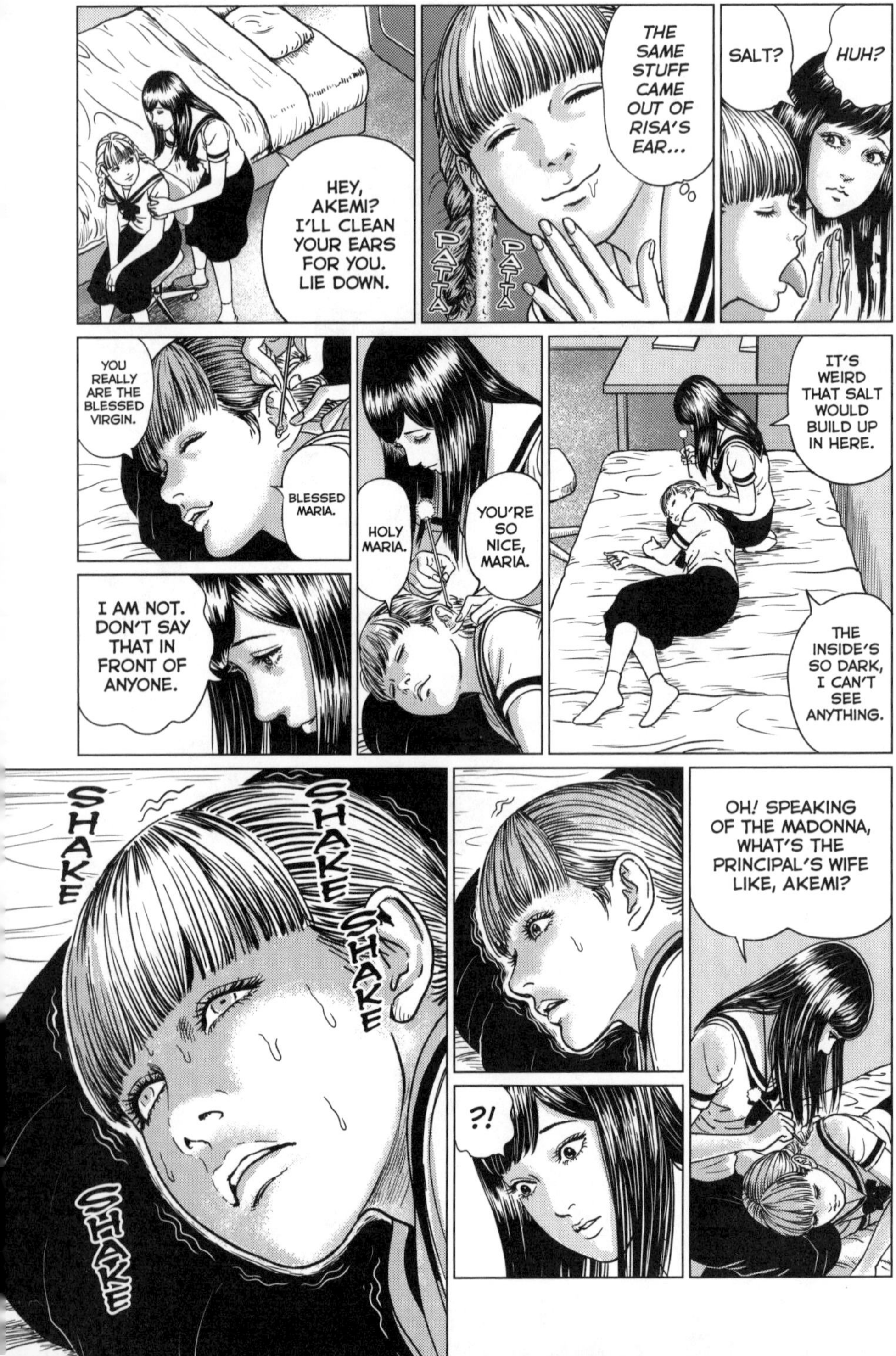
HUH?
SALT?
THE SAME STUFF CAME OUT OF RISA'S EAR...
PATTA
PATTA
HEY, AKEMI? I'LL CLEAN YOUR EARS FOR YOU. LIE DOWN.
IT'S WEIRD THAT SALT WOULD BUILD UP IN HERE.
THE INSIDE'S SO DARK, I CAN'T SEE ANYTHING.
YOU'RE SO NICE, MARIA.
HOLY MARIA.
YOU REALLY ARE THE BLESSED VIRGIN.
BLESSED MARIA.
I AM NOT. DON'T SAY THAT IN FRONT OF ANYONE.
OH! SPEAKING OF THE MADONNA, WHAT'S THE PRINCIPAL'S WIFE LIKE, AKEMI?
?!
SHAKE
SHAKE
SHAKE
SHAKE

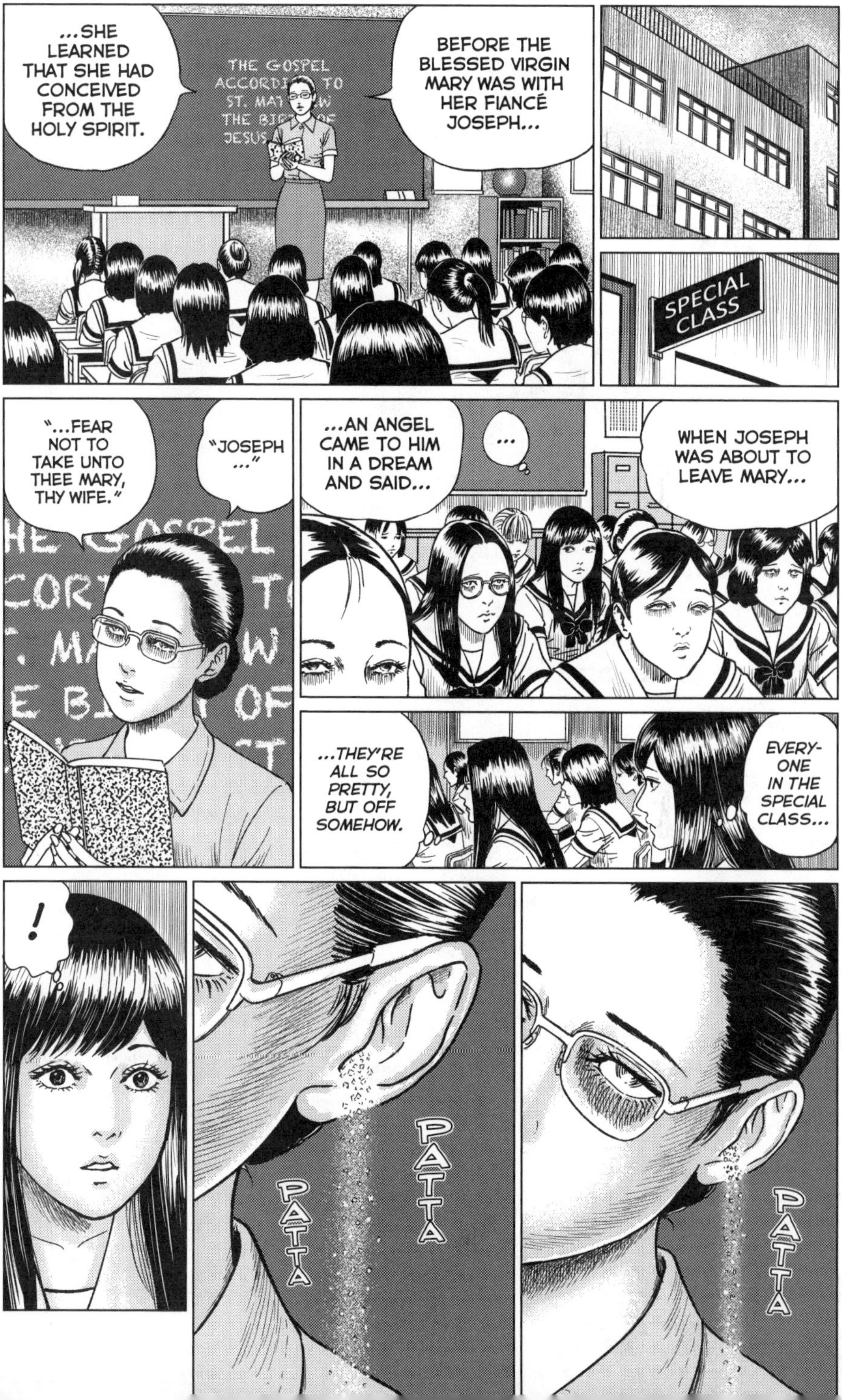
SPECIAL CLASS
BEFORE THE BLESSED VIRGIN MARY WAS WITH HER FIANCÉ JOSEPH...
...SHE LEARNED THAT SHE HAD CONCEIVED FROM THE HOLY SPIRIT.
THE GOSPEL
WHEN JOSEPH WAS ABOUT TO LEAVE MARY...
...
...AN ANGEL CAME TO HIM IN A DREAM AND SAID...
EVERY-ONE IN THE SPECIAL CLASS...
...THEY'RE ALL SO PRETTY, BUT OFF SOMEHOW.
"JOSEPH ..."
"...FEAR NOT TO TAKE UNTO THEE MARY, THY WIFE."
PATTA
PATTA
PATTA
PATTA
!

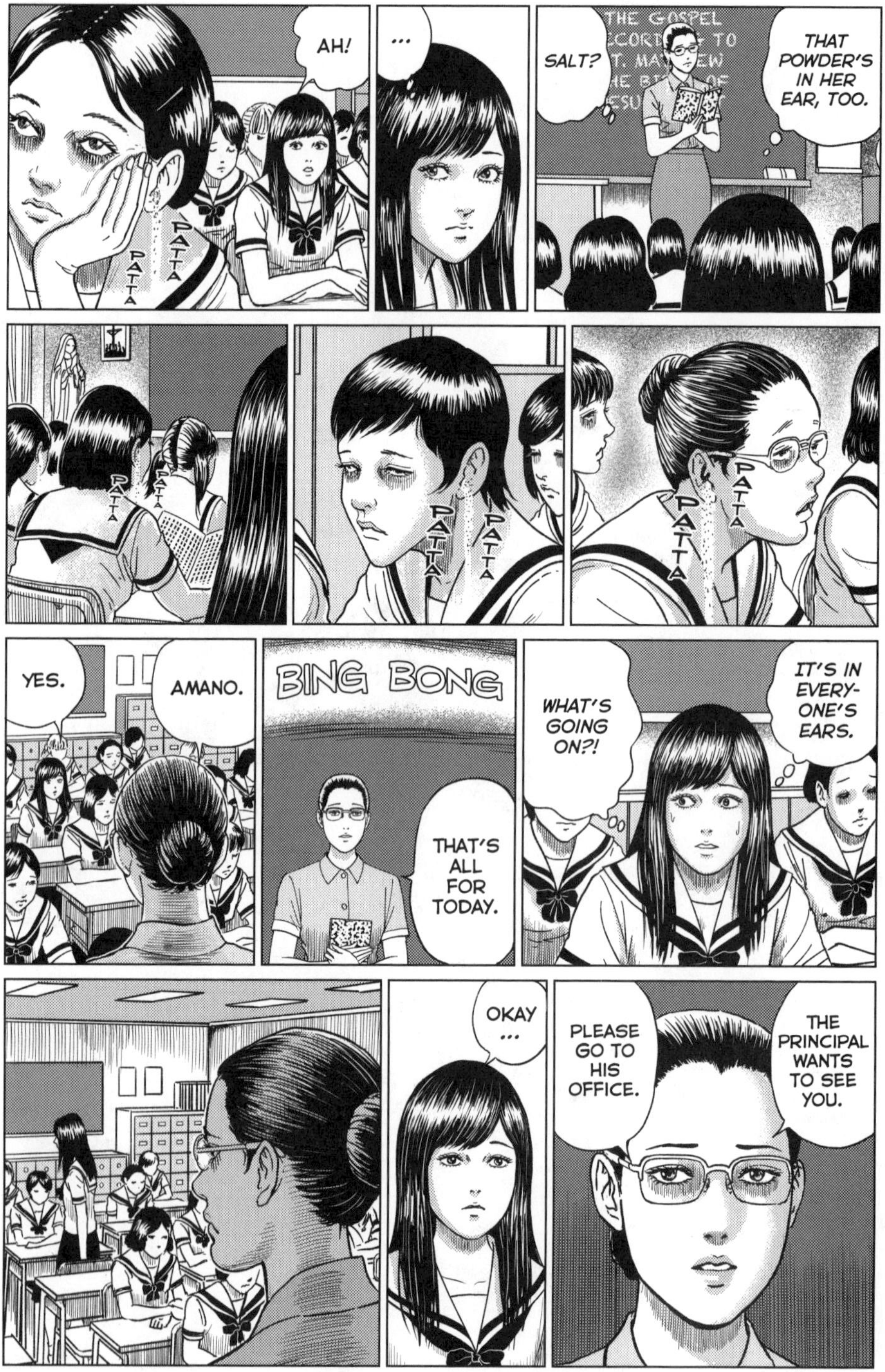
THE GOSPEL
THAT POWDER'S IN HER EAR, TOO.
SALT?
...
AH!
PATTA
PATTA
PATTA
PATTA
PATTA
PATTA
PATTA
PATTA
IT'S IN EVERY-ONE'S EARS.
WHAT'S GOING ON?!
BING BONG
THAT'S ALL FOR TODAY.
AMANO.
YES.
THE PRINCIPAL WANTS TO SEE YOU.
PLEASE GO TO HIS OFFICE.
OKAY ...

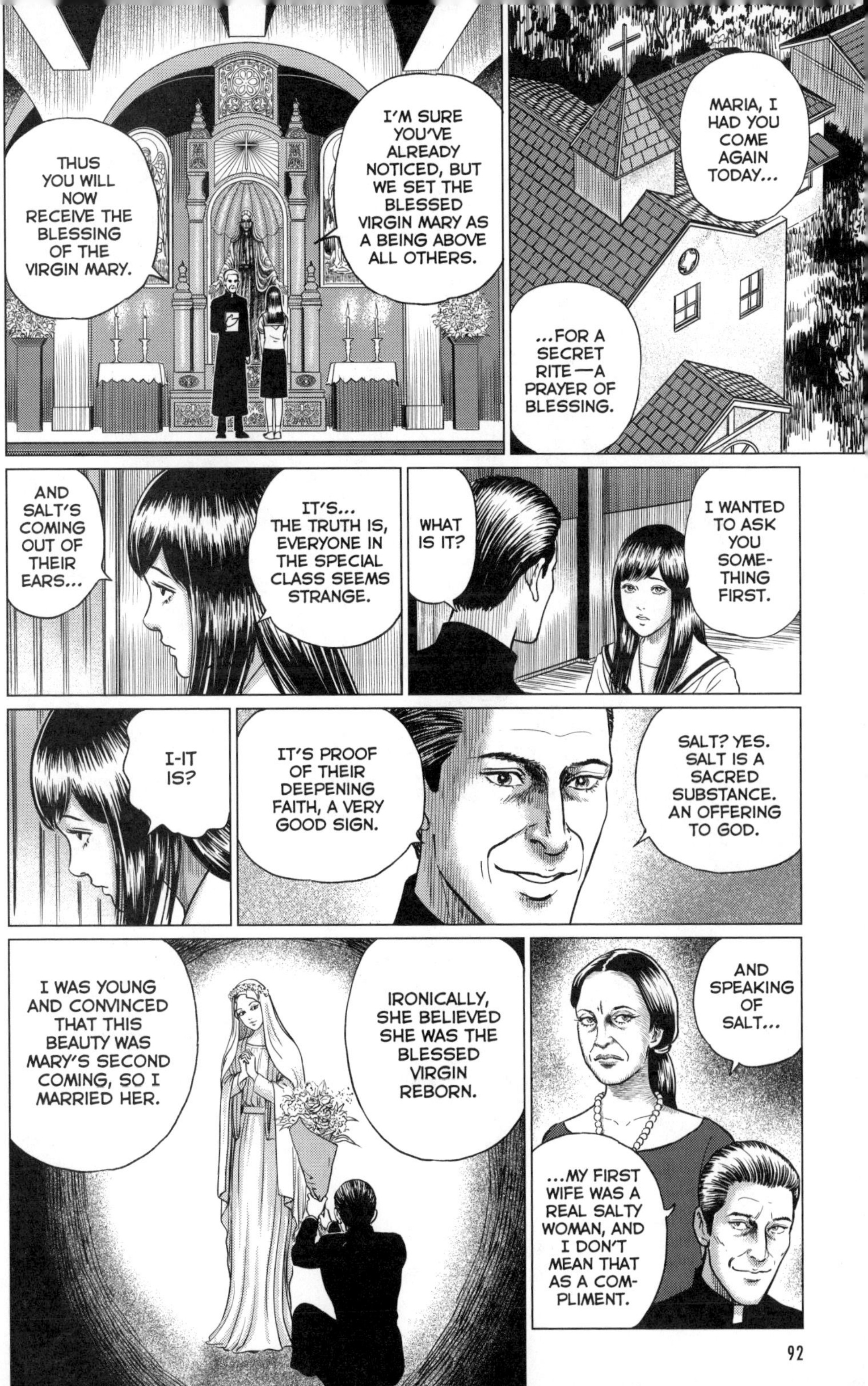
MARIA, I HAD YOU COME AGAIN TODAY...
...FOR A SECRET RITE—A PRAYER OF BLESSING.
I'M SURE YOU'VE ALREADY NOTICED, BUT WE SET THE BLESSED VIRGIN MARY AS A BEING ABOVE ALL OTHERS.
THUS YOU WILL NOW RECEIVE THE BLESSING OF THE VIRGIN MARY.
I WANTED TO ASK YOU SOMETHING FIRST.
WHAT IS IT?
IT'S... THE TRUTH IS, EVERYONE IN THE SPECIAL CLASS SEEMS STRANGE.
AND SALT'S COMING OUT OF THEIR EARS...
SALT? YES. SALT IS A SACRED SUBSTANCE. AN OFFERING TO GOD.
IT'S PROOF OF THEIR DEEPENING FAITH, A VERY GOOD SIGN.
I-IT IS?
AND SPEAKING OF SALT...
...MY FIRST WIFE WAS A REAL SALTY WOMAN, AND I DON'T MEAN THAT AS A COMPLIMENT.
IRONICALLY, SHE BELIEVED SHE WAS THE BLESSED VIRGIN REBORN.
I WAS YOUNG AND CONVINCED THAT THIS BEAUTY WAS MARY'S SECOND COMING, SO I MARRIED HER.

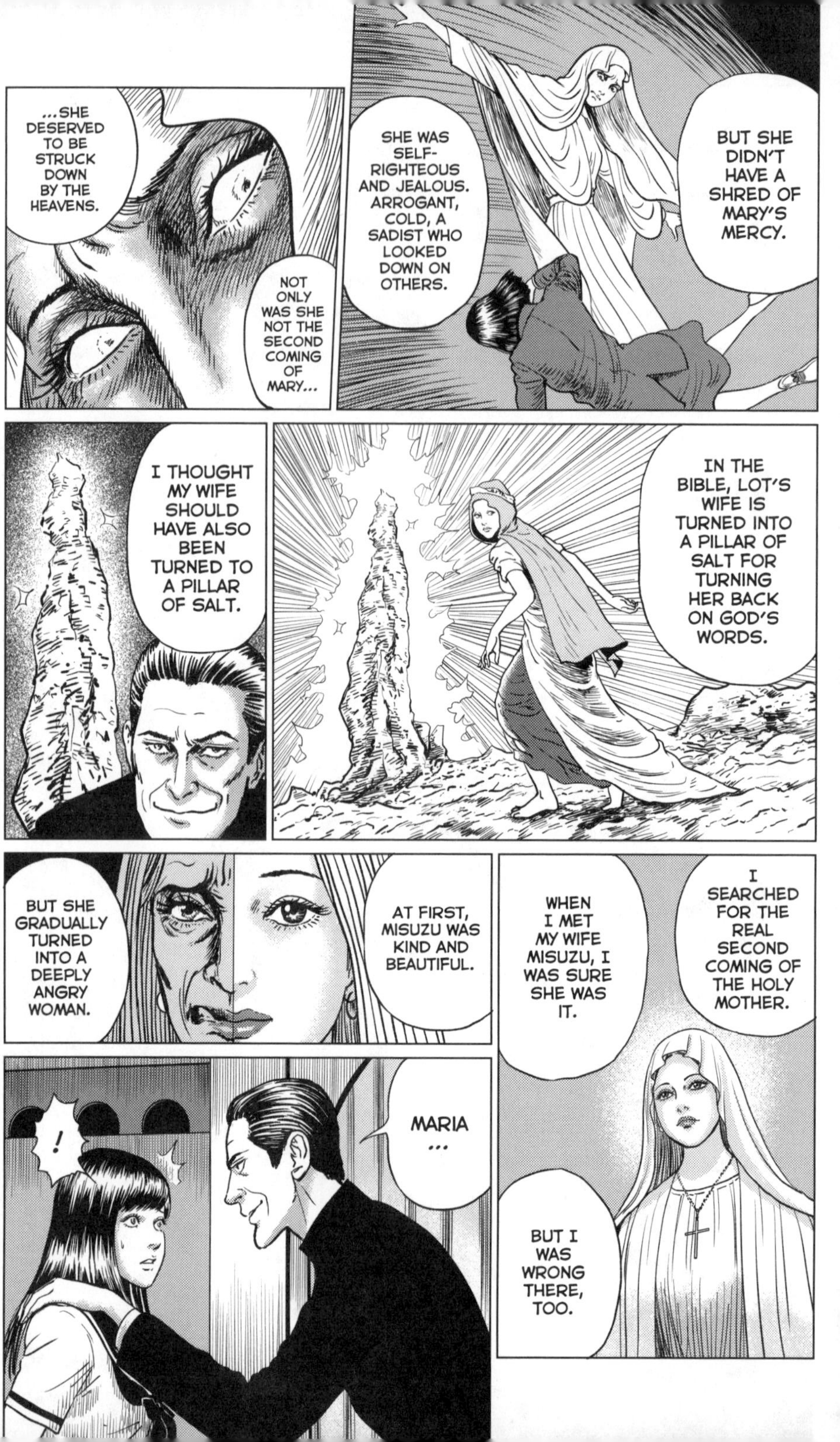
BUT SHE DIDN'T HAVE A SHRED OF MARY'S MERCY.
SHE WAS SELF-RIGHTEOUS AND JEALOUS. ARROGANT, COLD, A SADIST WHO LOOKED DOWN ON OTHERS.
NOT ONLY WAS SHE NOT THE SECOND COMING OF MARY...
...SHE DESERVED TO BE STRUCK DOWN BY THE HEAVENS.
IN THE BIBLE, LOT'S WIFE IS TURNED INTO A PILLAR OF SALT FOR TURNING HER BACK ON GOD'S WORDS.
I THOUGHT MY WIFE SHOULD HAVE ALSO BEEN TURNED TO A PILLAR OF SALT.
I SEARCHED FOR THE REAL SECOND COMING OF THE HOLY MOTHER.
WHEN I MET MY WIFE MISUZU, I WAS SURE SHE WAS IT.
BUT I WAS WRONG THERE, TOO.
AT FIRST, MISUZU WAS KIND AND BEAUTIFUL.
BUT SHE GRADUALLY TURNED INTO A DEEPLY ANGRY WOMAN.
MARIA ...
!

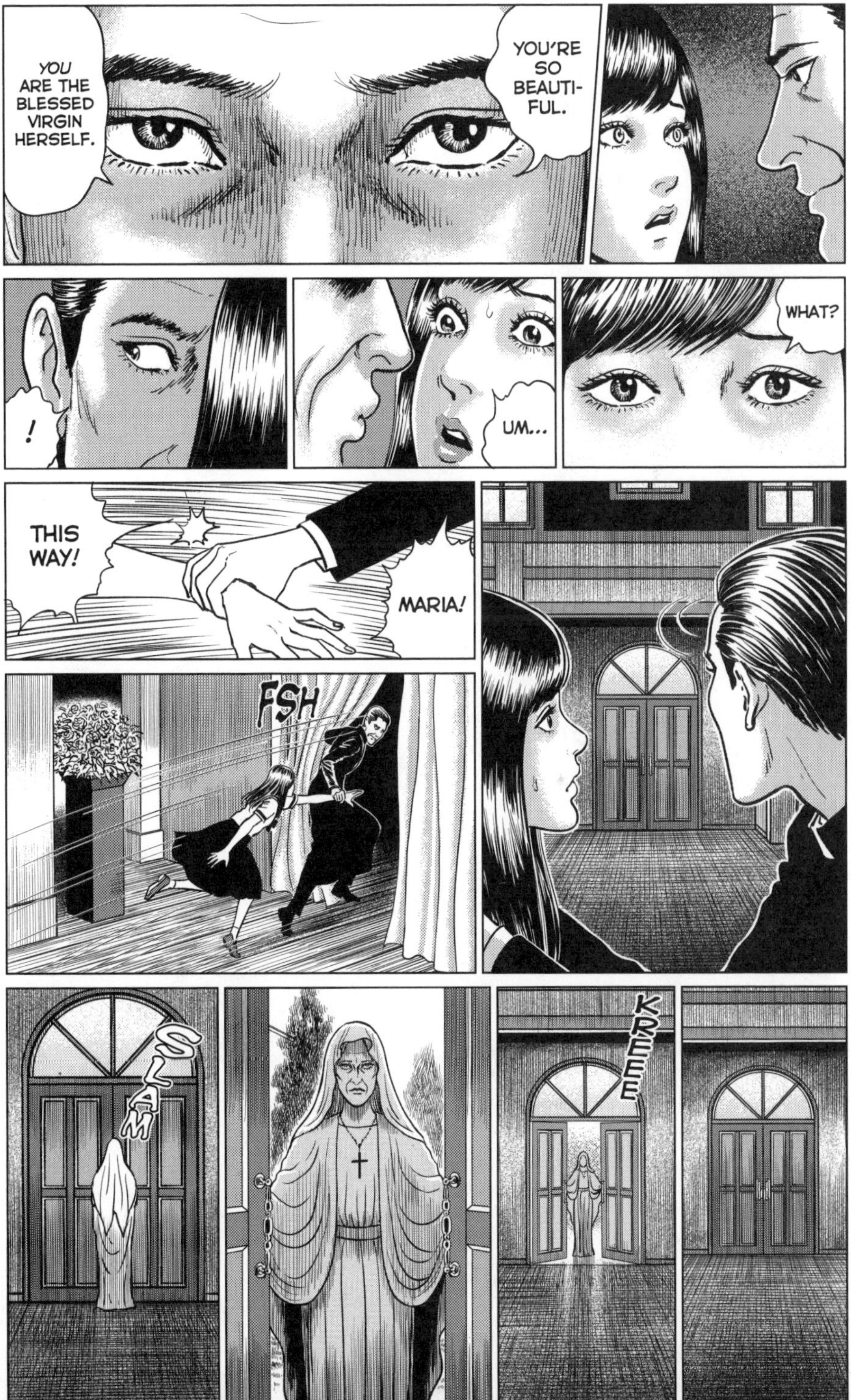
YOU'RE SO BEAUTIFUL.
YOU ARE THE BLESSED VIRGIN HERSELF.
WHAT?
UM...
!
MARIA!
THIS WAY!
FSH
KREEE
SLAM

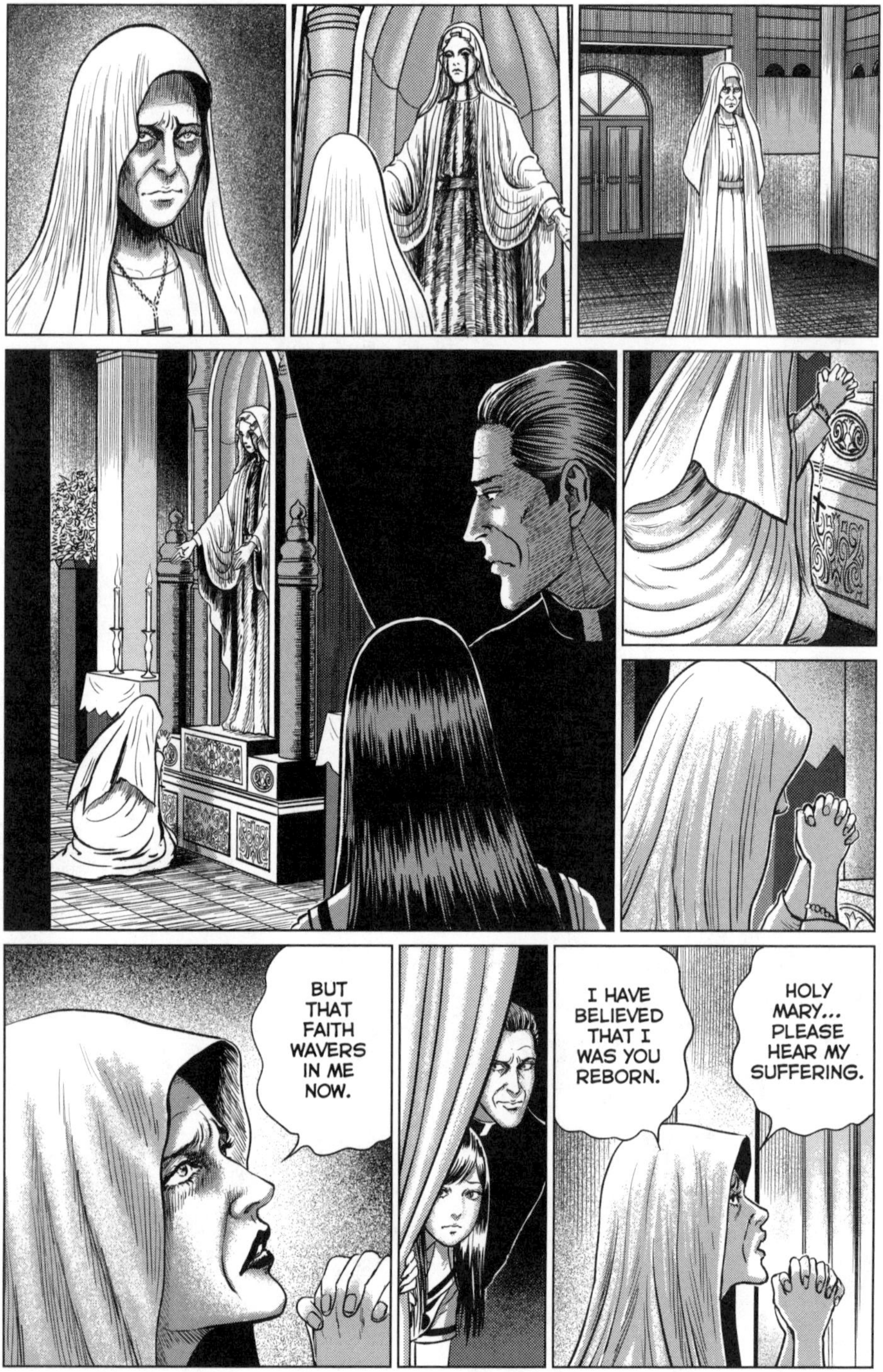
HOLY MARY... PLEASE HEAR MY SUFFERING.
I HAVE BELIEVED THAT I WAS YOU REBORN.
BUT THAT FAITH WAVERS IN ME NOW.

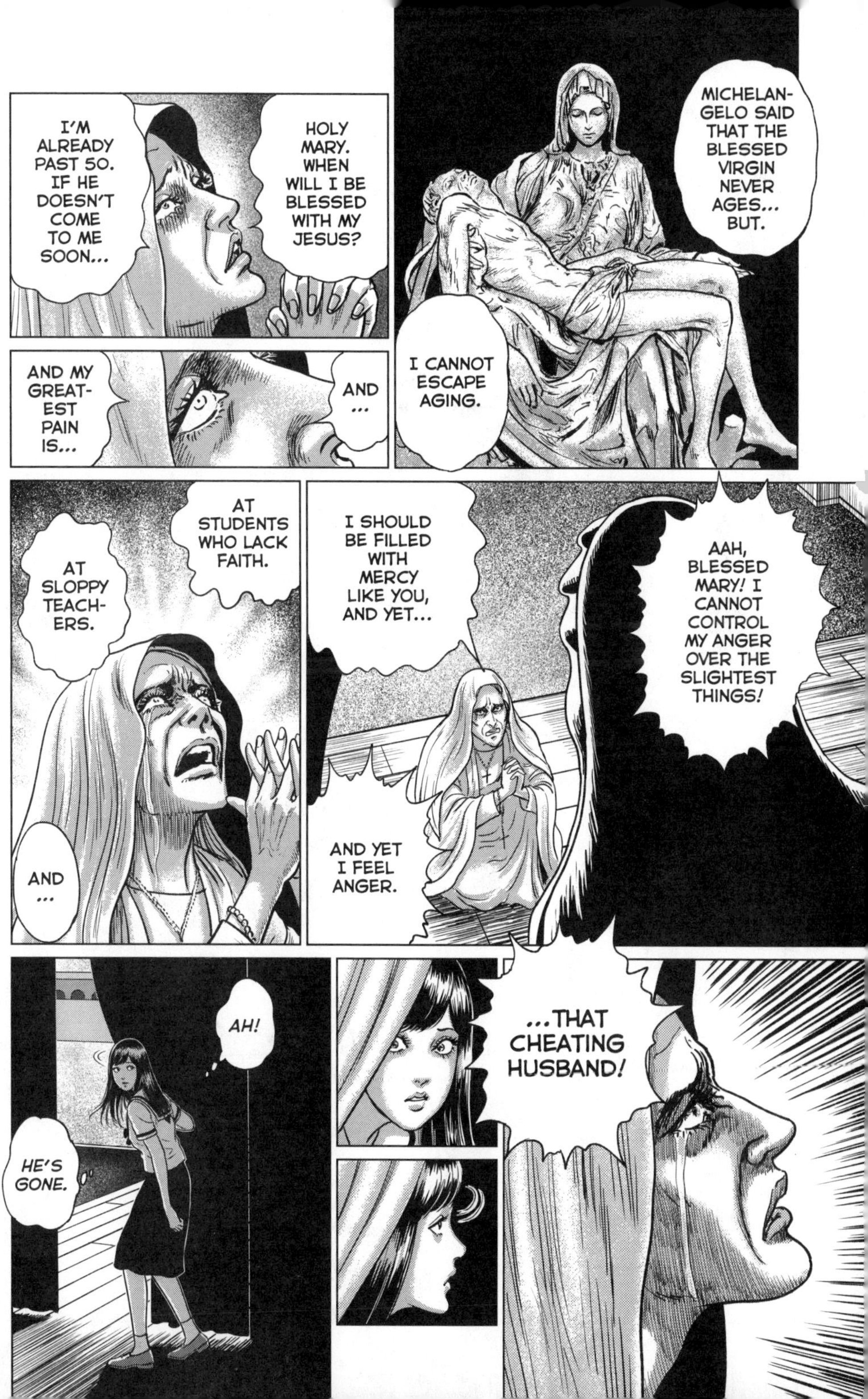
MICHELANGELO SAID THAT THE BLESSED VIRGIN NEVER AGES... BUT.
I CANNOT ESCAPE AGING.
HOLY MARY. WHEN WILL I BE BLESSED WITH MY JESUS?
I'M ALREADY PAST 50. IF HE DOESN'T COME TO ME SOON...
AND ...
AND MY GREATEST PAIN IS...
AAH, BLESSED MARY! I CANNOT CONTROL MY ANGER OVER THE SLIGHTEST THINGS!
I SHOULD BE FILLED WITH MERCY LIKE YOU, AND YET...
AND YET I FEEL ANGER.
AT STUDENTS WHO LACK FAITH.
AT SLOPPY TEACHERS.
AND ...
...THAT CHEATING HUSBAND!
AH!
HE'S GONE.

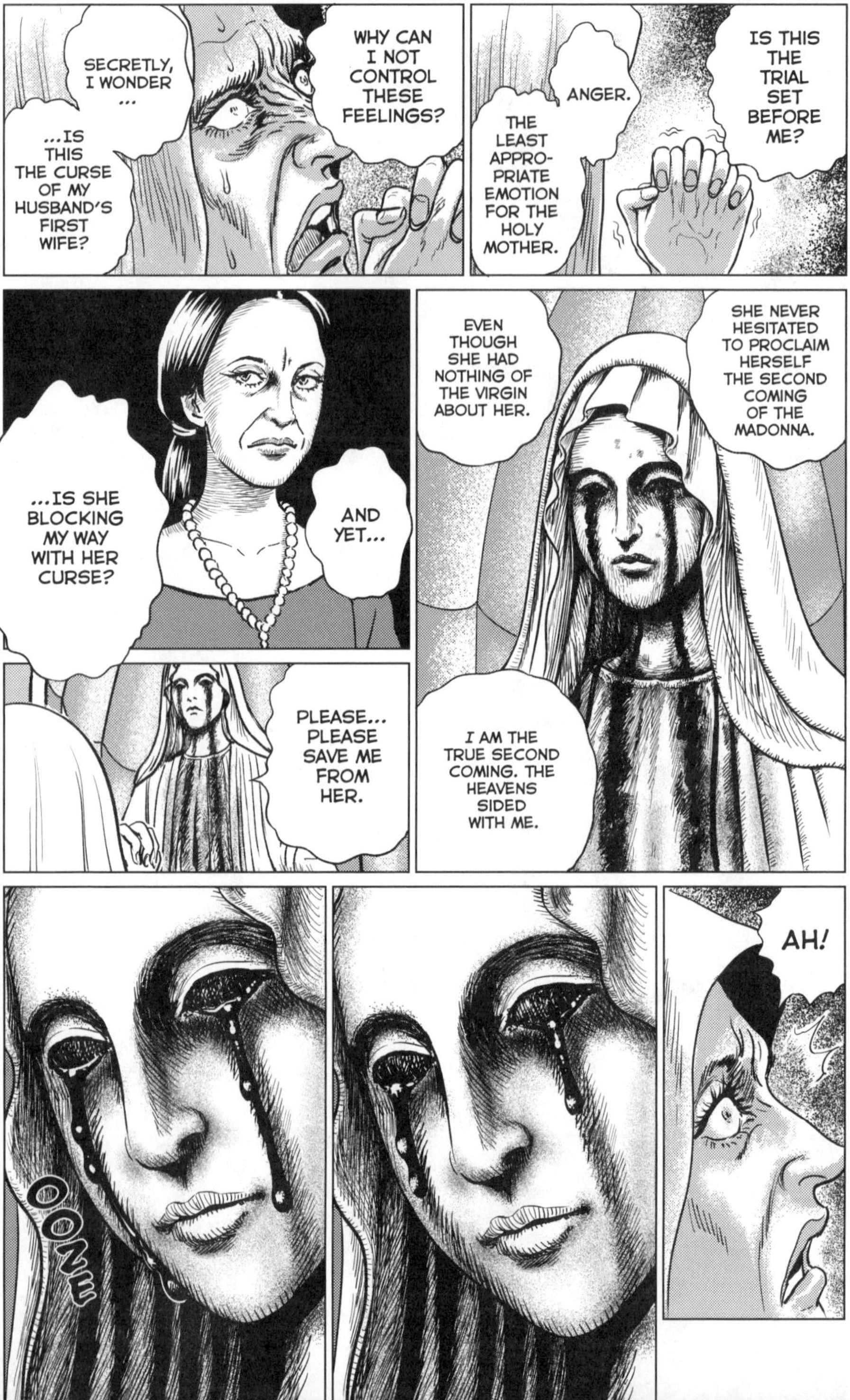
IS THIS THE TRIAL SET BEFORE ME?
ANGER.
THE LEAST APPROPRIATE EMOTION FOR THE HOLY MOTHER.
WHY CAN I NOT CONTROL THESE FEELINGS?
SECRETLY, I WONDER...
...IS THIS THE CURSE OF MY HUSBAND'S FIRST WIFE?
SHE NEVER HESITATED TO PROCLAIM HERSELF THE SECOND COMING OF THE MADONNA.
EVEN THOUGH SHE HAD NOTHING OF THE VIRGIN ABOUT HER.
I AM THE TRUE SECOND COMING. THE HEAVENS SIDED WITH ME.
AND YET...
...IS SHE BLOCKING MY WAY WITH HER CURSE?
PLEASE... PLEASE SAVE ME FROM HER.
AH!
OOZE

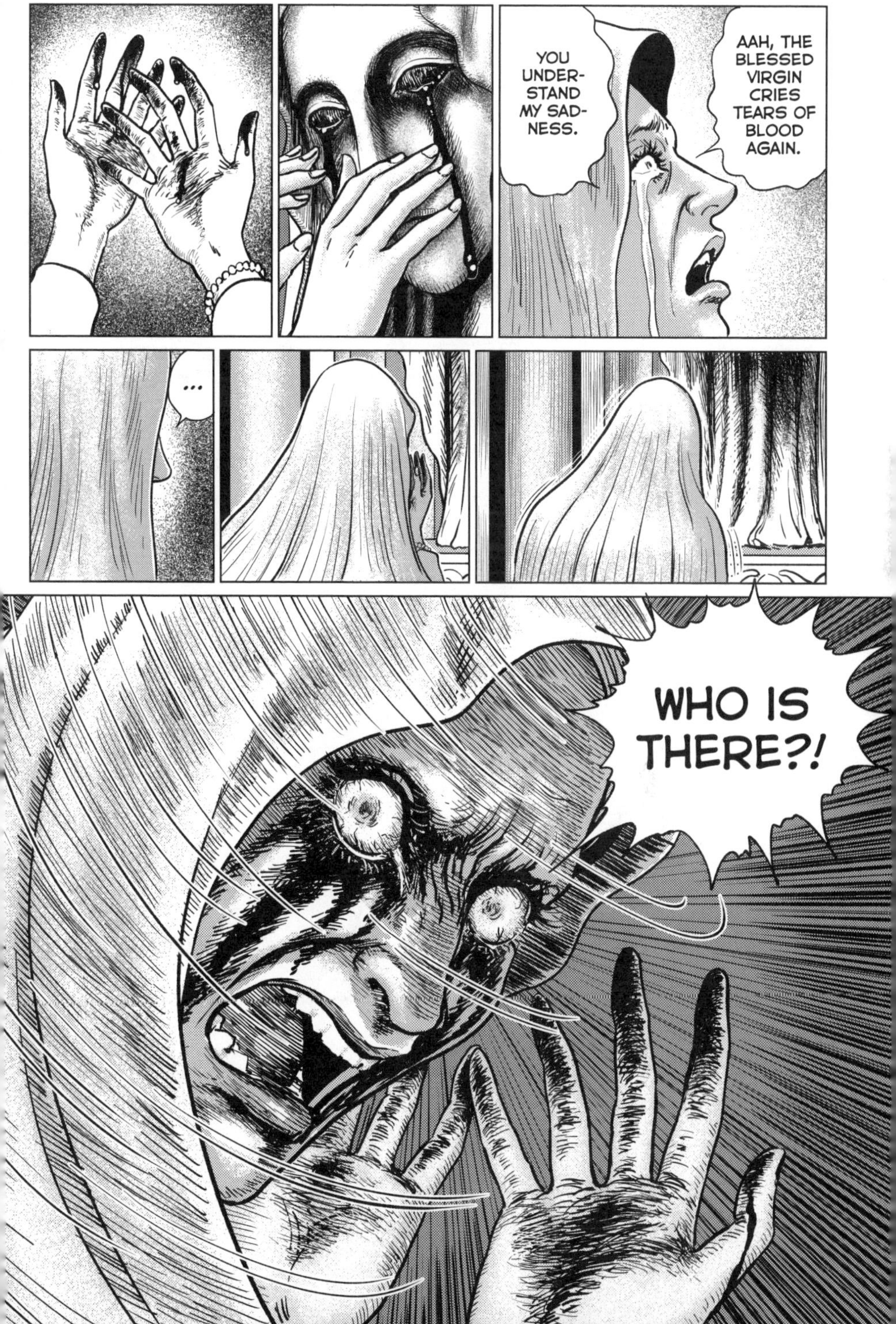
AAH, THE BLESSED VIRGIN CRIES TEARS OF BLOOD AGAIN.
YOU UNDER-STAND MY SAD-NESS.
...
WHO IS THERE?!

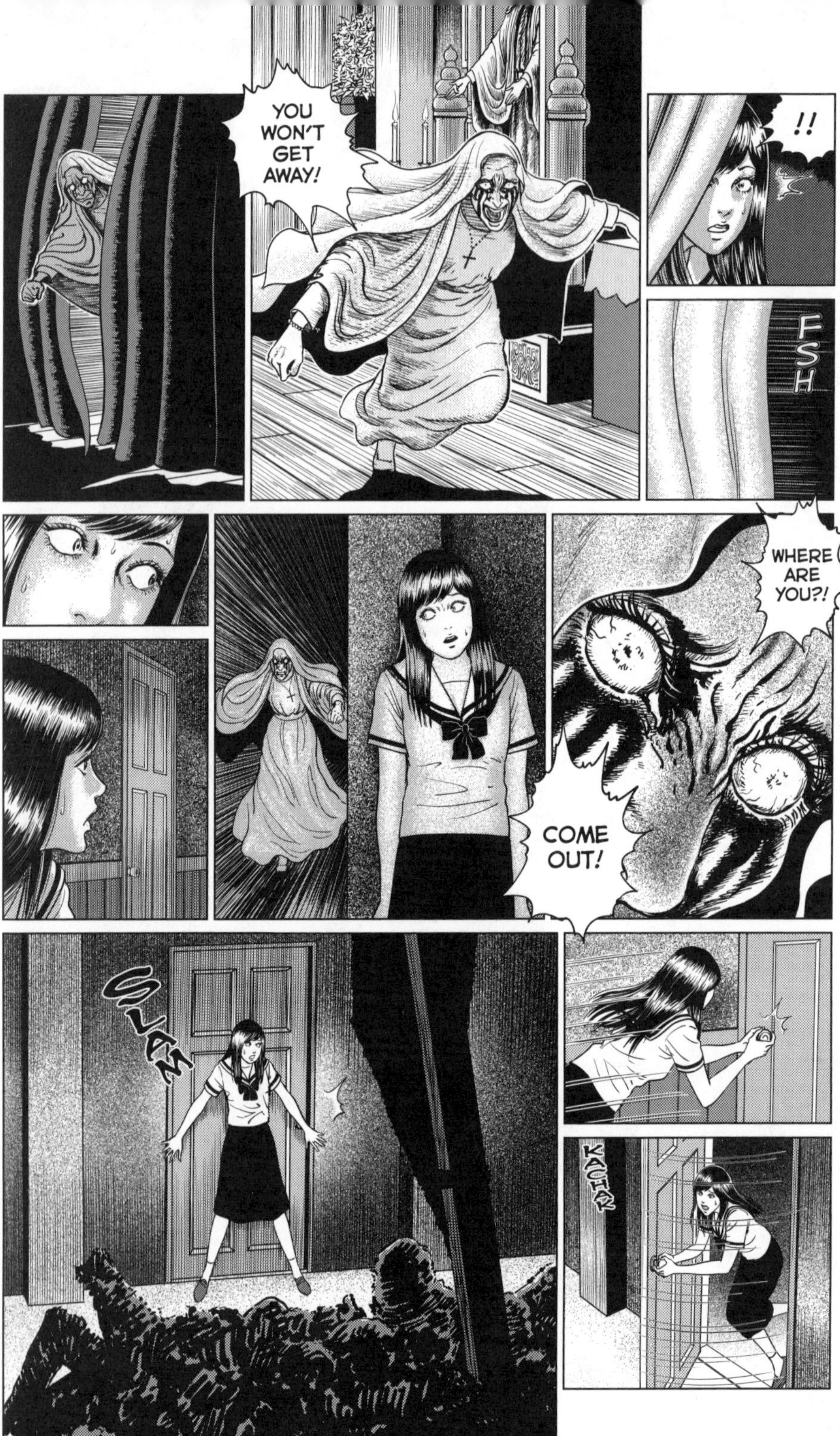
!!
FSH
YOU WON'T GET AWAY!
WHERE ARE YOU?!
COME OUT!
KACHAK
SLAM

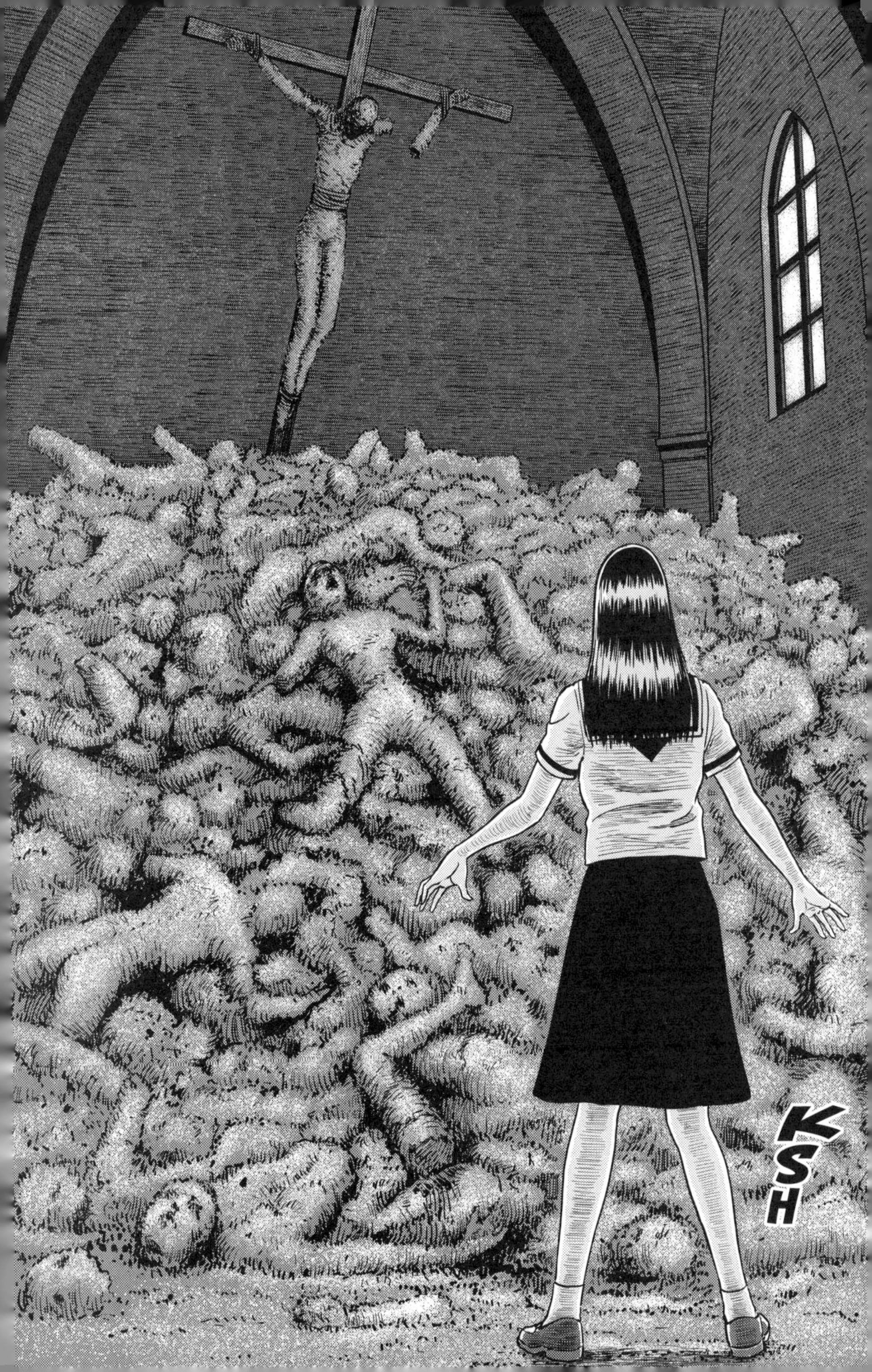
KSH

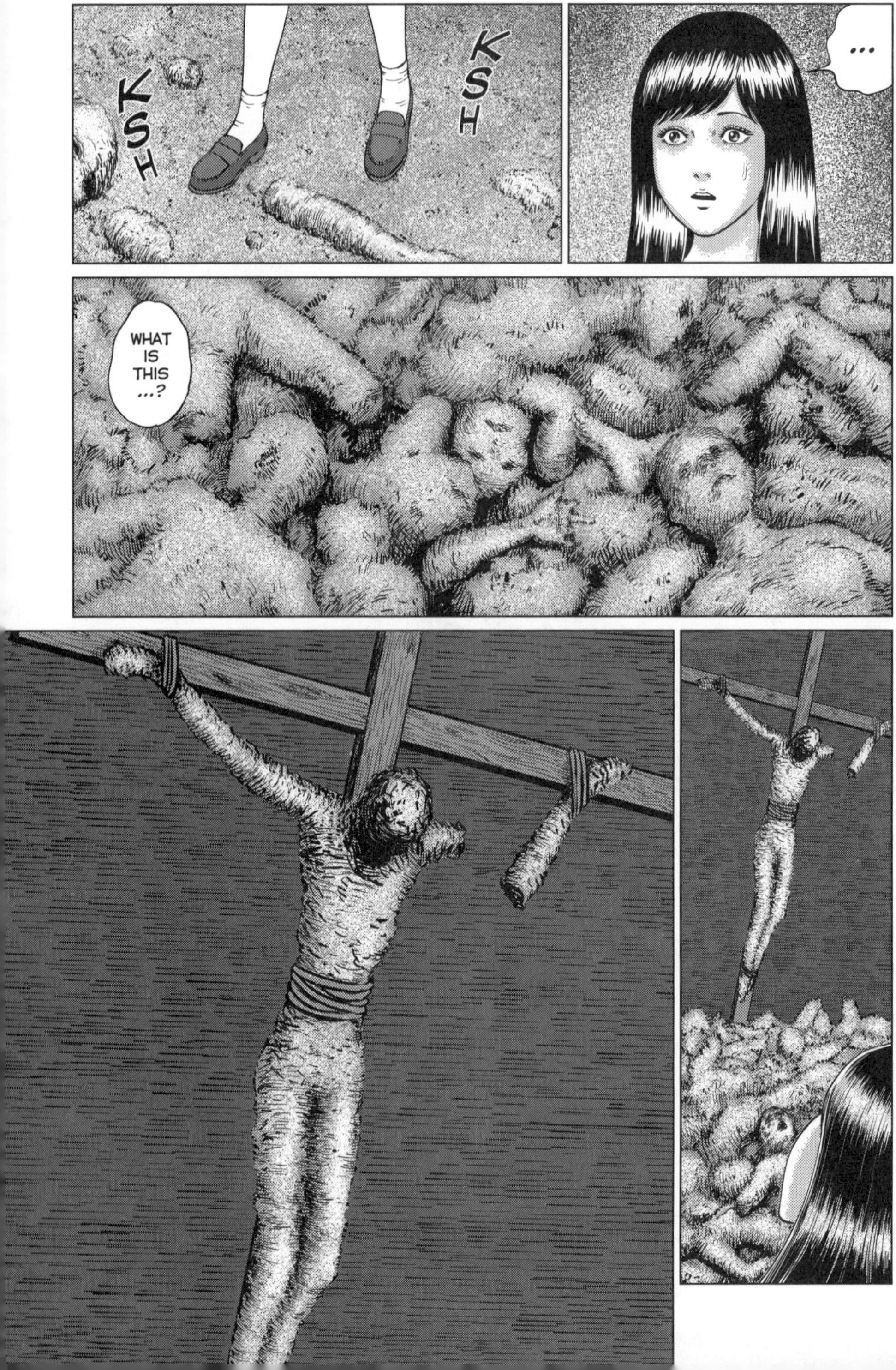
...
KSH
KSH
WHAT IS THIS ...?

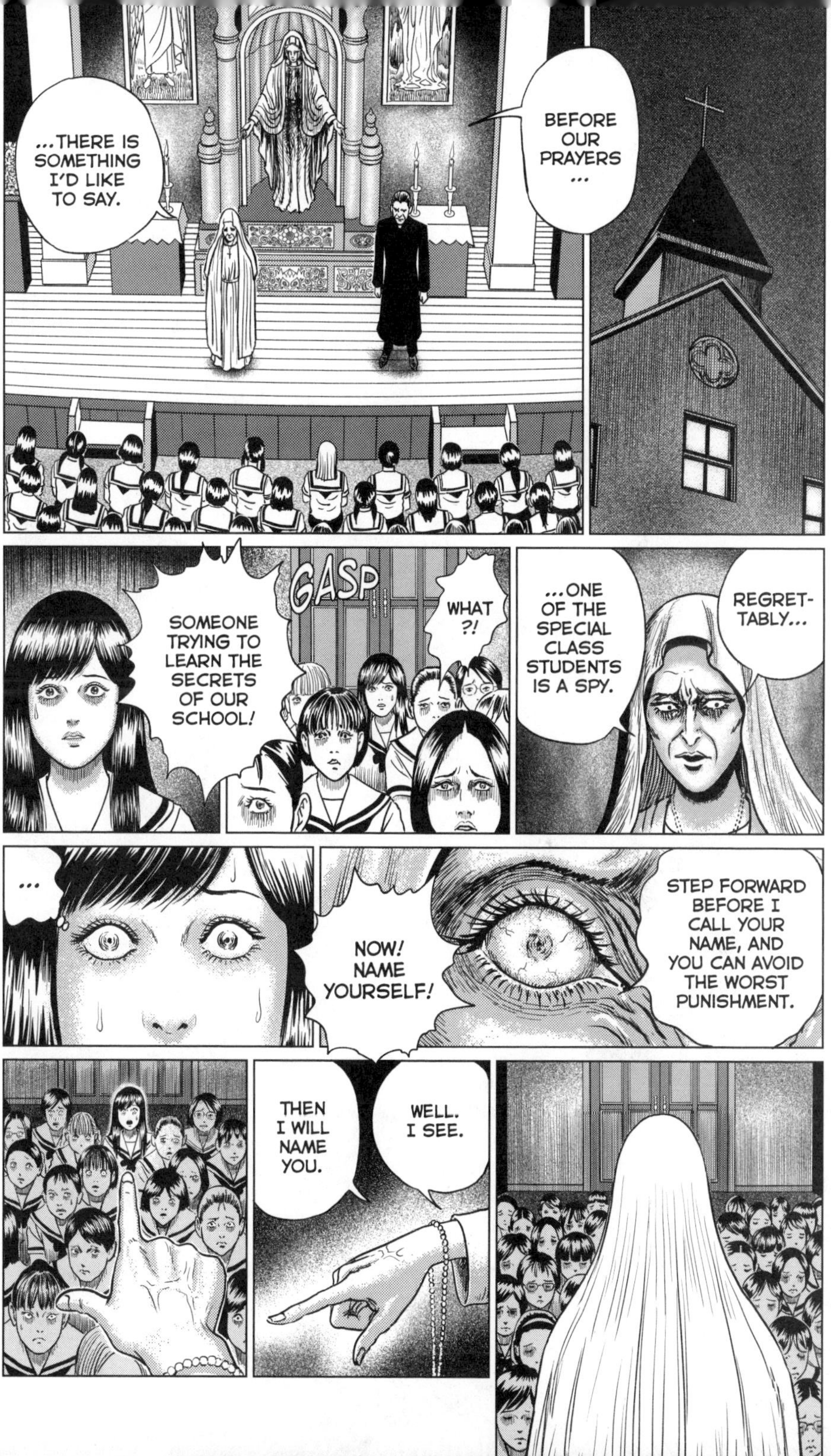
BEFORE OUR PRAYERS ...
...THERE IS SOMETHING I'D LIKE TO SAY.
REGRET-TABLY...
...ONE OF THE SPECIAL CLASS STUDENTS IS A SPY.
WHAT ?!
GASP
SOMEONE TRYING TO LEARN THE SECRETS OF OUR SCHOOL!
STEP FORWARD BEFORE I CALL YOUR NAME, AND YOU CAN AVOID THE WORST PUNISHMENT.
NOW! NAME YOURSELF!
...
WELL. I SEE.
THEN I WILL NAME YOU.

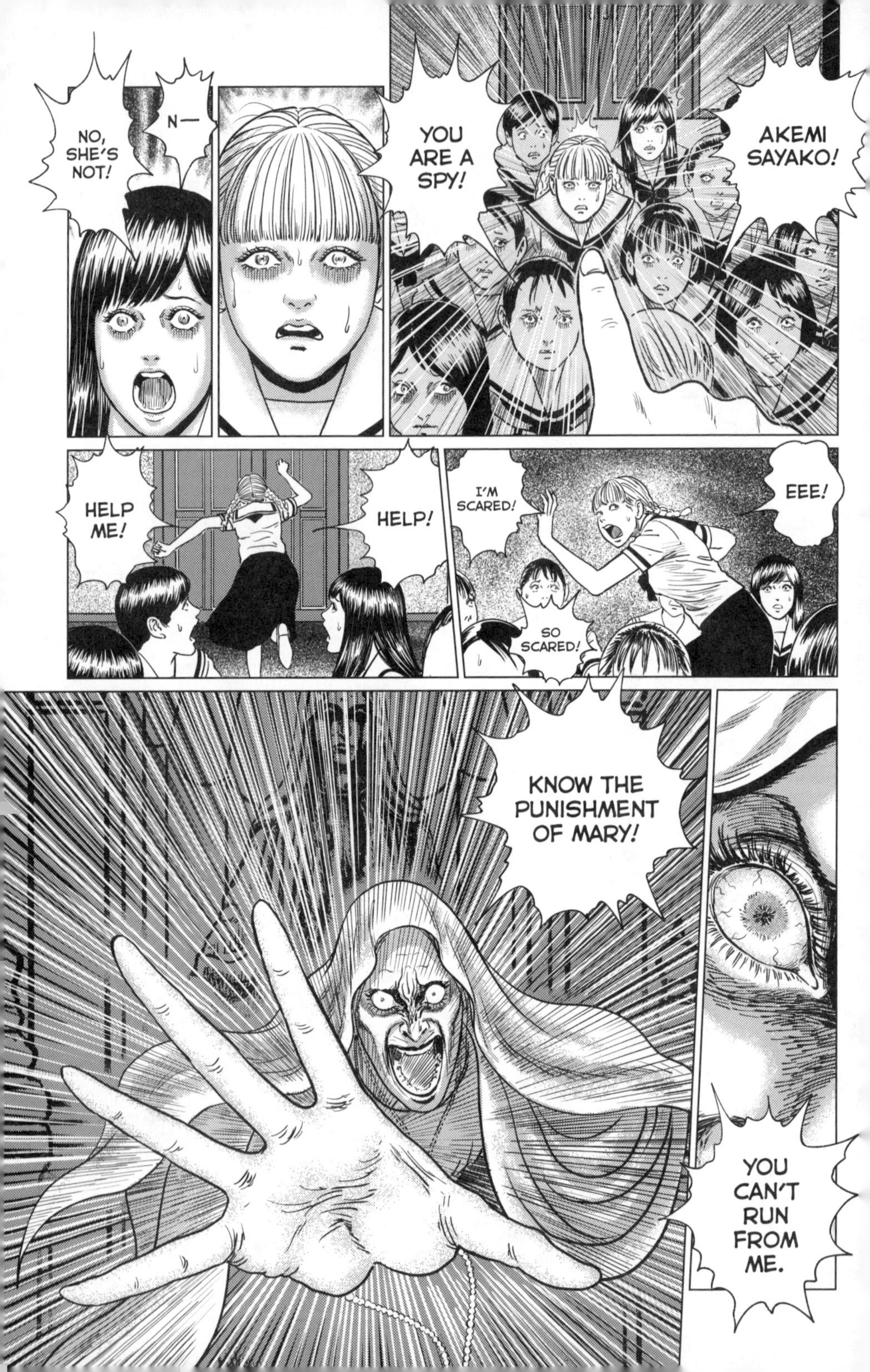
AKEMI SAYAKO!
YOU ARE A SPY!
N—
NO, SHE'S NOT!
EEE!
I'M SCARED!
SO SCARED!
HELP!
HELP ME!
KNOW THE PUNISHMENT OF MARY!
YOU CAN'T RUN FROM ME.

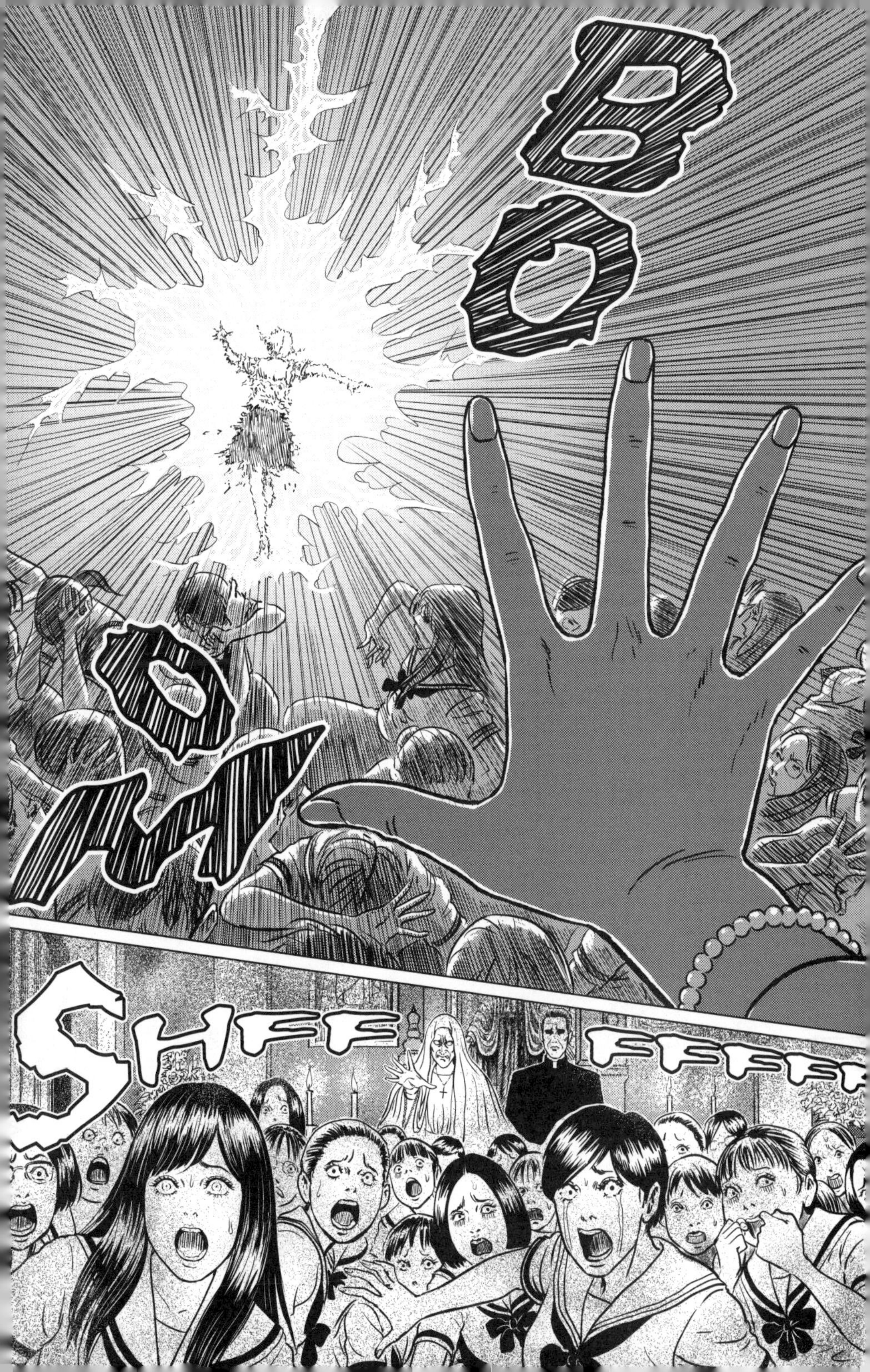
BOOM
SHFFF
FFFF

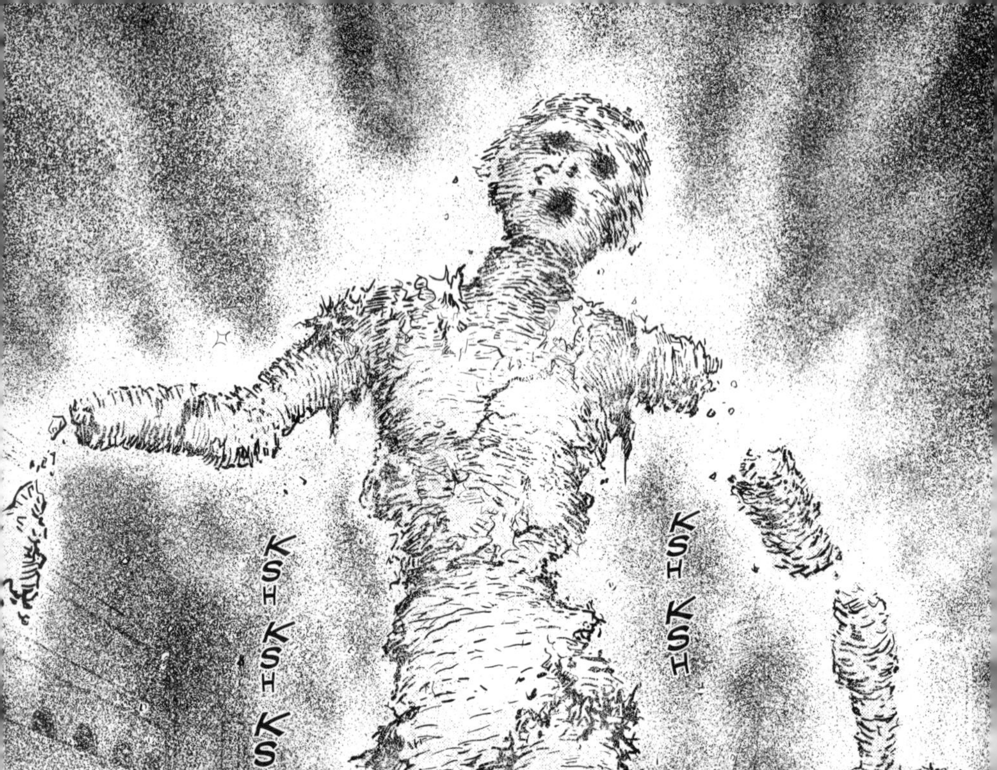
KSH KSH
KSH KSH KSH

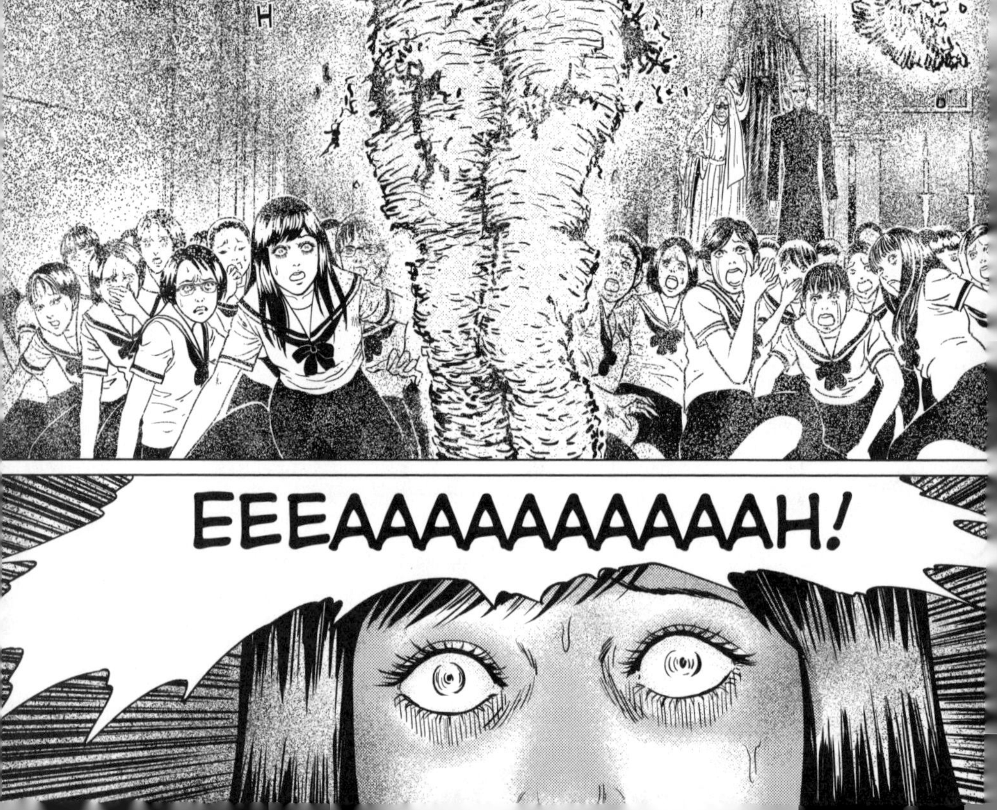
EEEAAAAAAAAAAAH!

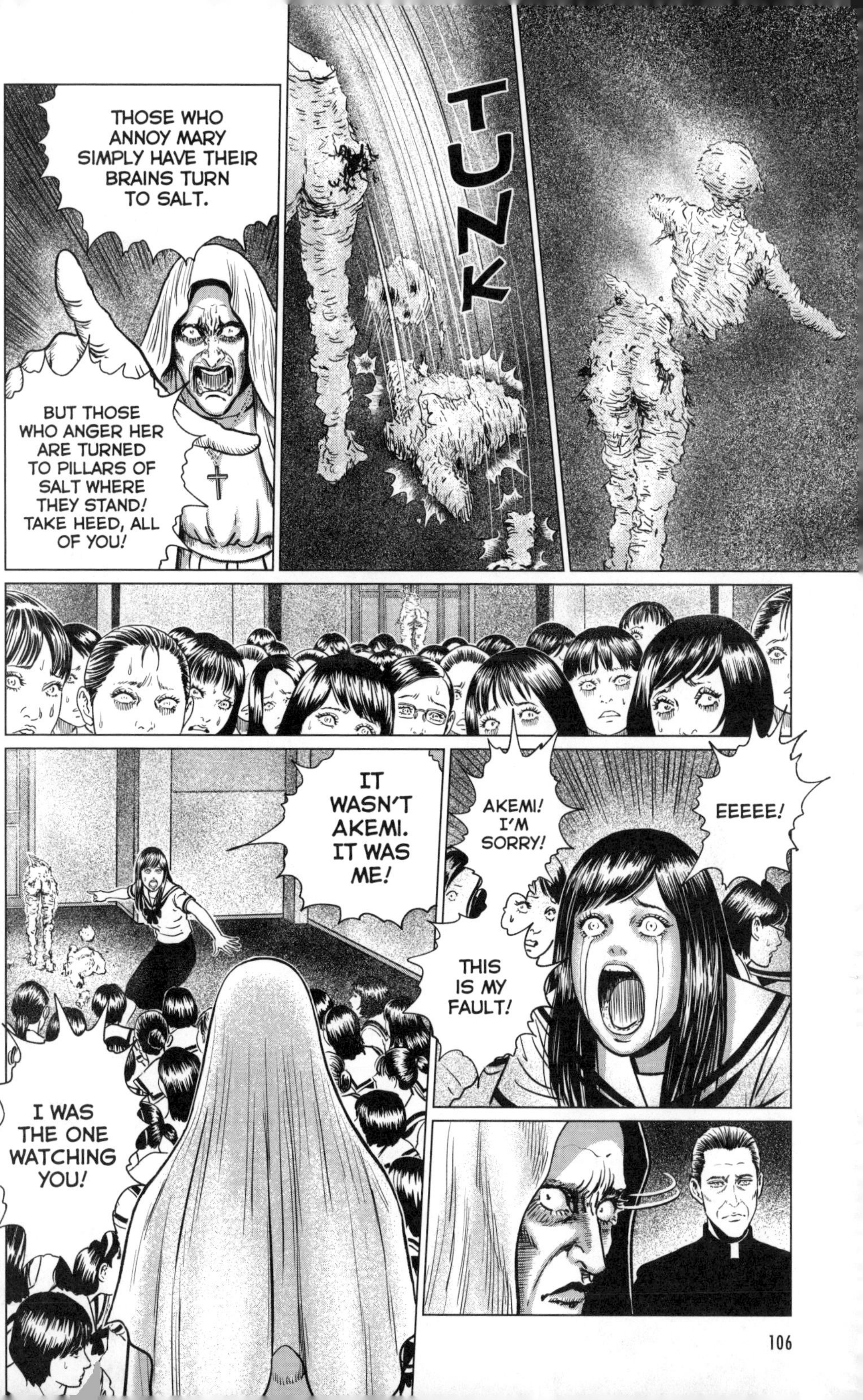
TUNK
THOSE WHO ANNOY MARY SIMPLY HAVE THEIR BRAINS TURN TO SALT.
BUT THOSE WHO ANGER HER ARE TURNED TO PILLARS OF SALT WHERE THEY STAND! TAKE HEED, ALL OF YOU!
EEEEE!
AKEMI! I'M SORRY!
THIS IS MY FAULT!
IT WASN'T AKEMI. IT WAS ME!
I WAS THE ONE WATCHING YOU!

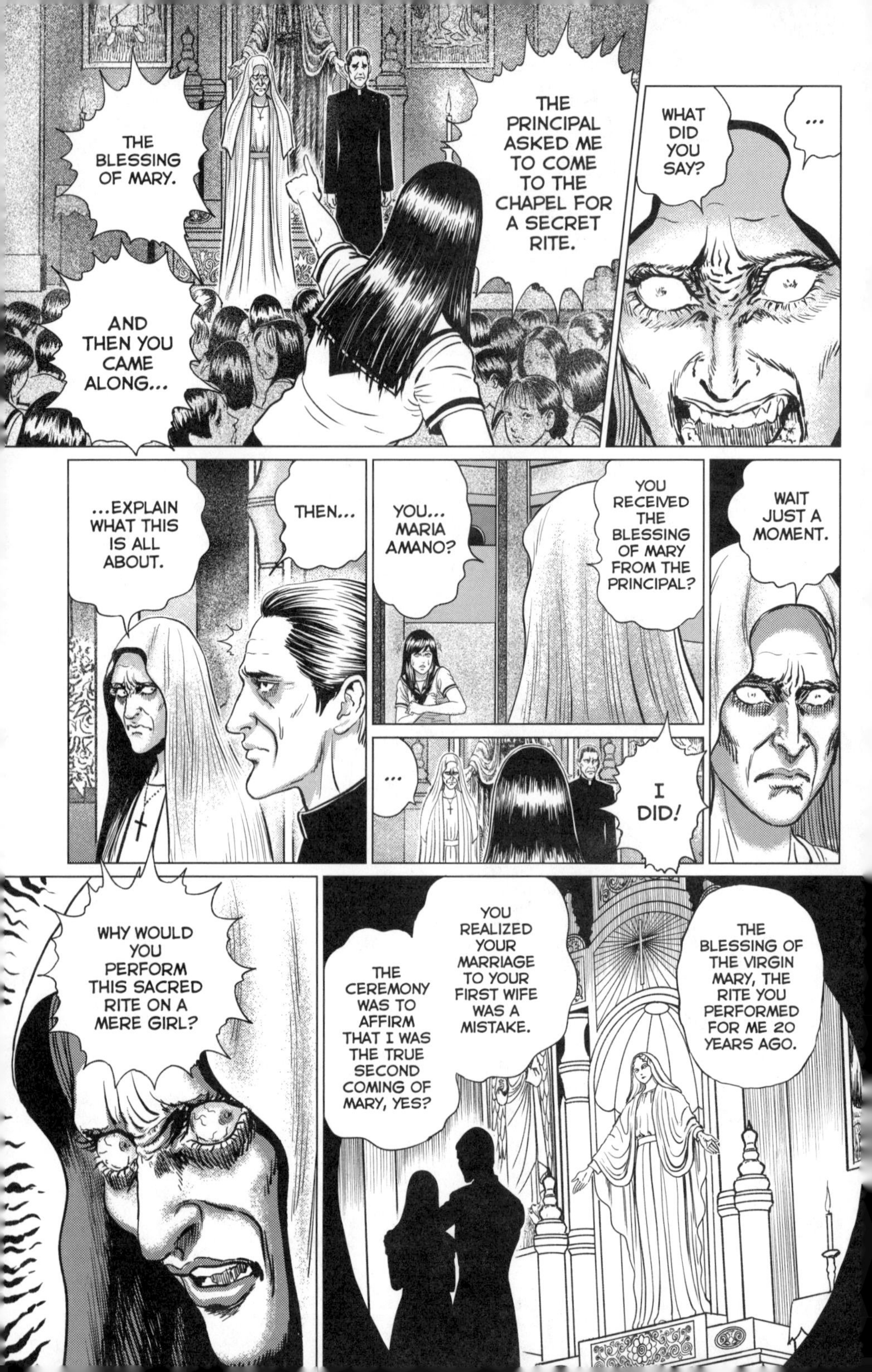
...
WHAT DID YOU SAY?
THE PRINCIPAL ASKED ME TO COME TO THE CHAPEL FOR A SECRET RITE.
THE BLESSING OF MARY.
AND THEN YOU CAME ALONG...
WAIT JUST A MOMENT.
YOU RECEIVED THE BLESSING OF MARY FROM THE PRINCIPAL?
YOU... MARIA AMANO?
I DID!
...
THEN...
...EXPLAIN WHAT THIS IS ALL ABOUT.
THE BLESSING OF THE VIRGIN MARY, THE RITE YOU PERFORMED FOR ME 20 YEARS AGO.
YOU REALIZED YOUR MARRIAGE TO YOUR FIRST WIFE WAS A MISTAKE.
THE CEREMONY WAS TO AFFIRM THAT I WAS THE TRUE SECOND COMING OF MARY, YES?
WHY WOULD YOU PERFORM THIS SACRED RITE ON A MERE GIRL?

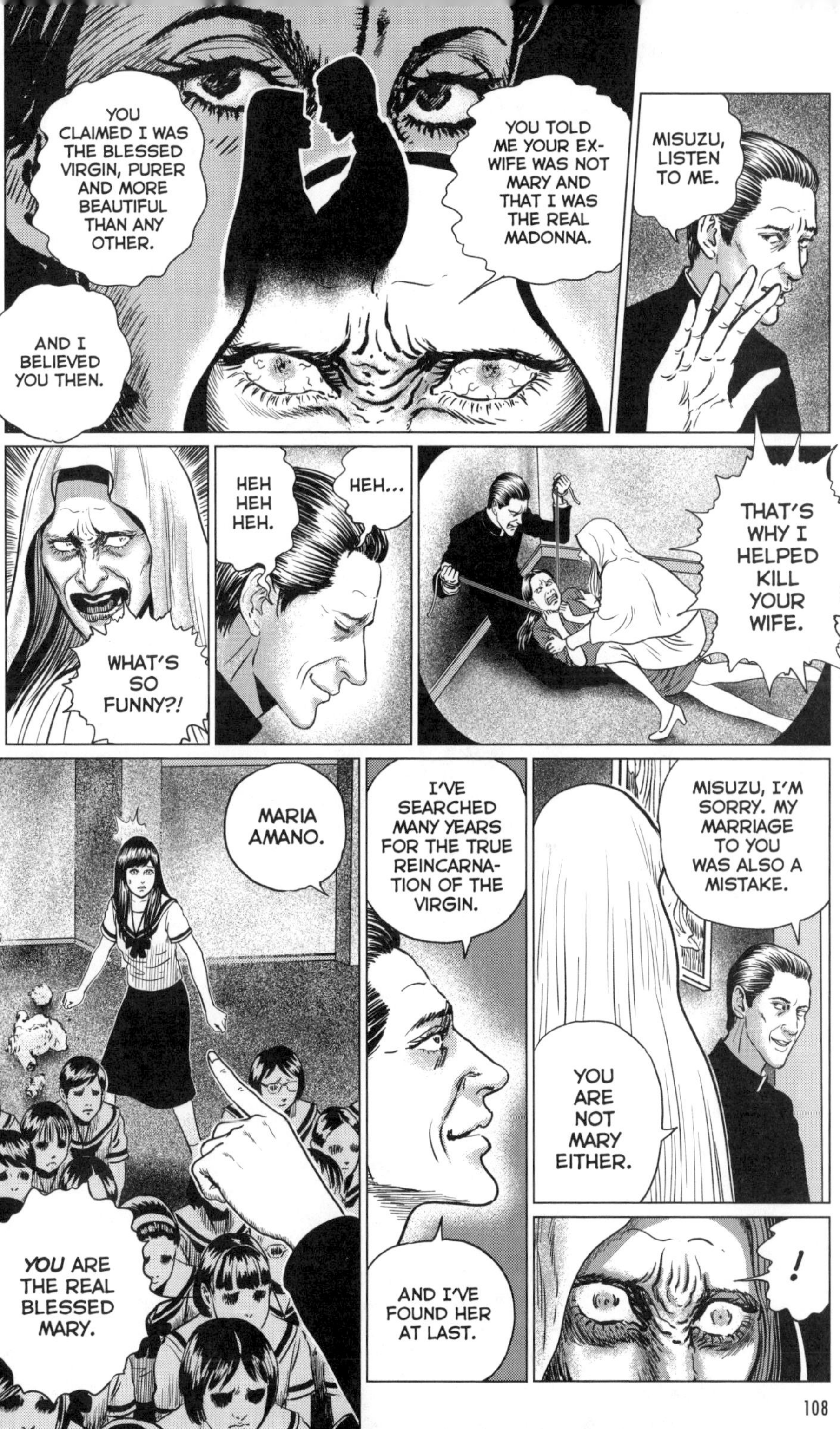
MISUZU, LISTEN TO ME.
YOU TOLD ME YOUR EX-WIFE WAS NOT MARY AND THAT I WAS THE REAL MADONNA.
YOU CLAIMED I WAS THE BLESSED VIRGIN, PURER AND MORE BEAUTIFUL THAN ANY OTHER.
AND I BELIEVED YOU THEN.
THAT'S WHY I HELPED KILL YOUR WIFE.
HEH...
HEH HEH HEH.
WHAT'S SO FUNNY?!
MISUZU, I'M SORRY. MY MARRIAGE TO YOU WAS ALSO A MISTAKE.
YOU ARE NOT MARY EITHER.
!
I'VE SEARCHED MANY YEARS FOR THE TRUE REINCARNATION OF THE VIRGIN.
AND I'VE FOUND HER AT LAST.
MARIA AMANO.
YOU ARE THE REAL BLESSED MARY.

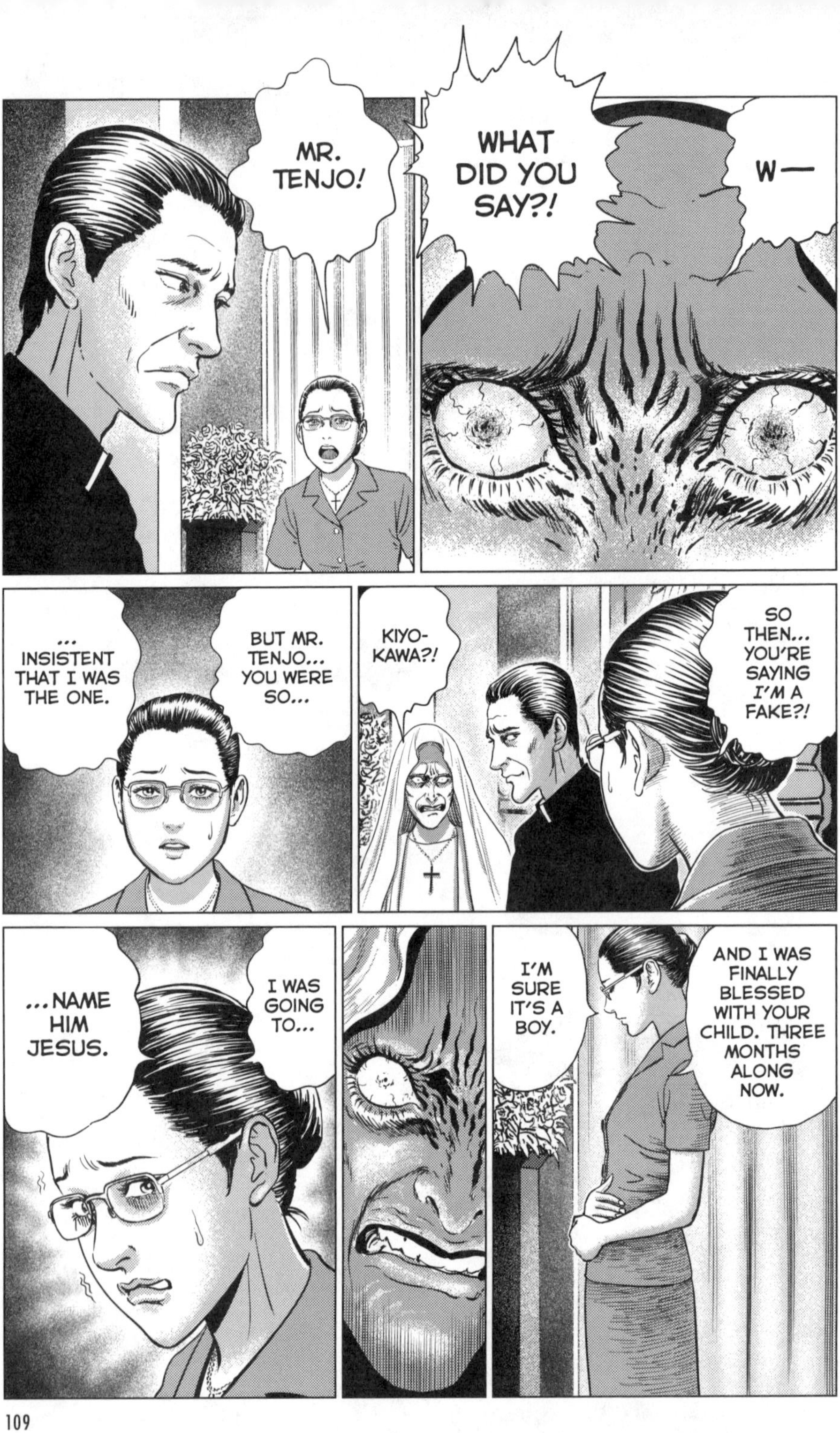
W—
WHAT DID YOU SAY?!
MR. TENJO!
SO THEN... YOU'RE SAYING I'M A FAKE?!
KIYO-KAWA?!
BUT MR. TENJO... YOU WERE SO...
... INSISTENT THAT I WAS THE ONE.
AND I WAS FINALLY BLESSED WITH YOUR CHILD. THREE MONTHS ALONG NOW.
I'M SURE IT'S A BOY.
I WAS GOING TO...
...NAME HIM JESUS.

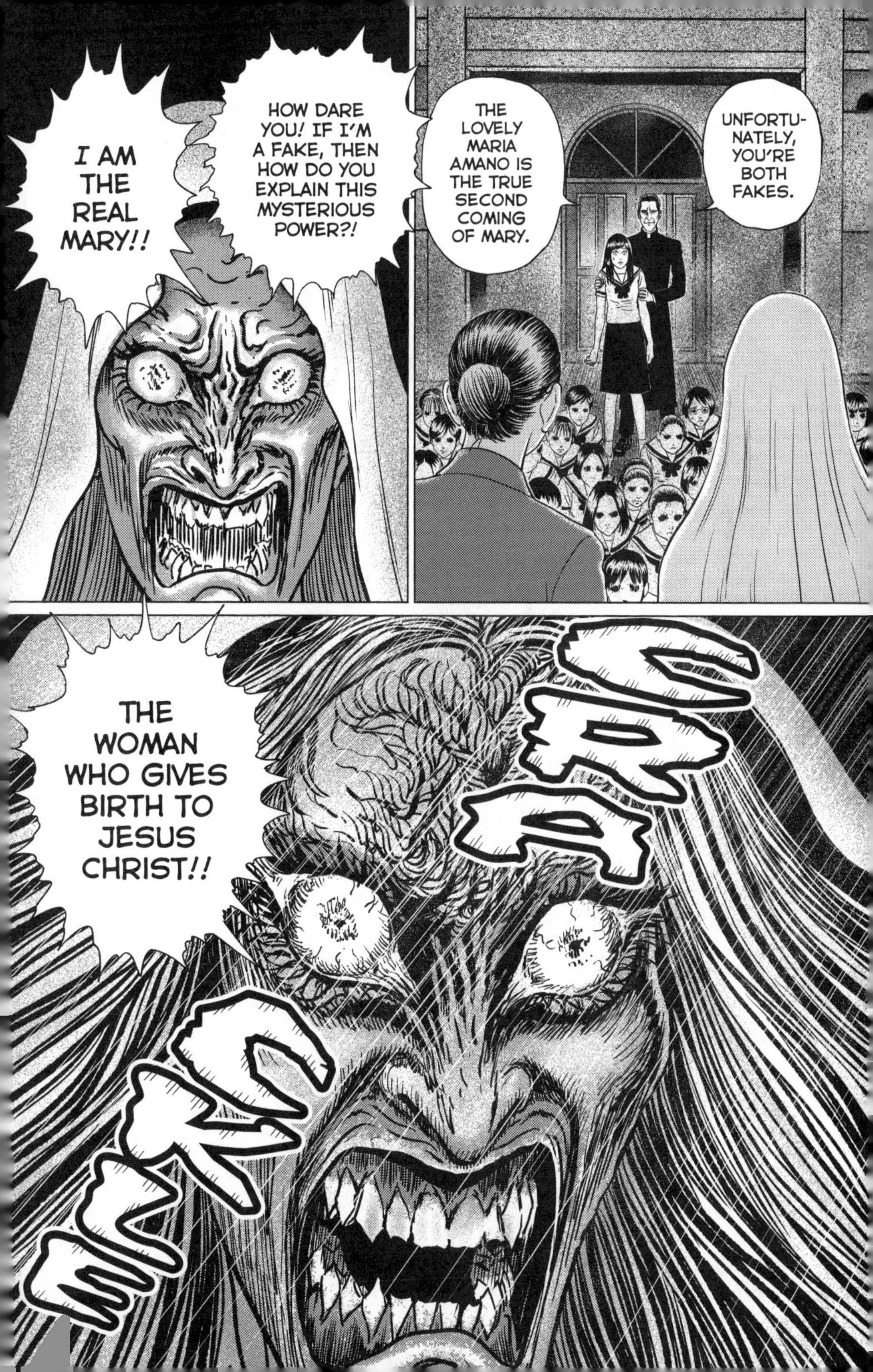
UNFORTUNATELY, YOU'RE BOTH FAKES.
THE LOVELY MARIA AMANO IS THE TRUE SECOND COMING OF MARY.
HOW DARE YOU! IF I'M A FAKE, THEN HOW DO YOU EXPLAIN THIS MYSTERIOUS POWER?!
I AM THE REAL MARY!!
THE WOMAN WHO GIVES BIRTH TO JESUS CHRIST!!

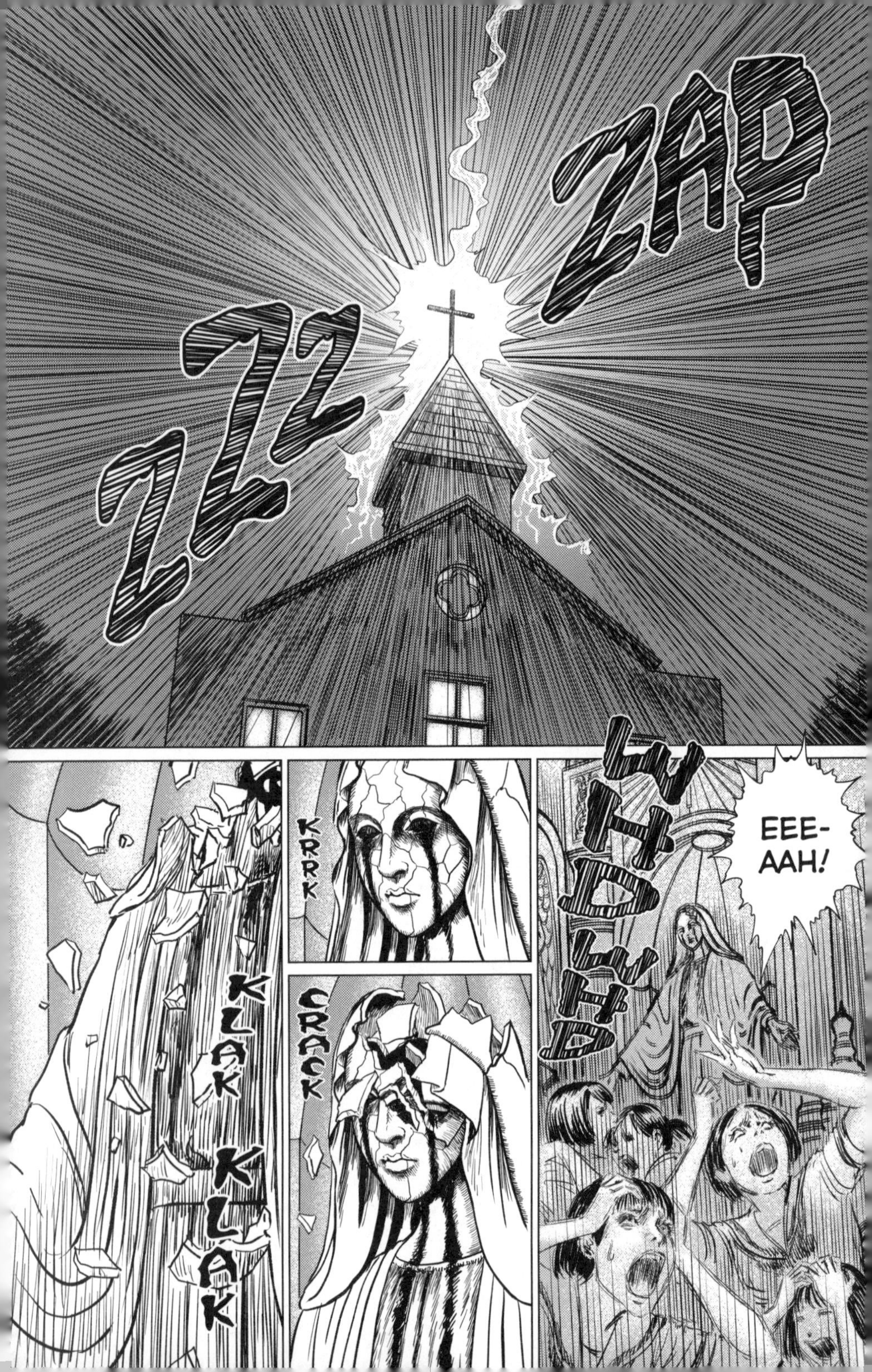
ZZZ ZAP
EEE-AAH!
WHD WHD
KRRRK
CRACK
KLAK KLAK

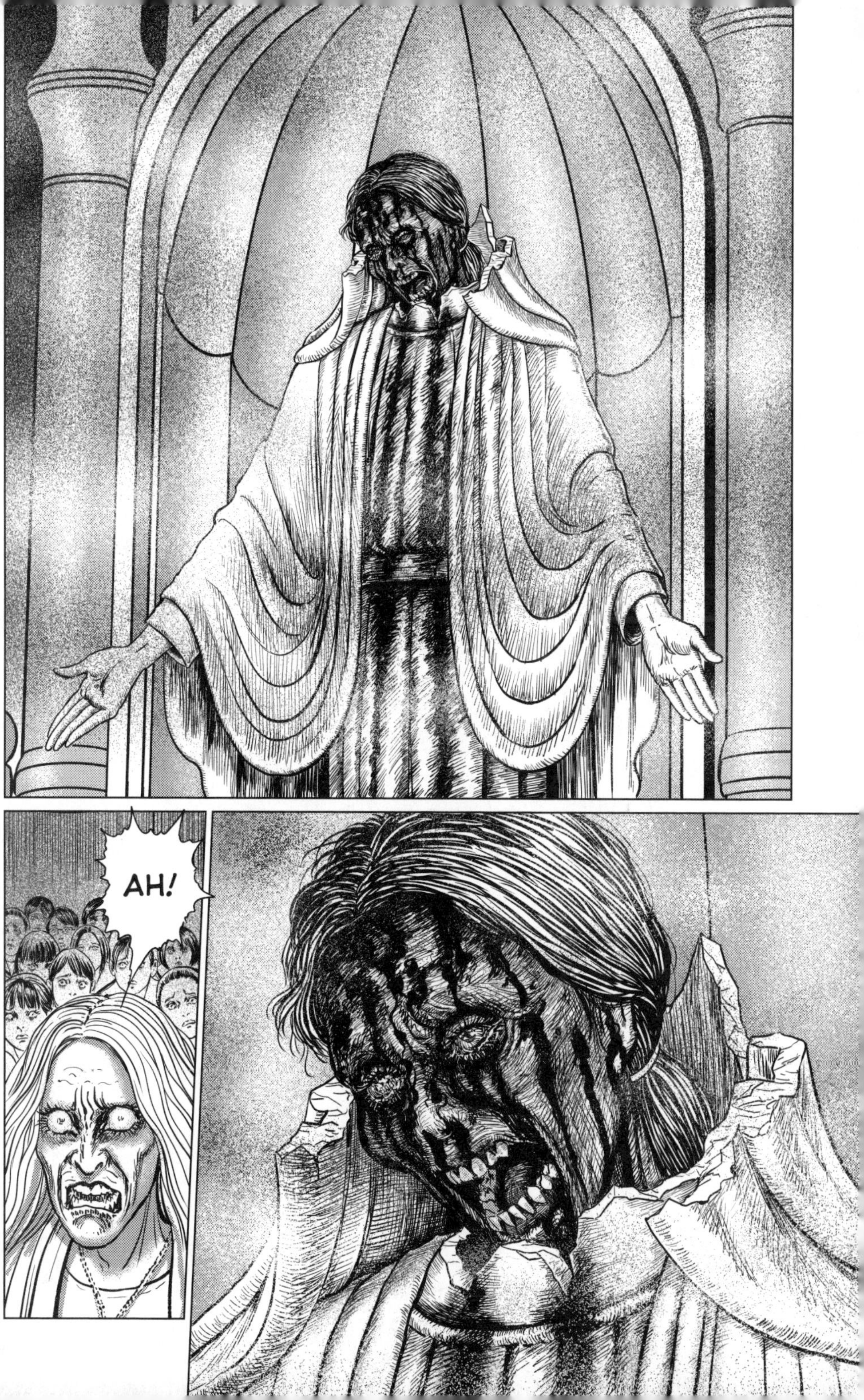
AH!

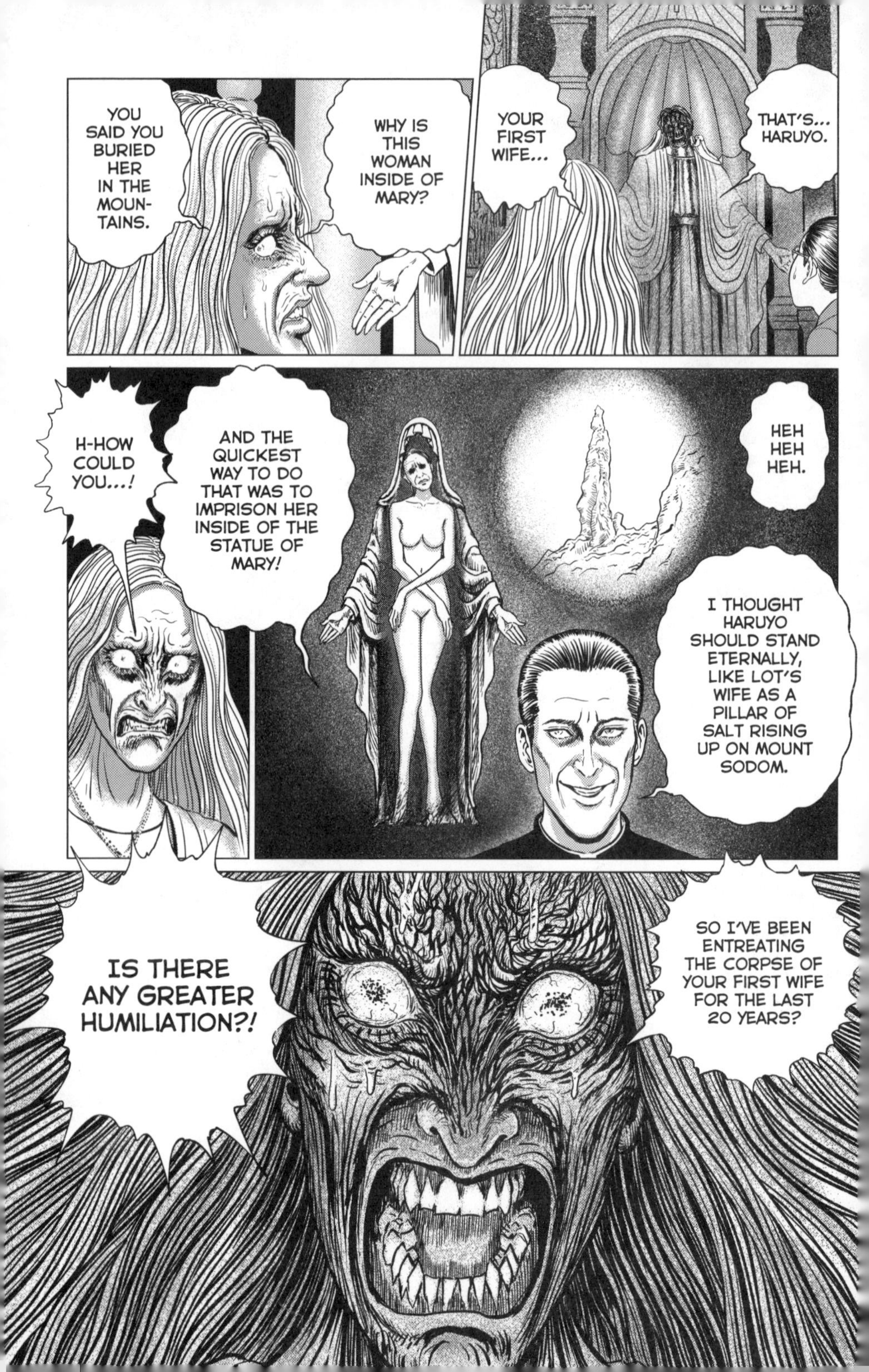
THAT'S... HARUYO.
YOUR FIRST WIFE...
WHY IS THIS WOMAN INSIDE OF MARY?
YOU SAID YOU BURIED HER IN THE MOUN-TAINS.
HEH HEH HEH.
I THOUGHT HARUYO SHOULD STAND ETERNALLY, LIKE LOT'S WIFE AS A PILLAR OF SALT RISING UP ON MOUNT SODOM.
AND THE QUICKEST WAY TO DO THAT WAS TO IMPRISON HER INSIDE OF THE STATUE OF MARY!
H-HOW COULD YOU...!
SO I'VE BEEN ENTREATING THE CORPSE OF YOUR FIRST WIFE FOR THE LAST 20 YEARS?
IS THERE ANY GREATER HUMILIATION?!

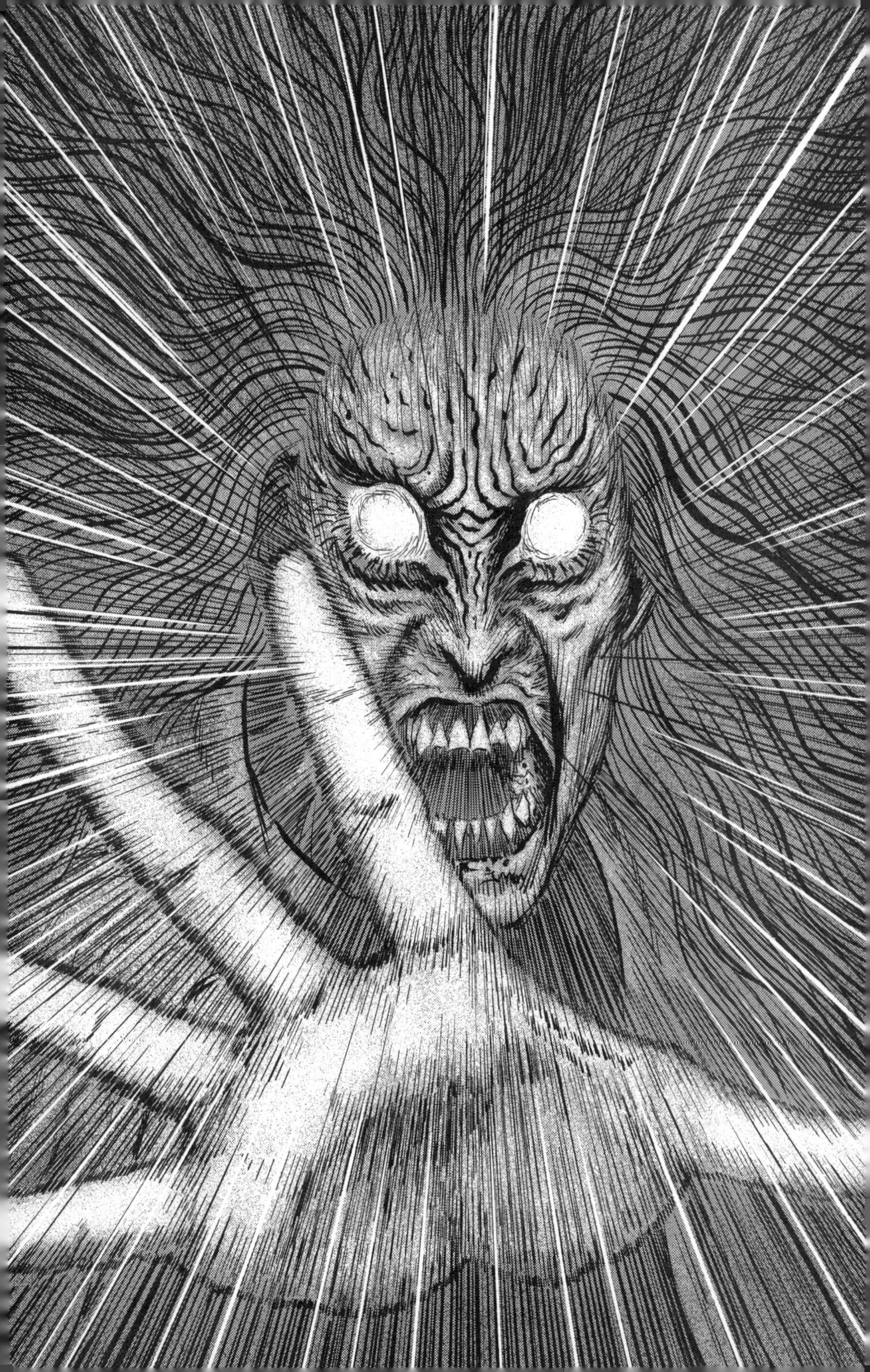

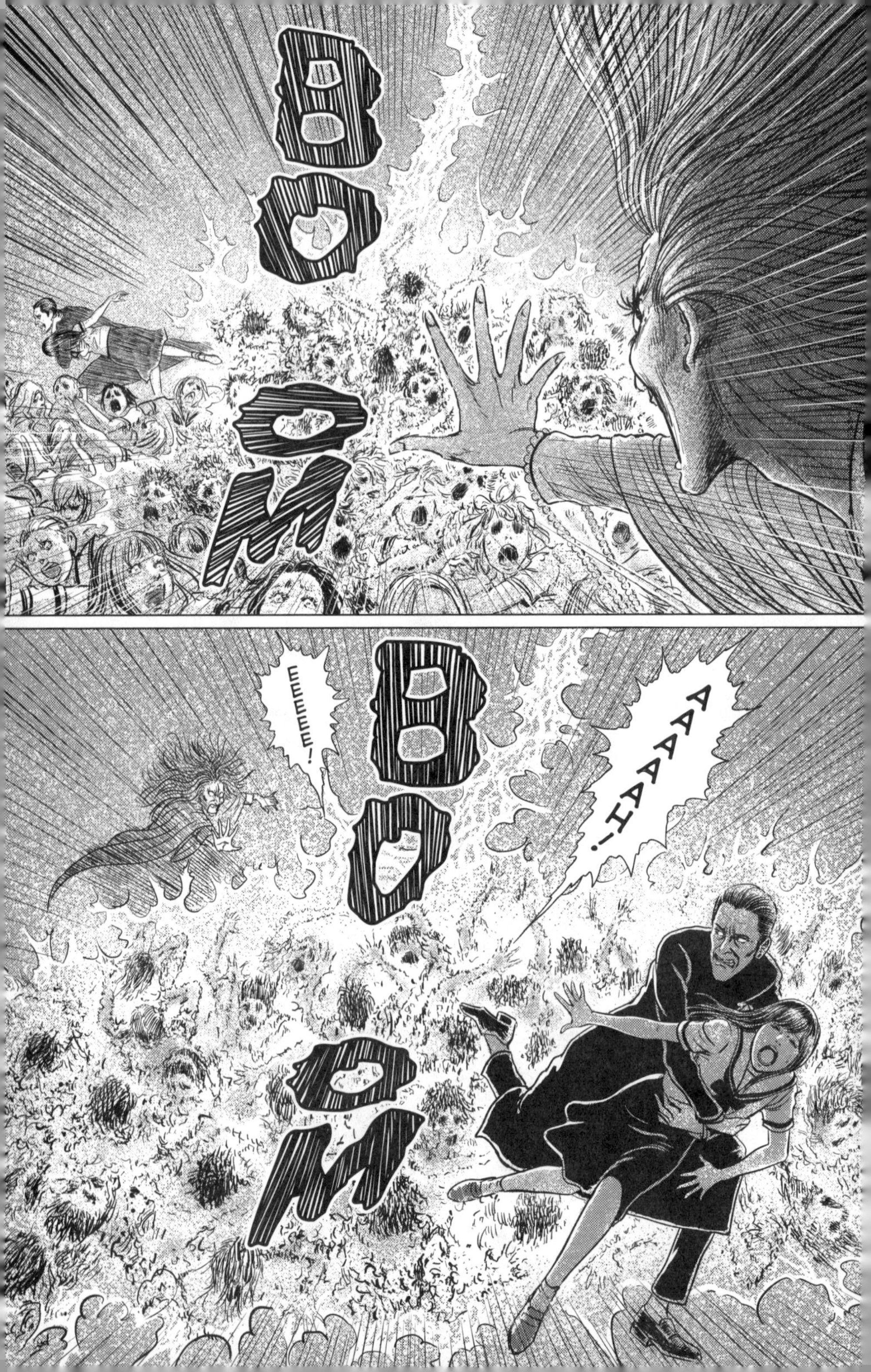
BOOM
AAAAAAH!
BOOM
EEEEE!

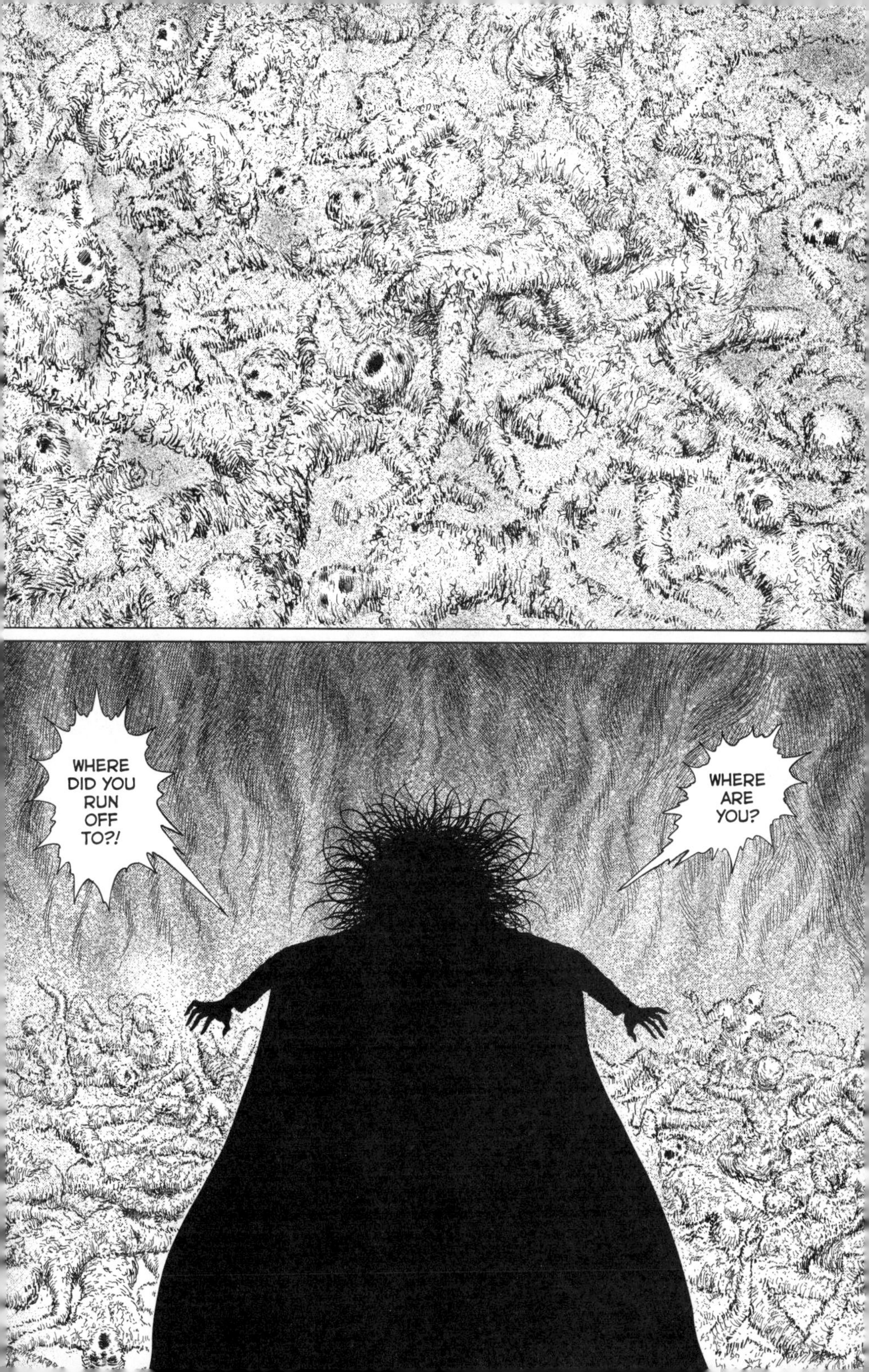
WHERE ARE YOU?
WHERE DID YOU RUN OFF TO?!

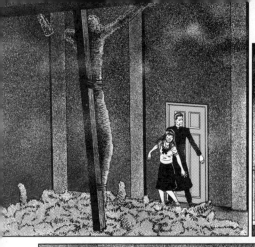

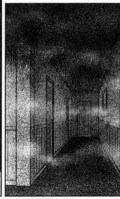

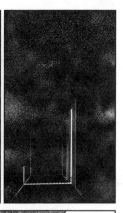

A TRULY TER-RIFYING WOMAN.
NO WONDER THEY CALL HER "ANGRY WITCH WOMAN."
THIS SMOKE ...
THE LIGHTNING STRIKE MUST HAVE STARTED A FIRE.
HMPH. BUT THAT DOESN'T MATTER.
BEHOLD. THIS MOUNTAIN OF SALT PILLARS.
THE FINAL RESTING PLACE OF ALL THOSE WHO ANGERED THAT WITCH WOMAN.

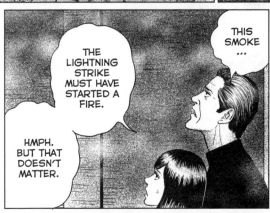

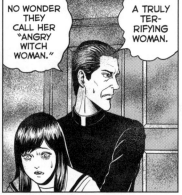

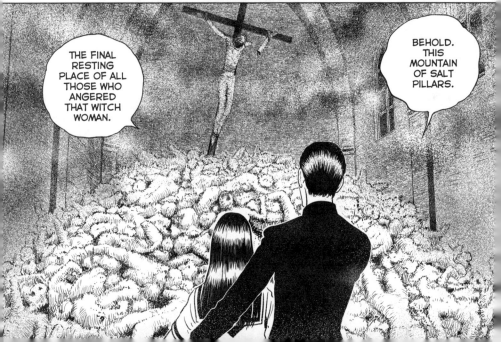

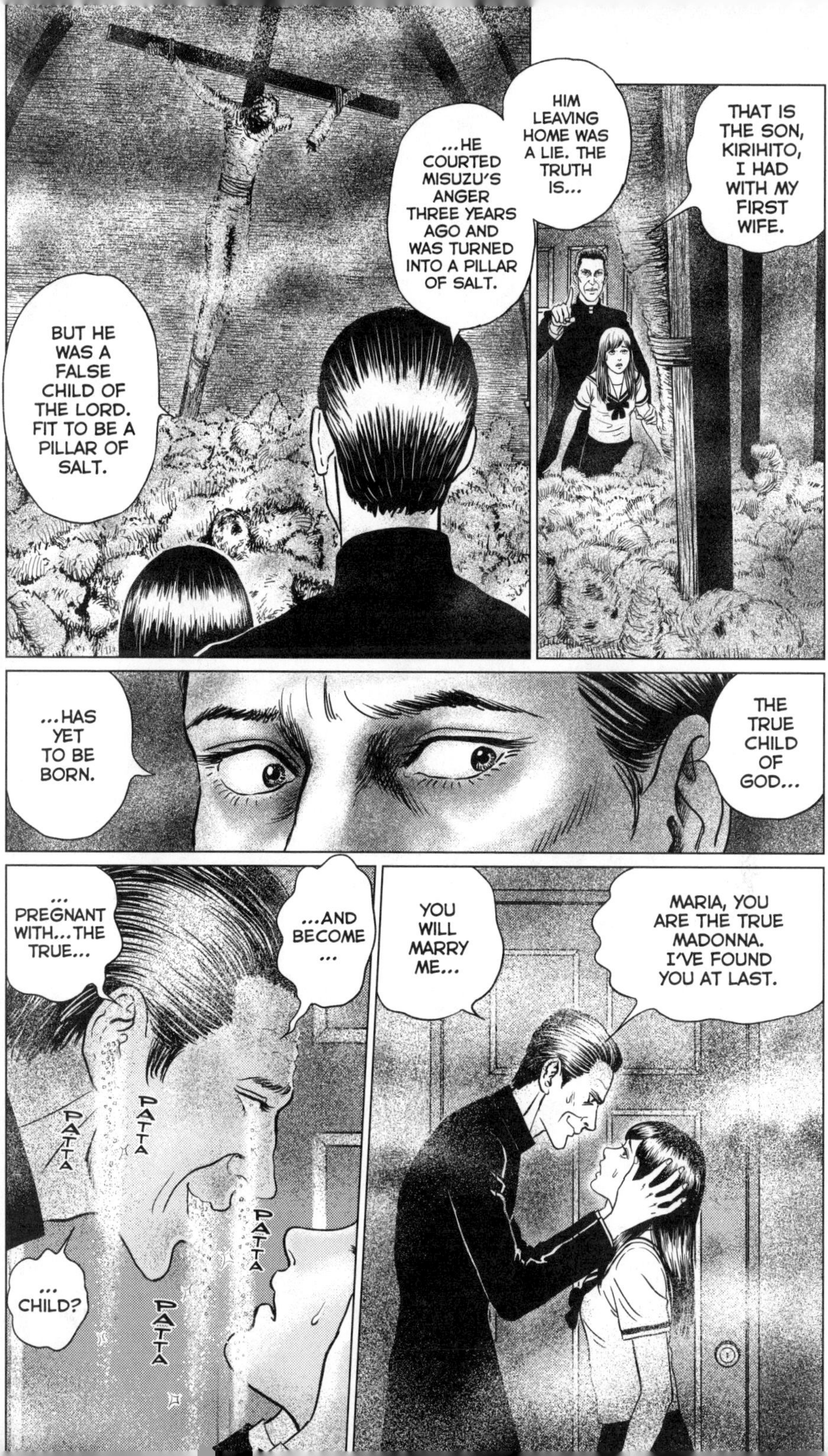
THAT IS THE SON, KIRIHITO, I HAD WITH MY FIRST WIFE.
HIM LEAVING HOME WAS A LIE. THE TRUTH IS...
...HE COURTED MISUZU'S ANGER THREE YEARS AGO AND WAS TURNED INTO A PILLAR OF SALT.
BUT HE WAS A FALSE CHILD OF THE LORD. FIT TO BE A PILLAR OF SALT.
THE TRUE CHILD OF GOD...
...HAS YET TO BE BORN.
MARIA, YOU ARE THE TRUE MADONNA. I'VE FOUND YOU AT LAST.
YOU WILL MARRY ME...
...AND BECOME...
...PREGNANT WITH...THE TRUE...
PATTA
PATTA
PATTA
PATTA
...CHILD?

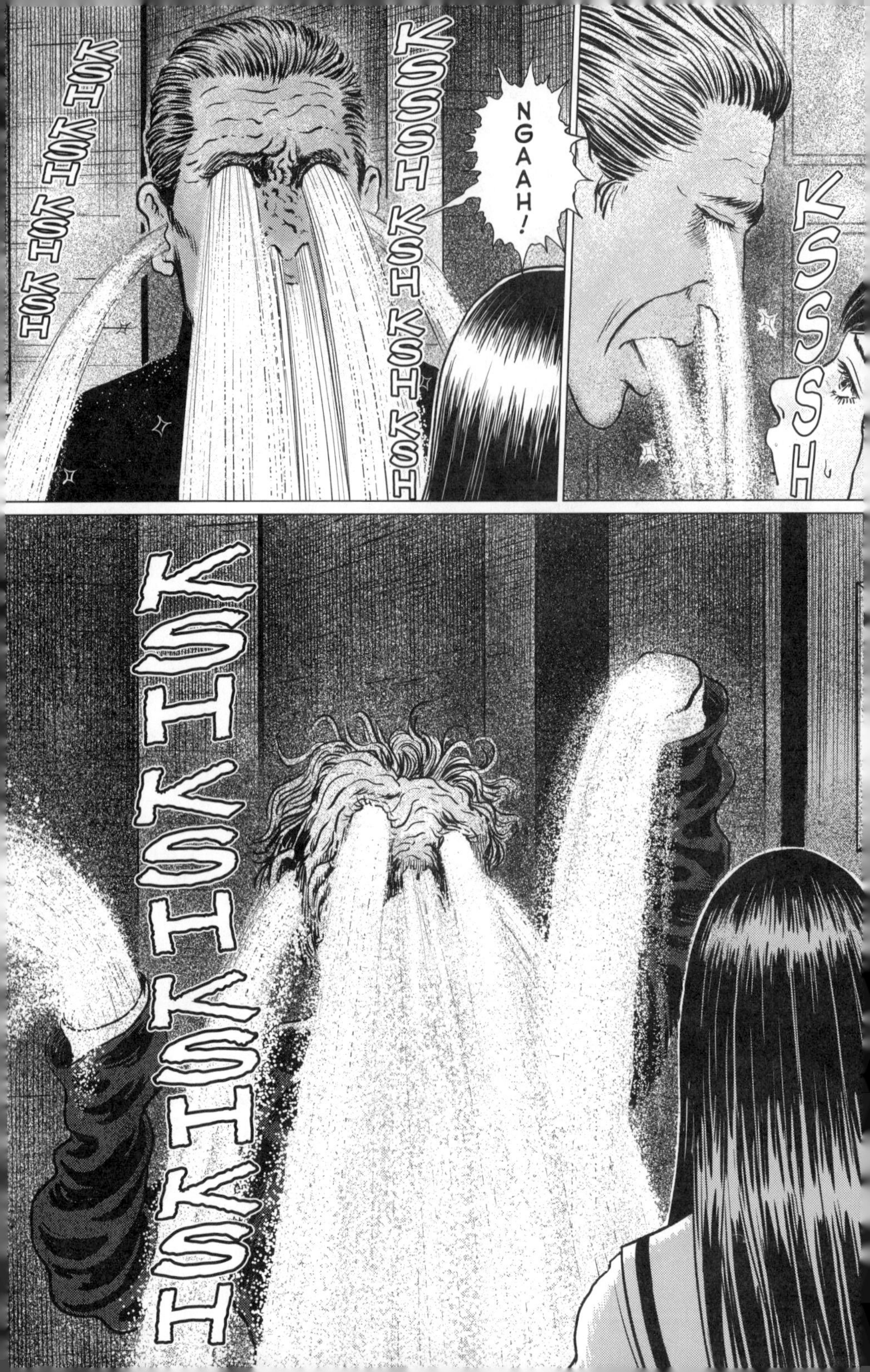
KSSSH
NGAAH!
KSSSH KSH KSH KSH
KSH KSH KSH KSH
KSH KSH KSH KSH

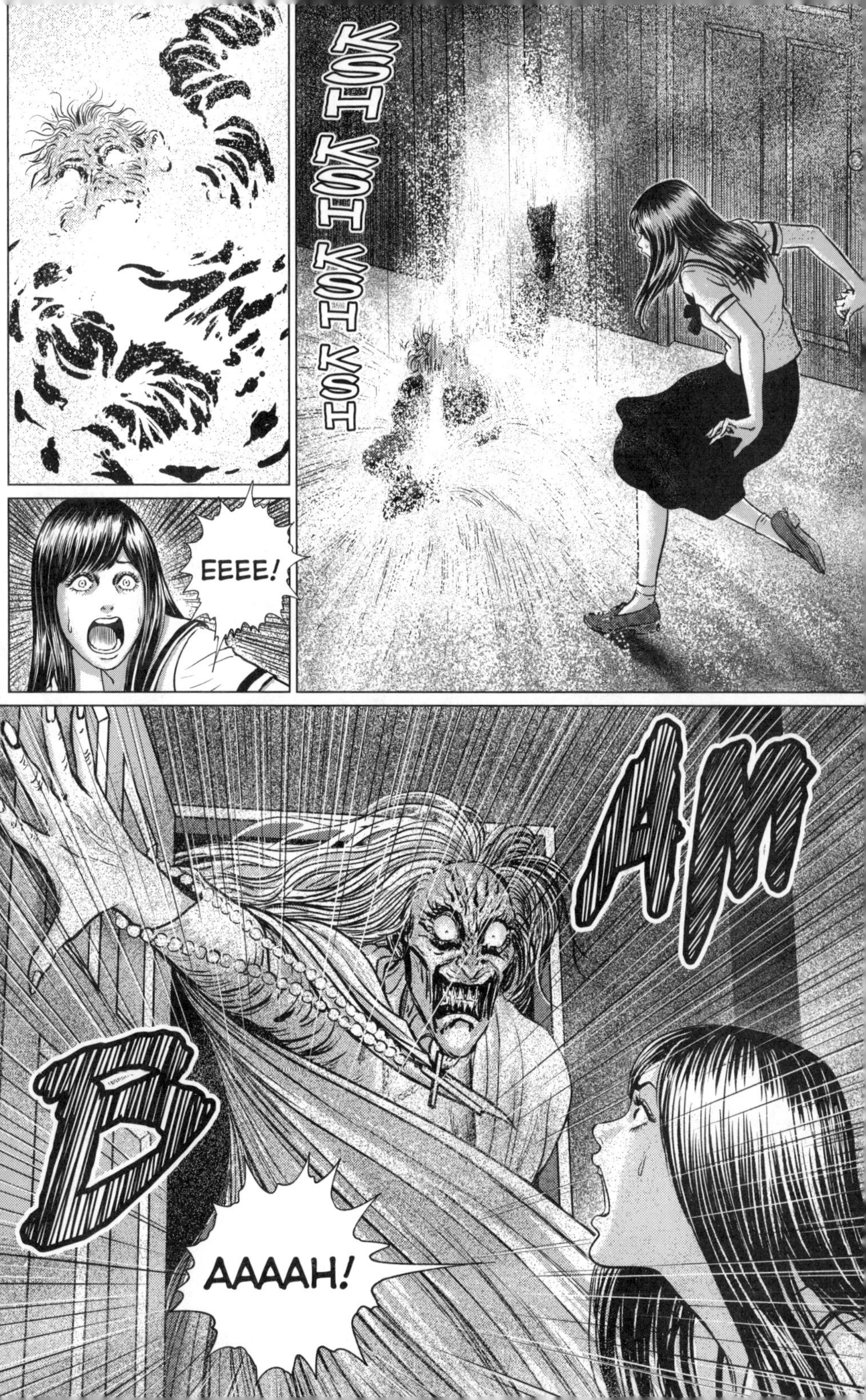
KSH KSH KSH KSH
EEEE!
BAM
AAAAH!

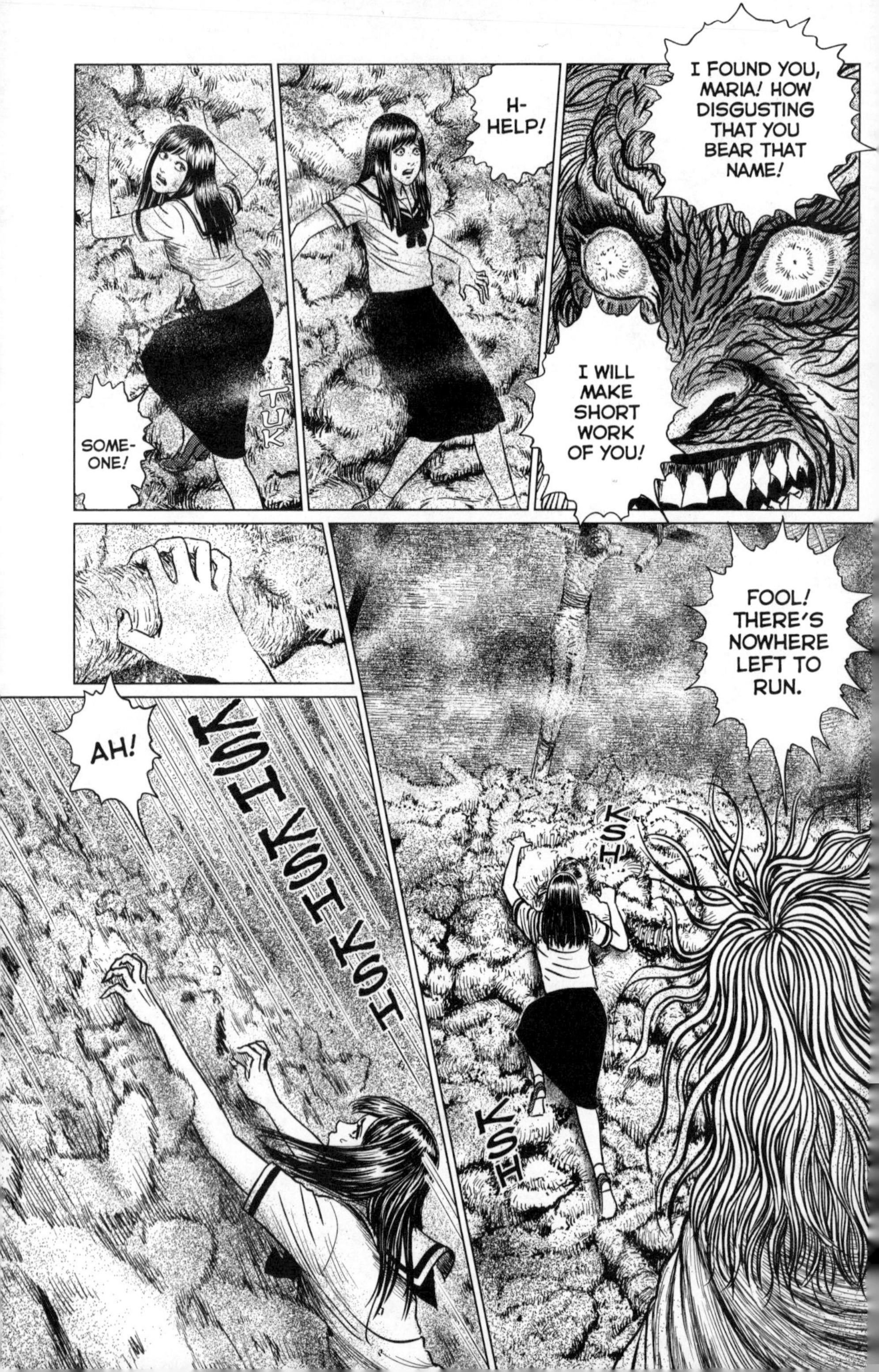
I FOUND YOU, MARIA! HOW DISGUSTING THAT YOU BEAR THAT NAME!
I WILL MAKE SHORT WORK OF YOU!
H- HELP!
TUK
SOME- ONE!
FOOL! THERE'S NOWHERE LEFT TO RUN.
KSH
KSH
AH!
KSH KSH KSH

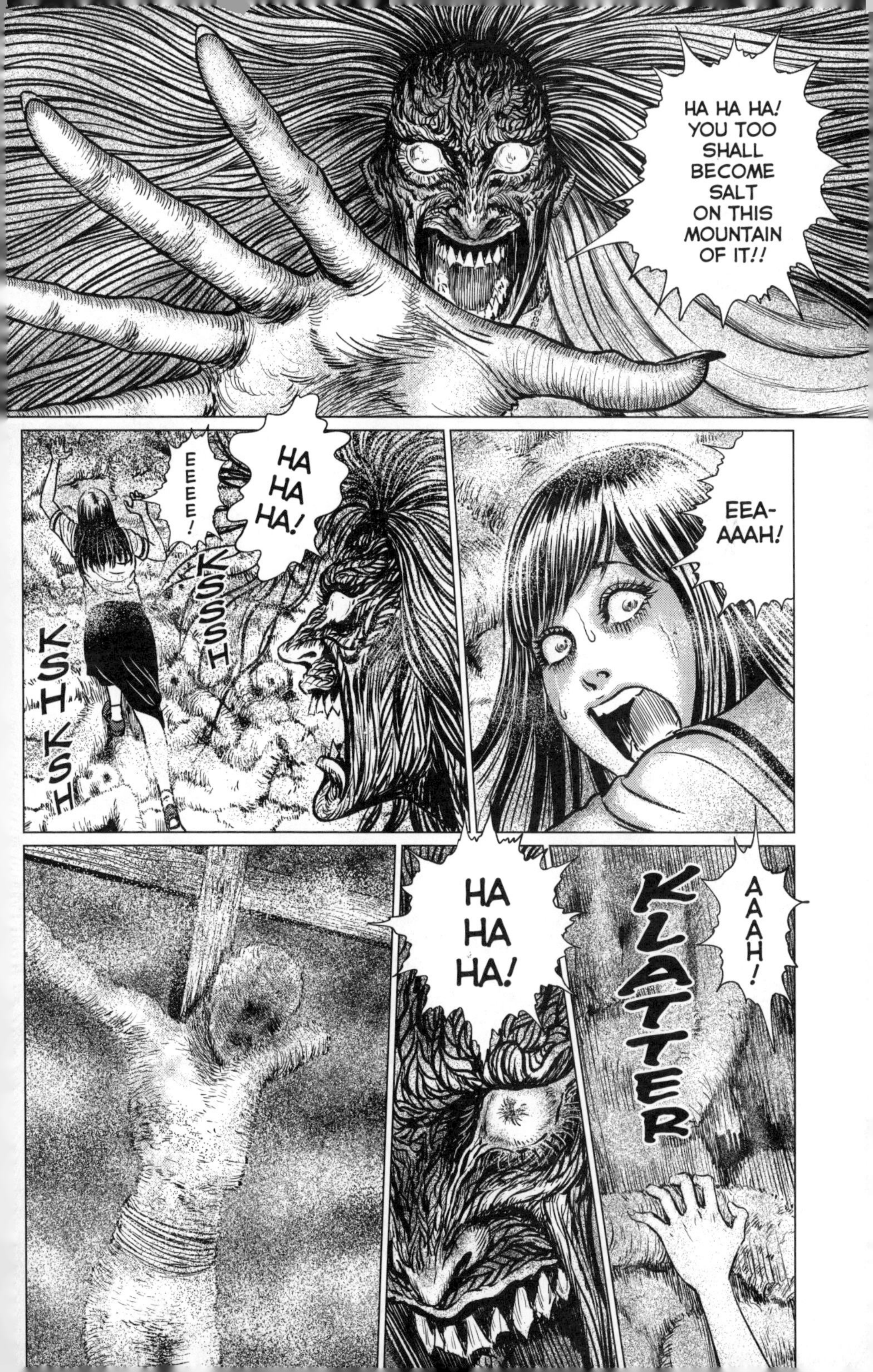
HA HA HA! YOU TOO SHALL BECOME SALT ON THIS MOUNTAIN OF IT!!
EEA-AAAH!
HA HA HA!
EEEE!
KSSSH
KSH KSH
AAAH!
KLATTER
HA HA HA!

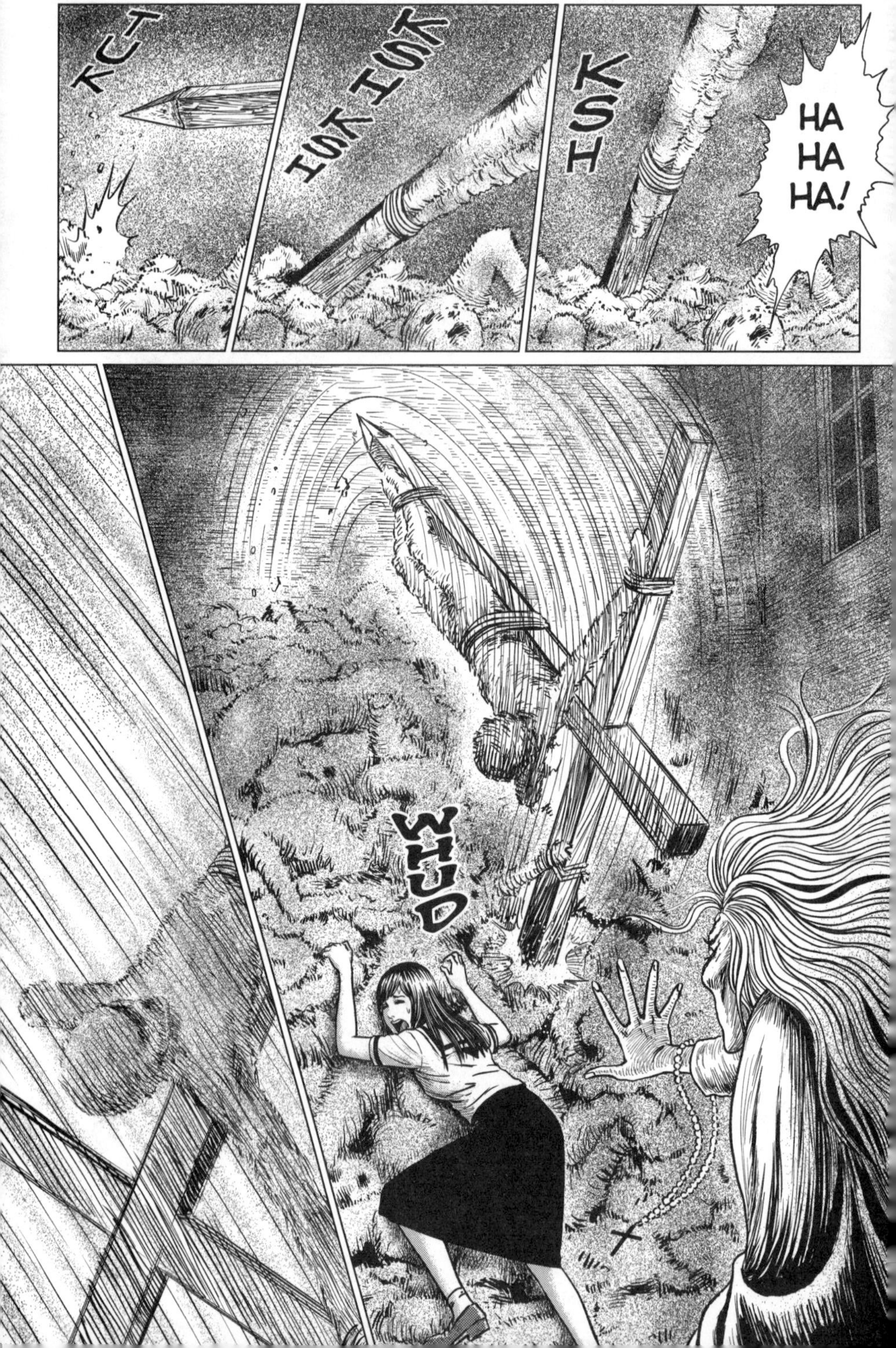
HA HA HA!
KSH
KSH KSH
TUK
WHUD

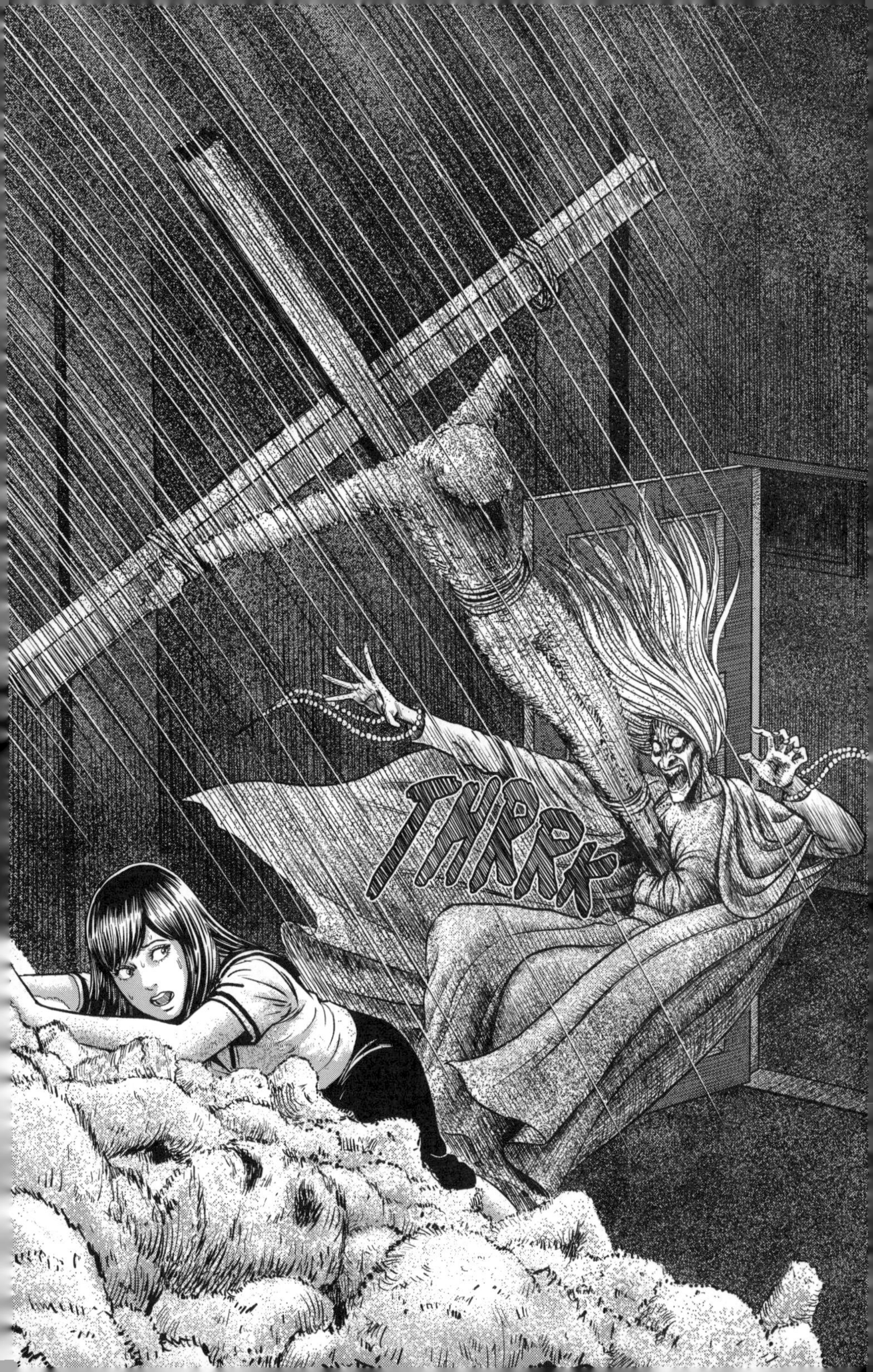
THRRK

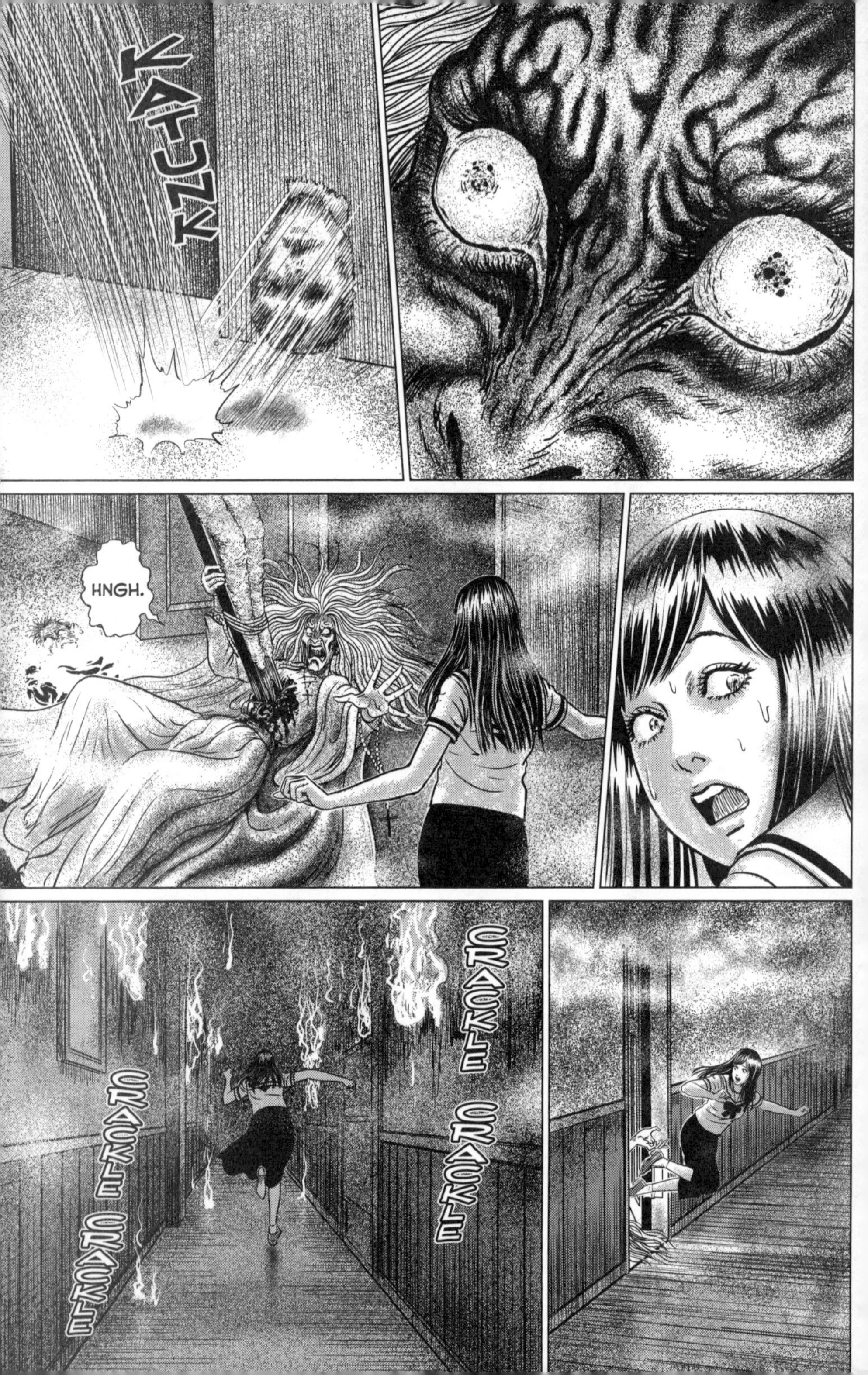
KATUNK
HNGH.
CRACKLE CRACKLE
CRACKLE CRACKLE

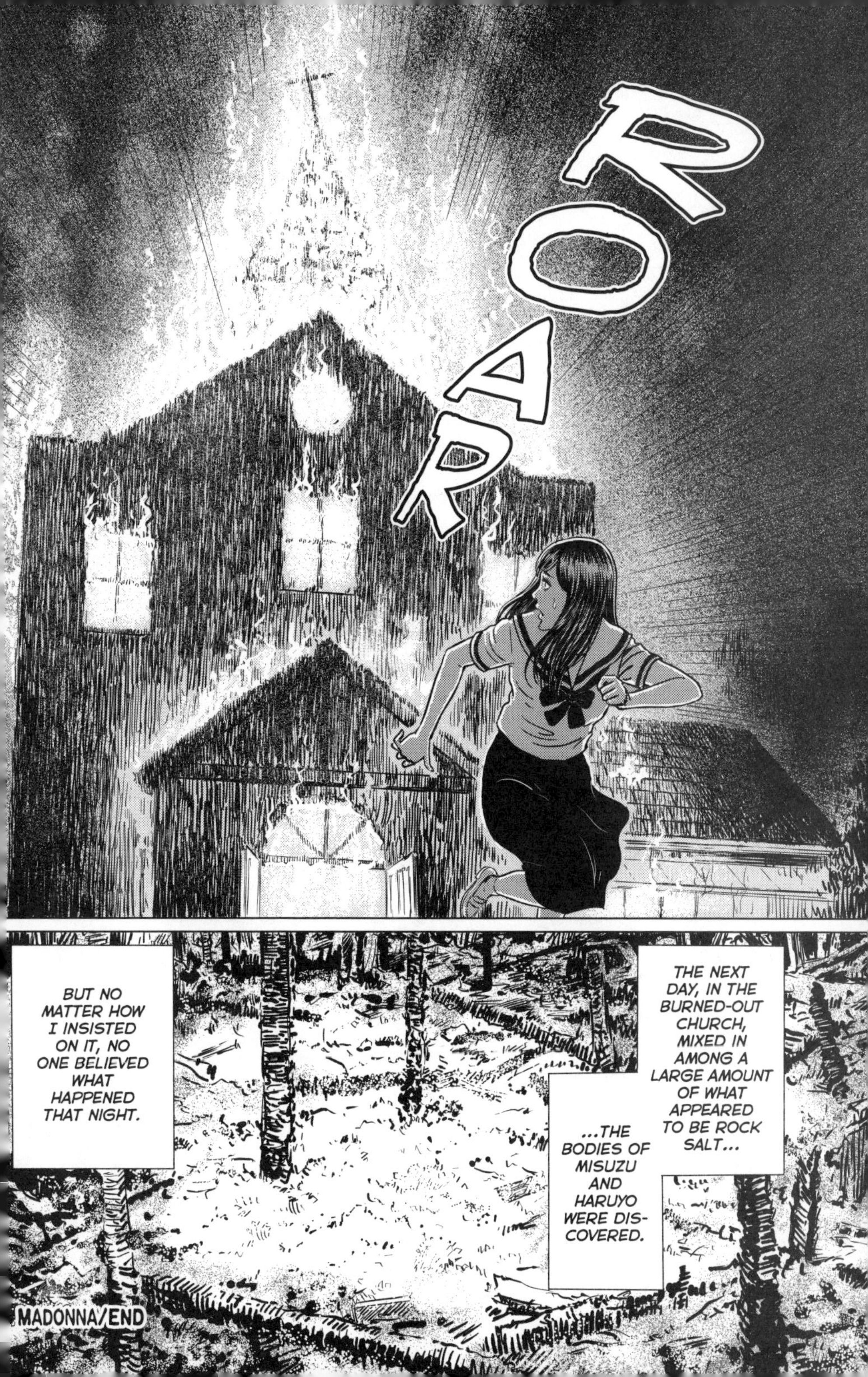
ROAR
THE NEXT DAY, IN THE BURNED-OUT CHURCH, MIXED IN AMONG A LARGE AMOUNT OF WHAT APPEARED TO BE ROCK SALT...
...THE BODIES OF MISUZU AND HARUYO WERE DISCOVERED.
BUT NO MATTER HOW I INSISTED ON IT, NO ONE BELIEVED WHAT HAPPENED THAT NIGHT.
MADONNA/END

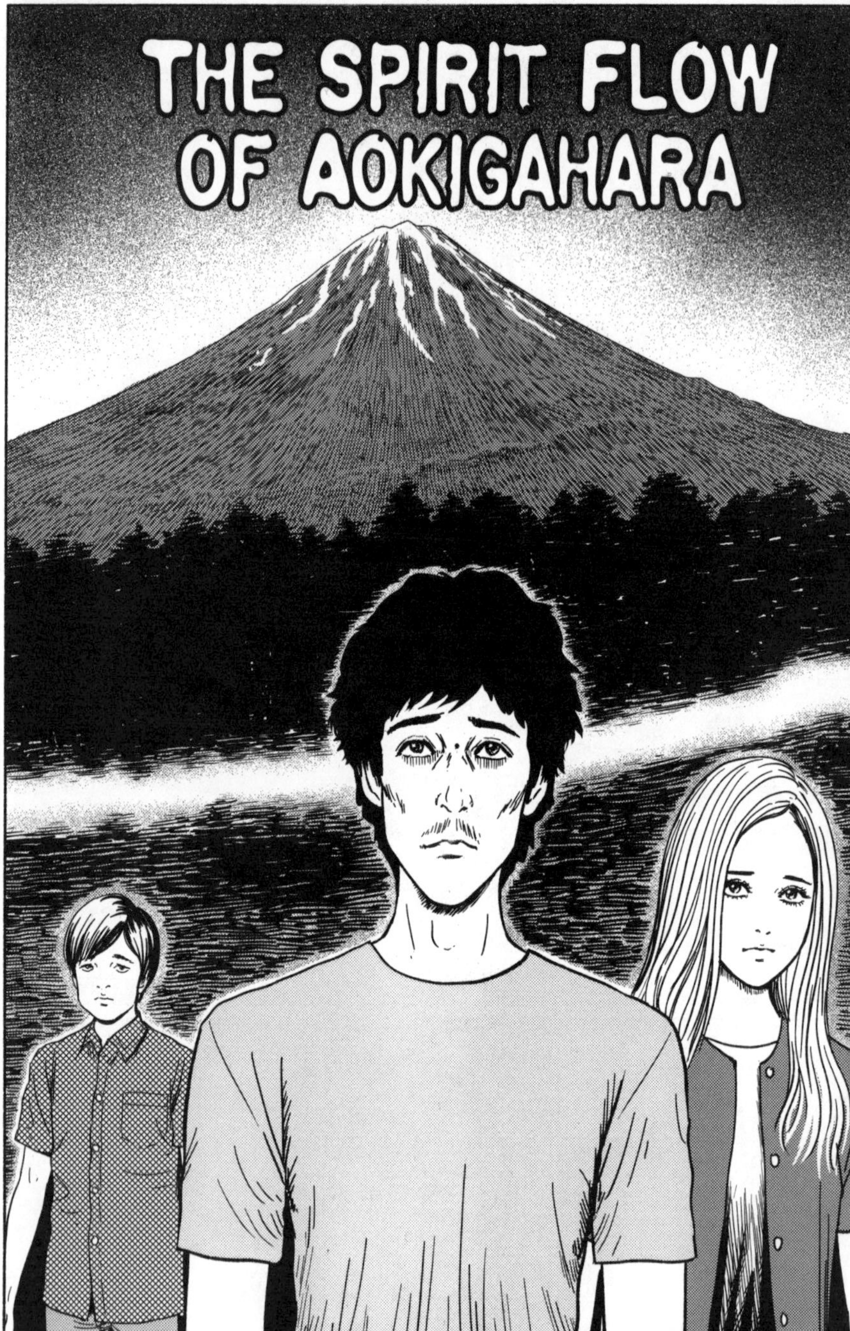
THE SPIRIT FLOW OF AOKIGAHARA

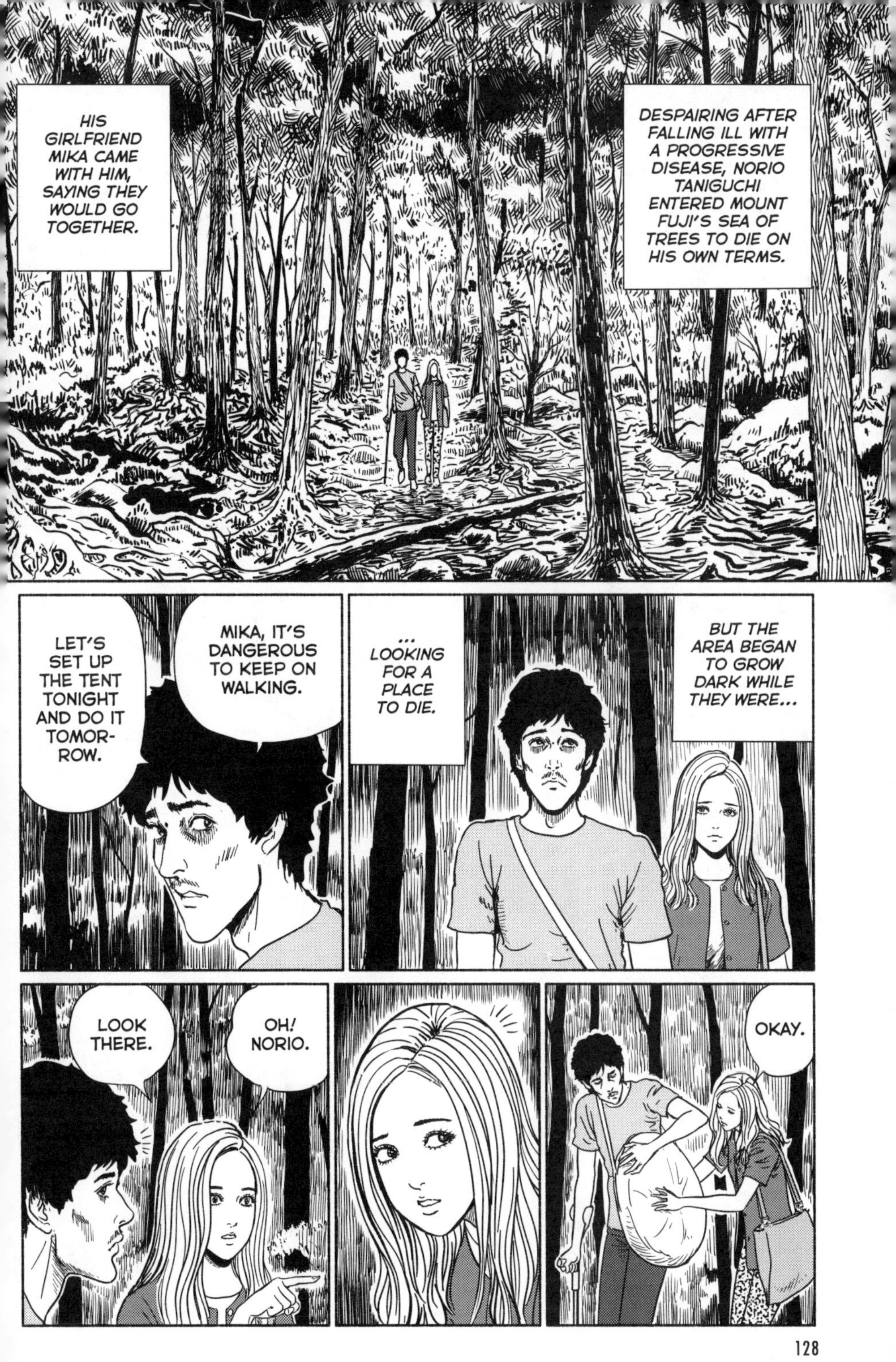
DESPAIRING AFTER FALLING ILL WITH A PROGRESSIVE DISEASE, NORIO TANIGUCHI ENTERED MOUNT FUJI'S SEA OF TREES TO DIE ON HIS OWN TERMS.
HIS GIRLFRIEND MIKA CAME WITH HIM, SAYING THEY WOULD GO TOGETHER.
BUT THE AREA BEGAN TO GROW DARK WHILE THEY WERE...
...LOOKING FOR A PLACE TO DIE.
MIKA, IT'S DANGEROUS TO KEEP ON WALKING.
LET'S SET UP THE TENT TONIGHT AND DO IT TOMOR-ROW.
OKAY.
OH! NORIO.
LOOK THERE.

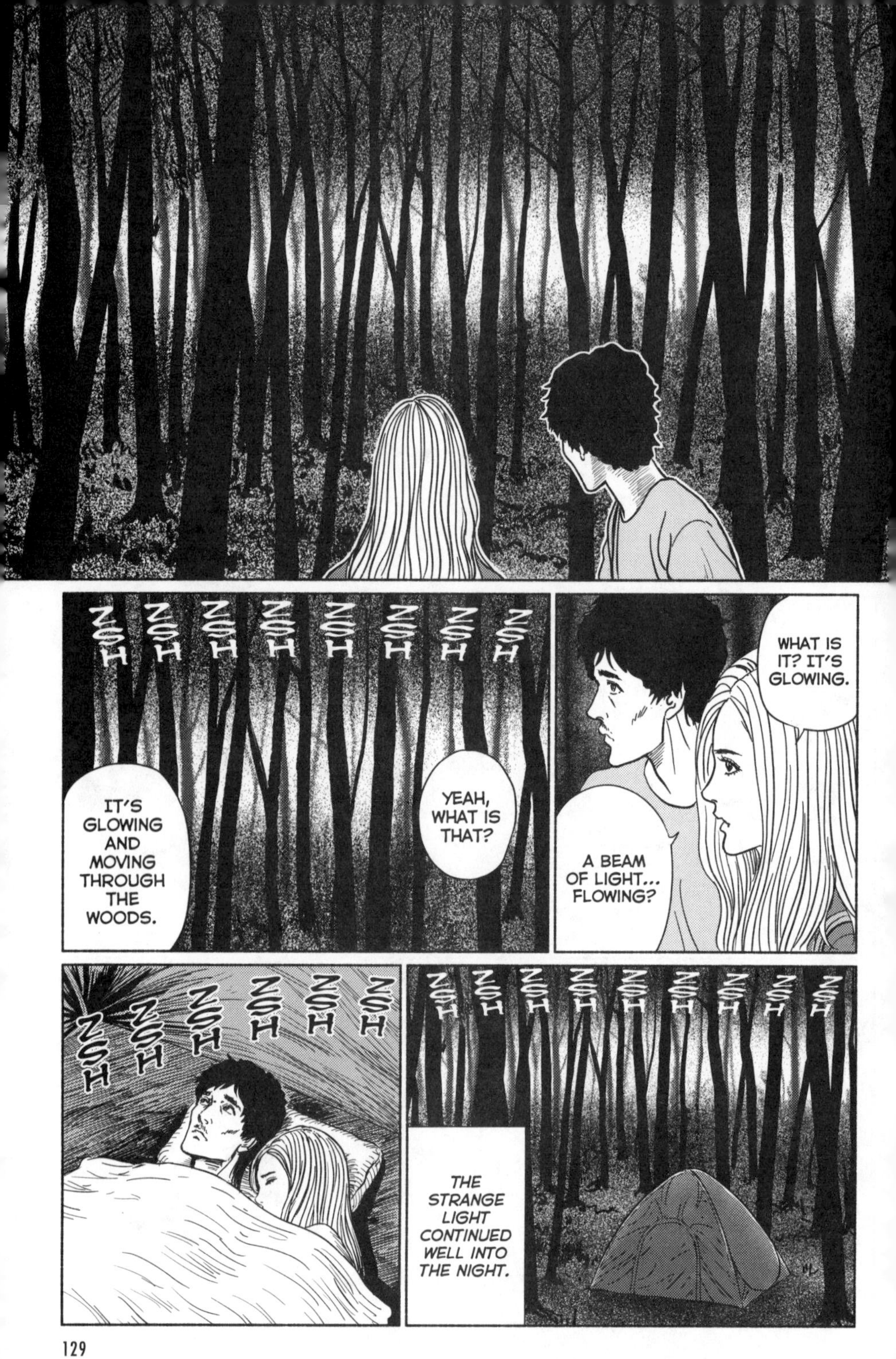
WHAT IS IT? IT'S GLOWING.
A BEAM OF LIGHT... FLOWING?
ZSH ZSH ZSH ZSH ZSH ZSH ZSH ZSH
YEAH, WHAT IS THAT?
IT'S GLOWING AND MOVING THROUGH THE WOODS.
ZSH ZSH ZSH ZSH ZSH ZSH ZSH ZSH ZSH
THE STRANGE LIGHT CONTINUED WELL INTO THE NIGHT.
ZSH ZSH ZSH ZSH ZSH ZSH

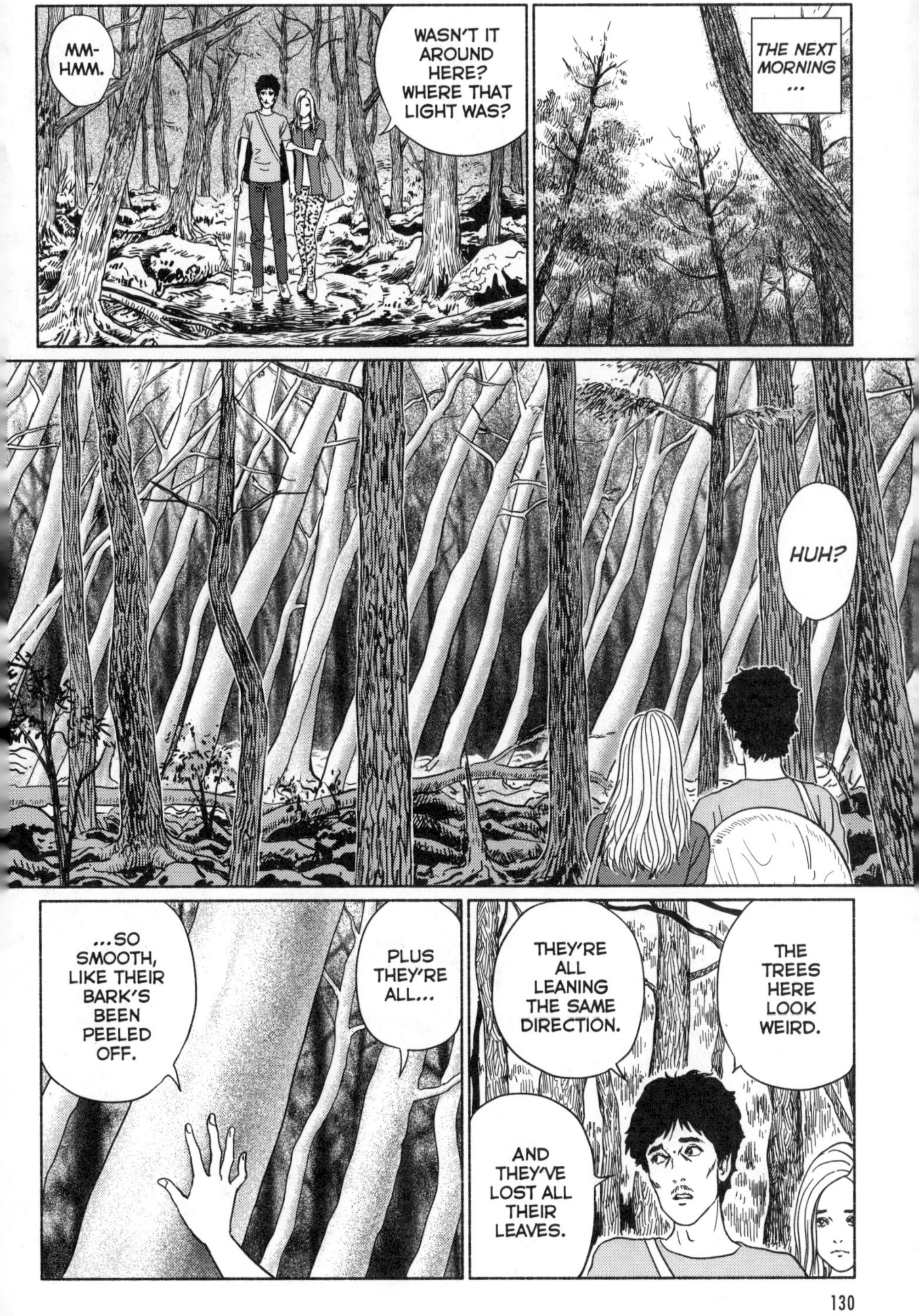
THE NEXT MORNING ...
WASN'T IT AROUND HERE? WHERE THAT LIGHT WAS?
MM-HMM.
HUH?
THE TREES HERE LOOK WEIRD.
THEY'RE ALL LEANING THE SAME DIRECTION.
AND THEY'VE LOST ALL THEIR LEAVES.
PLUS THEY'RE ALL...
...SO SMOOTH, LIKE THEIR BARK'S BEEN PEELED OFF.

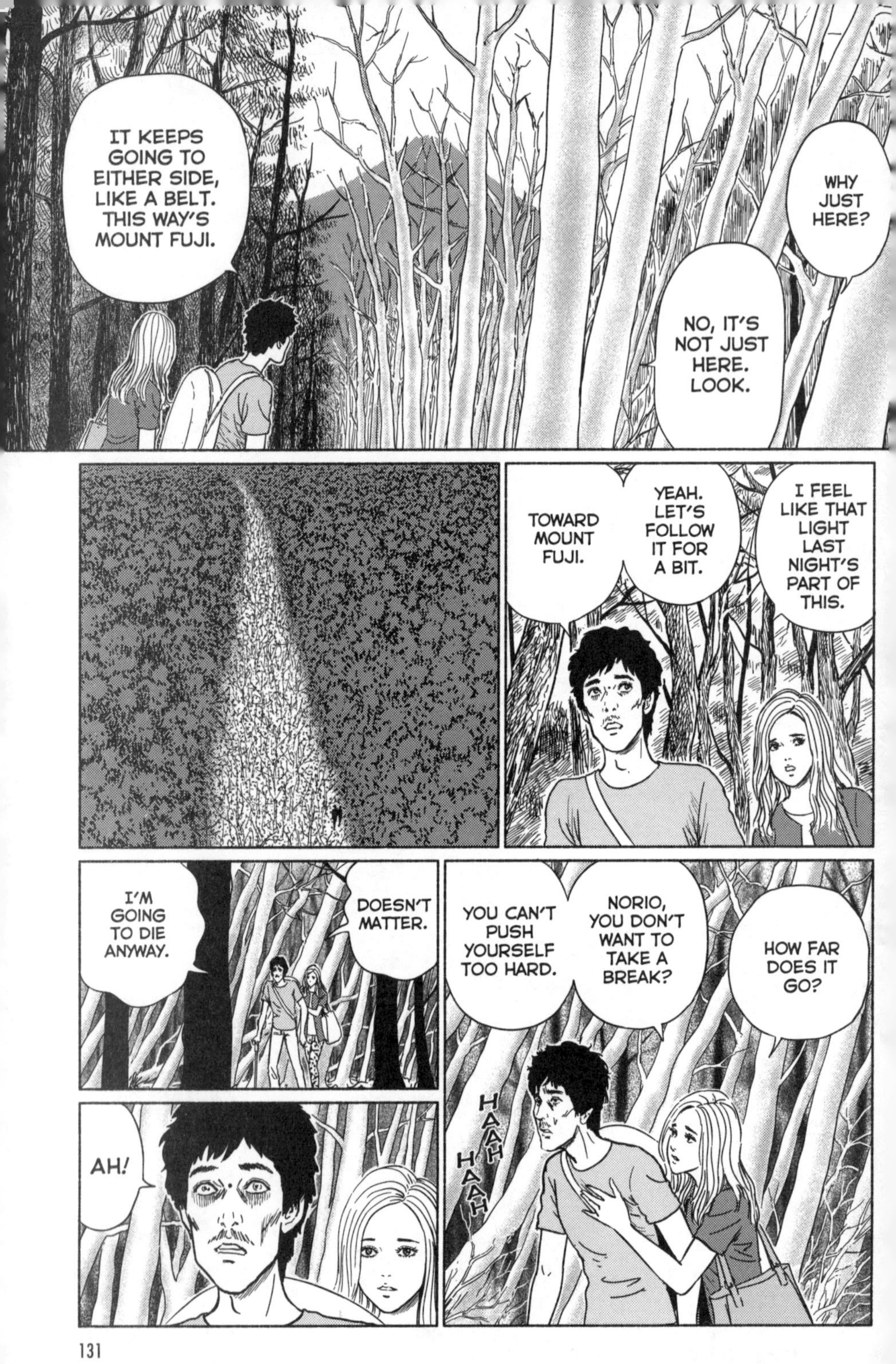
WHY JUST HERE?
NO, IT'S NOT JUST HERE. LOOK.
IT KEEPS GOING TO EITHER SIDE, LIKE A BELT. THIS WAY'S MOUNT FUJI.
I FEEL LIKE THAT LIGHT LAST NIGHT'S PART OF THIS.
YEAH. LET'S FOLLOW IT FOR A BIT.
TOWARD MOUNT FUJI.
HOW FAR DOES IT GO?
NORIO, YOU DON'T WANT TO TAKE A BREAK?
YOU CAN'T PUSH YOURSELF TOO HARD.
HAAH HAAH
DOESN'T MATTER.
I'M GOING TO DIE ANYWAY.
AH!

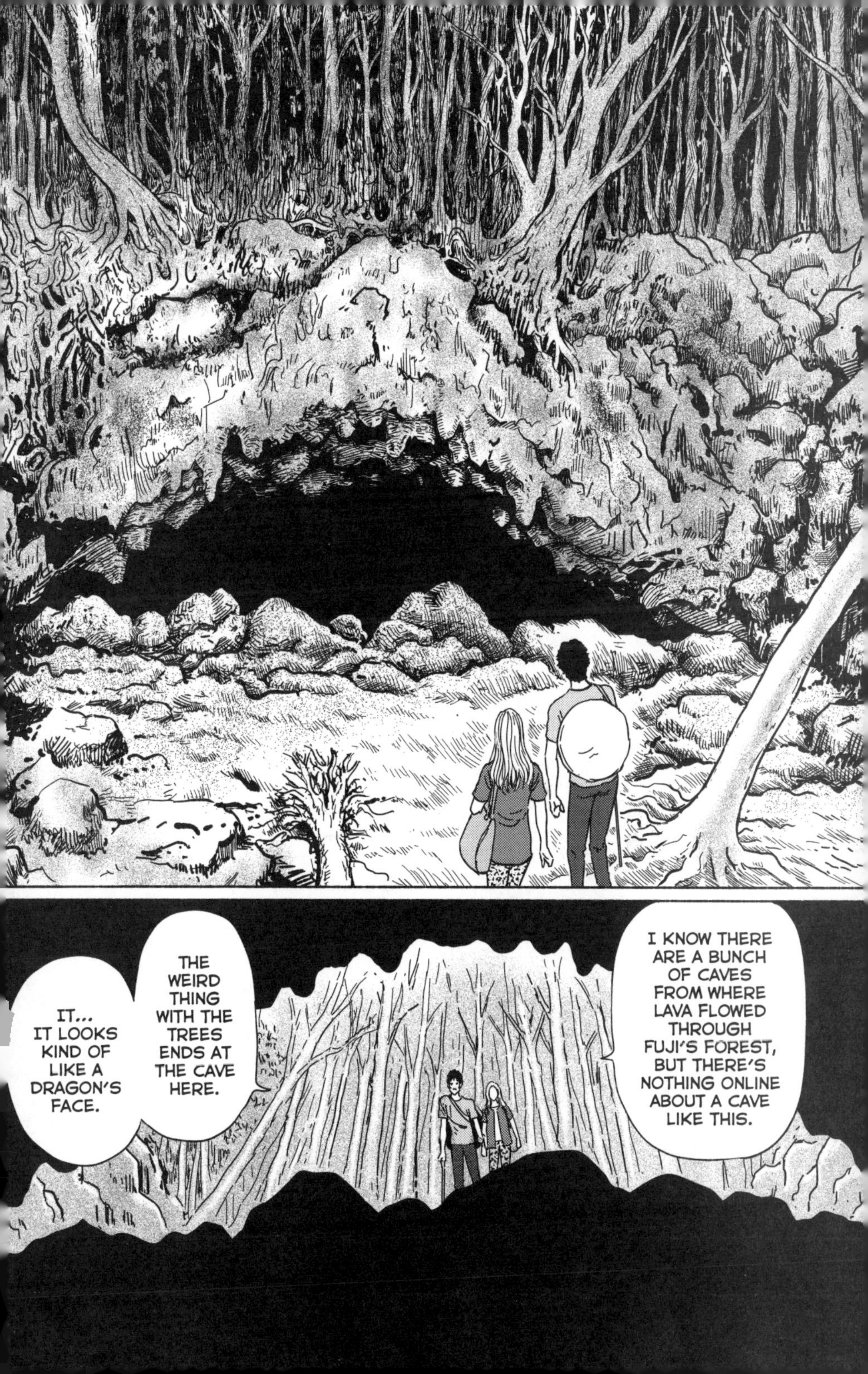
I KNOW THERE ARE A BUNCH OF CAVES FROM WHERE LAVA FLOWED THROUGH FUJI'S FOREST, BUT THERE'S NOTHING ONLINE ABOUT A CAVE LIKE THIS.
THE WEIRD THING WITH THE TREES ENDS AT THE CAVE HERE.
IT... IT LOOKS KIND OF LIKE A DRAGON'S FACE.

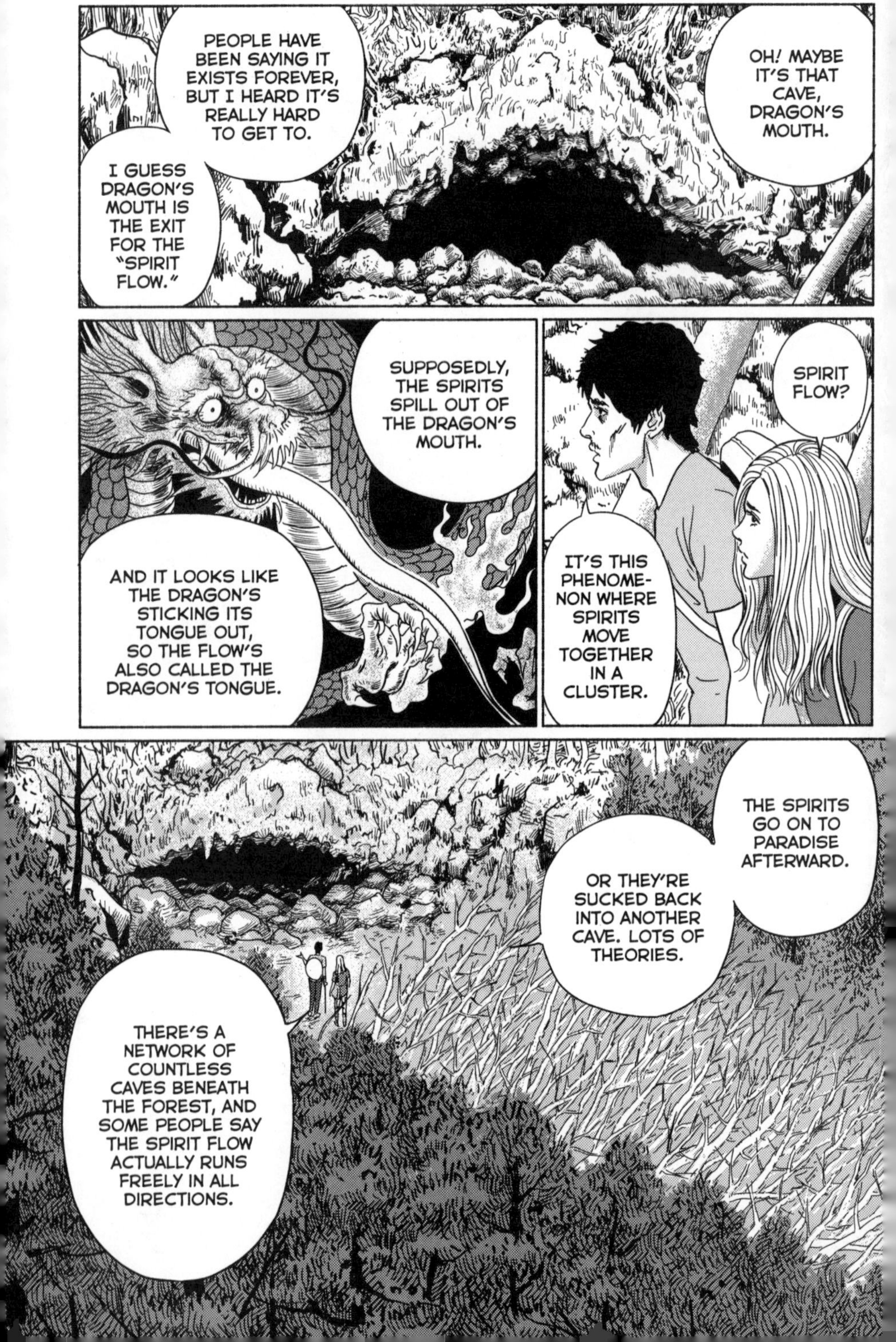
OH! MAYBE IT'S THAT CAVE, DRAGON'S MOUTH.
PEOPLE HAVE BEEN SAYING IT EXISTS FOREVER, BUT I HEARD IT'S REALLY HARD TO GET TO.
I GUESS DRAGON'S MOUTH IS THE EXIT FOR THE "SPIRIT FLOW."
SPIRIT FLOW?
IT'S THIS PHENOMENON WHERE SPIRITS MOVE TOGETHER IN A CLUSTER.
SUPPOSEDLY, THE SPIRITS SPILL OUT OF THE DRAGON'S MOUTH.
AND IT LOOKS LIKE THE DRAGON'S STICKING ITS TONGUE OUT, SO THE FLOW'S ALSO CALLED THE DRAGON'S TONGUE.
THE SPIRITS GO ON TO PARADISE AFTERWARD.
OR THEY'RE SUCKED BACK INTO ANOTHER CAVE. LOTS OF THEORIES.
THERE'S A NETWORK OF COUNTLESS CAVES BENEATH THE FOREST, AND SOME PEOPLE SAY THE SPIRIT FLOW ACTUALLY RUNS FREELY IN ALL DIRECTIONS.

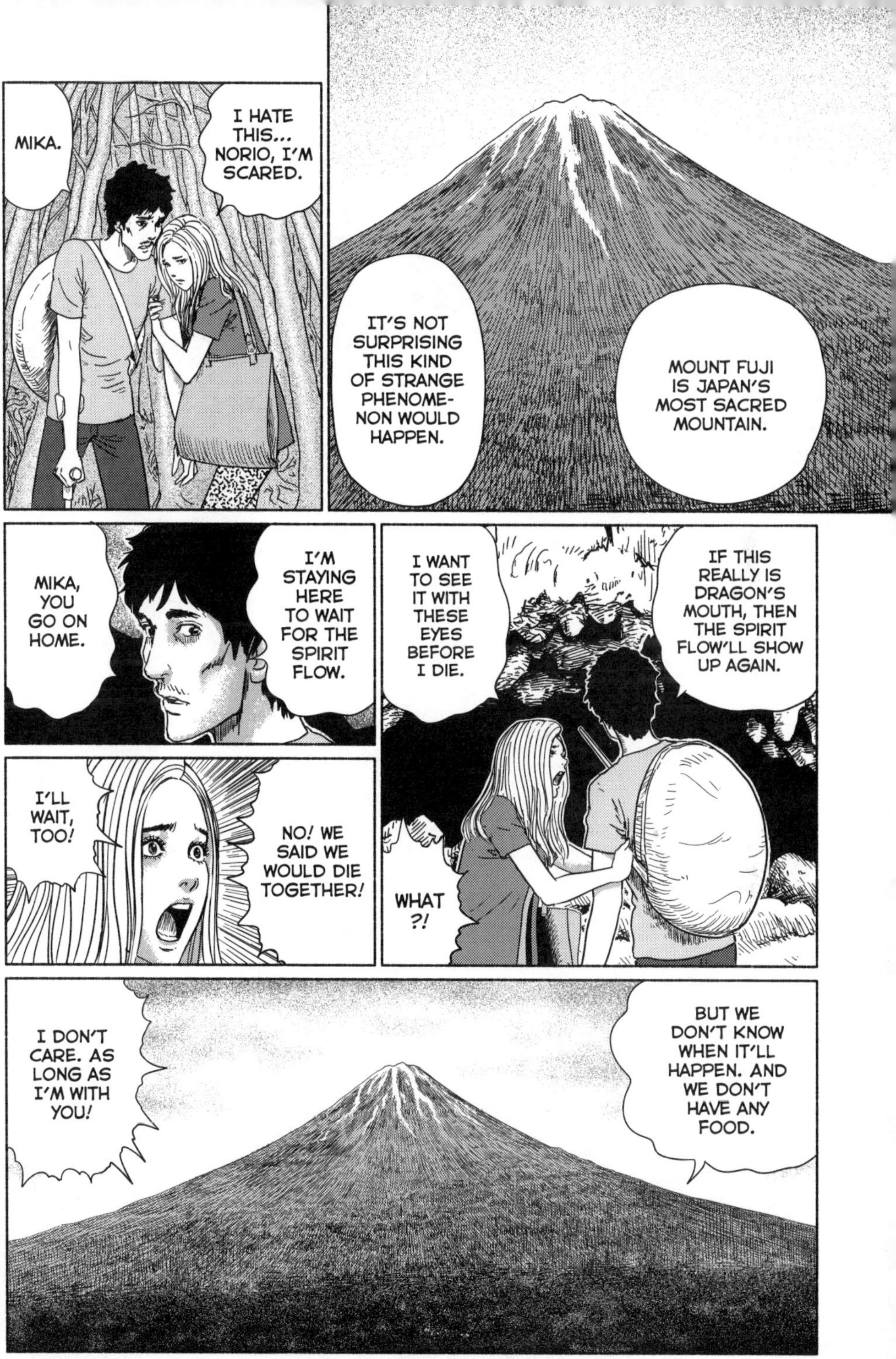
MOUNT FUJI IS JAPAN'S MOST SACRED MOUNTAIN.
IT'S NOT SURPRISING THIS KIND OF STRANGE PHENOME-NON WOULD HAPPEN.
I HATE THIS... NORIO, I'M SCARED.
MIKA.
IF THIS REALLY IS DRAGON'S MOUTH, THEN THE SPIRIT FLOW'LL SHOW UP AGAIN.
I WANT TO SEE IT WITH THESE EYES BEFORE I DIE.
WHAT?!
I'M STAYING HERE TO WAIT FOR THE SPIRIT FLOW.
MIKA, YOU GO ON HOME.
NO! WE SAID WE WOULD DIE TOGETHER!
I'LL WAIT, TOO!
BUT WE DON'T KNOW WHEN IT'LL HAPPEN. AND WE DON'T HAVE ANY FOOD.
I DON'T CARE. AS LONG AS I'M WITH YOU!

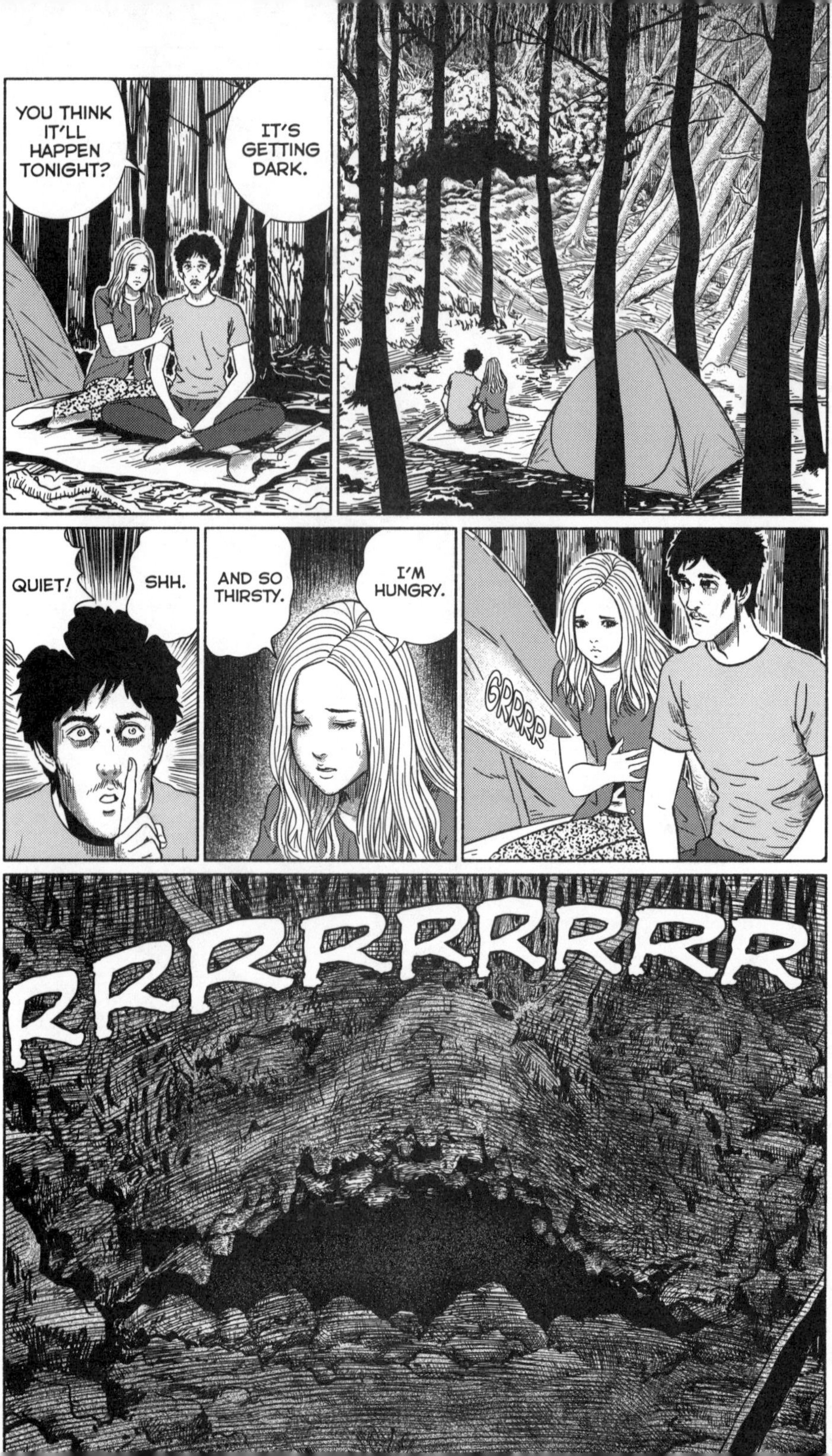
IT'S GETTING DARK.
YOU THINK IT'LL HAPPEN TONIGHT?
GRRRR
I'M HUNGRY.
AND SO THIRSTY.
SHH.
QUIET!
RRRRRRRRRR

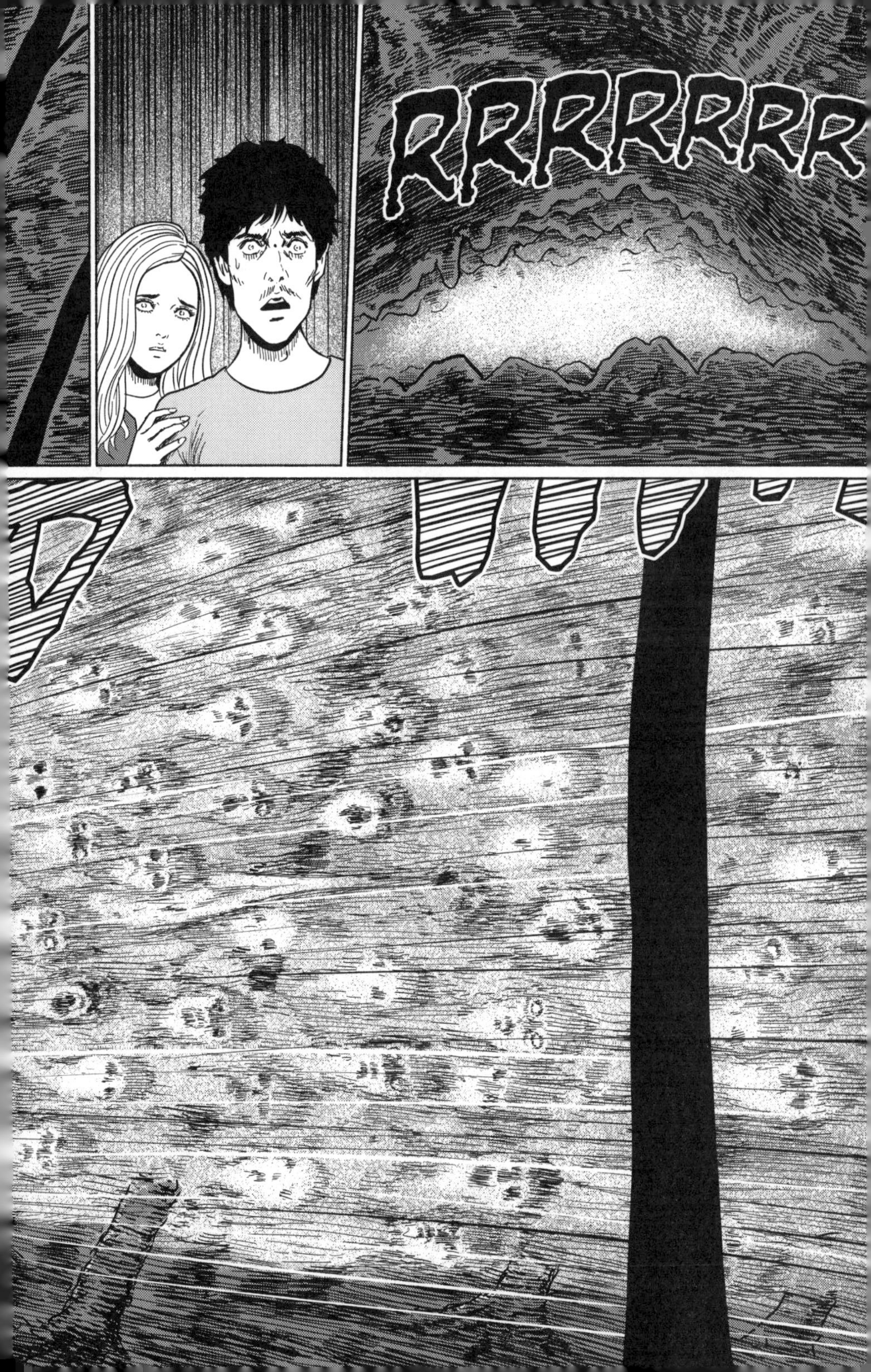
RRRRRRR

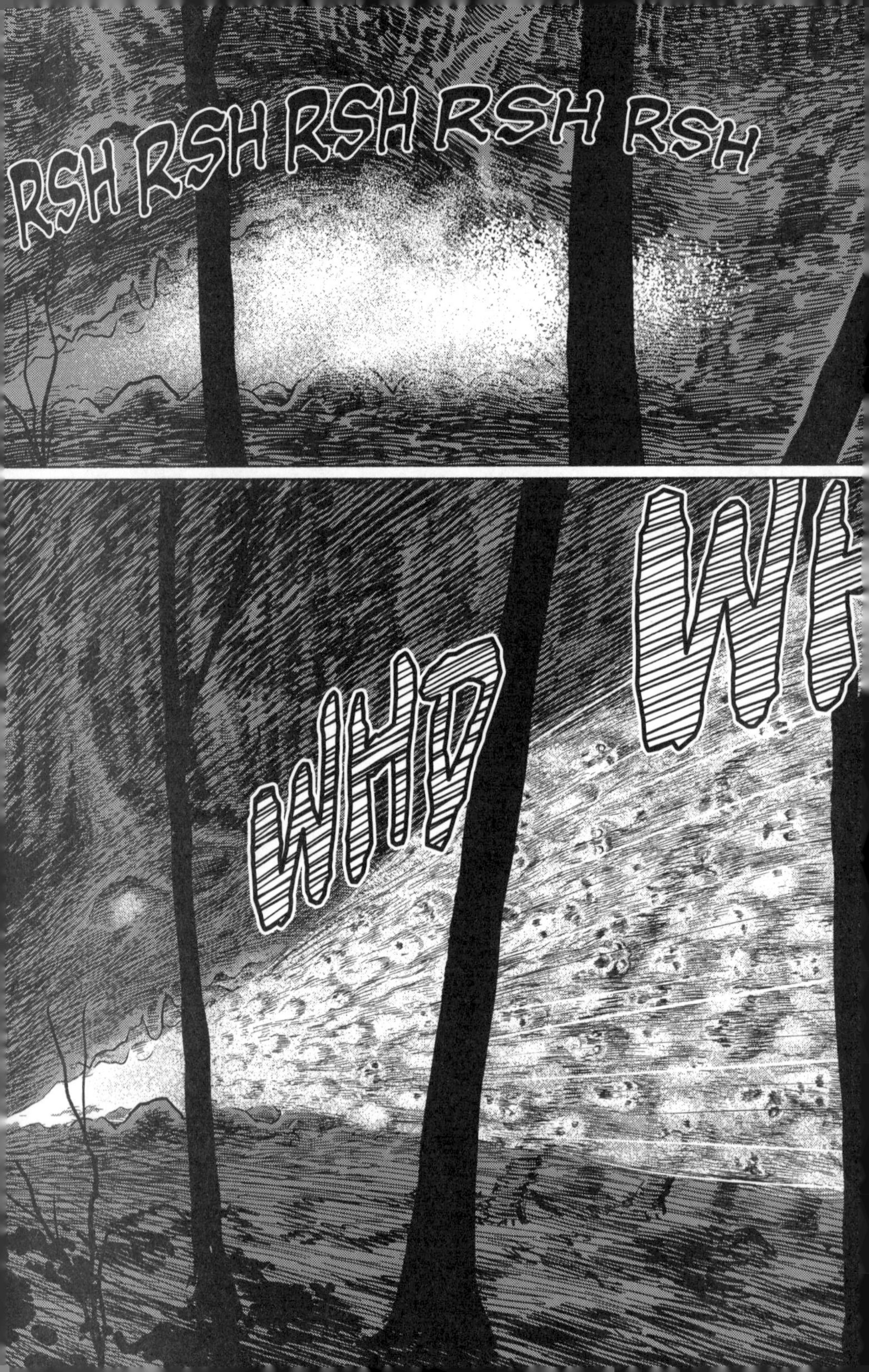
RSH RSH RSH RSH RSH
WHD

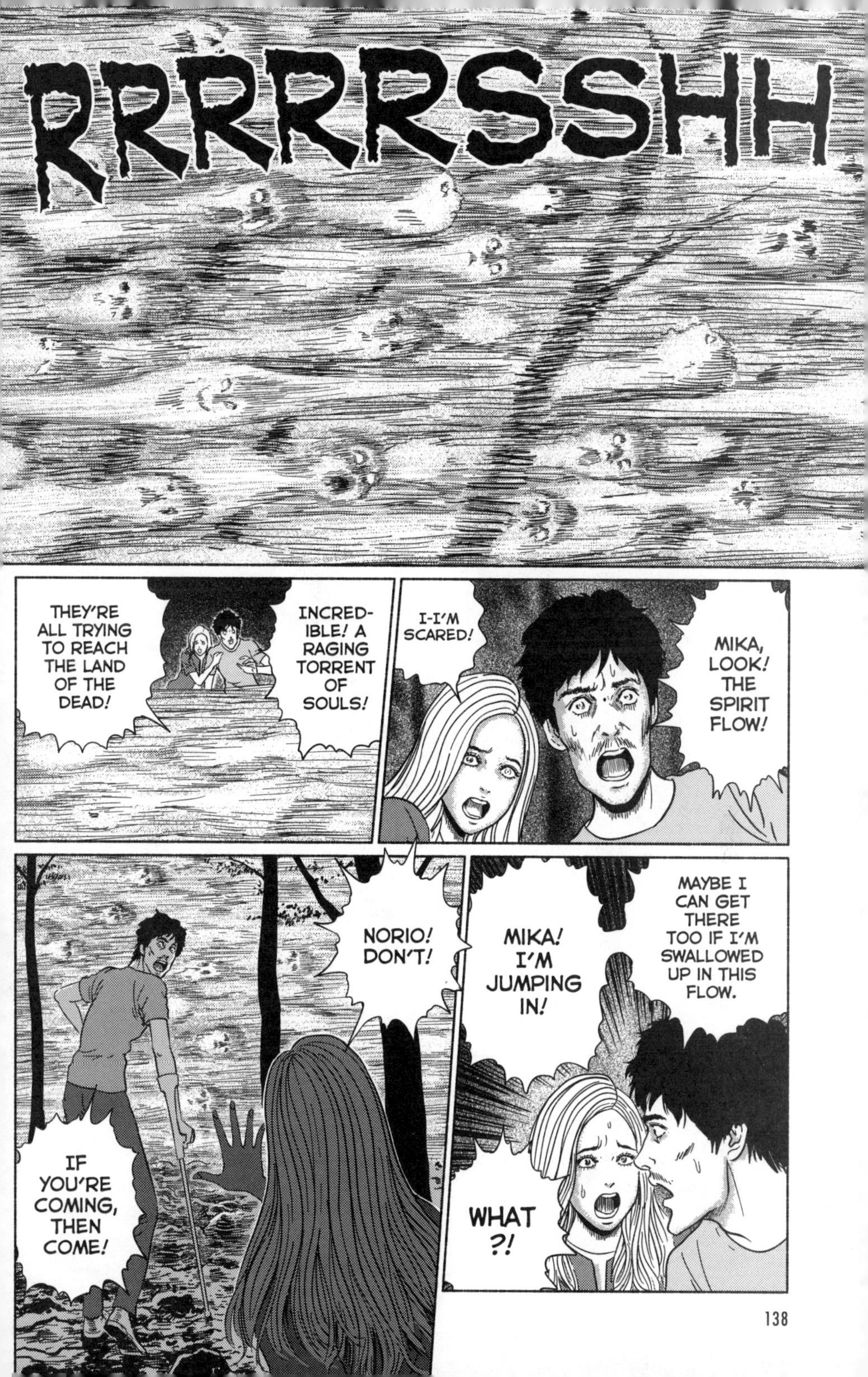
RRRRRSSHH
MIKA, LOOK! THE SPIRIT FLOW!
I-I'M SCARED!
INCRED-IBLE! A RAGING TORRENT OF SOULS!
THEY'RE ALL TRYING TO REACH THE LAND OF THE DEAD!
MAYBE I CAN GET THERE TOO IF I'M SWALLOWED UP IN THIS FLOW.
MIKA! I'M JUMPING IN!
WHAT?!
NORIO! DON'T!
IF YOU'RE COMING, THEN COME!

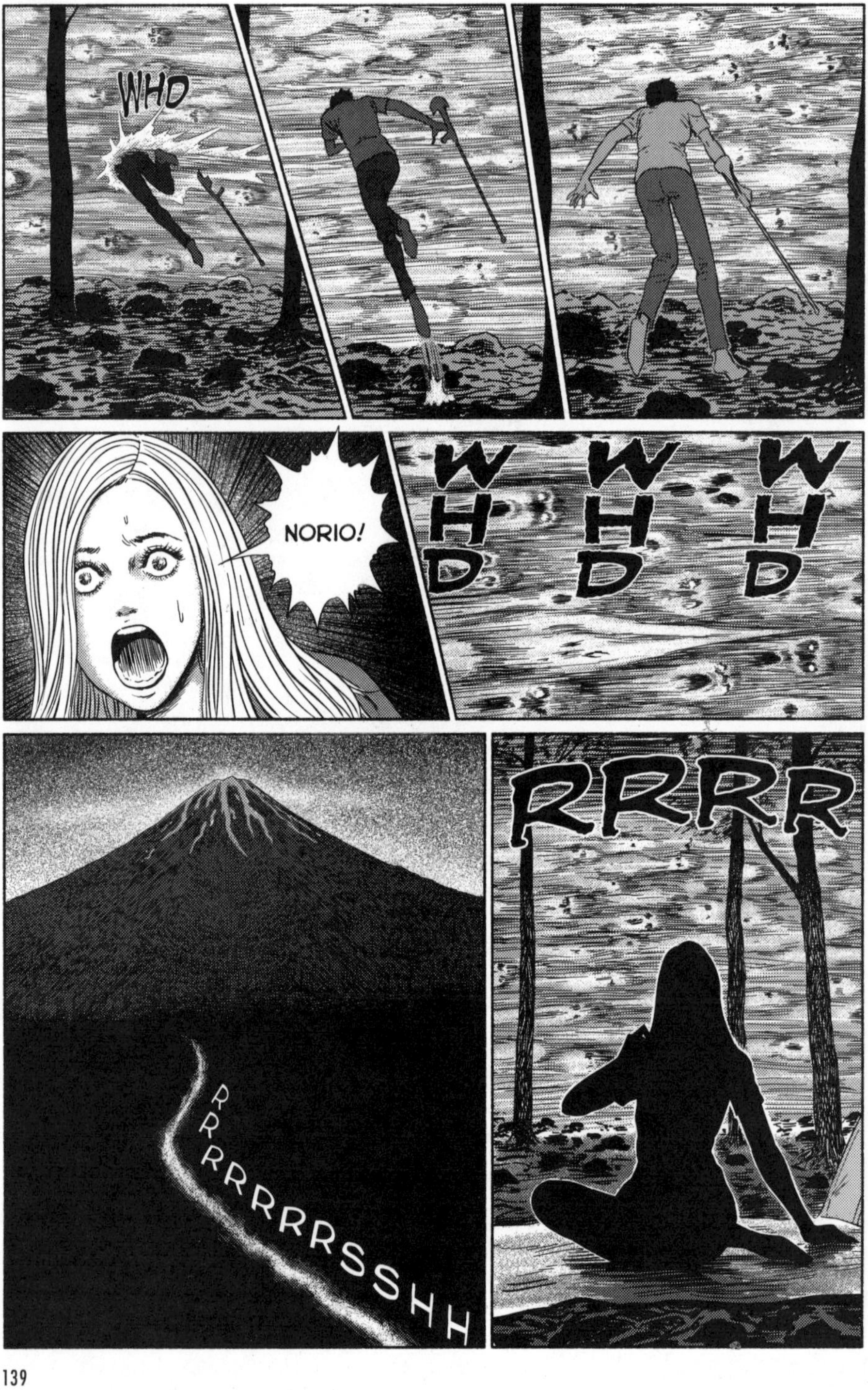
WHD
WHD WHD WHD
NORIO!
RRRR
RRRRRRRSSHH

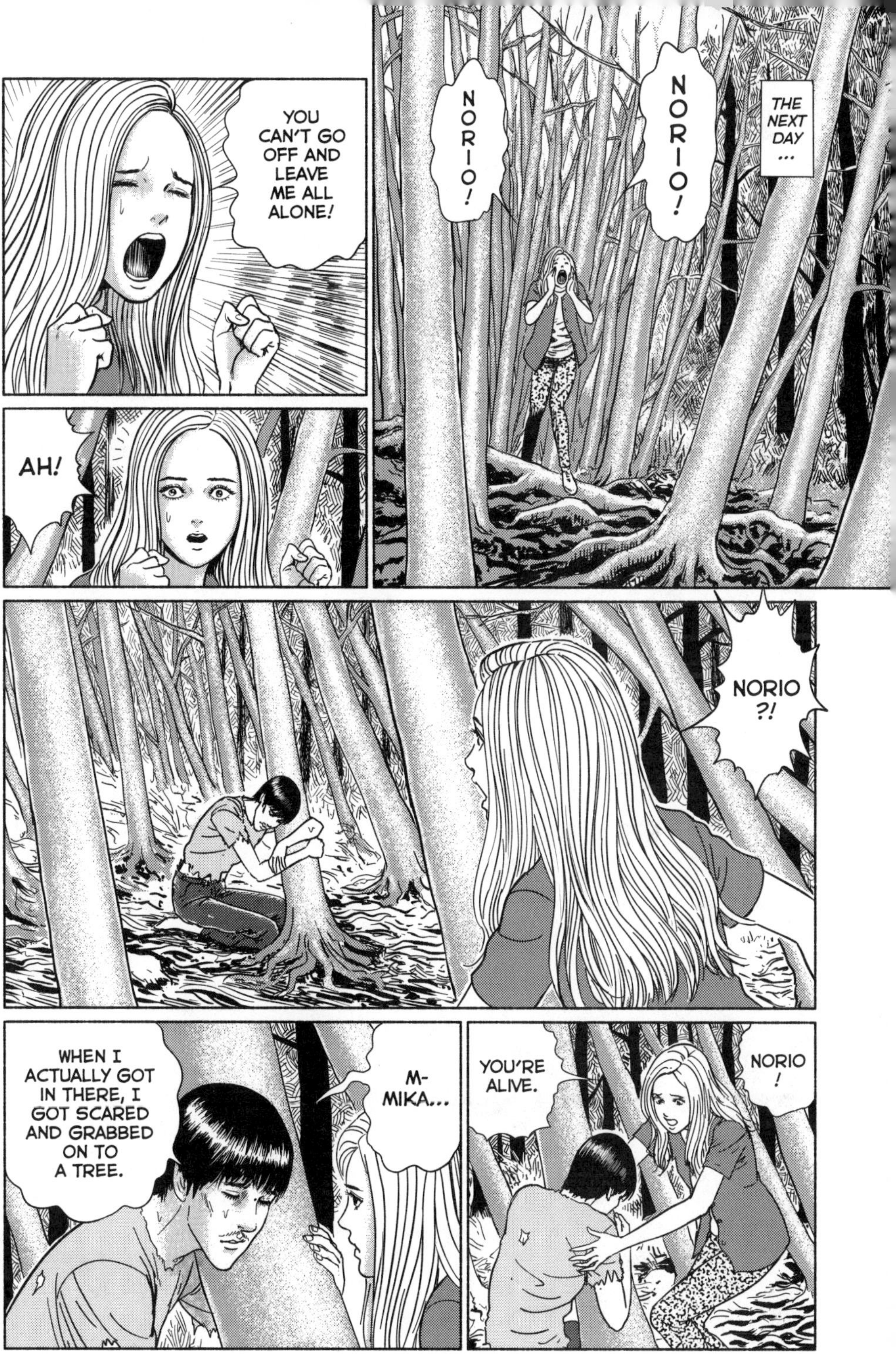

THE NEXT DAY ...
NORIO!
NORIO!
YOU CAN'T GO OFF AND LEAVE ME ALL ALONE!
AH!
NORIO ?!
NORIO !
YOU'RE ALIVE.
M-MIKA...
WHEN I ACTUALLY GOT IN THERE, I GOT SCARED AND GRABBED ON TO A TREE.

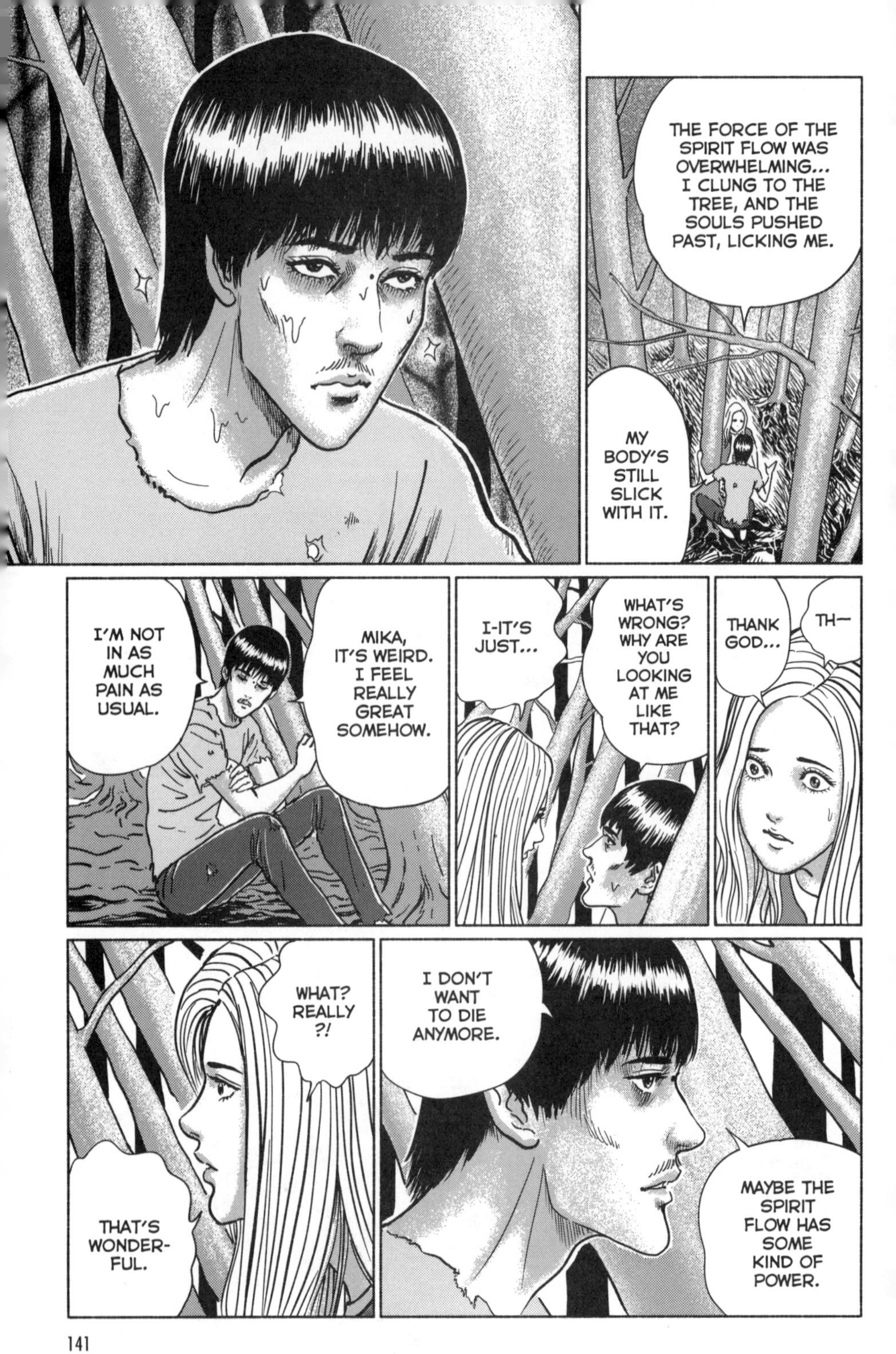
THE FORCE OF THE SPIRIT FLOW WAS OVERWHELMING... I CLUNG TO THE TREE, AND THE SOULS PUSHED PAST, LICKING ME.
MY BODY'S STILL SLICK WITH IT.
TH—
THANK GOD...
WHAT'S WRONG? WHY ARE YOU LOOKING AT ME LIKE THAT?
I-IT'S JUST...
MIKA, IT'S WEIRD. I FEEL REALLY GREAT SOMEHOW.
I'M NOT IN AS MUCH PAIN AS USUAL.
I DON'T WANT TO DIE ANYMORE.
MAYBE THE SPIRIT FLOW HAS SOME KIND OF POWER.
WHAT? REALLY?!
THAT'S WONDERFUL.

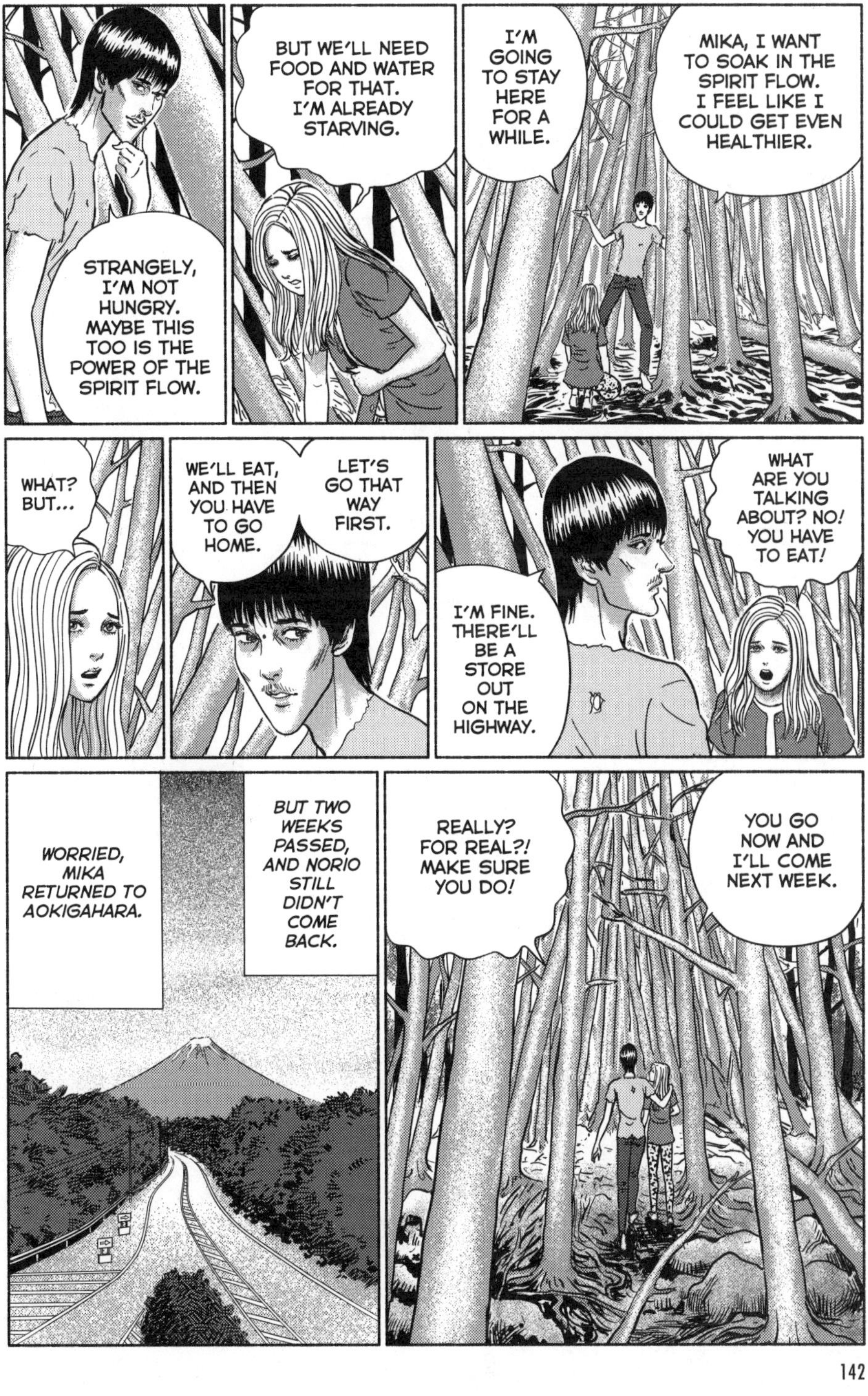
MIKA, I WANT TO SOAK IN THE SPIRIT FLOW. I FEEL LIKE I COULD GET EVEN HEALTHIER.
I'M GOING TO STAY HERE FOR A WHILE.
BUT WE'LL NEED FOOD AND WATER FOR THAT. I'M ALREADY STARVING.
STRANGELY, I'M NOT HUNGRY. MAYBE THIS TOO IS THE POWER OF THE SPIRIT FLOW.
WHAT ARE YOU TALKING ABOUT? NO! YOU HAVE TO EAT!
I'M FINE. THERE'LL BE A STORE OUT ON THE HIGHWAY.
LET'S GO THAT WAY FIRST.
WE'LL EAT, AND THEN YOU HAVE TO GO HOME.
WHAT? BUT...
YOU GO NOW AND I'LL COME NEXT WEEK.
REALLY? FOR REAL?! MAKE SURE YOU DO!
BUT TWO WEEKS PASSED, AND NORIO STILL DIDN'T COME BACK.
WORRIED, MIKA RETURNED TO AOKIGAHARA.

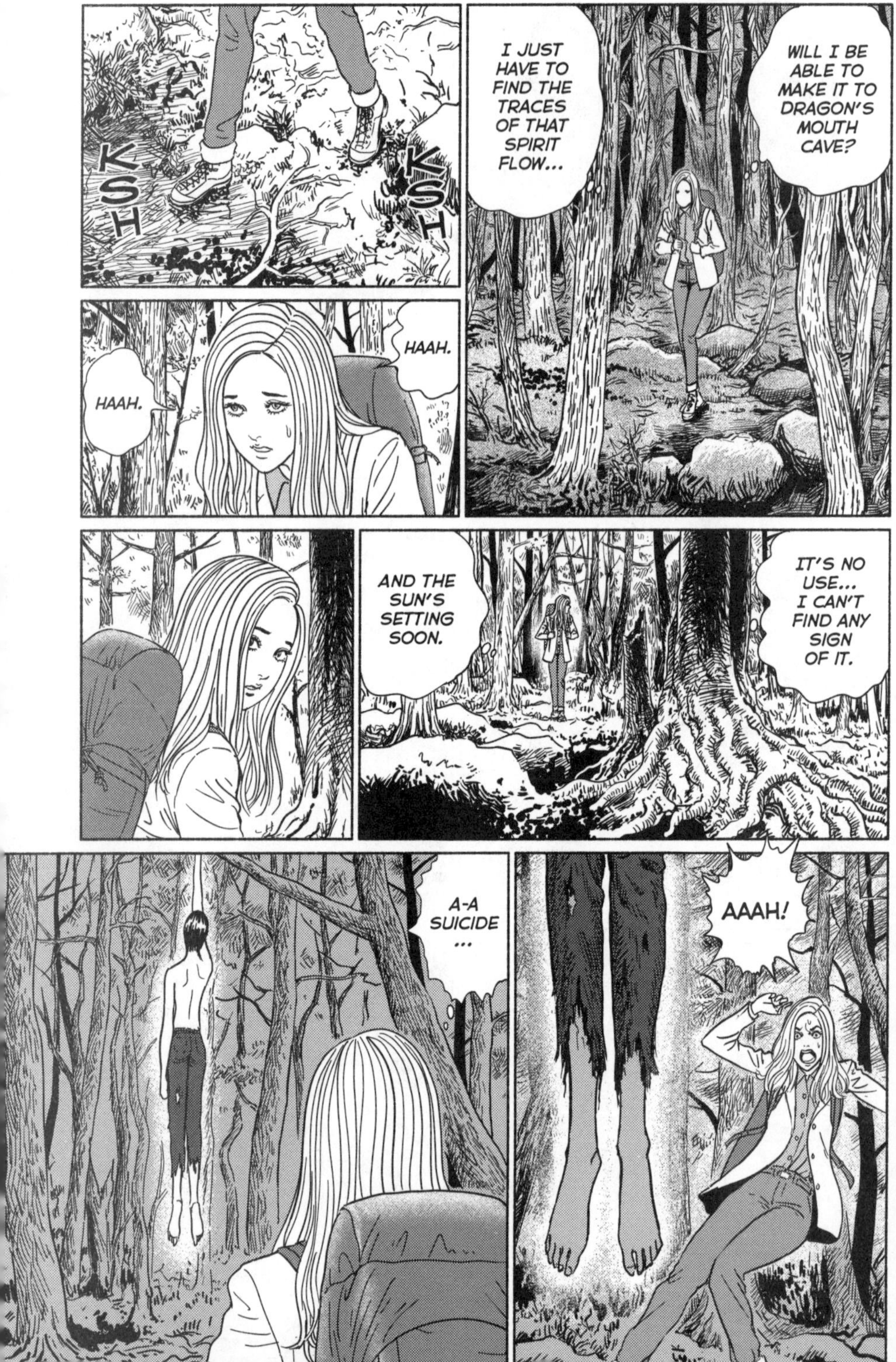
WILL I BE ABLE TO MAKE IT TO DRAGON'S MOUTH CAVE?
I JUST HAVE TO FIND THE TRACES OF THAT SPIRIT FLOW...
KSH
KSH
HAAH.
HAAH.
IT'S NO USE... I CAN'T FIND ANY SIGN OF IT.
AND THE SUN'S SETTING SOON.
AAAH!
A-A SUICIDE ...

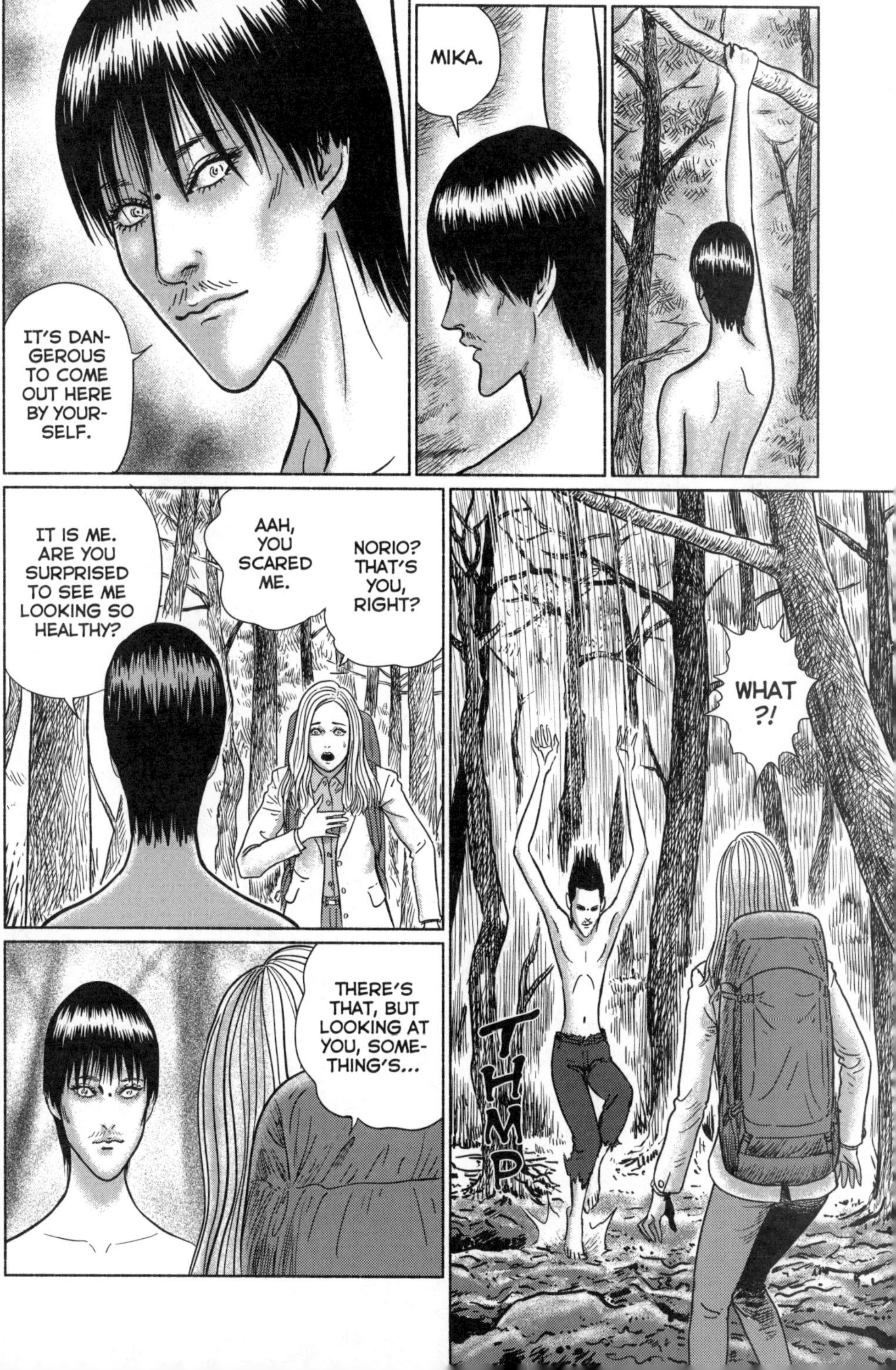
MIKA.
IT'S DAN-GEROUS TO COME OUT HERE BY YOUR-SELF.
WHAT ?!
THMP
NORIO? THAT'S YOU, RIGHT?
AAH, YOU SCARED ME.
IT IS ME. ARE YOU SURPRISED TO SEE ME LOOKING SO HEALTHY?
THERE'S THAT, BUT LOOKING AT YOU, SOME-THING'S...

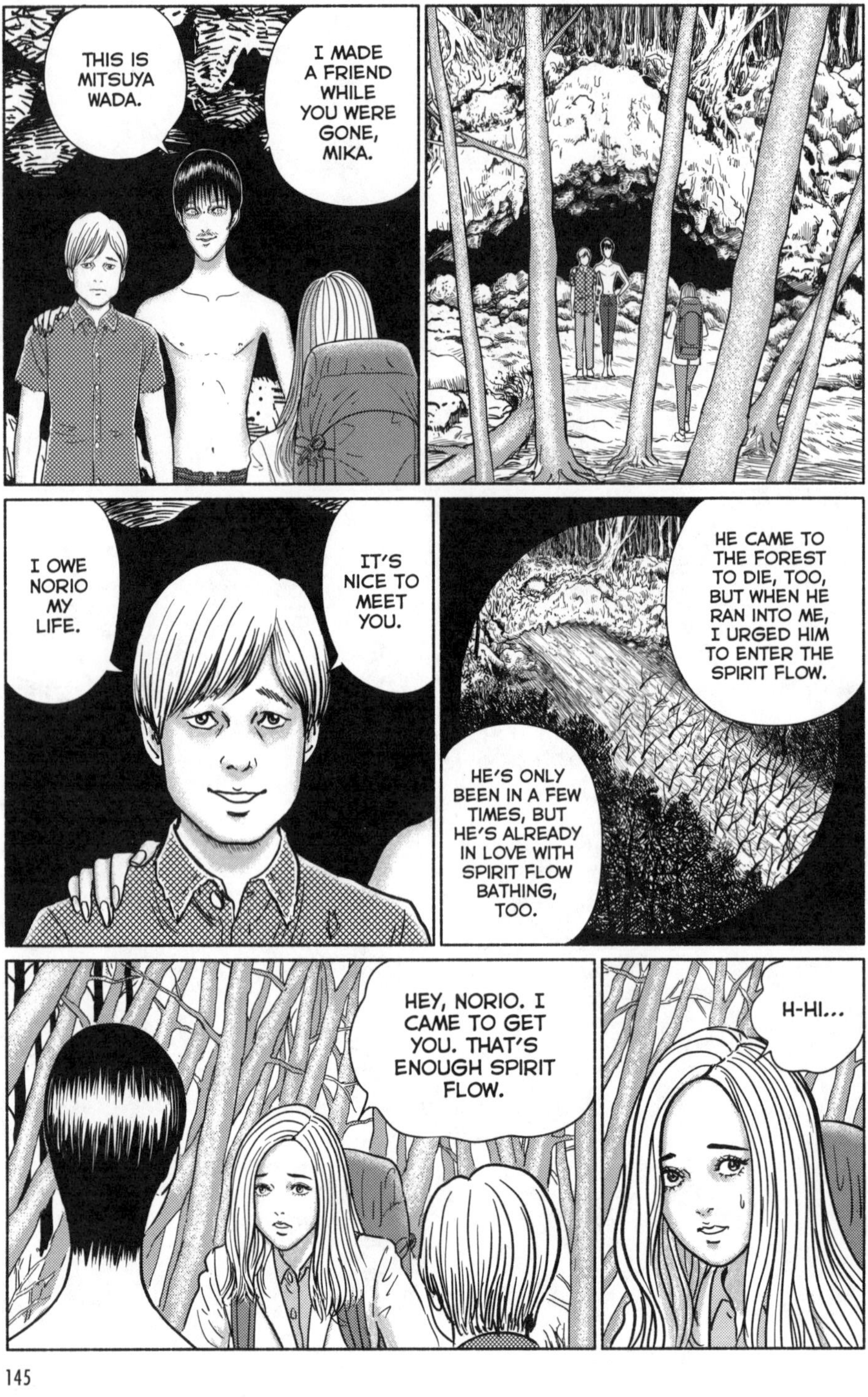
I MADE A FRIEND WHILE YOU WERE GONE, MIKA.
THIS IS MITSUYA WADA.
HE CAME TO THE FOREST TO DIE, TOO, BUT WHEN HE RAN INTO ME, I URGED HIM TO ENTER THE SPIRIT FLOW.
HE'S ONLY BEEN IN A FEW TIMES, BUT HE'S ALREADY IN LOVE WITH SPIRIT FLOW BATHING, TOO.
IT'S NICE TO MEET YOU.
I OWE NORIO MY LIFE.
H-HI...
HEY, NORIO. I CAME TO GET YOU. THAT'S ENOUGH SPIRIT FLOW.

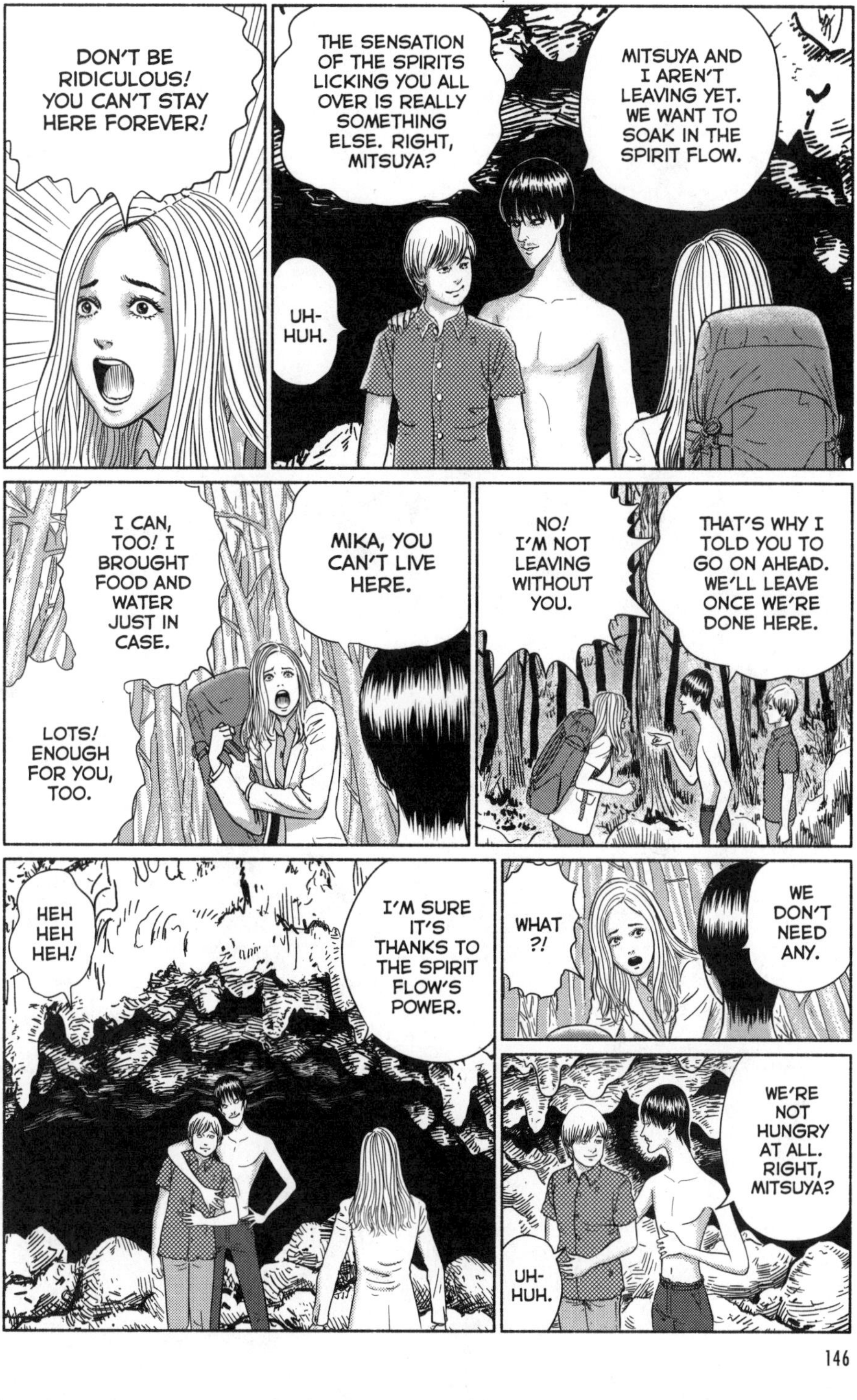
MITSUYA AND I AREN'T LEAVING YET. WE WANT TO SOAK IN THE SPIRIT FLOW.
THE SENSATION OF THE SPIRITS LICKING YOU ALL OVER IS REALLY SOMETHING ELSE. RIGHT, MITSUYA?
UH-HUH.
DON'T BE RIDICULOUS! YOU CAN'T STAY HERE FOREVER!
THAT'S WHY I TOLD YOU TO GO ON AHEAD. WE'LL LEAVE ONCE WE'RE DONE HERE.
NO! I'M NOT LEAVING WITHOUT YOU.
MIKA, YOU CAN'T LIVE HERE.
I CAN, TOO! I BROUGHT FOOD AND WATER JUST IN CASE.
LOTS! ENOUGH FOR YOU, TOO.
WE DON'T NEED ANY.
WHAT?!
WE'RE NOT HUNGRY AT ALL. RIGHT, MITSUYA?
UH-HUH.
I'M SURE IT'S THANKS TO THE SPIRIT FLOW'S POWER.
HEH HEH HEH!

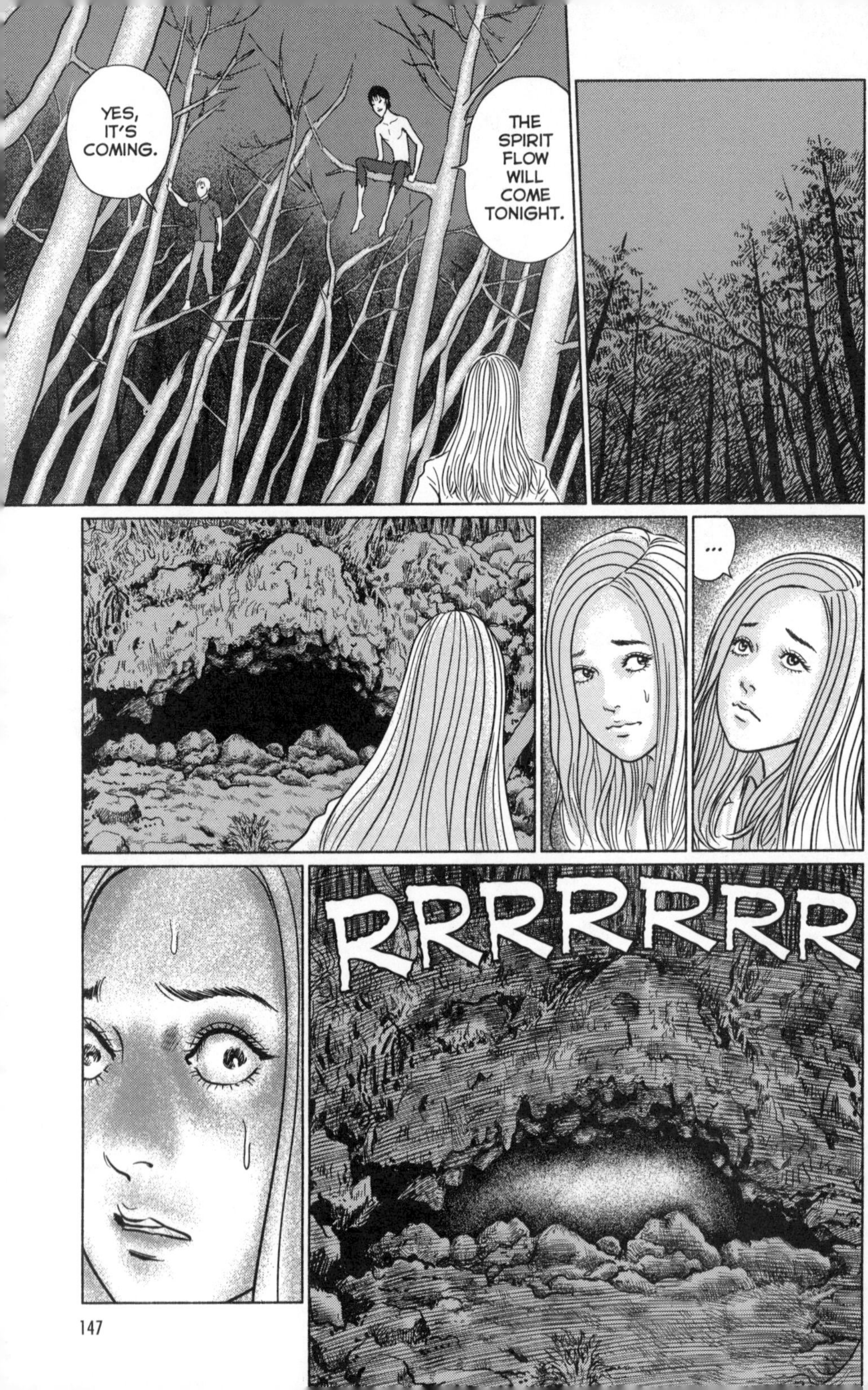
THE SPIRIT FLOW WILL COME TONIGHT.
YES, IT'S COMING.
...
RRRRRRR

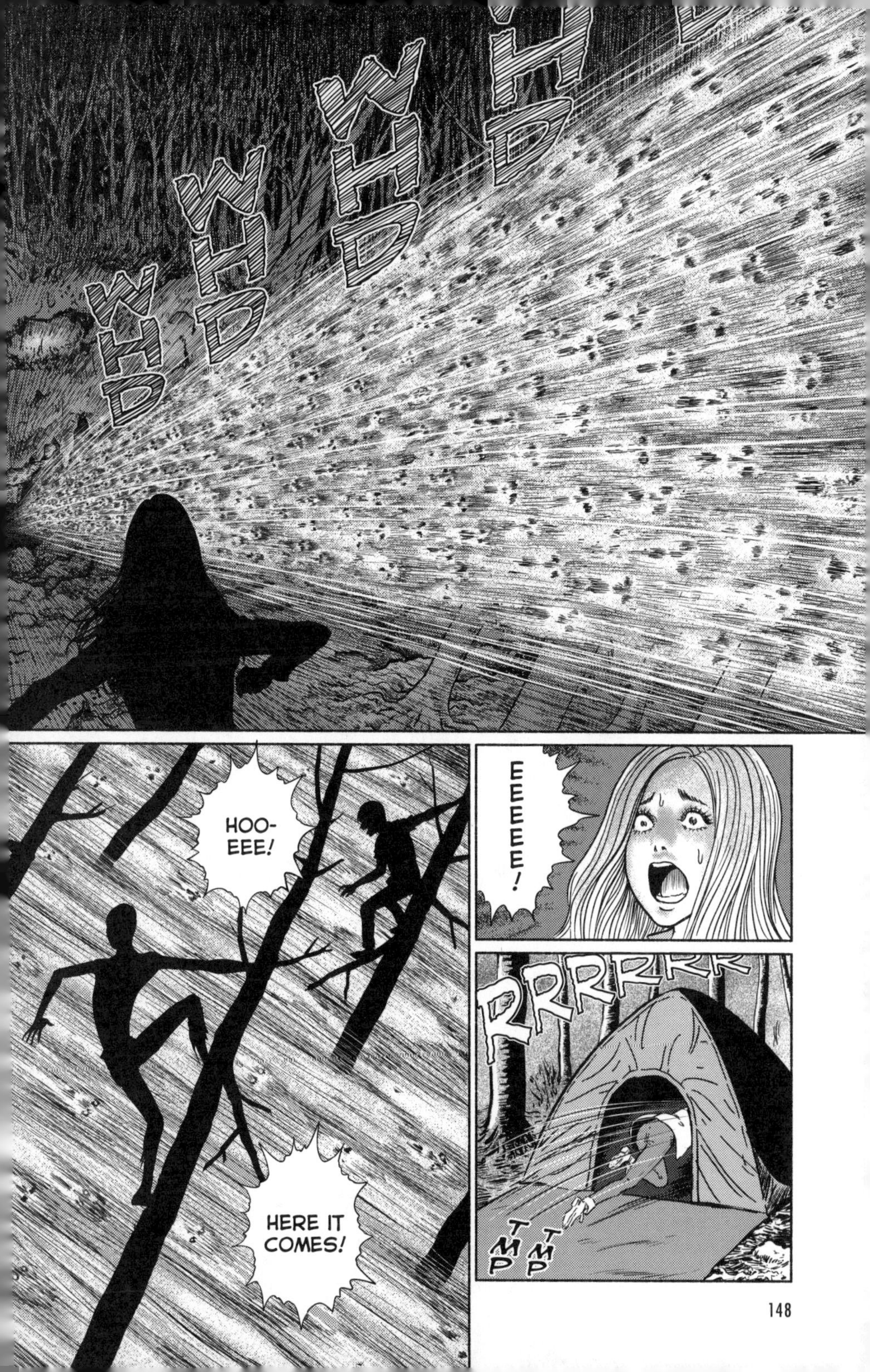
WHD
WHD
WHD
EEEEEE!
RRRRRR
TMP
TMP
HOO-EEE!
HERE IT COMES!

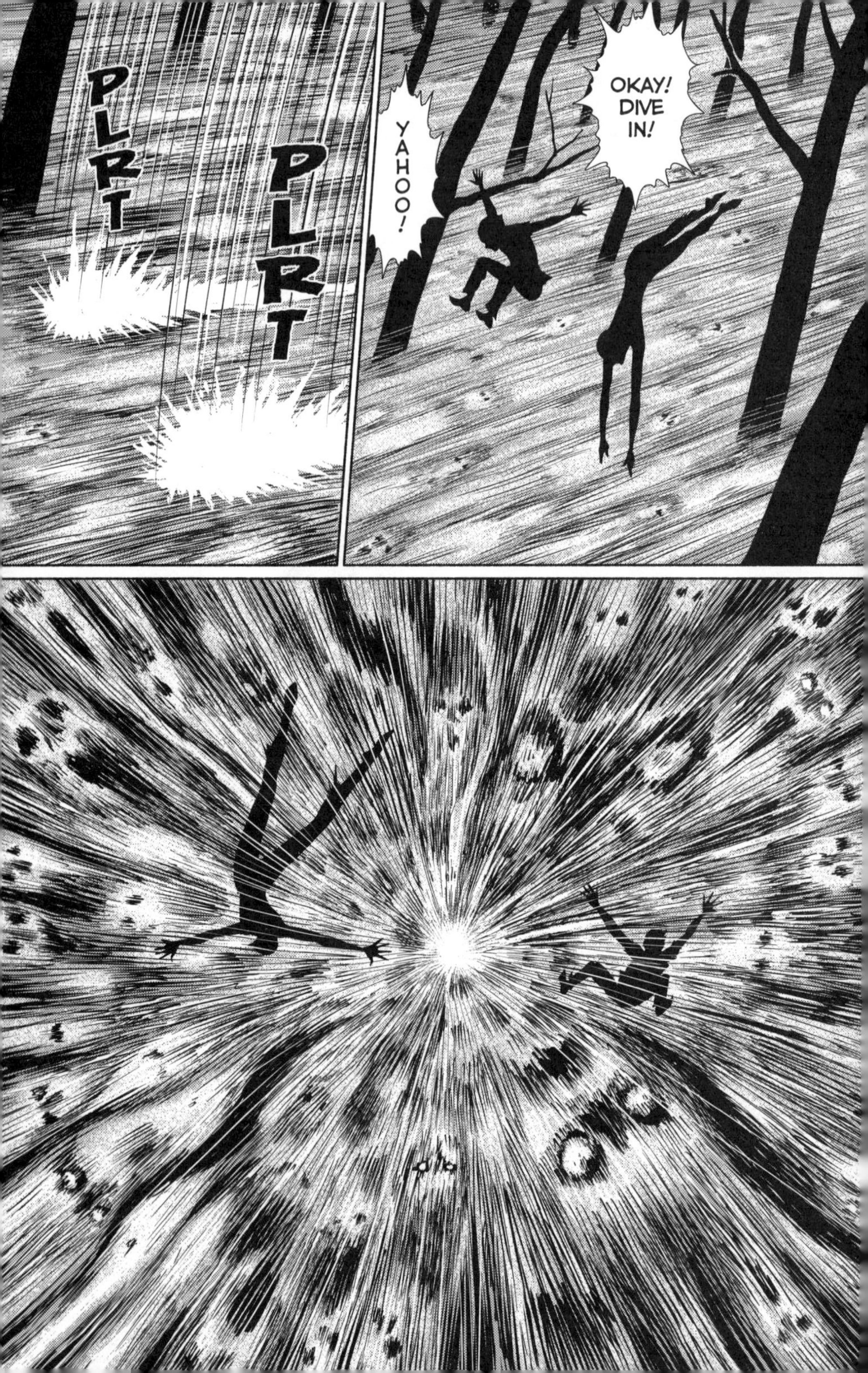
OKAY! DIVE IN!
YAHOO!
PLRT
PLRT

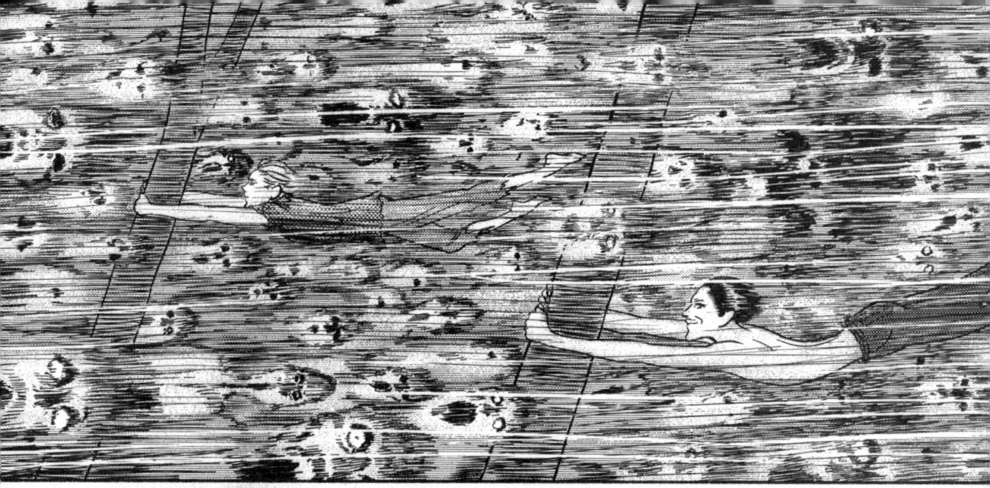
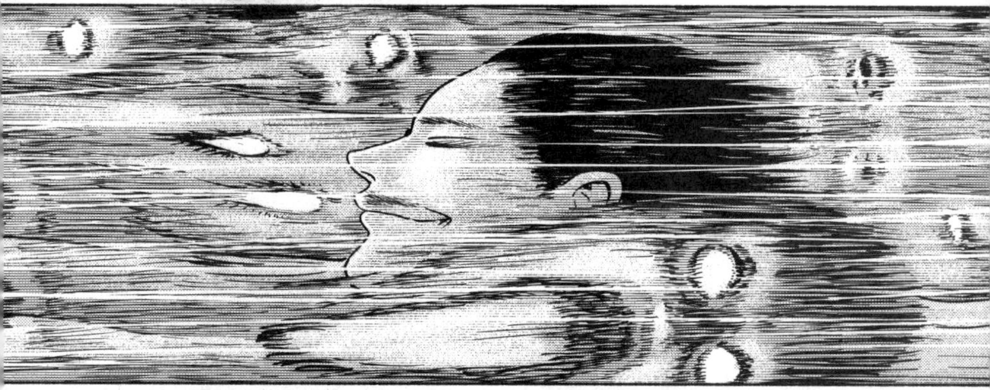
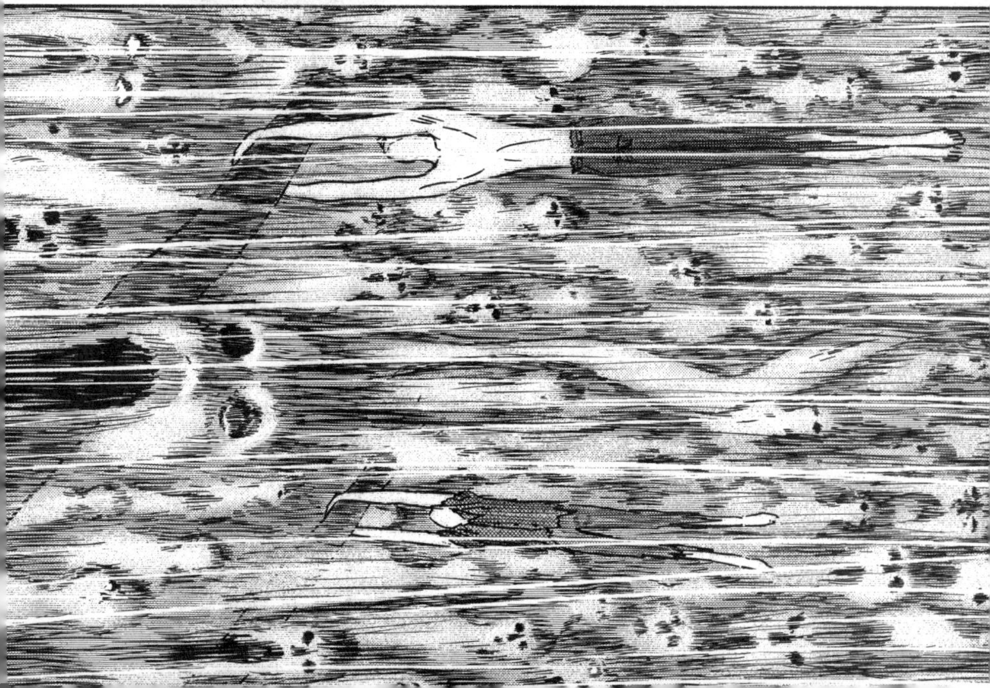

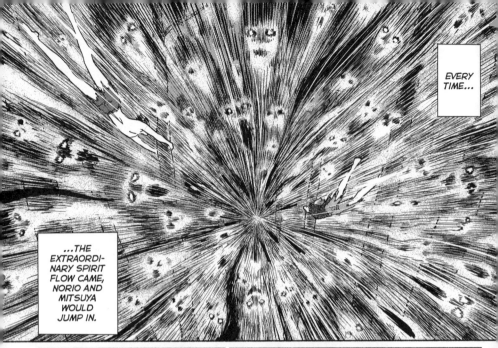

EVERY TIME...

...THE EXTRAORDINARY SPIRIT FLOW CAME, NORIO AND MITSUYA WOULD JUMP IN.

CURIOUSLY, WITH EACH DIVE, THE PAIR SEEMED TO BECOME MORE AND MORE POLISHED.

ONE DAY, A STRANGE MAN CAME ALONG.

HE SAID HE WAS A YOU-TUBER.

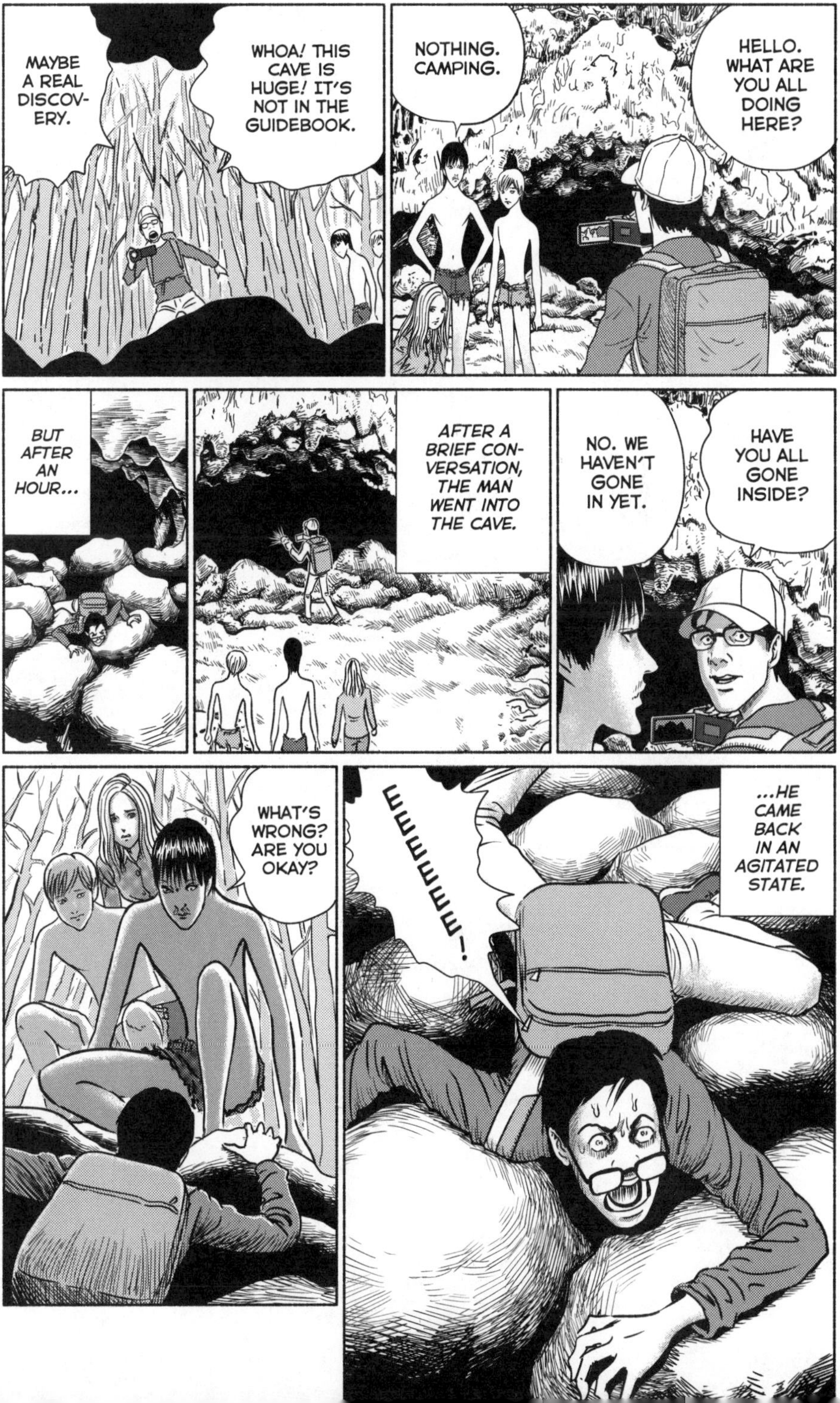
HELLO. WHAT ARE YOU ALL DOING HERE?
NOTHING. CAMPING.
WHOA! THIS CAVE IS HUGE! IT'S NOT IN THE GUIDEBOOK.
MAYBE A REAL DISCOVERY.
HAVE YOU ALL GONE INSIDE?
NO. WE HAVEN'T GONE IN YET.
AFTER A BRIEF CONVERSATION, THE MAN WENT INTO THE CAVE.
BUT AFTER AN HOUR...
...HE CAME BACK IN AN AGITATED STATE.
EEEEEEE!
WHAT'S WRONG? ARE YOU OKAY?

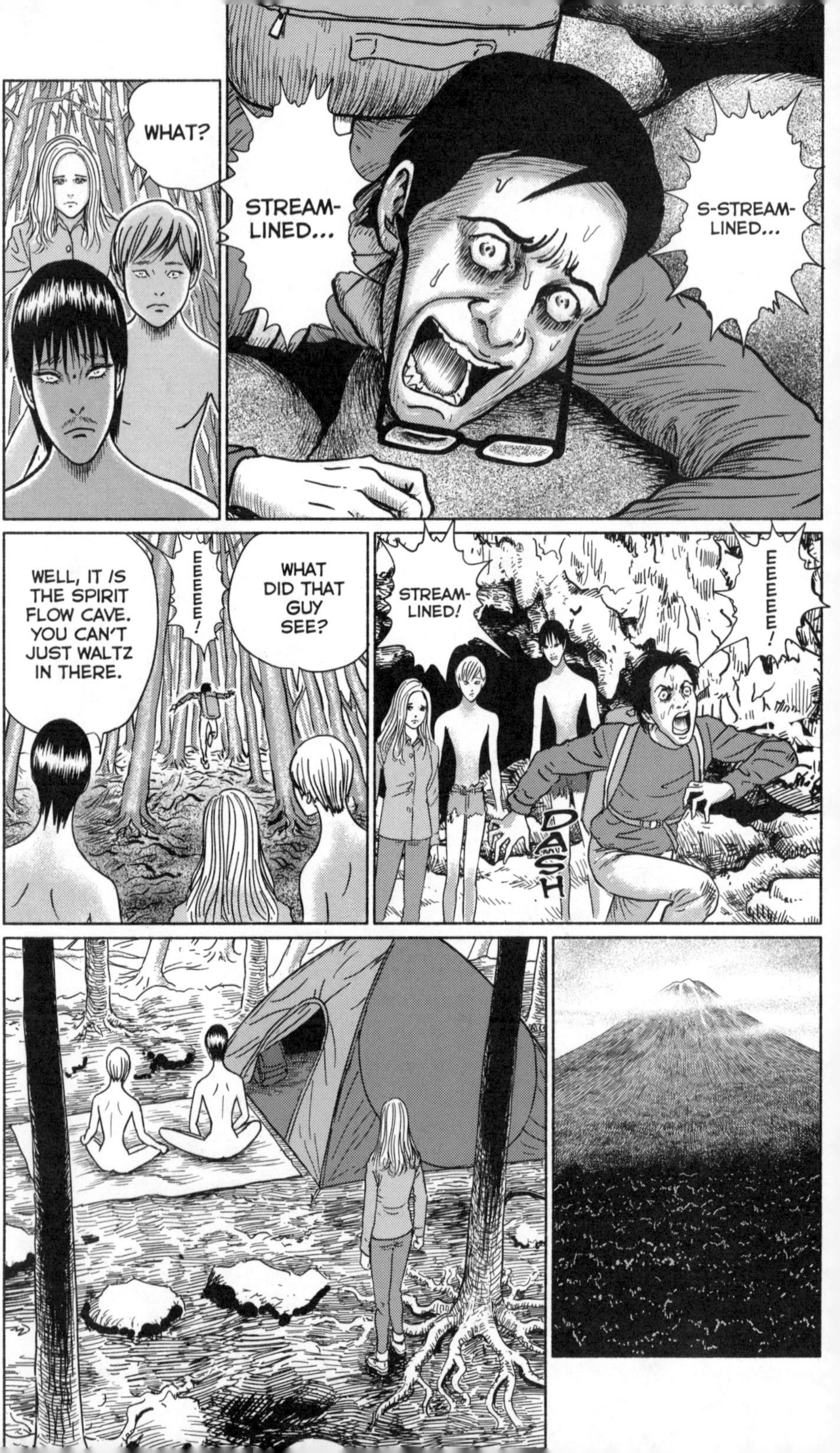
S-STREAM-LINED...
STREAM-LINED...
WHAT?
EEEEE!
STREAM-LINED!
DASH
WHAT DID THAT GUY SEE?
EEEEE!
WELL, IT IS THE SPIRIT FLOW CAVE. YOU CAN'T JUST WALTZ IN THERE.

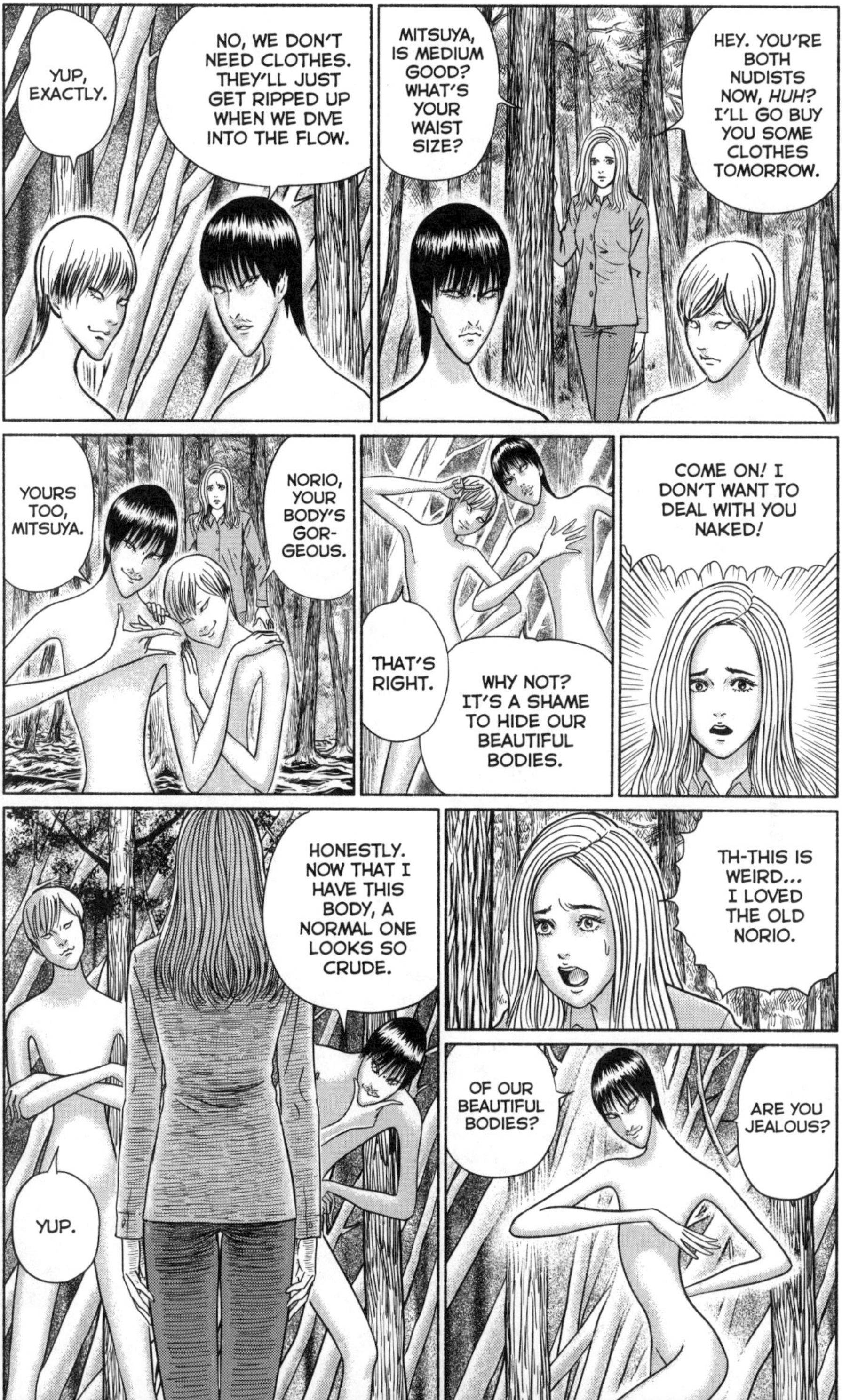
HEY. YOU'RE BOTH NUDISTS NOW, *HUH*? I'LL GO BUY YOU SOME CLOTHES TOMORROW.
MITSUYA, IS MEDIUM GOOD? WHAT'S YOUR WAIST SIZE?
NO, WE DON'T NEED CLOTHES. THEY'LL JUST GET RIPPED UP WHEN WE DIVE INTO THE FLOW.
YUP, EXACTLY.
COME ON! I DON'T WANT TO DEAL WITH YOU NAKED!
WHY NOT? IT'S A SHAME TO HIDE OUR BEAUTIFUL BODIES.
THAT'S RIGHT.
NORIO, YOUR BODY'S GORGEOUS.
YOURS TOO, MITSUYA.
TH-THIS IS WEIRD... I LOVED THE OLD NORIO.
ARE YOU JEALOUS?
OF OUR BEAUTIFUL BODIES?
HONESTLY. NOW THAT I HAVE THIS BODY, A NORMAL ONE LOOKS SO CRUDE.
YUP.

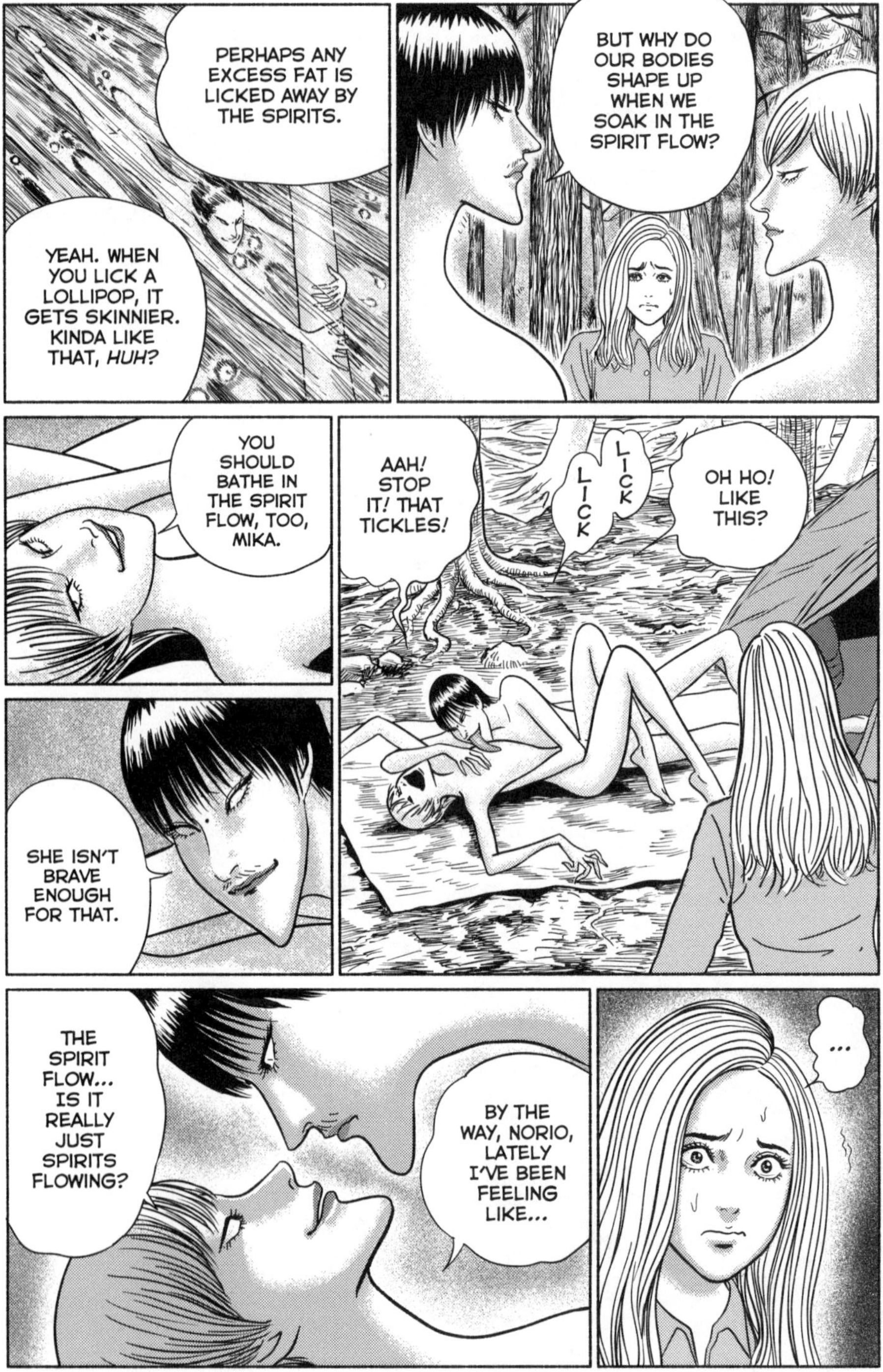
BUT WHY DO OUR BODIES SHAPE UP WHEN WE SOAK IN THE SPIRIT FLOW?
PERHAPS ANY EXCESS FAT IS LICKED AWAY BY THE SPIRITS.
YEAH. WHEN YOU LICK A LOLLIPOP, IT GETS SKINNIER. KINDA LIKE THAT, *HUH*?
OH HO! LIKE THIS?
LICK LICK
AAH! STOP IT! THAT TICKLES!
YOU SHOULD BATHE IN THE SPIRIT FLOW, TOO, MIKA.
SHE ISN'T BRAVE ENOUGH FOR THAT.
...
BY THE WAY, NORIO, LATELY I'VE BEEN FEELING LIKE...
THE SPIRIT FLOW... IS IT REALLY JUST SPIRITS FLOWING?

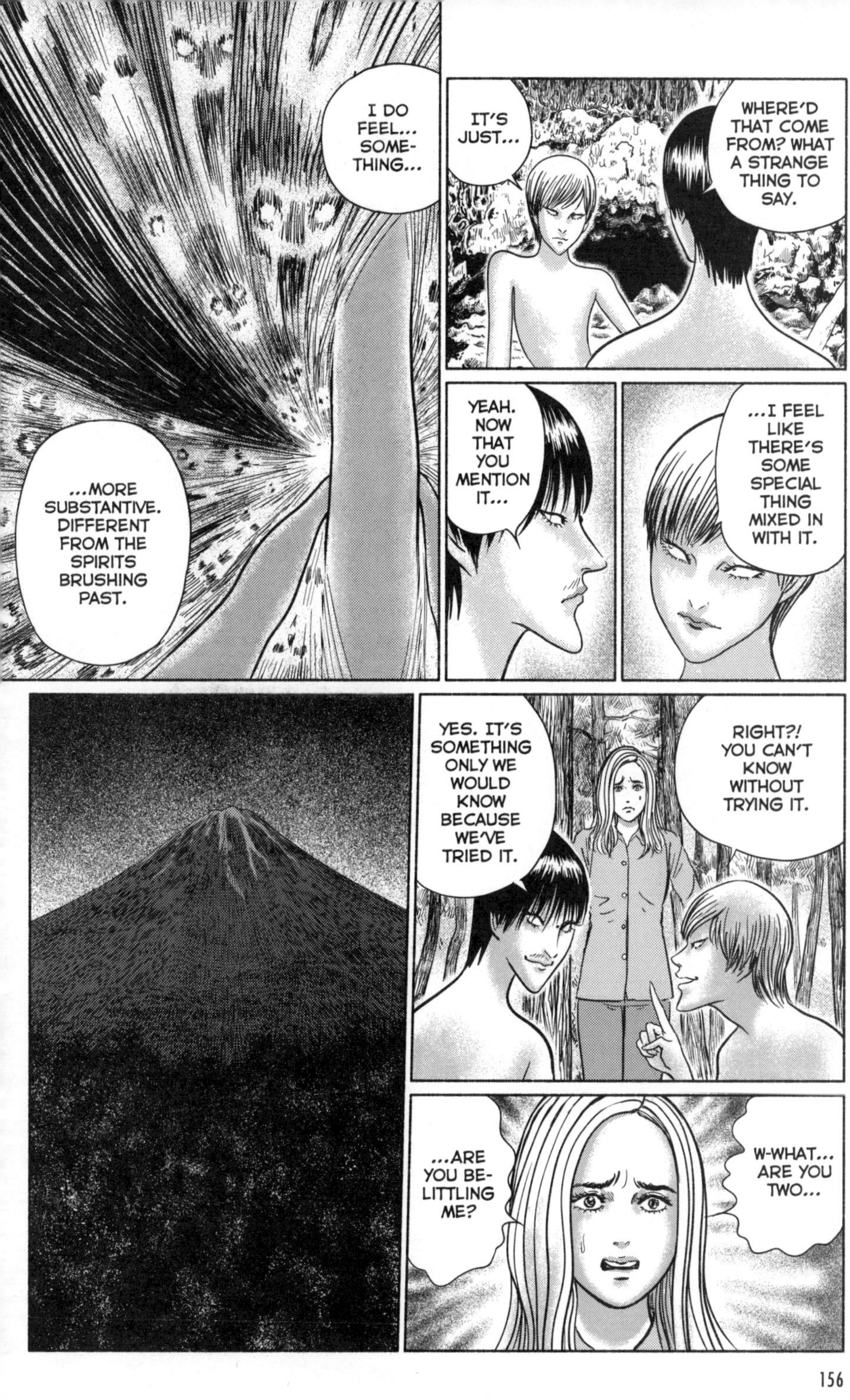
WHERE'D THAT COME FROM? WHAT A STRANGE THING TO SAY.
IT'S JUST...
...I FEEL LIKE THERE'S SOME SPECIAL THING MIXED IN WITH IT.
YEAH. NOW THAT YOU MENTION IT...
I DO FEEL... SOME-THING...
...MORE SUBSTANTIVE. DIFFERENT FROM THE SPIRITS BRUSHING PAST.
RIGHT?! YOU CAN'T KNOW WITHOUT TRYING IT.
YES. IT'S SOMETHING ONLY WE WOULD KNOW BECAUSE WE'VE TRIED IT.
W-WHAT... ARE YOU TWO...
...ARE YOU BE-LITTLING ME?

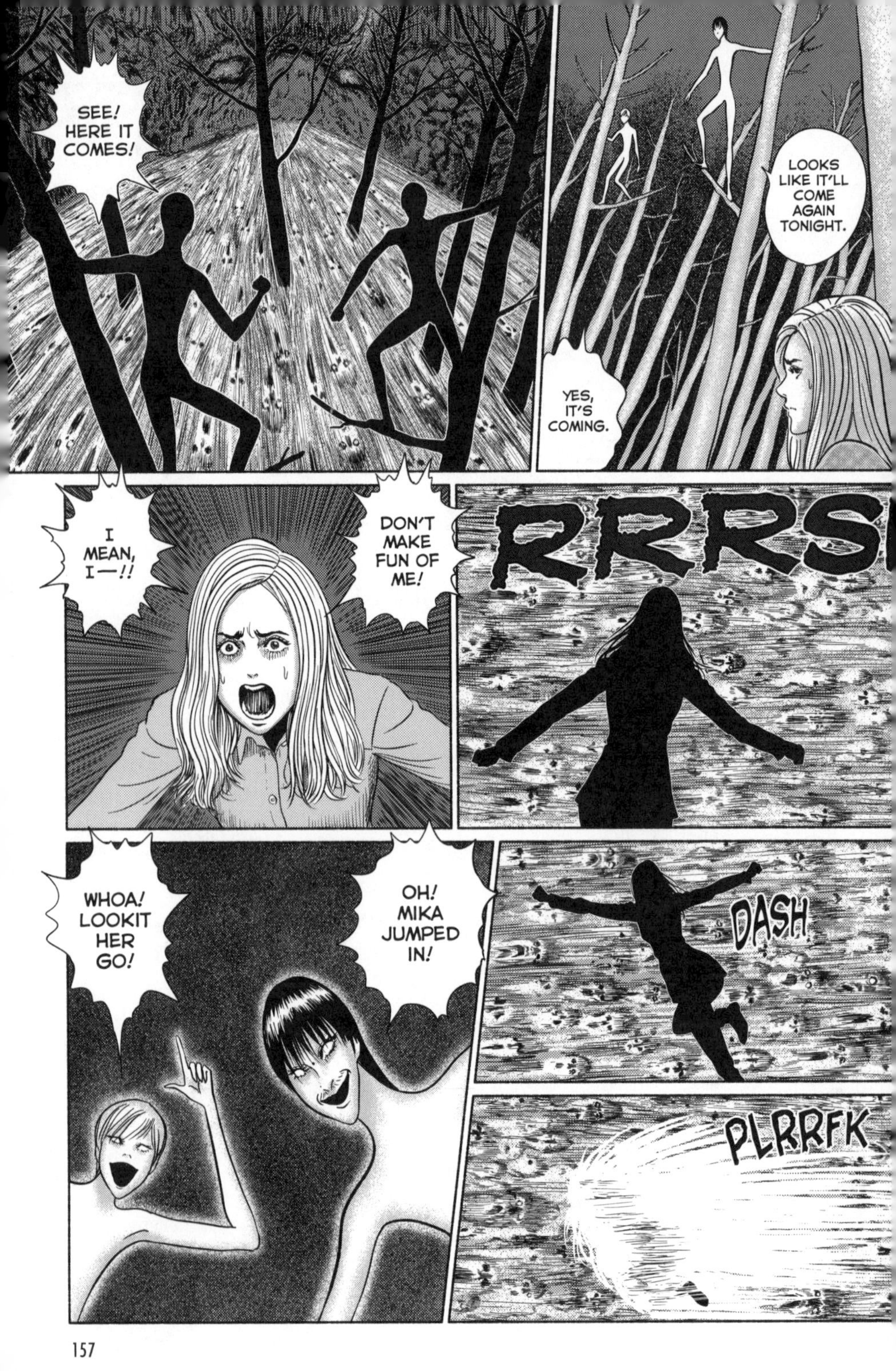
LOOKS LIKE IT'LL COME AGAIN TONIGHT.
YES, IT'S COMING.
SEE! HERE IT COMES!
RRRS
DON'T MAKE FUN OF ME!
I MEAN, I—!!
DASH
PLRRFK
OH! MIKA JUMPED IN!
WHOA! LOOKIT HER GO!

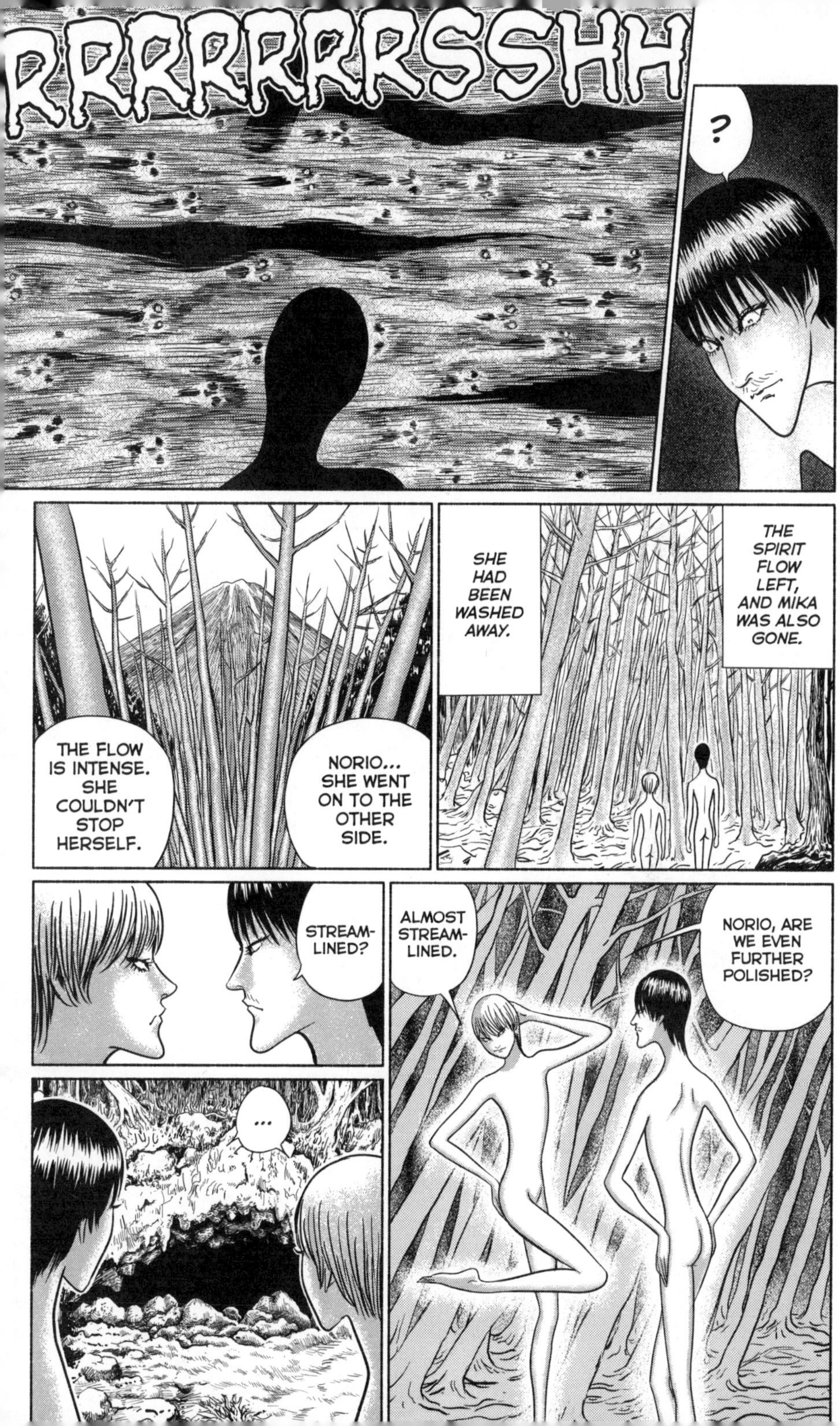
?
RRRRRRRSSHH
THE SPIRIT FLOW LEFT, AND MIKA WAS ALSO GONE.
SHE HAD BEEN WASHED AWAY.
NORIO... SHE WENT ON TO THE OTHER SIDE.
THE FLOW IS INTENSE. SHE COULDN'T STOP HERSELF.
NORIO, ARE WE EVEN FURTHER POLISHED?
ALMOST STREAM-LINED.
STREAM-LINED?
...

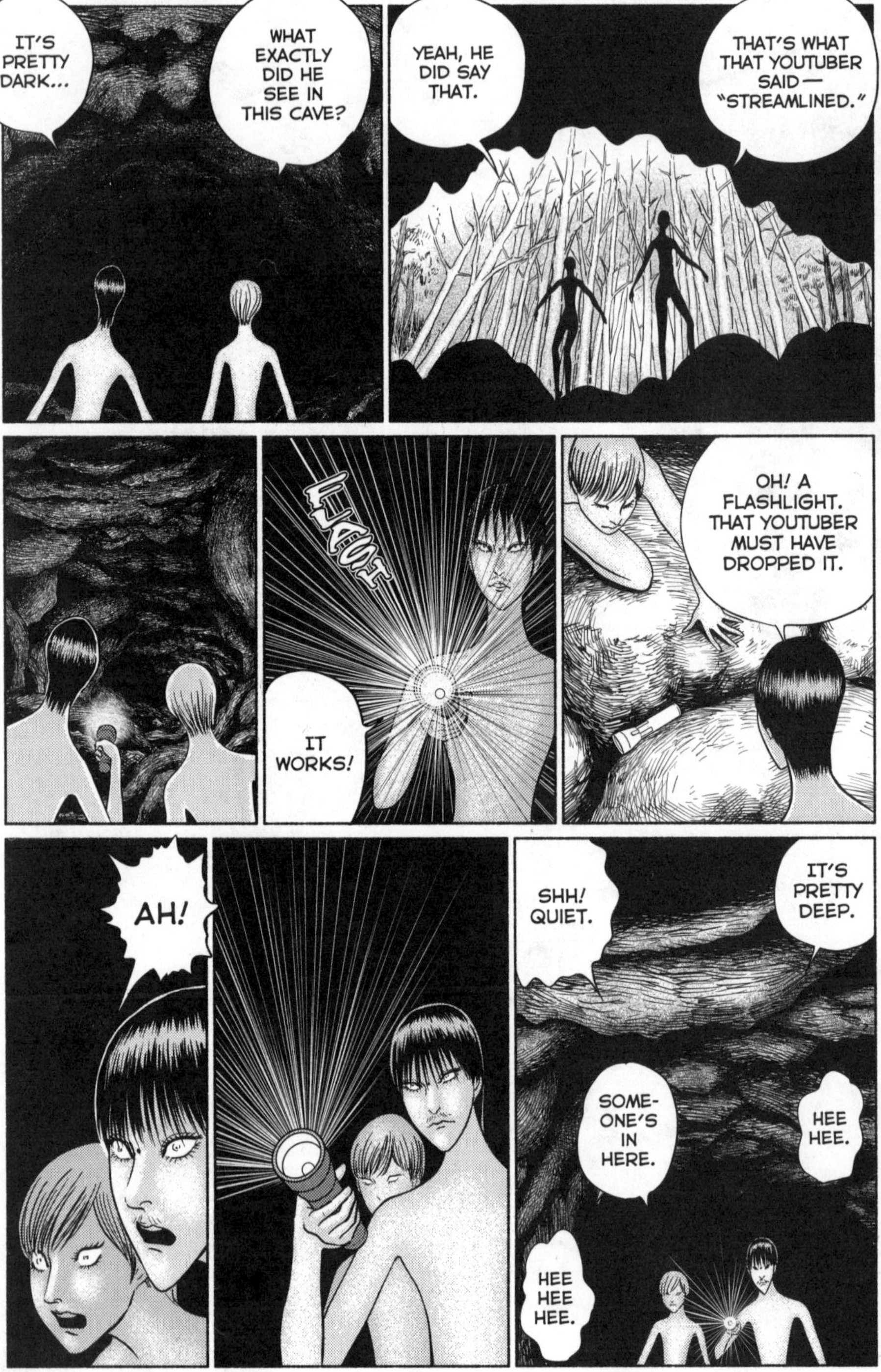
THAT'S WHAT THAT YOUTUBER SAID—"STREAMLINED."
YEAH, HE DID SAY THAT.
WHAT EXACTLY DID HE SEE IN THIS CAVE?
IT'S PRETTY DARK...
OH! A FLASHLIGHT. THAT YOUTUBER MUST HAVE DROPPED IT.
FLASH
IT WORKS!
IT'S PRETTY DEEP.
SHH! QUIET.
HEE HEE.
SOME-ONE'S IN HERE.
HEE HEE HEE.
AH!

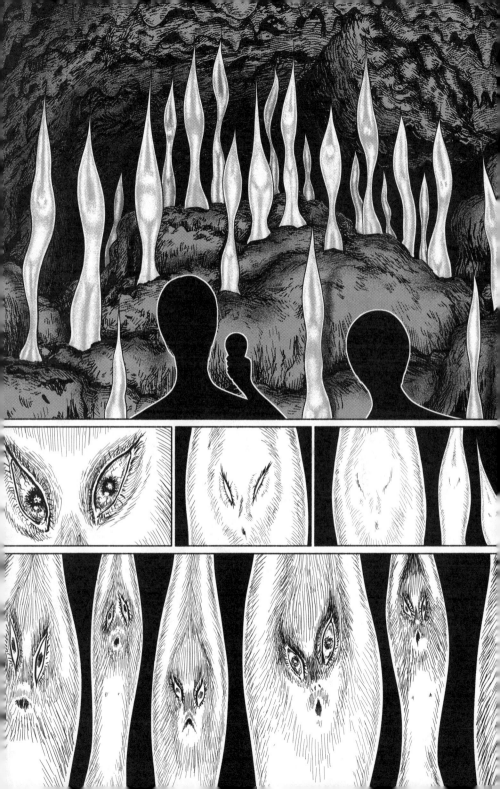

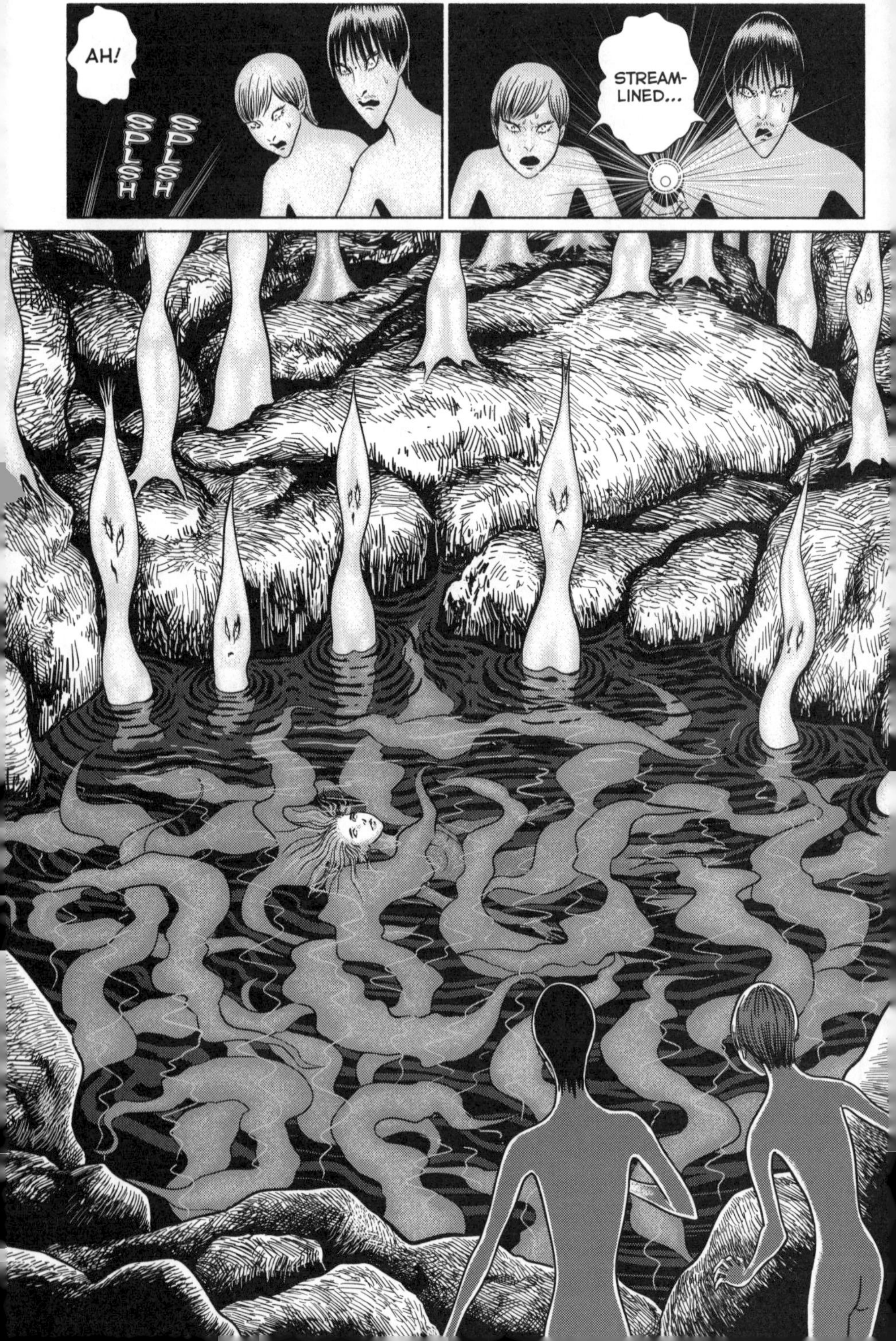
STREAM-LINED...
AH!
SPLSH SPLSH

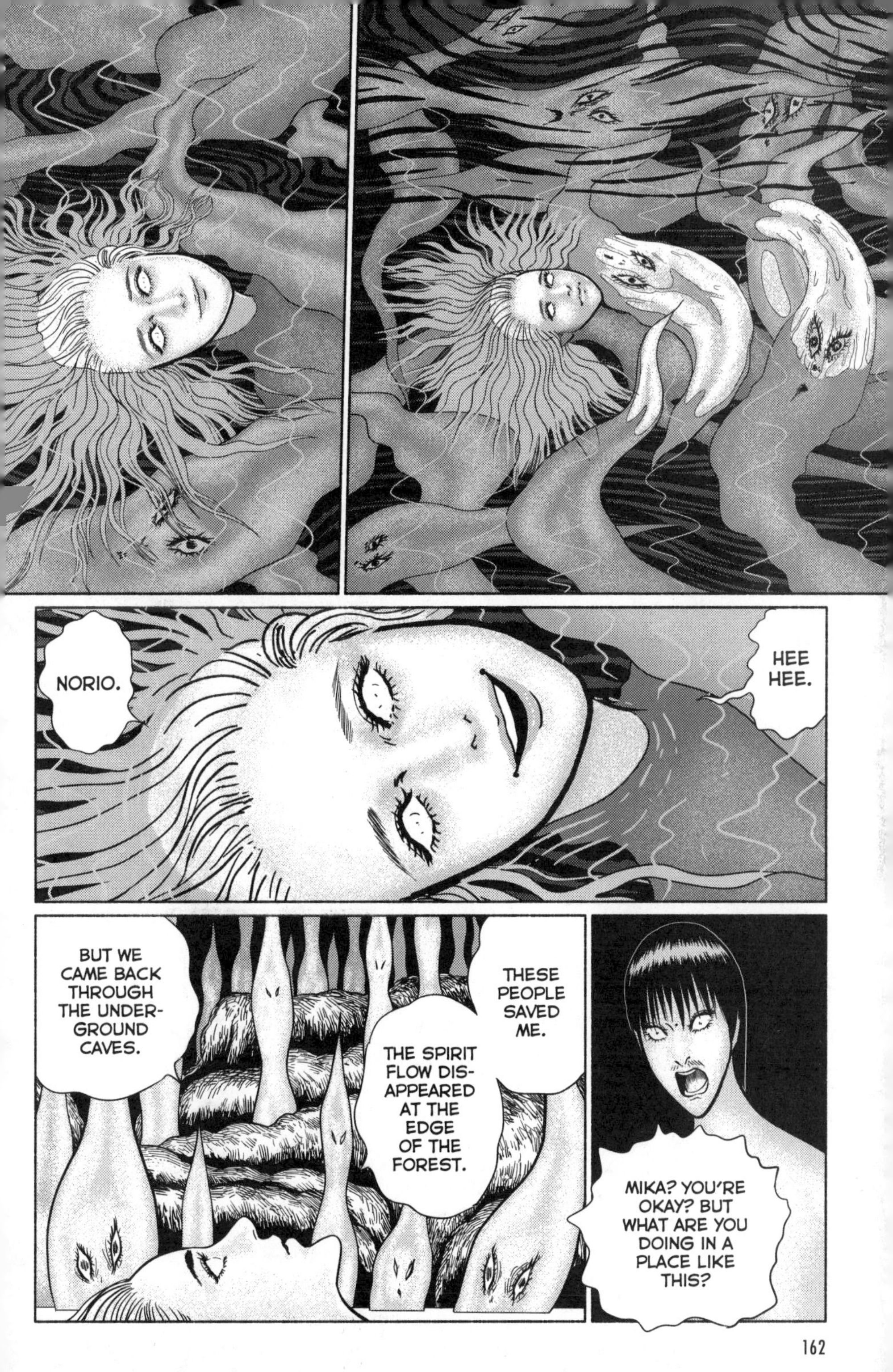
HEE HEE.
NORIO.
MIKA? YOU'RE OKAY? BUT WHAT ARE YOU DOING IN A PLACE LIKE THIS?
THESE PEOPLE SAVED ME.
THE SPIRIT FLOW DIS-APPEARED AT THE EDGE OF THE FOREST.
BUT WE CAME BACK THROUGH THE UNDER-GROUND CAVES.

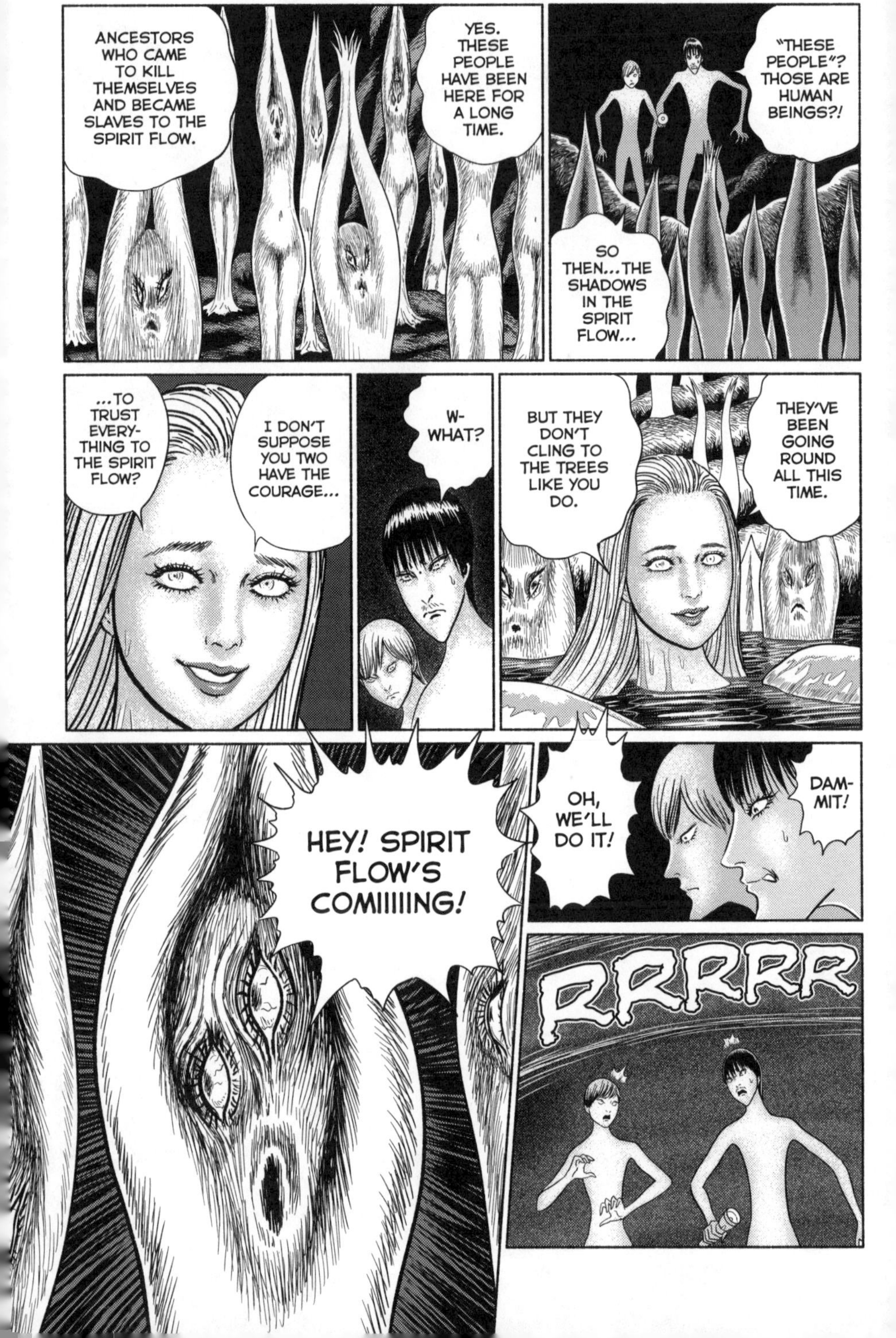
"THESE PEOPLE"? THOSE ARE HUMAN BEINGS?!
SO THEN...THE SHADOWS IN THE SPIRIT FLOW...
YES. THESE PEOPLE HAVE BEEN HERE FOR A LONG TIME.
ANCESTORS WHO CAME TO KILL THEMSELVES AND BECAME SLAVES TO THE SPIRIT FLOW.
THEY'VE BEEN GOING ROUND ALL THIS TIME.
BUT THEY DON'T CLING TO THE TREES LIKE YOU DO.
W-WHAT?
I DON'T SUPPOSE YOU TWO HAVE THE COURAGE...
...TO TRUST EVERYTHING TO THE SPIRIT FLOW?
DAMMIT!
OH, WE'LL DO IT!
RRRRR
HEY! SPIRIT FLOW'S COMIIIIING!

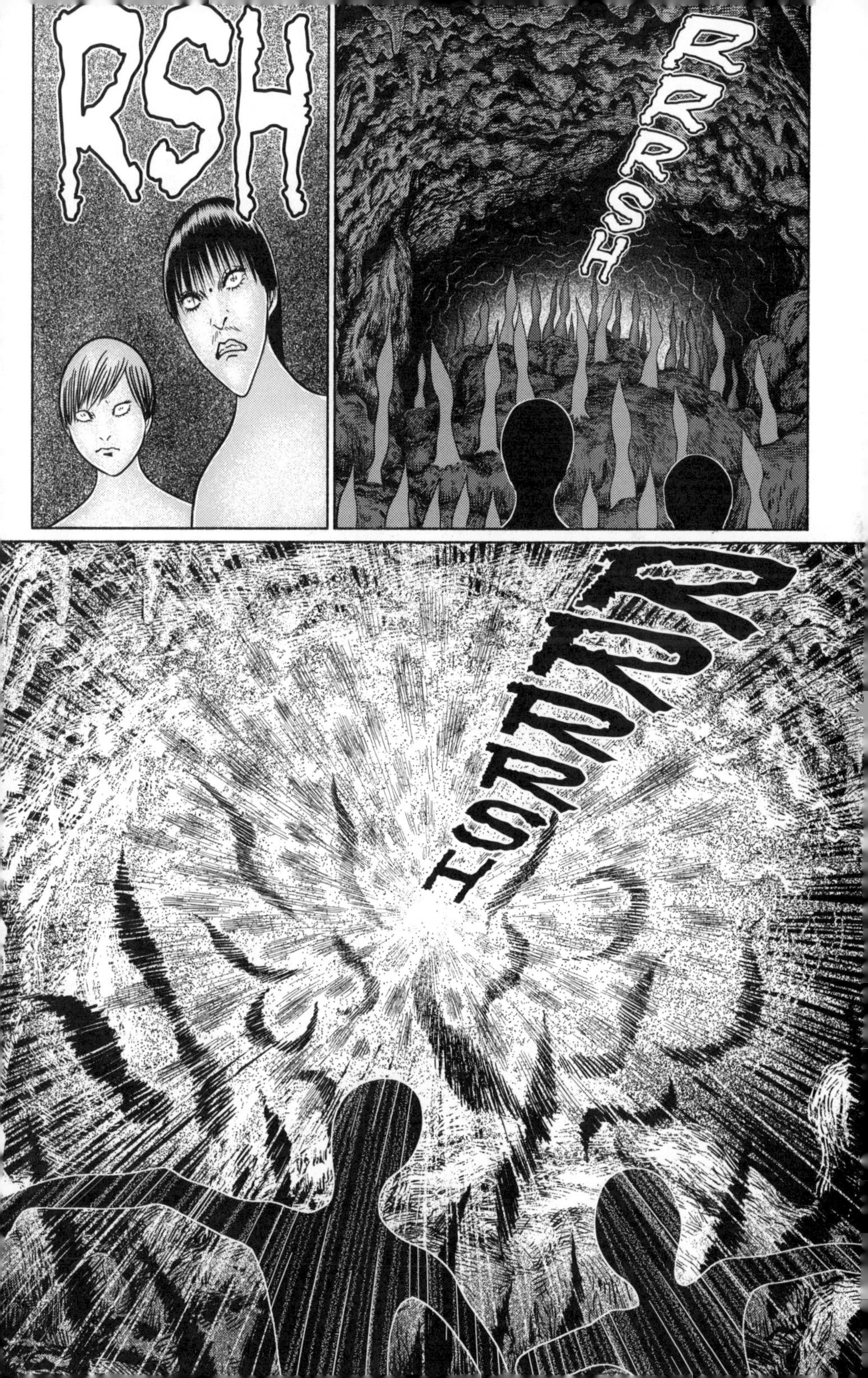
RRRSH
RSH
RRRRSH

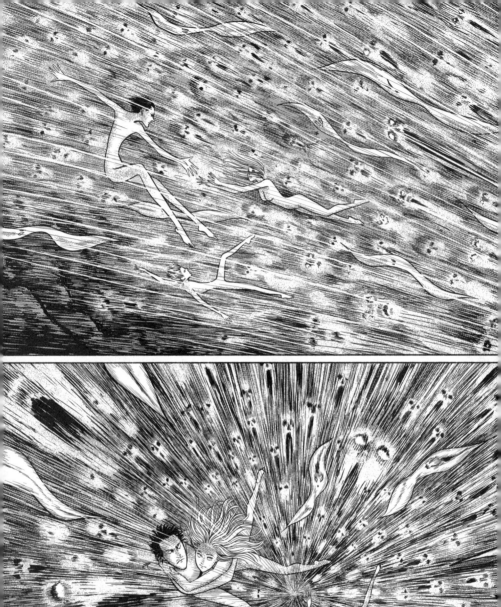
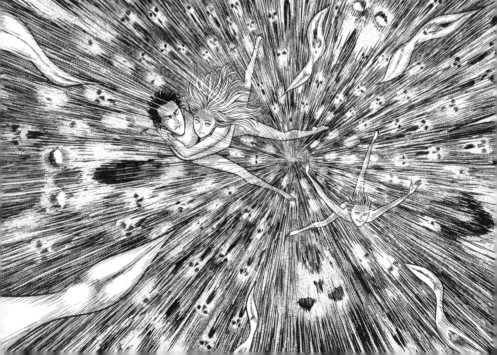

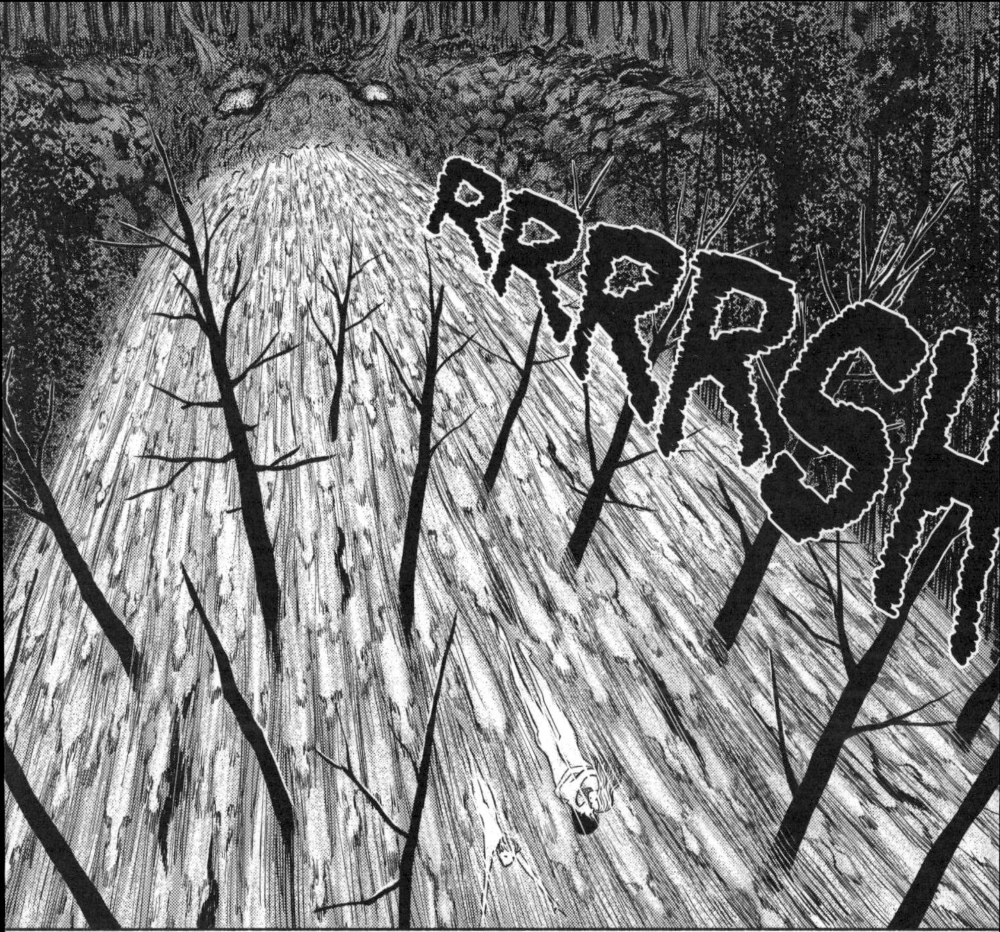
RRRRRSHH

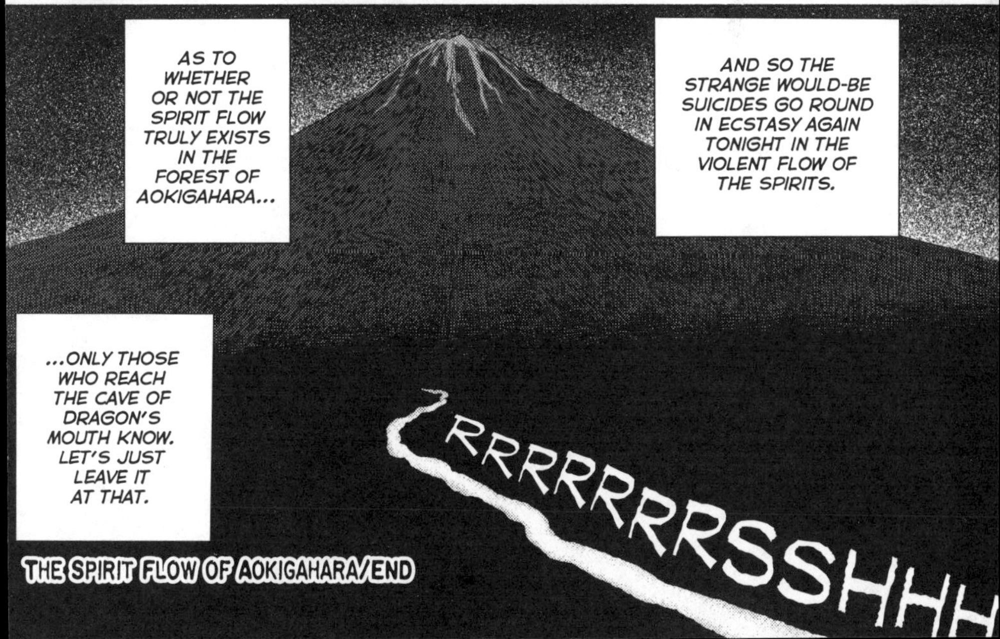
AND SO THE STRANGE WOULD-BE SUICIDES GO ROUND IN ECSTASY AGAIN TONIGHT IN THE VIOLENT FLOW OF THE SPIRITS.
AS TO WHETHER OR NOT THE SPIRIT FLOW TRULY EXISTS IN THE FOREST OF AOKIGAHARA...
...ONLY THOSE WHO REACH THE CAVE OF DRAGON'S MOUTH KNOW. LET'S JUST LEAVE IT AT THAT.
RRRRRRRRSSHHH
THE SPIRIT FLOW OF AOKIGAHARA/END

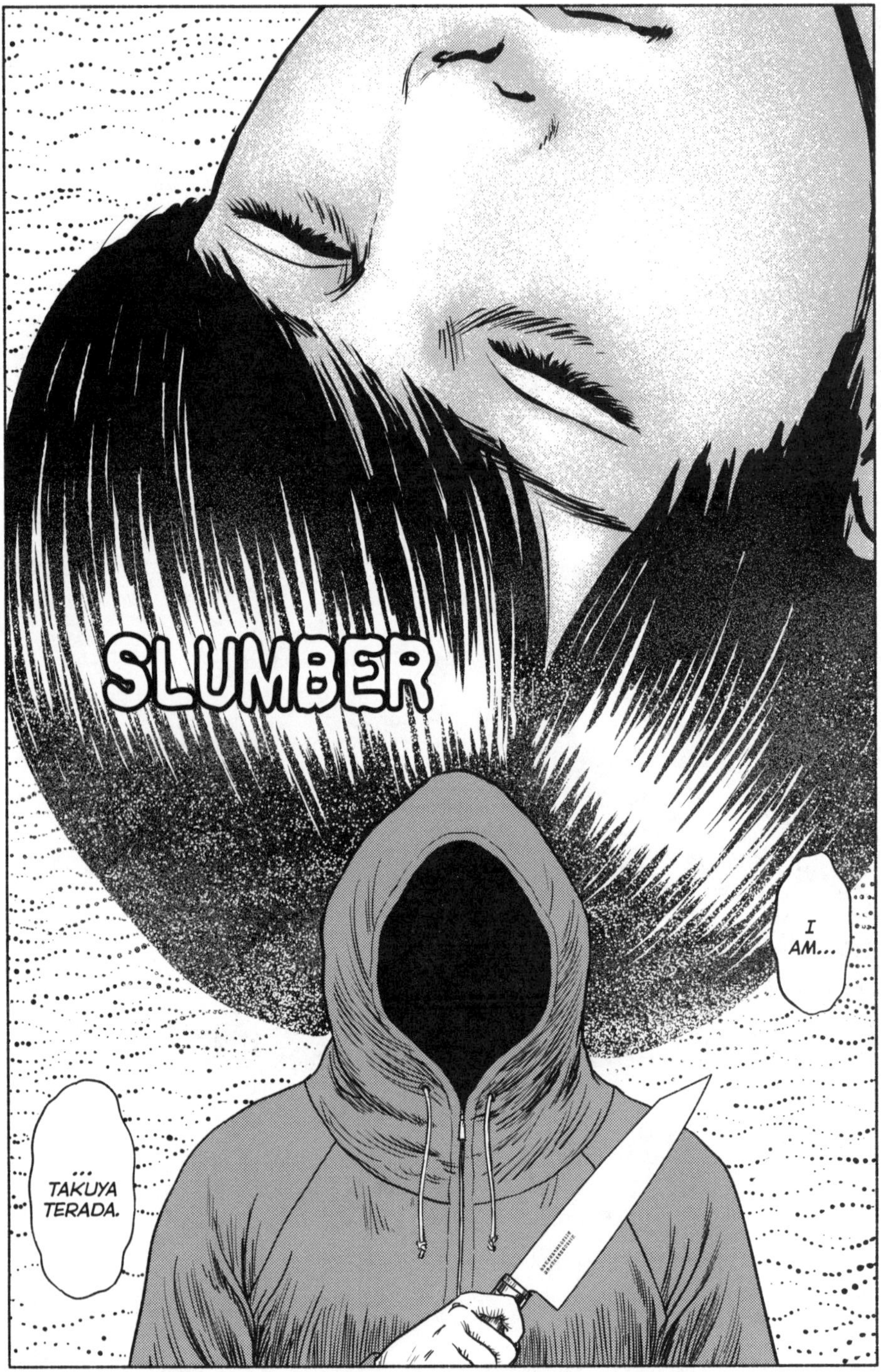
SLUMBER
I AM...
...TAKUYA TERADA.

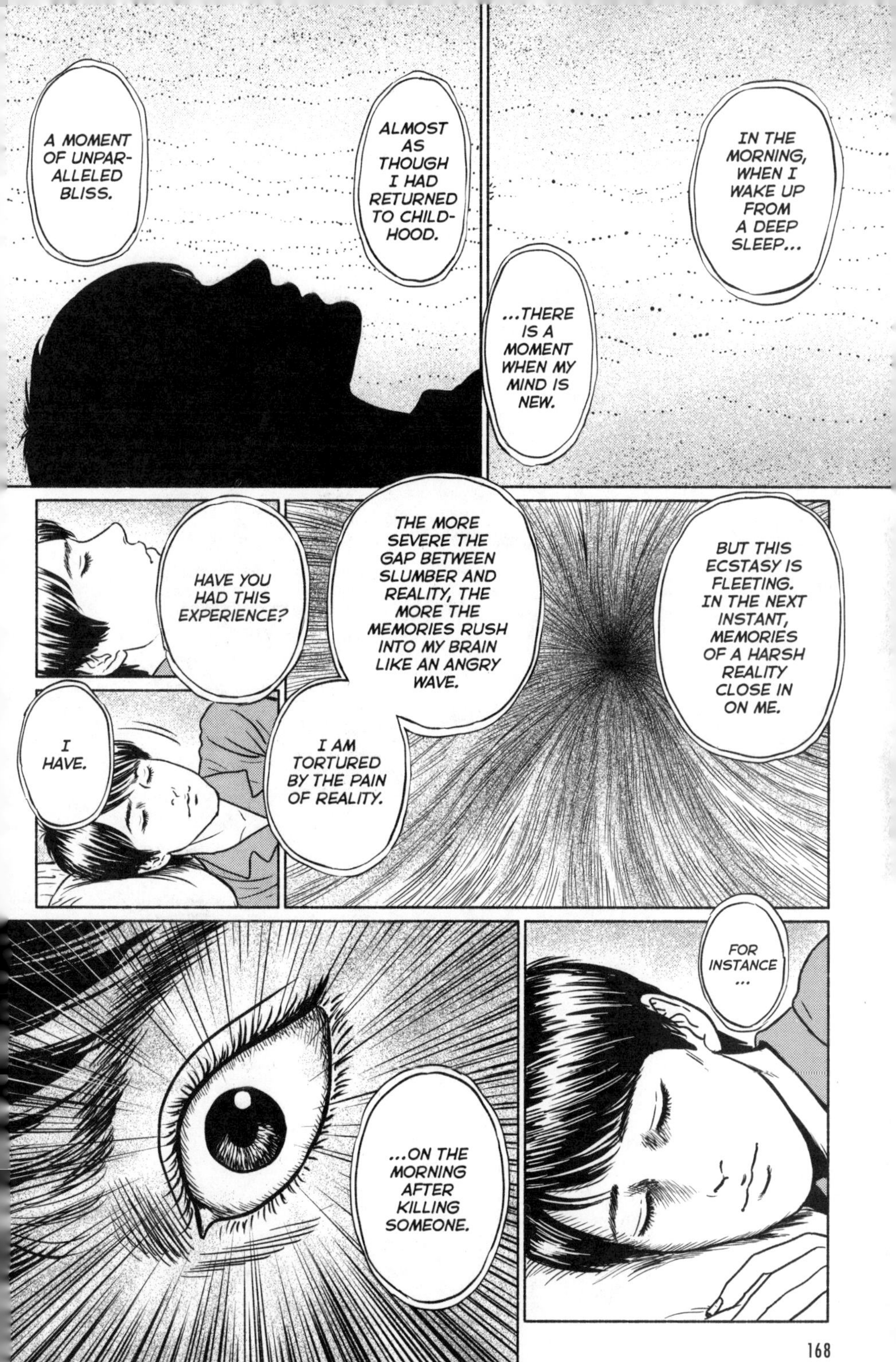
IN THE MORNING, WHEN I WAKE UP FROM A DEEP SLEEP...
...THERE IS A MOMENT WHEN MY MIND IS NEW.
ALMOST AS THOUGH I HAD RETURNED TO CHILD-HOOD.
A MOMENT OF UNPAR-ALLELED BLISS.
BUT THIS ECSTASY IS FLEETING. IN THE NEXT INSTANT, MEMORIES OF A HARSH REALITY CLOSE IN ON ME.
THE MORE SEVERE THE GAP BETWEEN SLUMBER AND REALITY, THE MORE THE MEMORIES RUSH INTO MY BRAIN LIKE AN ANGRY WAVE.
I AM TORTURED BY THE PAIN OF REALITY.
HAVE YOU HAD THIS EXPERIENCE?
I HAVE.
FOR INSTANCE ...
...ON THE MORNING AFTER KILLING SOMEONE.

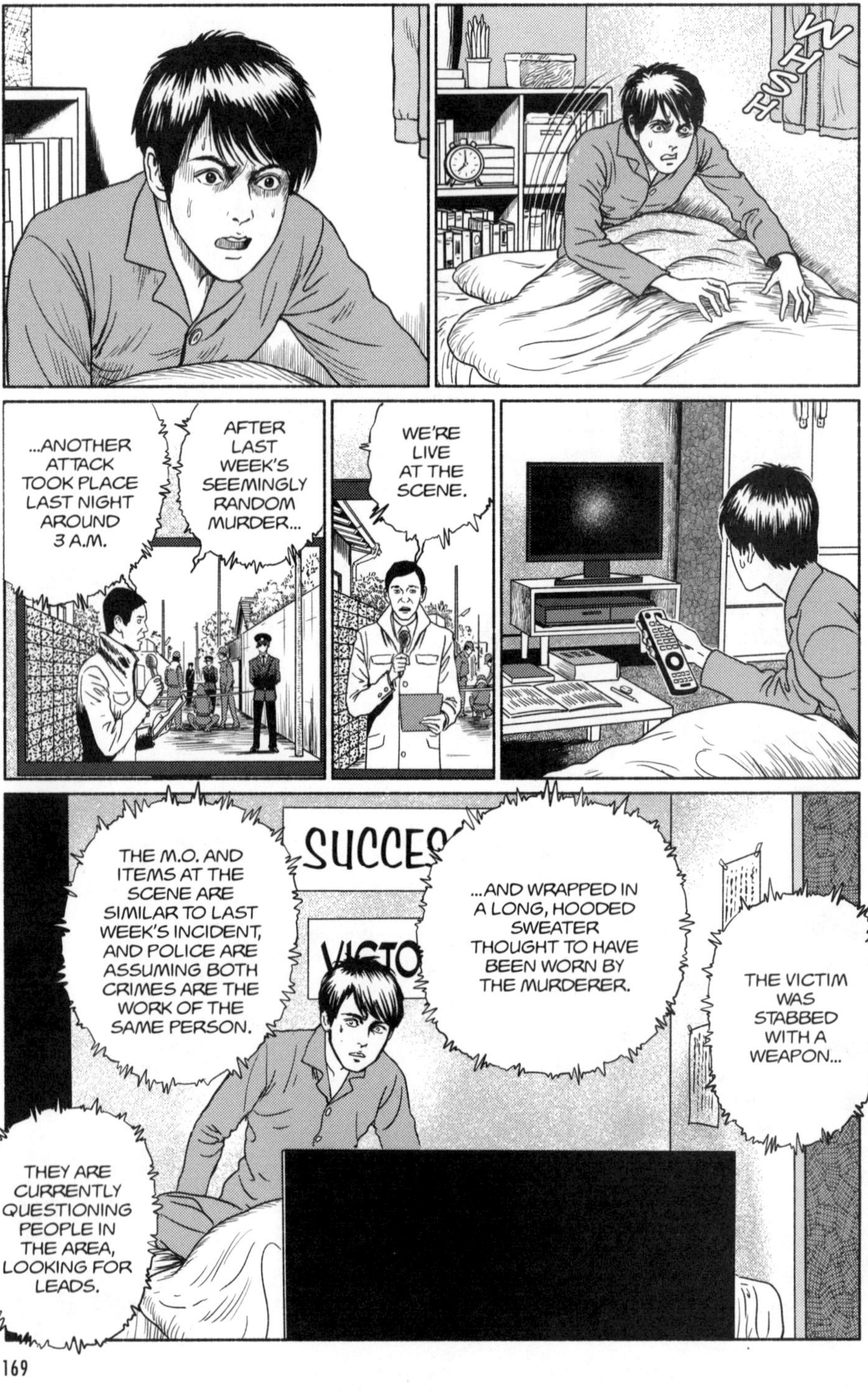
WHSH
WE'RE LIVE AT THE SCENE.
AFTER LAST WEEK'S SEEMINGLY RANDOM MURDER...
...ANOTHER ATTACK TOOK PLACE LAST NIGHT AROUND 3 A.M.
THE VICTIM WAS STABBED WITH A WEAPON...
...AND WRAPPED IN A LONG, HOODED SWEATER THOUGHT TO HAVE BEEN WORN BY THE MURDERER.
SUCCES
THE M.O. AND ITEMS AT THE SCENE ARE SIMILAR TO LAST WEEK'S INCIDENT, AND POLICE ARE ASSUMING BOTH CRIMES ARE THE WORK OF THE SAME PERSON.
VICTO
THEY ARE CURRENTLY QUESTIONING PEOPLE IN THE AREA, LOOKING FOR LEADS.

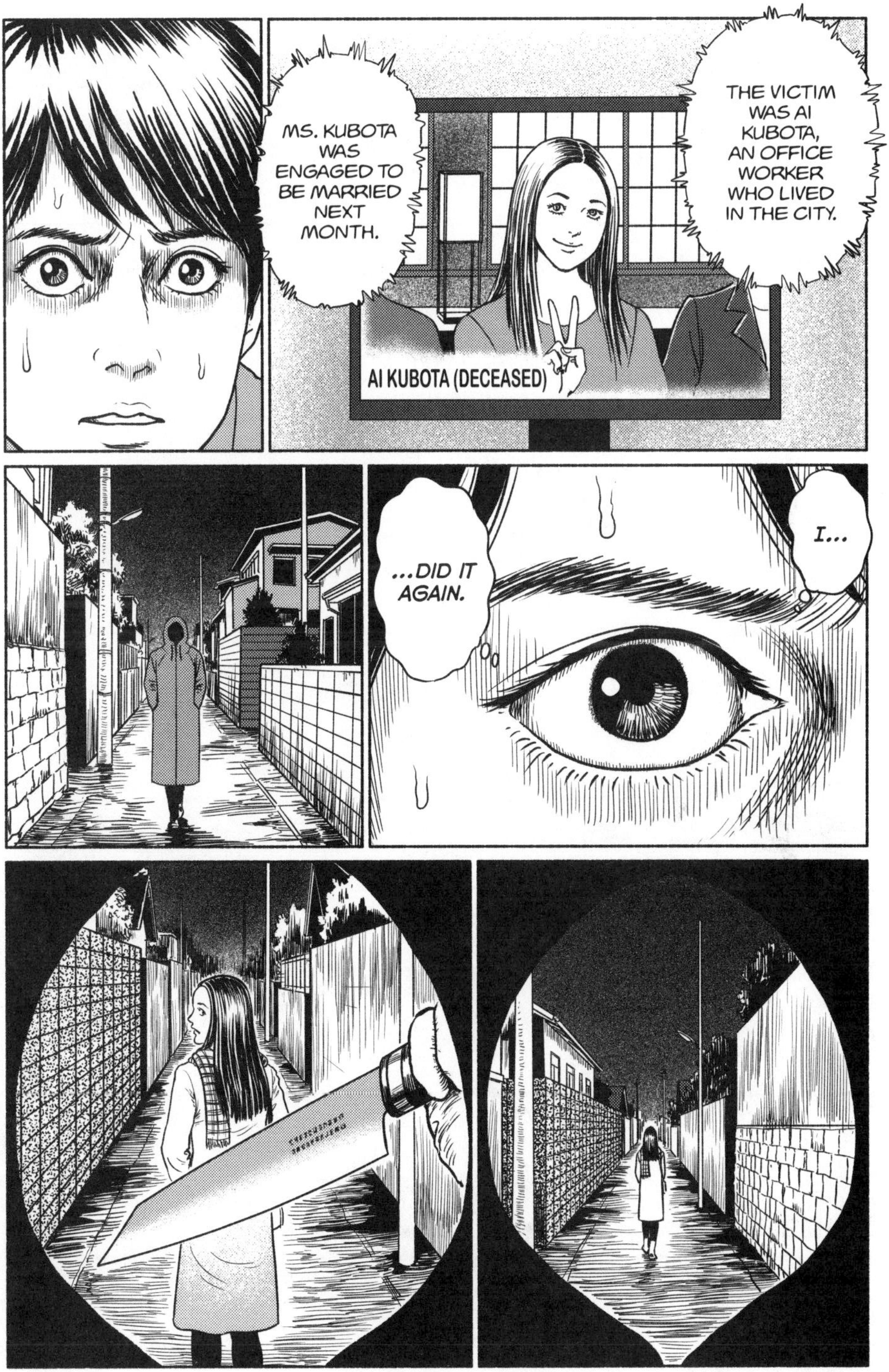
THE VICTIM WAS AI KUBOTA, AN OFFICE WORKER WHO LIVED IN THE CITY.
MS. KUBOTA WAS ENGAGED TO BE MARRIED NEXT MONTH.
AI KUBOTA (DECEASED)
I...
...DID IT AGAIN.

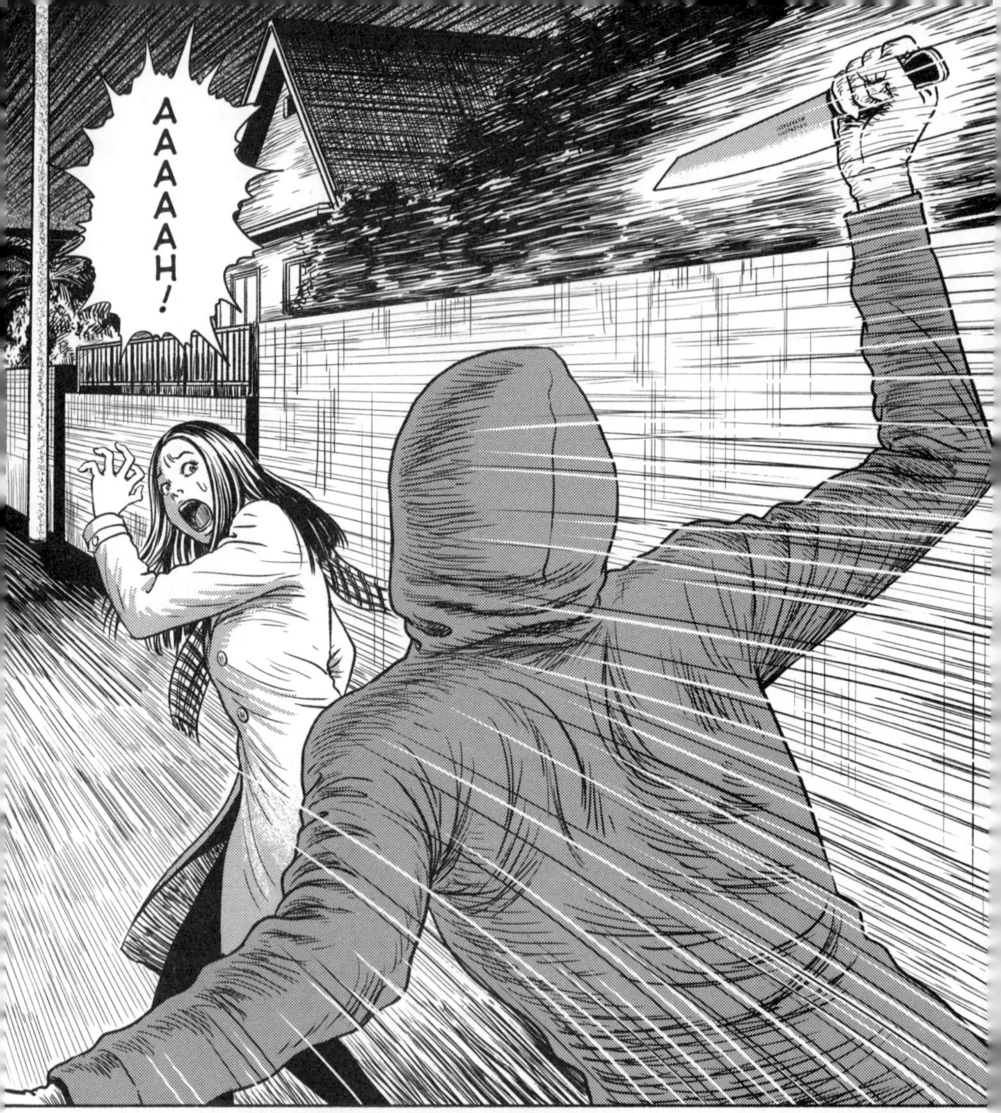
AAAAAAH!

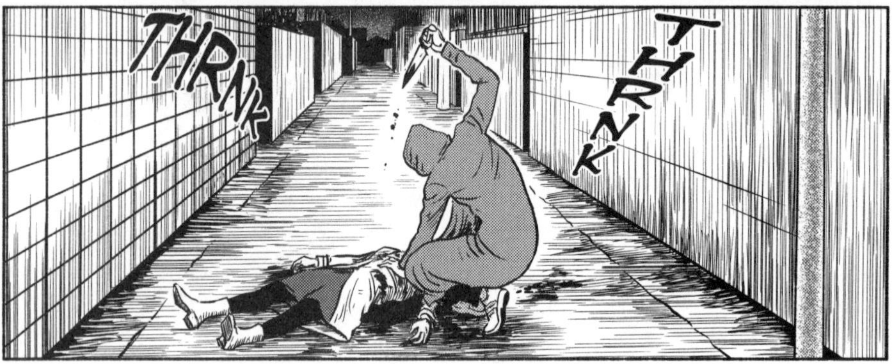
THRNK
THRNK

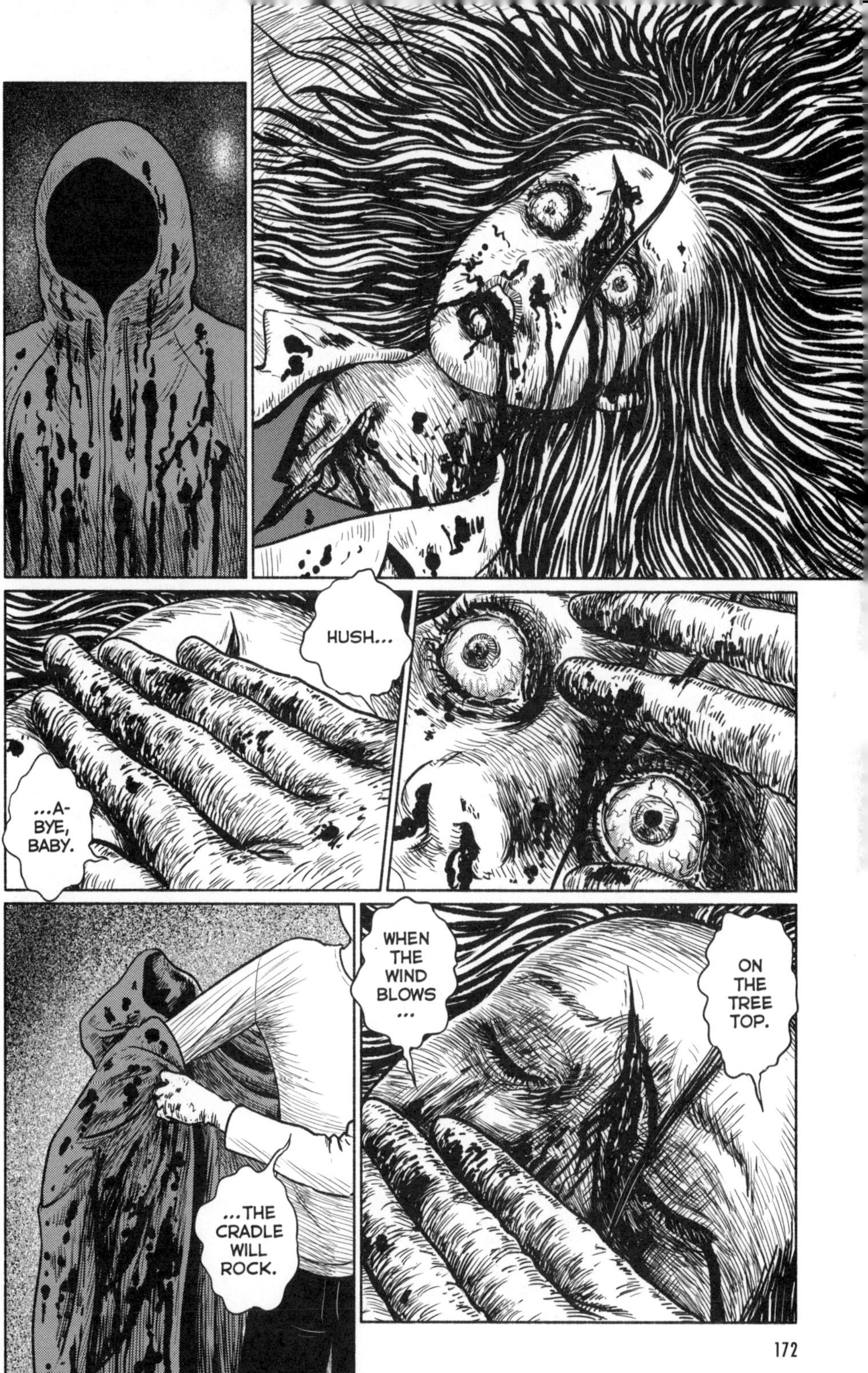
HUSH...
...A-BYE, BABY.
ON THE TREE TOP.
WHEN THE WIND BLOWS ...
...THE CRADLE WILL ROCK.

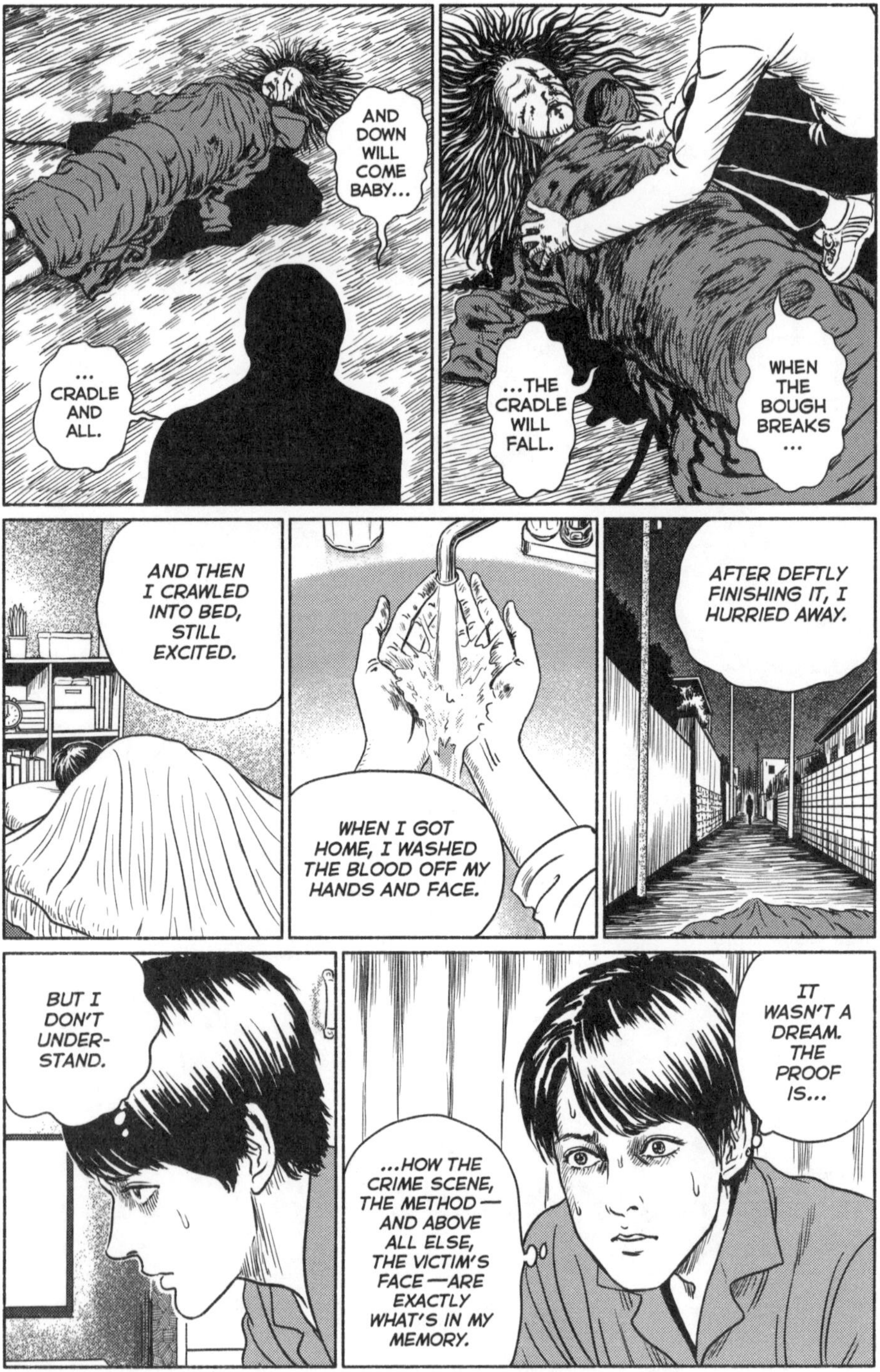
WHEN THE BOUGH BREAKS...
...THE CRADLE WILL FALL.
AND DOWN WILL COME BABY...
...CRADLE AND ALL.
AFTER DEFTLY FINISHING IT, I HURRIED AWAY.
WHEN I GOT HOME, I WASHED THE BLOOD OFF MY HANDS AND FACE.
AND THEN I CRAWLED INTO BED, STILL EXCITED.
IT WASN'T A DREAM. THE PROOF IS...
...HOW THE CRIME SCENE, THE METHOD— AND ABOVE ALL ELSE, THE VICTIM'S FACE—ARE EXACTLY WHAT'S IN MY MEMORY.
BUT I DON'T UNDERSTAND.

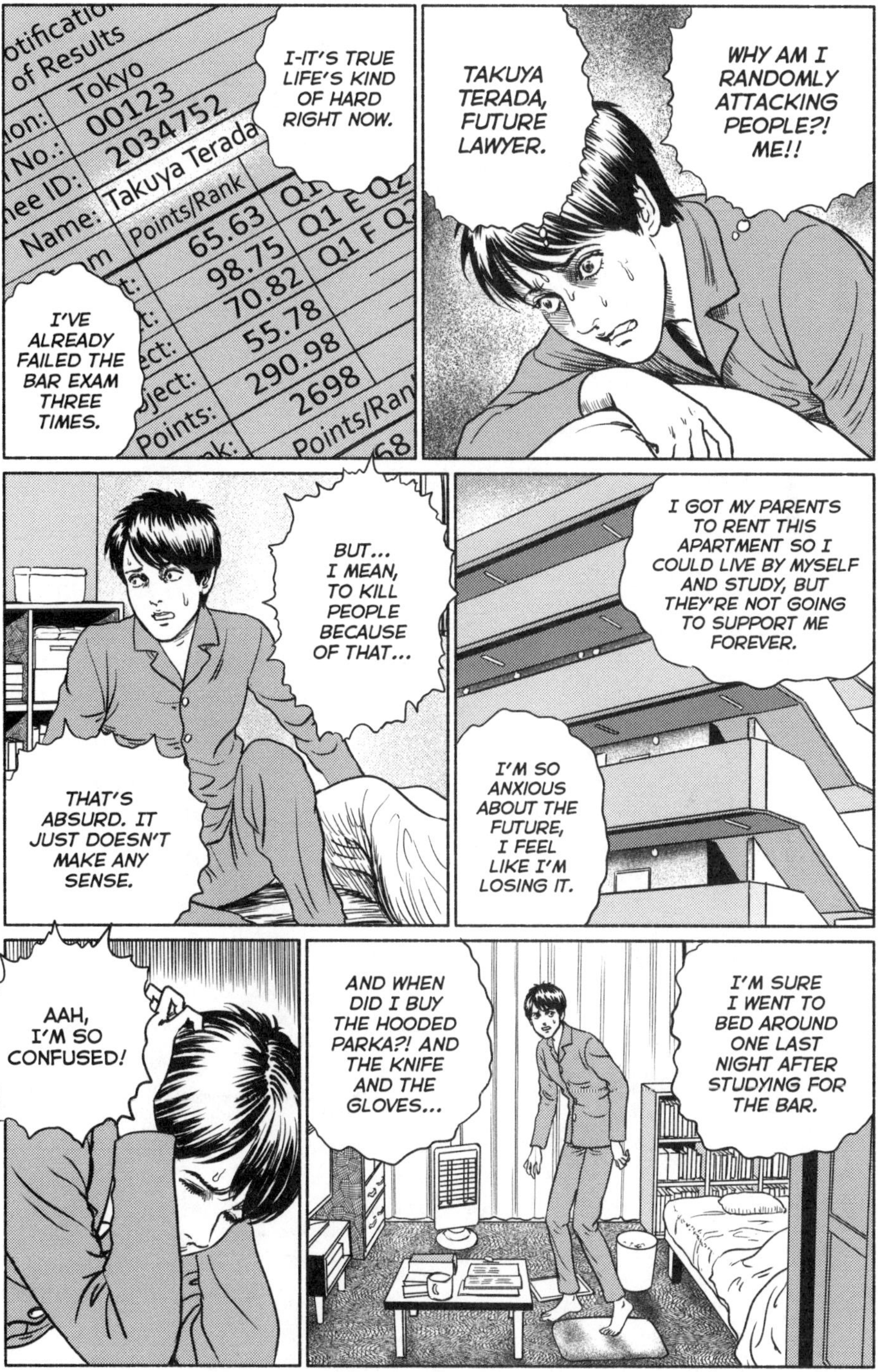
WHY AM I RANDOMLY ATTACKING PEOPLE?! ME!!
TAKUYA TERADA, FUTURE LAWYER.
I-IT'S TRUE LIFE'S KIND OF HARD RIGHT NOW.
of Results
Tokyo
00123
2034752
Name: Takuya Terada
Points/Rank
65.63
98.75
70.82
55.78
290.98
2698
Points:
I'VE ALREADY FAILED THE BAR EXAM THREE TIMES.
I GOT MY PARENTS TO RENT THIS APARTMENT SO I COULD LIVE BY MYSELF AND STUDY, BUT THEY'RE NOT GOING TO SUPPORT ME FOREVER.
I'M SO ANXIOUS ABOUT THE FUTURE, I FEEL LIKE I'M LOSING IT.
BUT... I MEAN, TO KILL PEOPLE BECAUSE OF THAT...
THAT'S ABSURD. IT JUST DOESN'T MAKE ANY SENSE.
I'M SURE I WENT TO BED AROUND ONE LAST NIGHT AFTER STUDYING FOR THE BAR.
AND WHEN DID I BUY THE HOODED PARKA?! AND THE KNIFE AND THE GLOVES...
AAH, I'M SO CONFUSED!

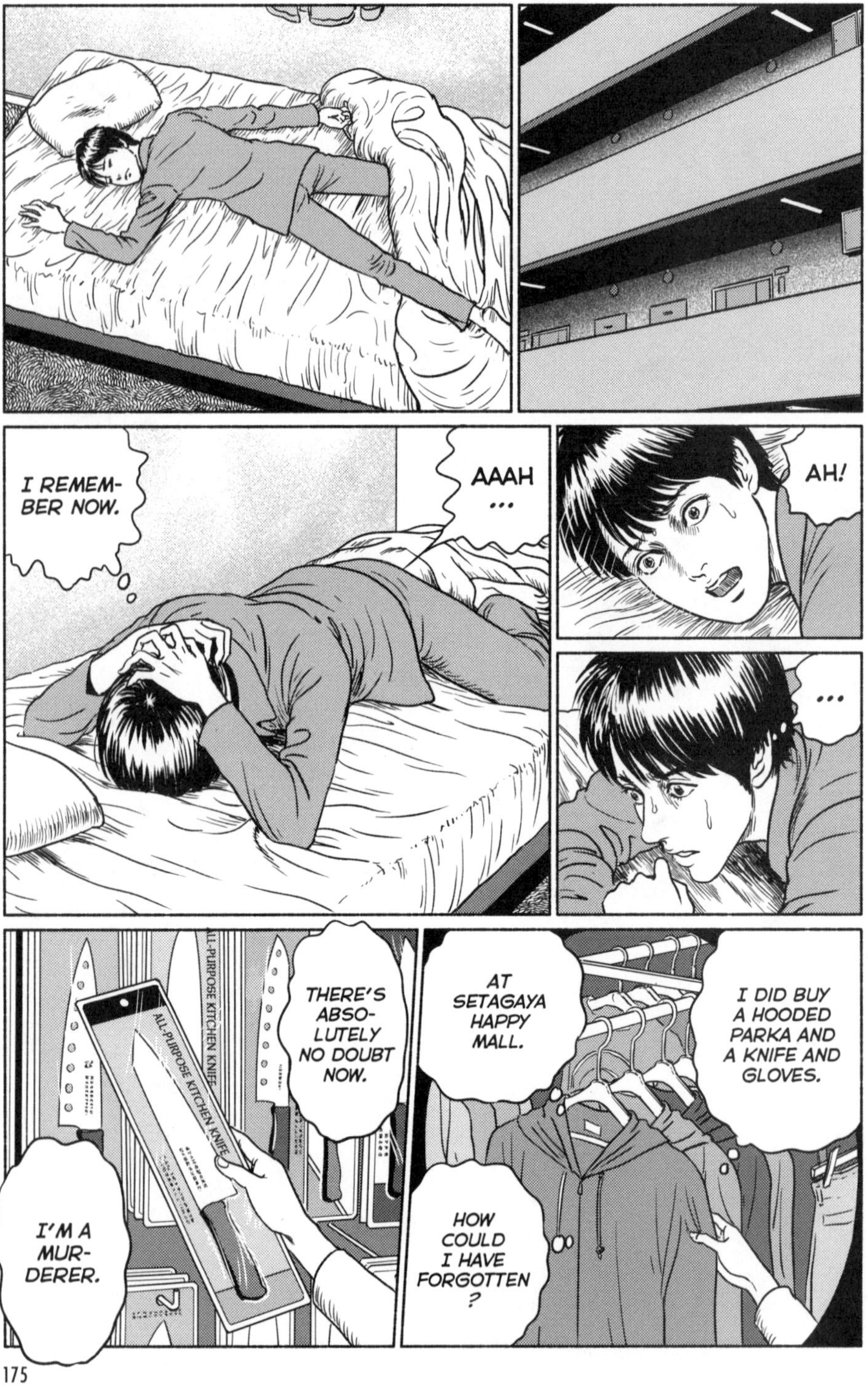
AH!
...
AAAH ...
I REMEMBER NOW.
I DID BUY A HOODED PARKA AND A KNIFE AND GLOVES.
AT SETAGAYA HAPPY MALL.
HOW COULD I HAVE FORGOTTEN?
THERE'S ABSOLUTELY NO DOUBT NOW.
ALL-PURPOSE KITCHEN KNIFE
I'M A MURDERER.

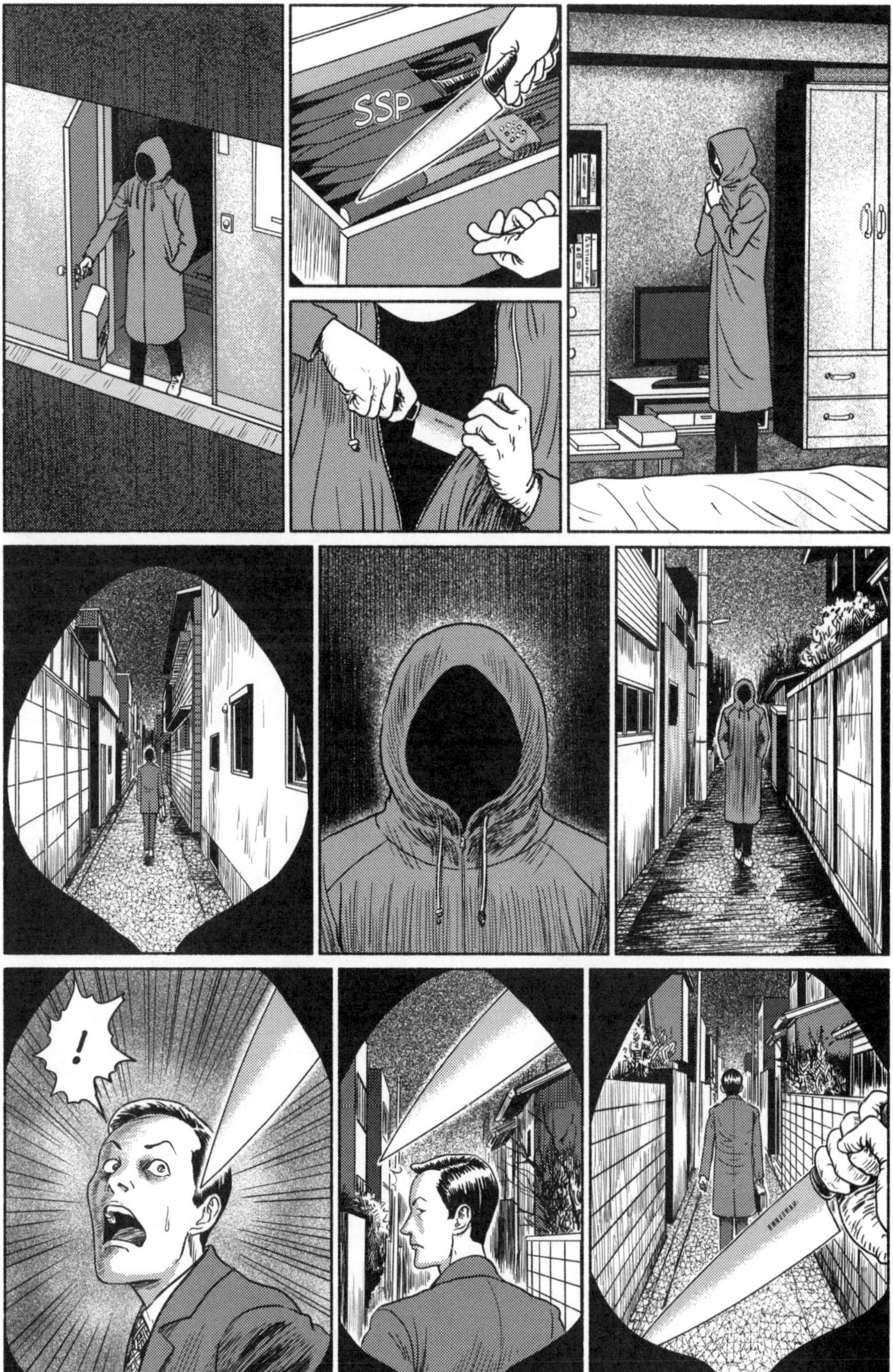
SSP
!

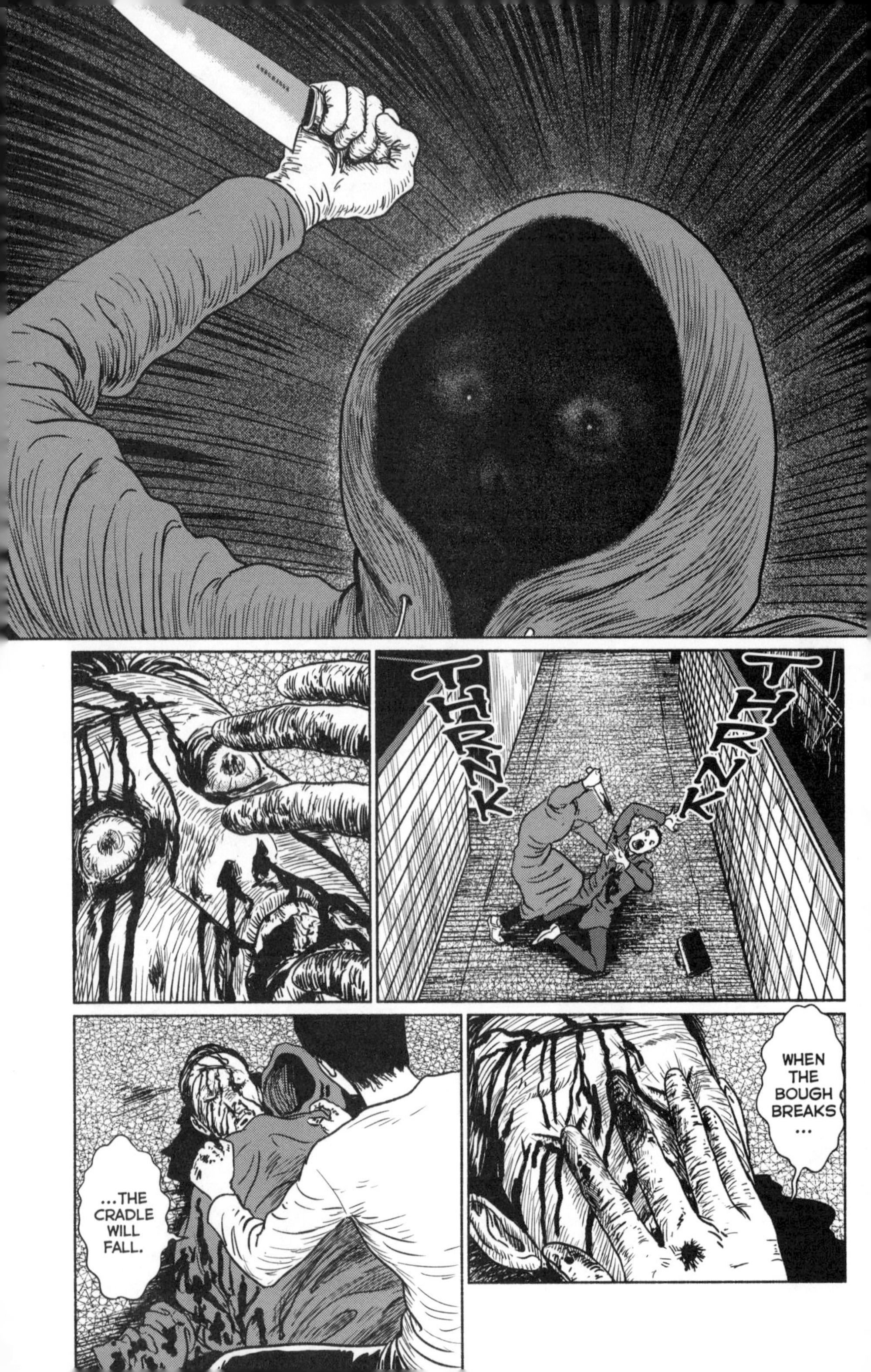
THRNK
THRNK
WHEN THE BOUGH BREAKS...
...THE CRADLE WILL FALL.

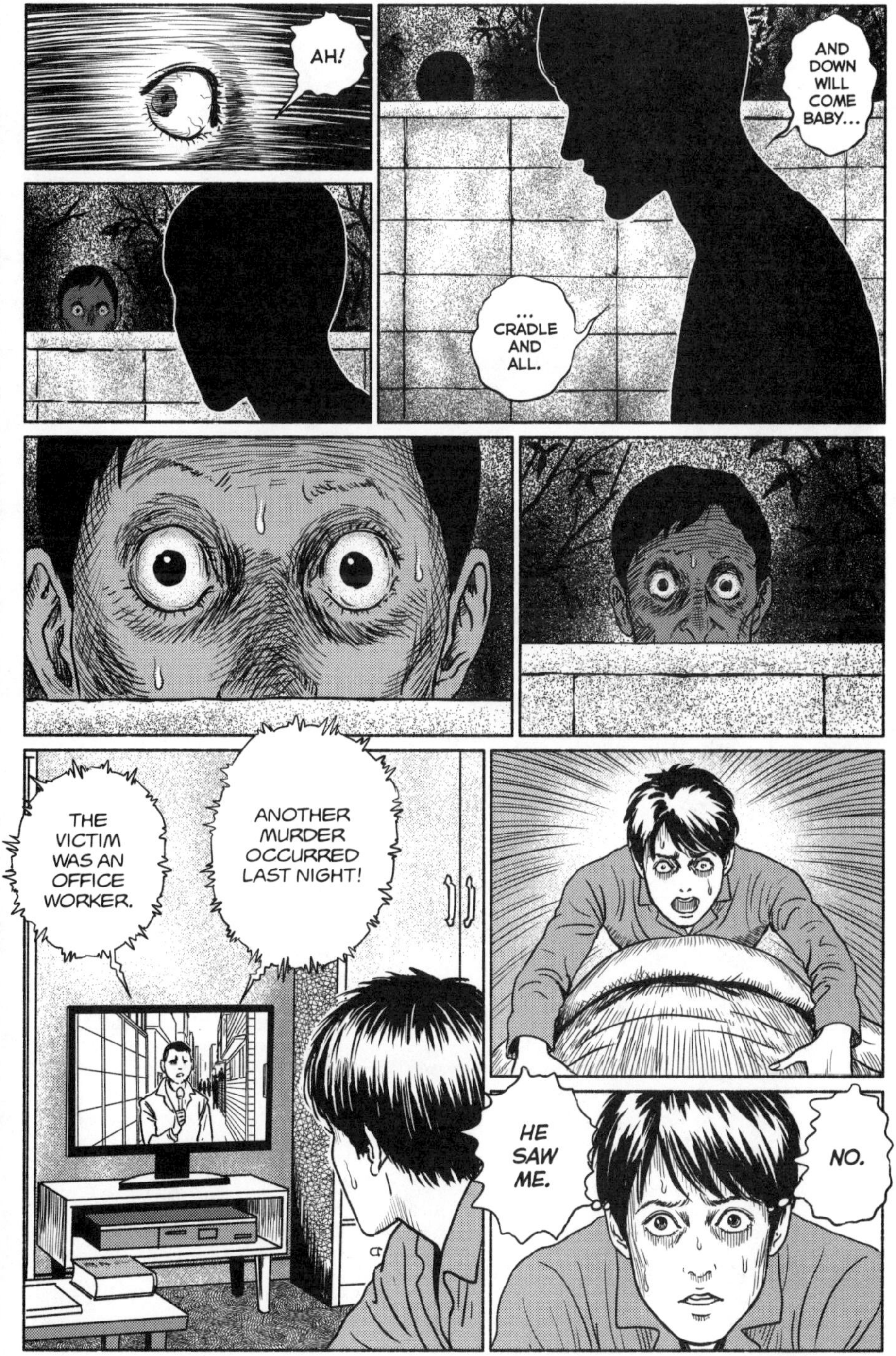
AND DOWN WILL COME BABY...
...CRADLE AND ALL.
AH!
NO.
HE SAW ME.
ANOTHER MURDER OCCURRED LAST NIGHT!
THE VICTIM WAS AN OFFICE WORKER.

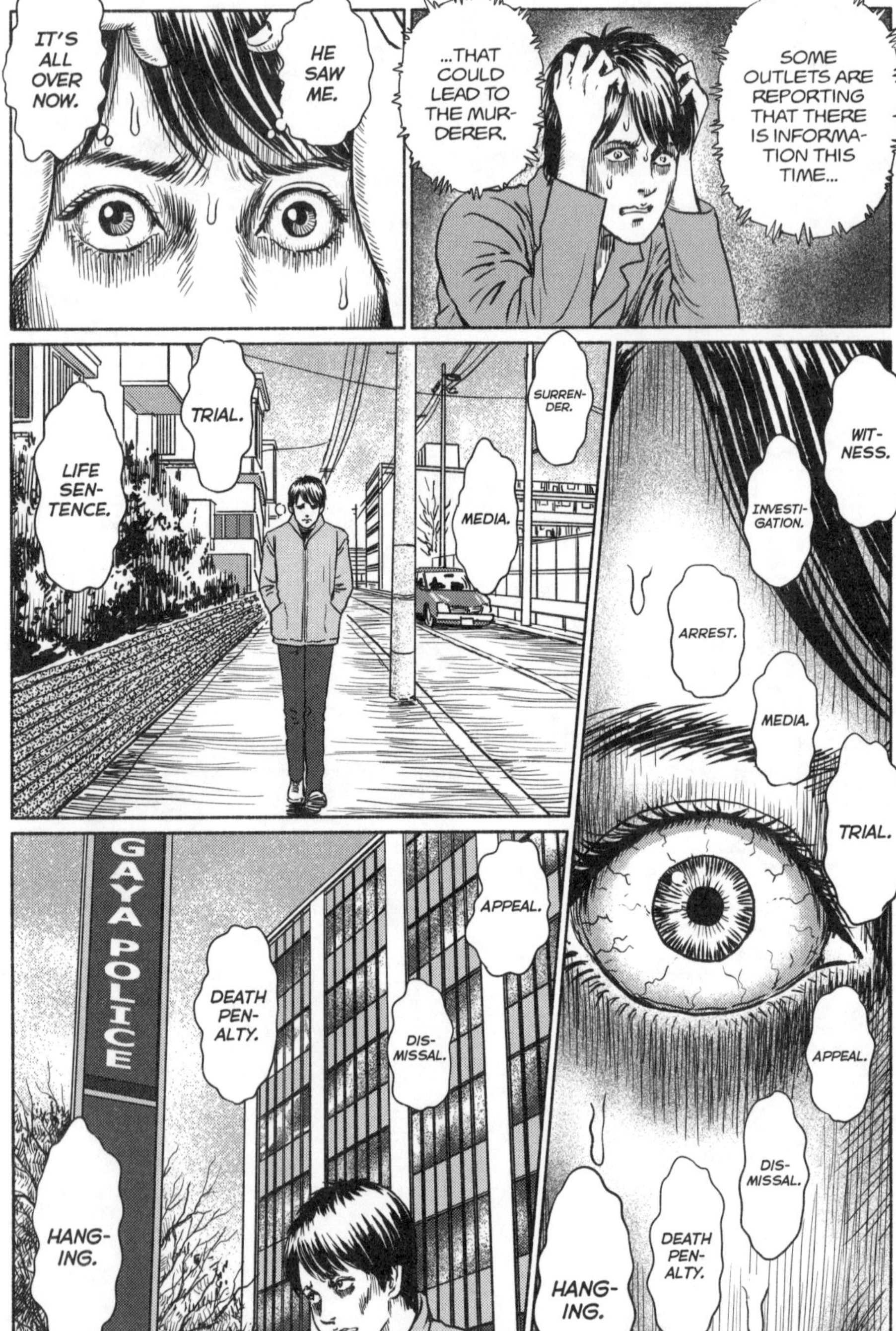
SOME OUTLETS ARE REPORTING THAT THERE IS INFORMATION THIS TIME...
...THAT COULD LEAD TO THE MUR-DERER.
HE SAW ME.
IT'S ALL OVER NOW.
WIT-NESS.
INVESTI-GATION.
ARREST.
MEDIA.
TRIAL.
APPEAL.
DIS-MISSAL.
DEATH PEN-ALTY.
HANG-ING.
SURREN-DER.
MEDIA.
TRIAL.
LIFE SEN-TENCE.
APPEAL.
GAYA POLICE
DEATH PEN-ALTY.
DIS-MISSAL.
HANG-ING.

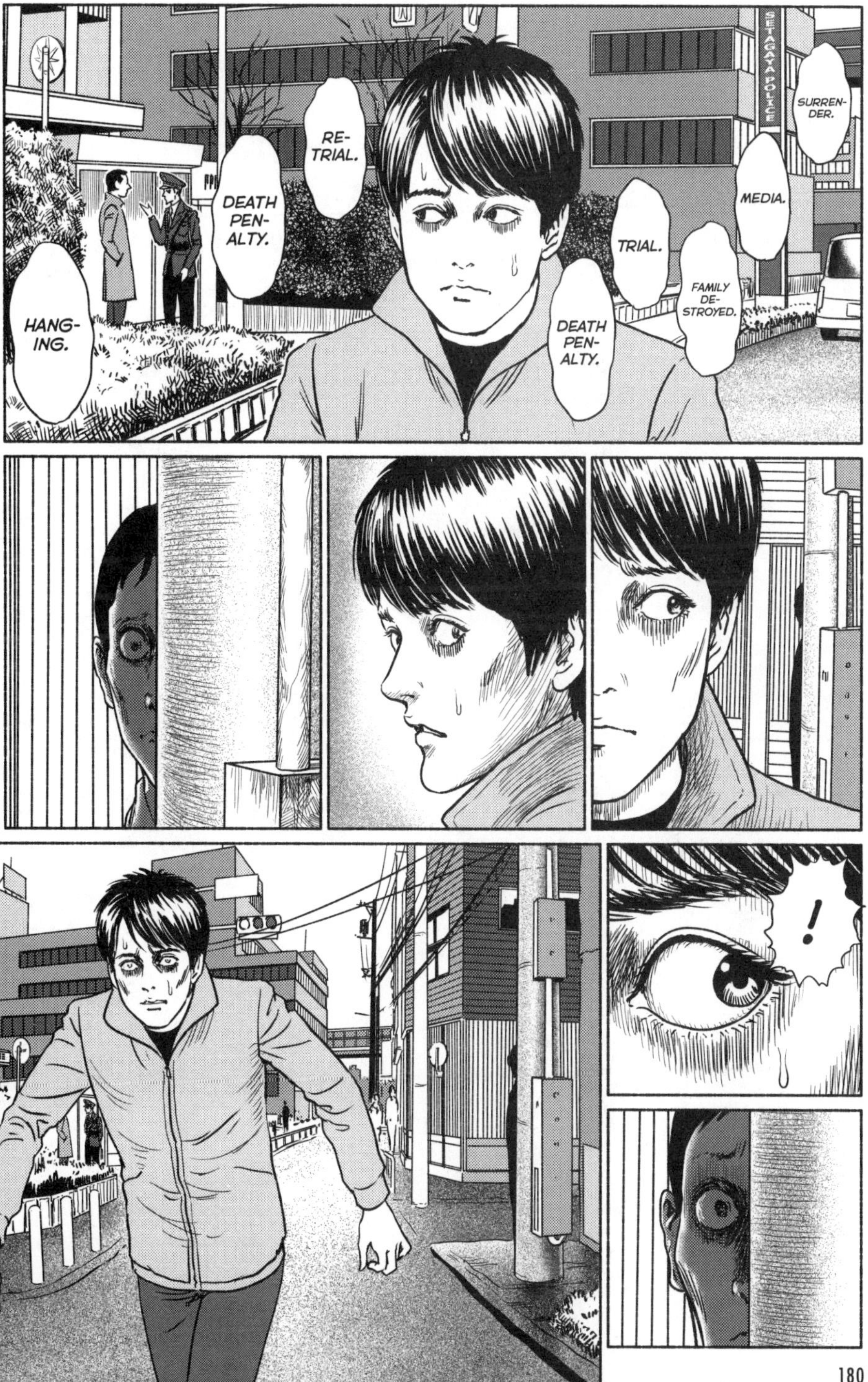
SURRENDER.
MEDIA.
TRIAL.
FAMILY DESTROYED.
DEATH PENALTY.
RETRIAL.
DEATH PENALTY.
HANGING.
!

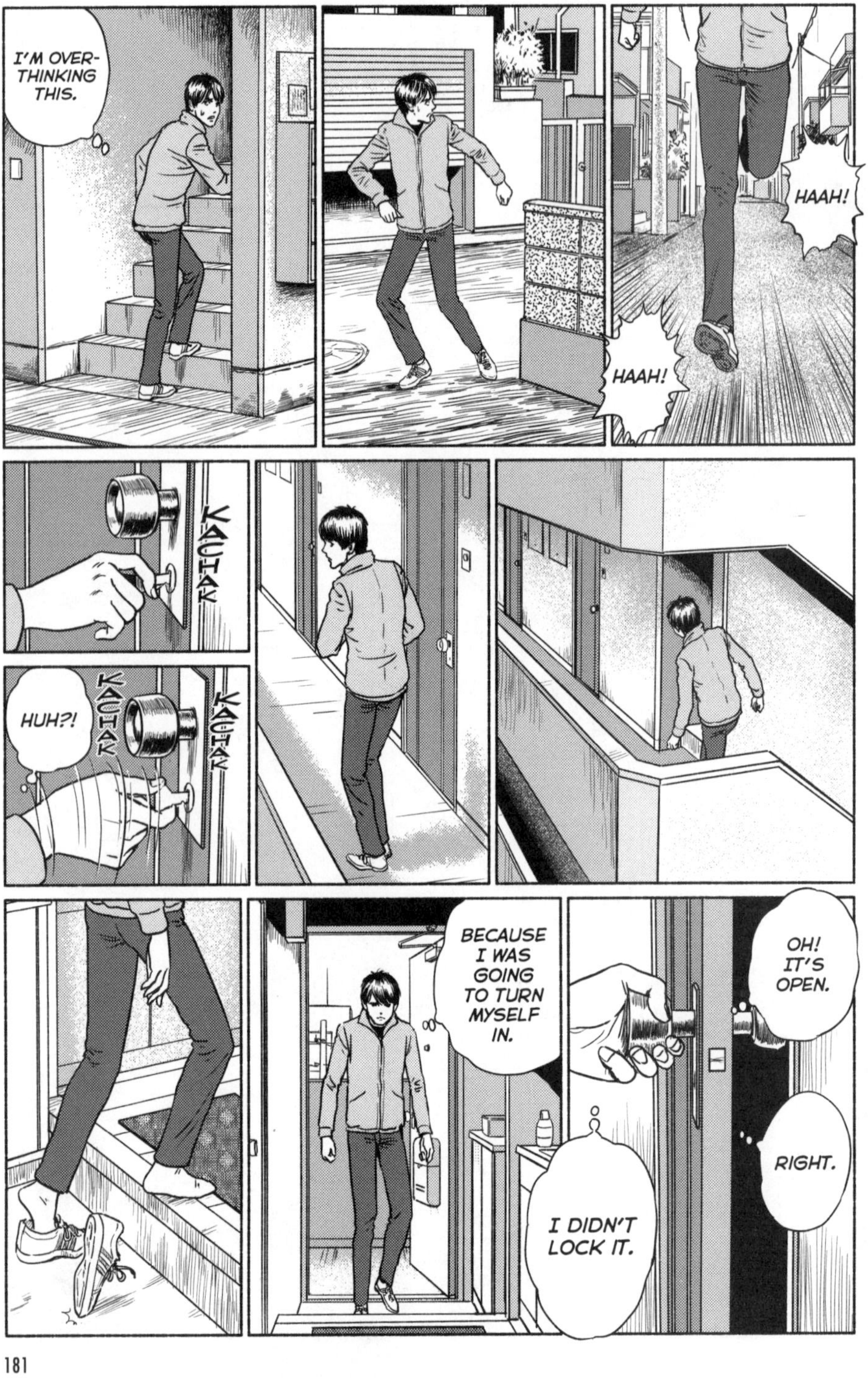
HAAH!
HAAH!
I'M OVER-THINKING THIS.
KACHAK
KACHAK
KACHAK
HUH?!
OH! IT'S OPEN.
RIGHT.
I DIDN'T LOCK IT.
BECAUSE I WAS GOING TO TURN MYSELF IN.

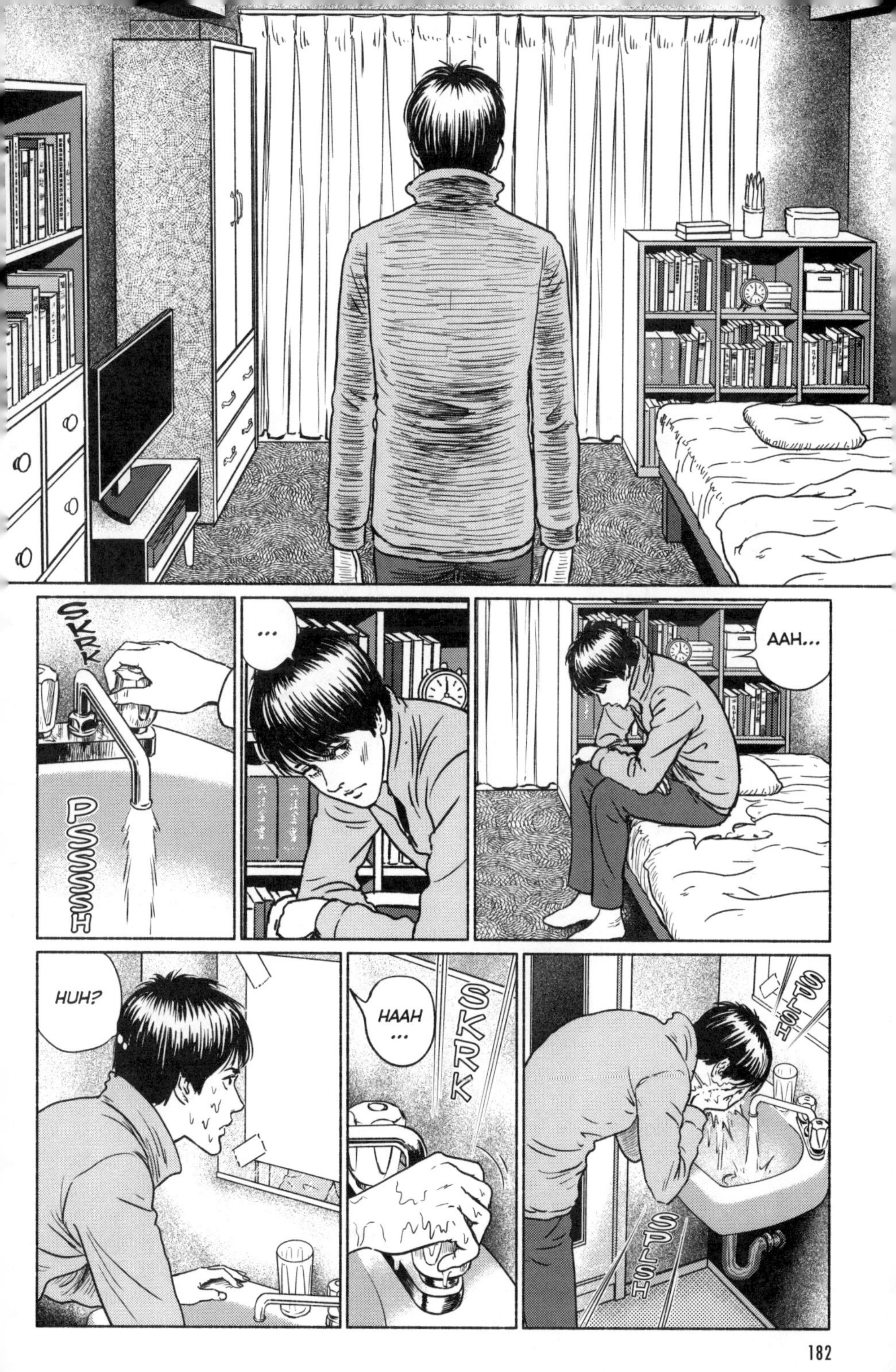
AAH...
...
SKRK
PSSSSH
SPLSH
SPLSH
HAAH ...
SKRK
HUH?

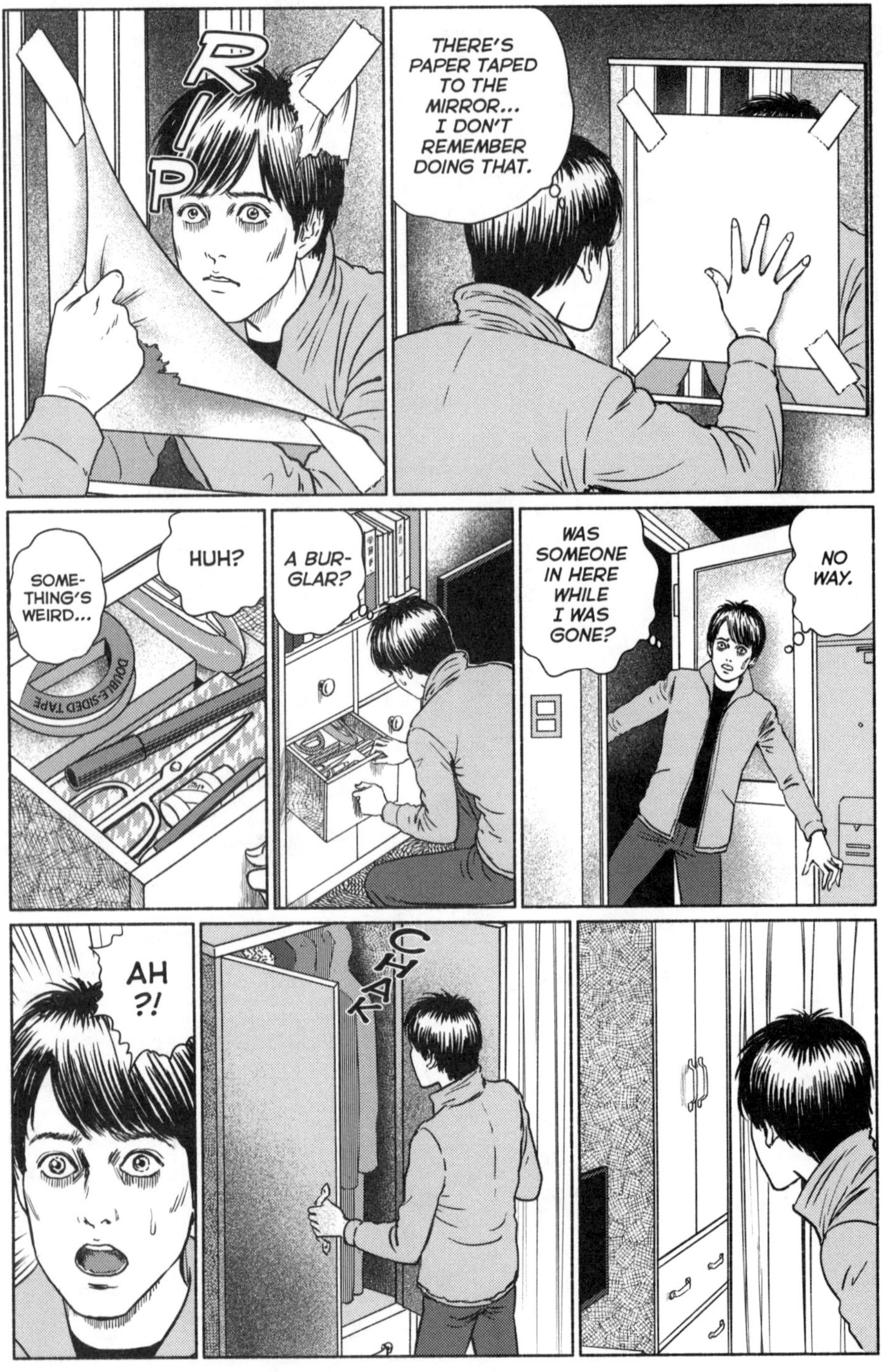
THERE'S PAPER TAPED TO THE MIRROR... I DON'T REMEMBER DOING THAT.
RIP
WAS SOMEONE IN HERE WHILE I WAS GONE?
NO WAY.
A BUR-GLAR?
HUH?
SOME-THING'S WEIRD...
DOUBLE-SIDED TAPE
CHAK
AH ?!

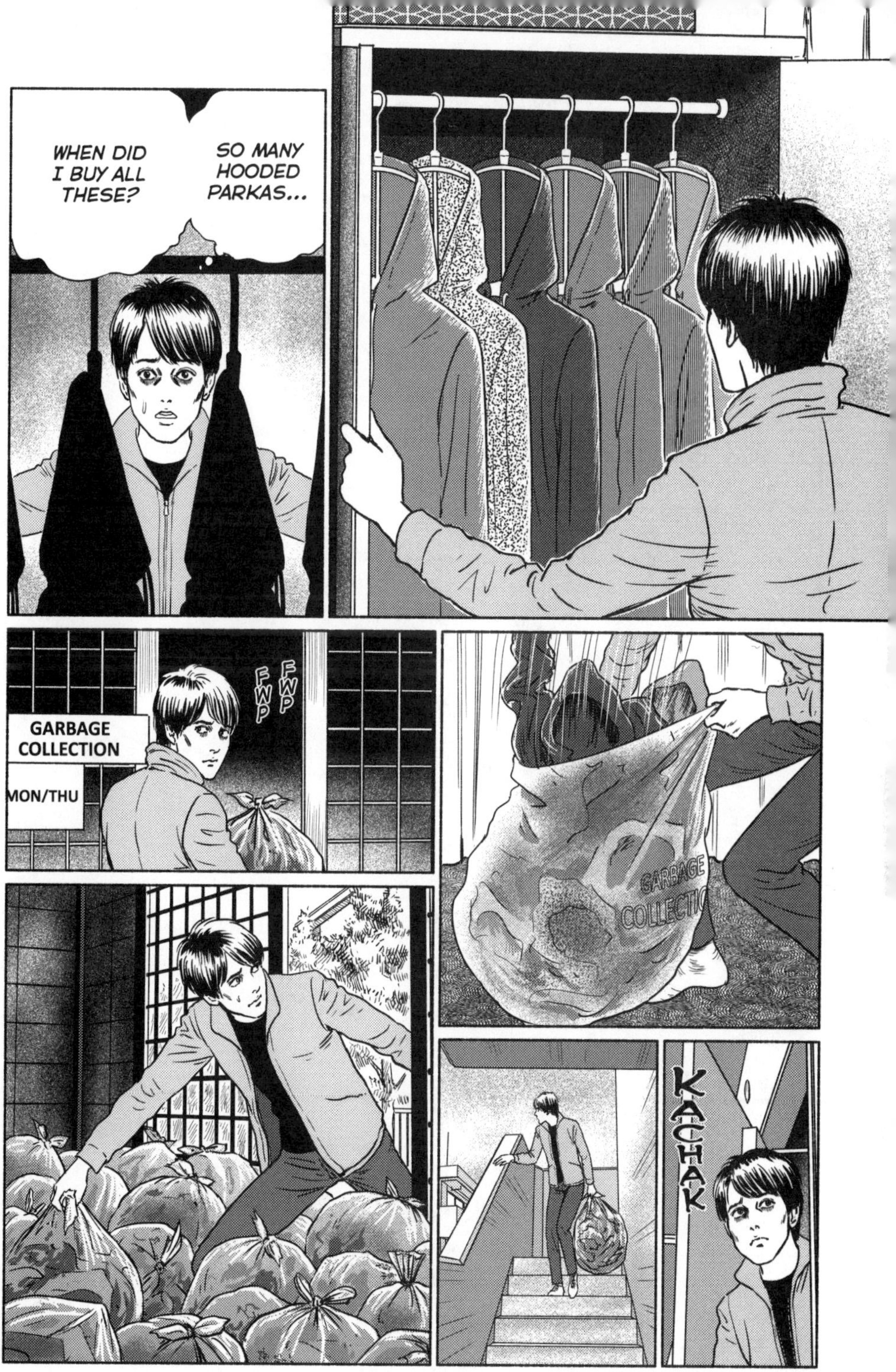
SO MANY HOODED PARKAS...
WHEN DID I BUY ALL THESE?
GARBAGE COLLECTIO
FWP FWP
GARBAGE COLLECTION
MON/THU
KACHAK

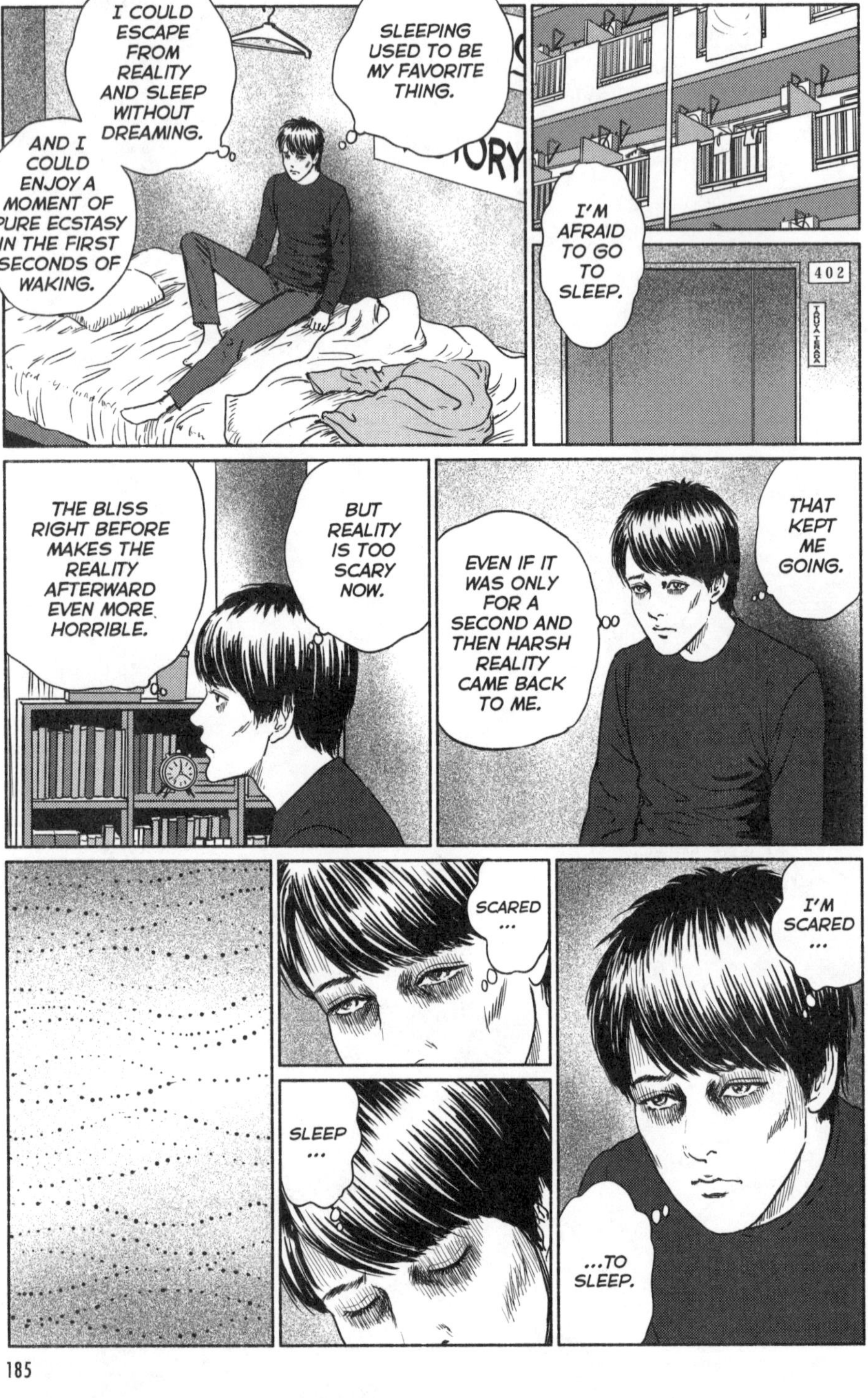
402
I'M AFRAID TO GO TO SLEEP.
SLEEPING USED TO BE MY FAVORITE THING.
I COULD ESCAPE FROM REALITY AND SLEEP WITHOUT DREAMING.
AND I COULD ENJOY A MOMENT OF PURE ECSTASY IN THE FIRST SECONDS OF WAKING.
THAT KEPT ME GOING.
EVEN IF IT WAS ONLY FOR A SECOND AND THEN HARSH REALITY CAME BACK TO ME.
BUT REALITY IS TOO SCARY NOW.
THE BLISS RIGHT BEFORE MAKES THE REALITY AFTERWARD EVEN MORE HORRIBLE.
I'M SCARED...
...TO SLEEP.
SCARED...
SLEEP...

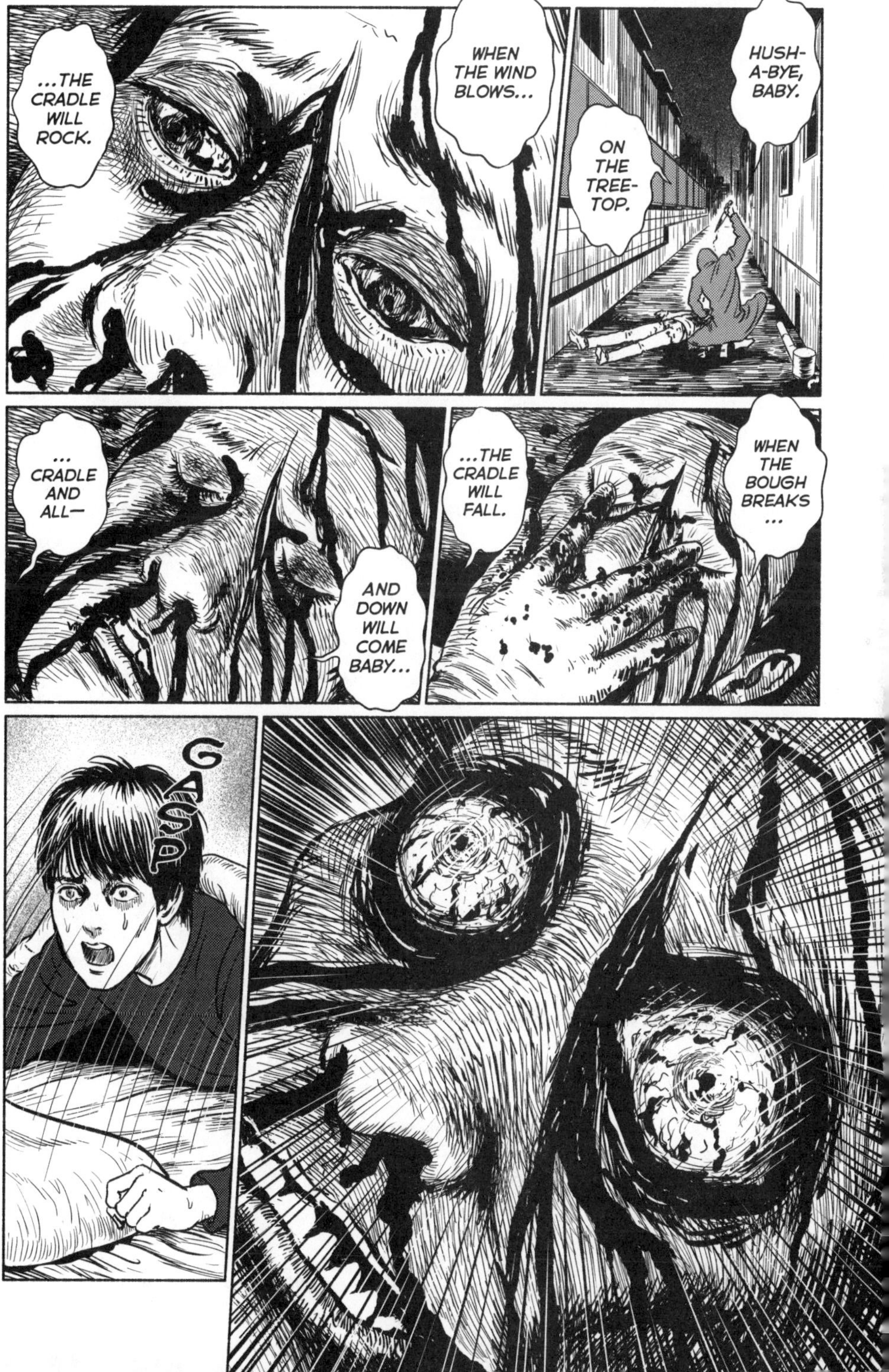
HUSH-A-BYE, BABY.
ON THE TREE-TOP.
WHEN THE WIND BLOWS...
...THE CRADLE WILL ROCK.
WHEN THE BOUGH BREAKS...
...THE CRADLE WILL FALL.
AND DOWN WILL COME BABY...
...CRADLE AND ALL—
GASP

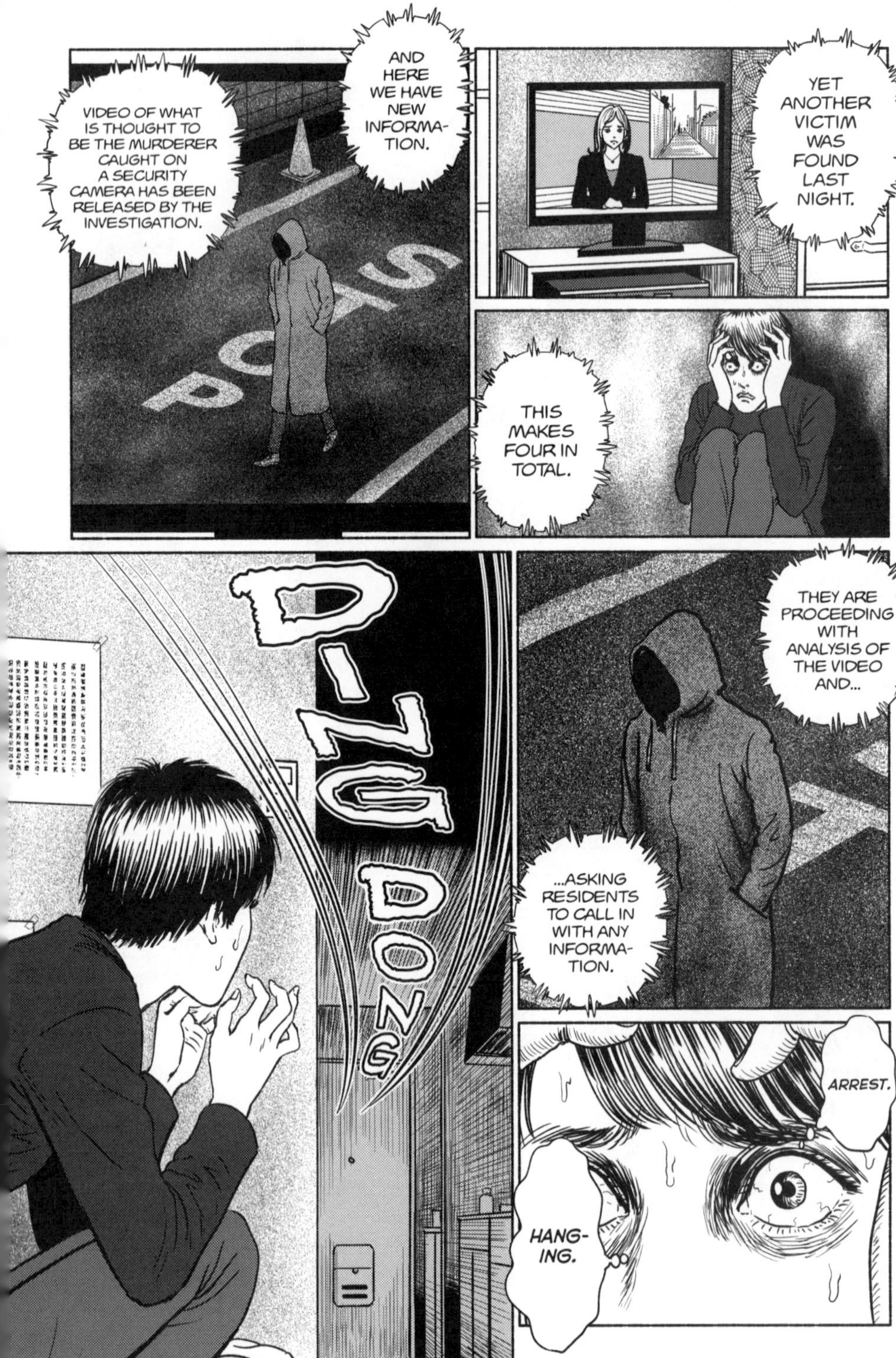
YET ANOTHER VICTIM WAS FOUND LAST NIGHT.
THIS MAKES FOUR IN TOTAL.
AND HERE WE HAVE NEW INFORMATION.
VIDEO OF WHAT IS THOUGHT TO BE THE MURDERER CAUGHT ON A SECURITY CAMERA HAS BEEN RELEASED BY THE INVESTIGATION.
STOP
THEY ARE PROCEEDING WITH ANALYSIS OF THE VIDEO AND...
...ASKING RESIDENTS TO CALL IN WITH ANY INFORMATION.
ARREST.
HANGING.
DING DONG

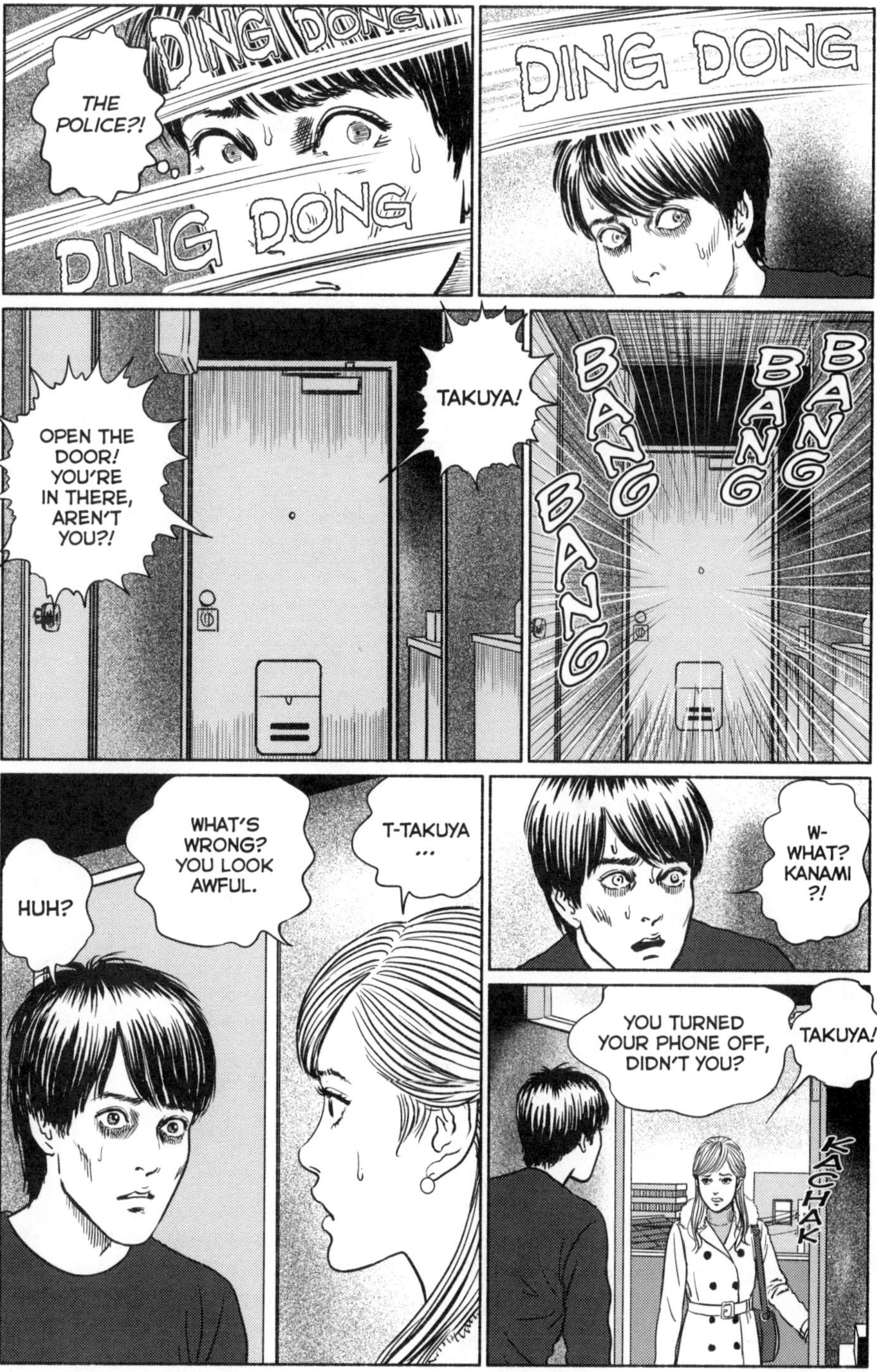
DING DONG
DING DONG
THE POLICE?!
DING DONG
BANG
BANG
BANG BANG
TAKUYA!
OPEN THE DOOR! YOU'RE IN THERE, AREN'T YOU?!
W-WHAT? KANAMI?!
TAKUYA!
YOU TURNED YOUR PHONE OFF, DIDN'T YOU?
KACHAK
T-TAKUYA...
WHAT'S WRONG? YOU LOOK AWFUL.
HUH?

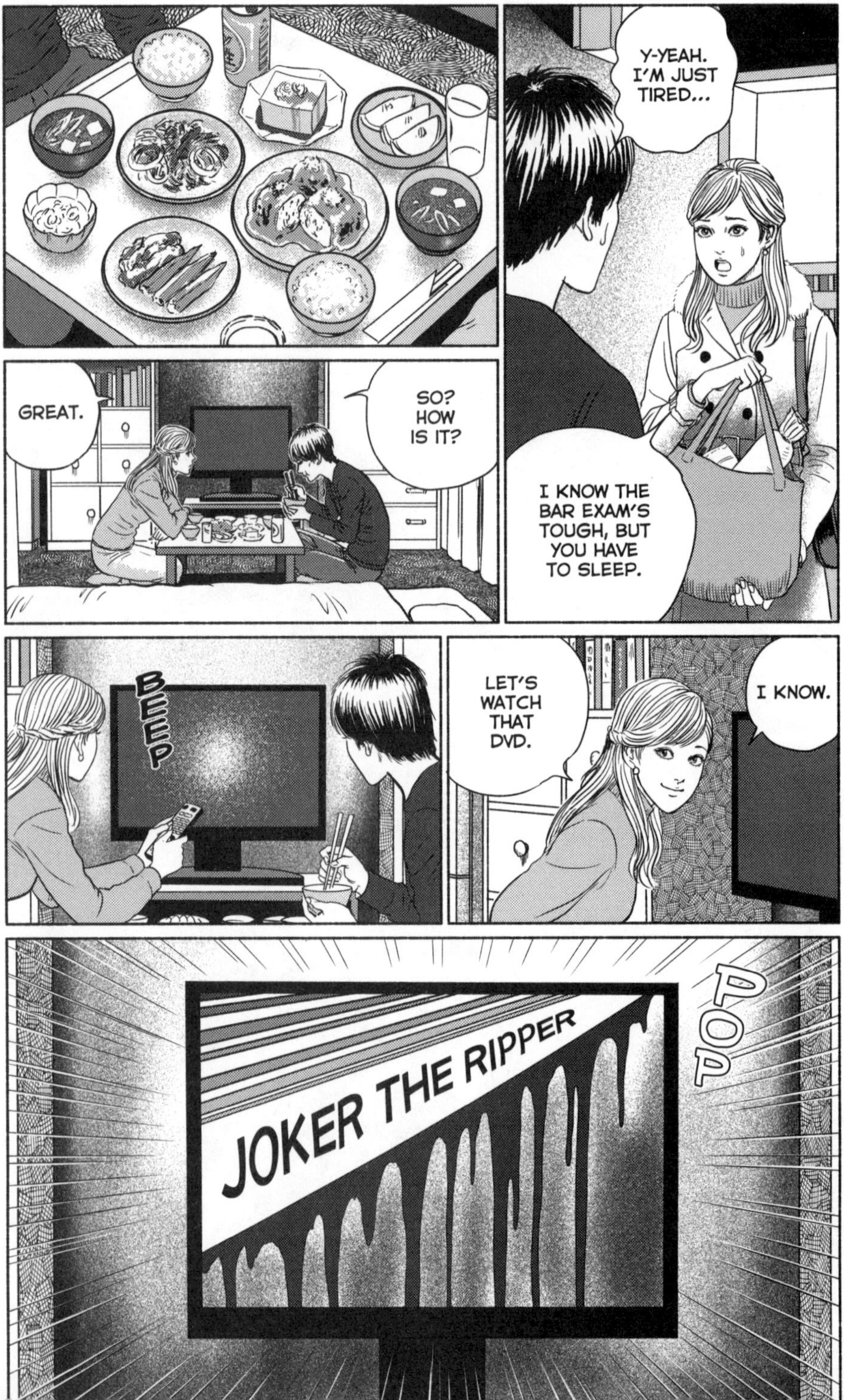
Y-YEAH. I'M JUST TIRED...
I KNOW THE BAR EXAM'S TOUGH, BUT YOU HAVE TO SLEEP.
SO? HOW IS IT?
GREAT.
I KNOW.
LET'S WATCH THAT DVD.
BEEEP
POP
JOKER THE RIPPER

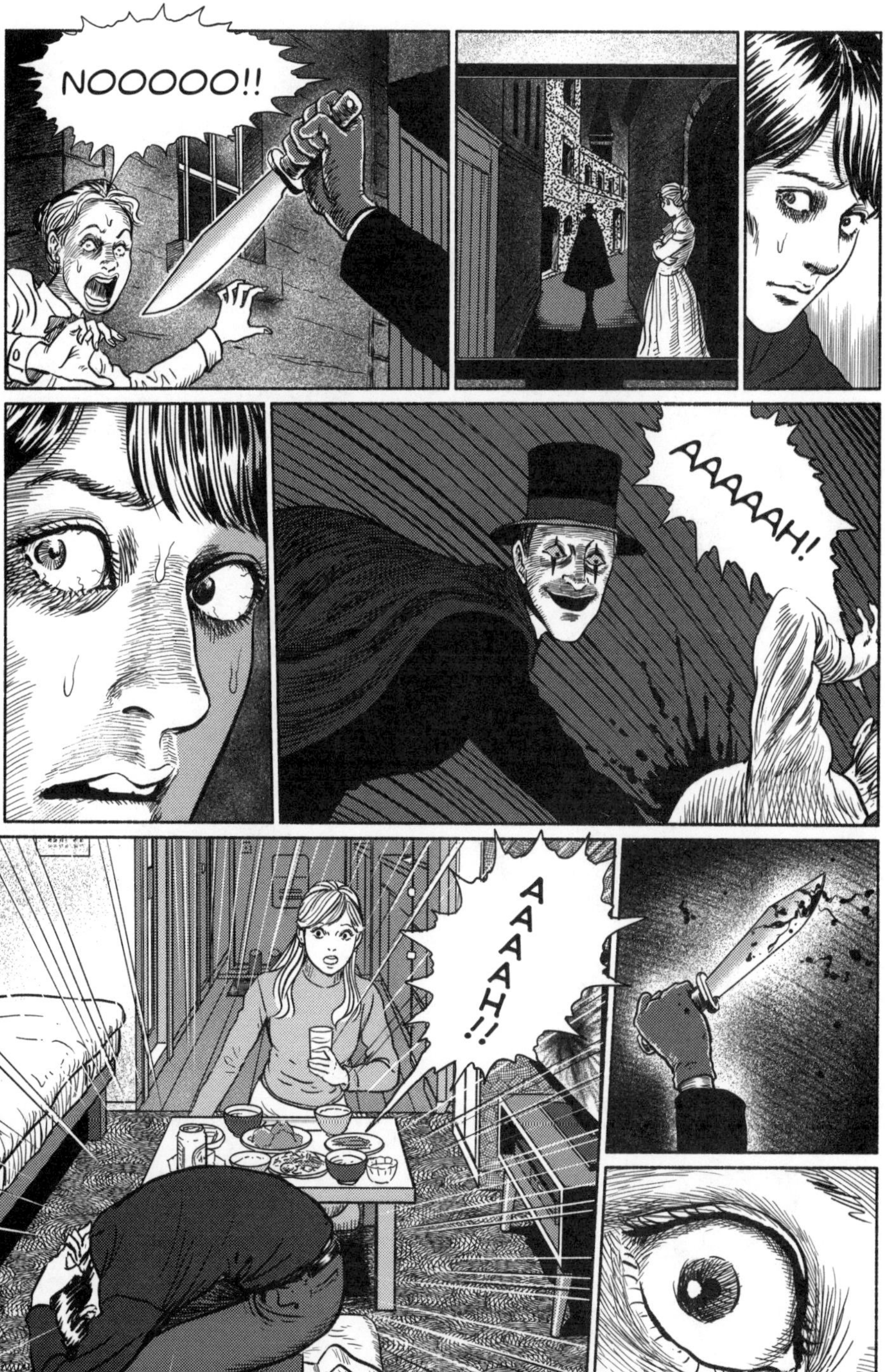
NOOOOO!!
AAAAAH!
AAAAAH!!

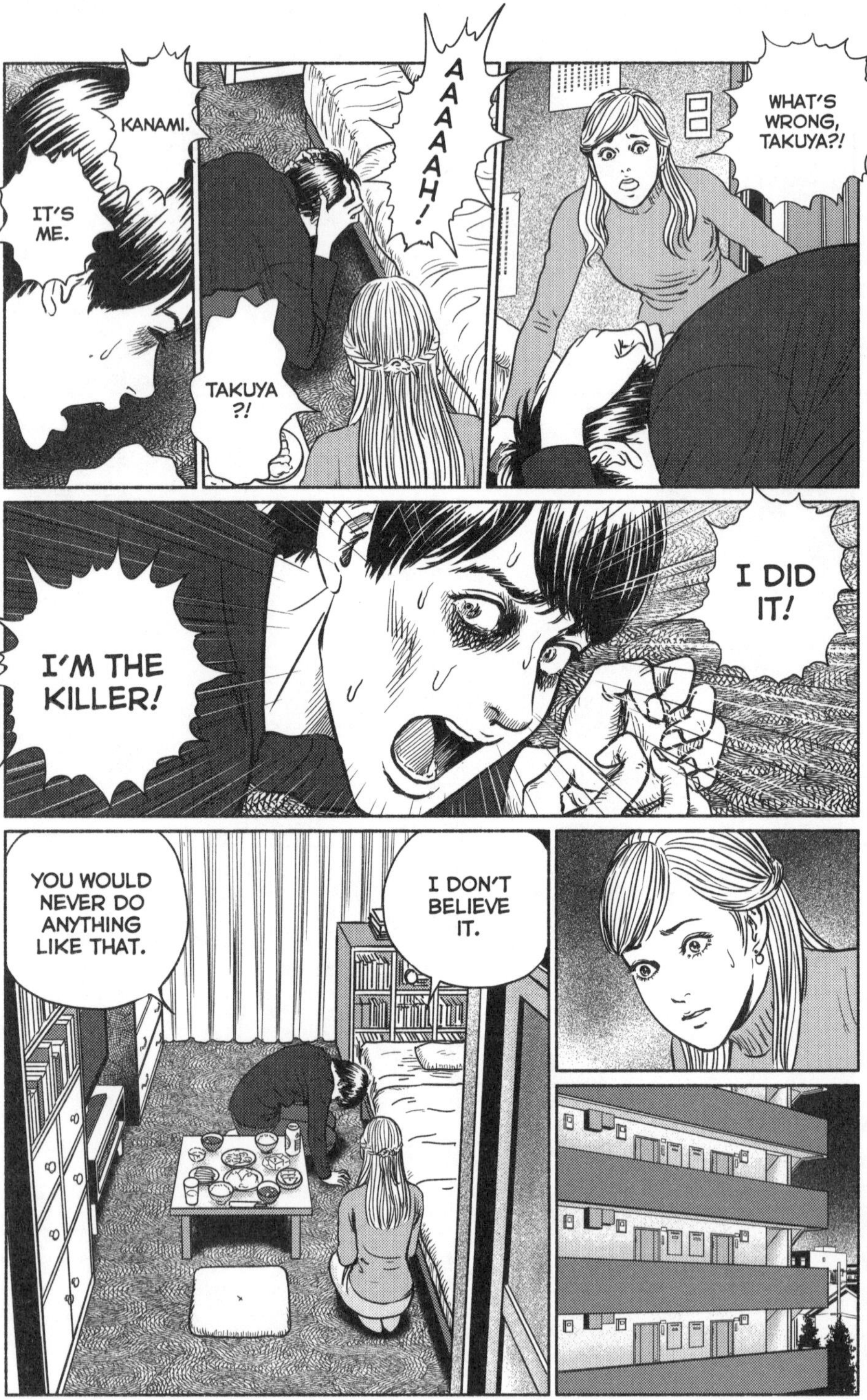
WHAT'S WRONG, TAKUYA?!
AAAAAH!
TAKUYA?!
KANAMI.
IT'S ME.
I DID IT!
I'M THE KILLER!
I DON'T BELIEVE IT.
YOU WOULD NEVER DO ANYTHING LIKE THAT.

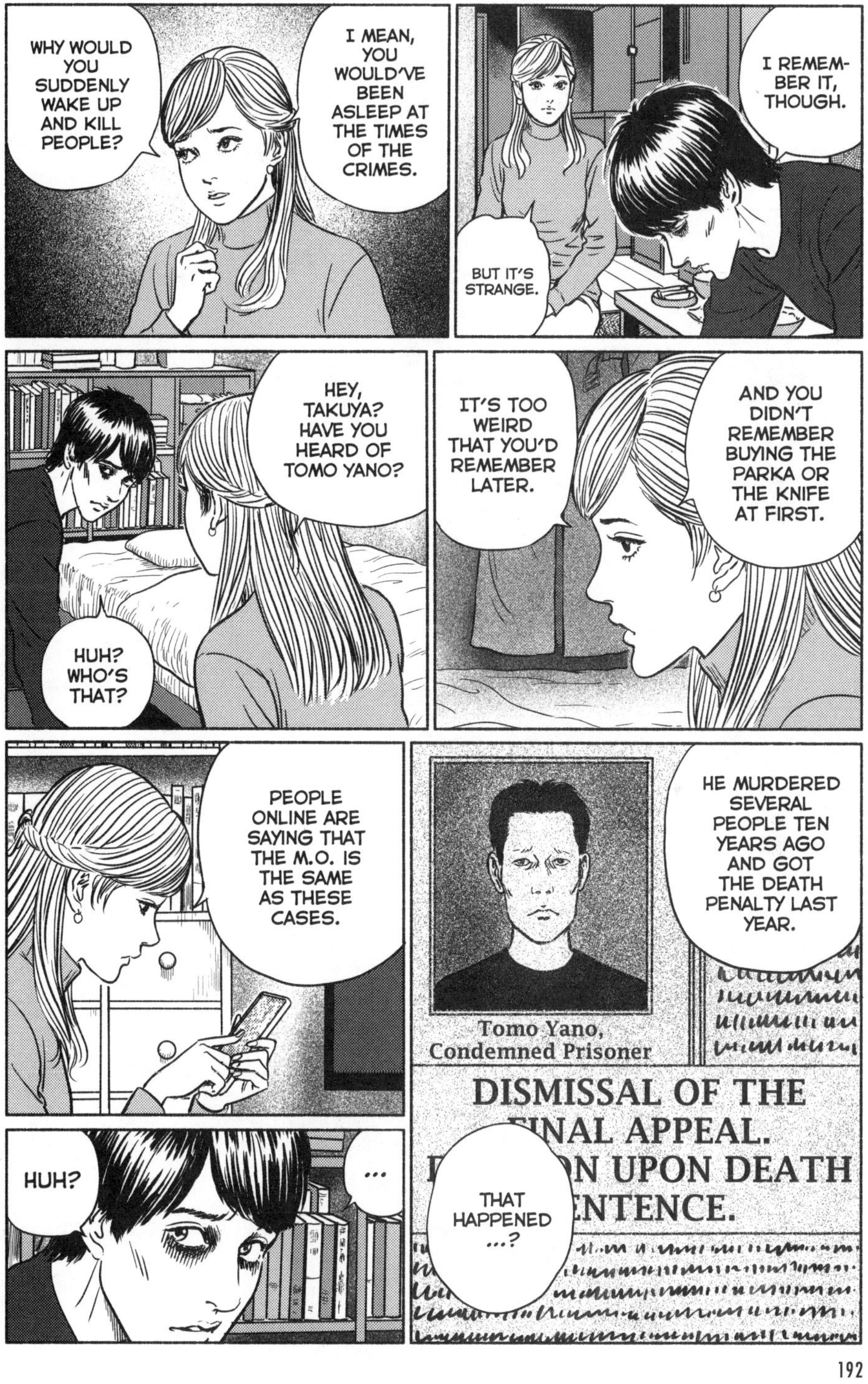
I REMEMBER IT, THOUGH.
BUT IT'S STRANGE.
WHY WOULD YOU SUDDENLY WAKE UP AND KILL PEOPLE?
I MEAN, YOU WOULD'VE BEEN ASLEEP AT THE TIMES OF THE CRIMES.
AND YOU DIDN'T REMEMBER BUYING THE PARKA OR THE KNIFE AT FIRST.
IT'S TOO WEIRD THAT YOU'D REMEMBER LATER.
HEY, TAKUYA? HAVE YOU HEARD OF TOMO YANO?
HUH? WHO'S THAT?
HE MURDERED SEVERAL PEOPLE TEN YEARS AGO AND GOT THE DEATH PENALTY LAST YEAR.
Tomo Yano, Condemned Prisoner
DISMISSAL OF THE
INAL APPEAL.
ON UPON DEATH
ENTENCE.
THAT HAPPENED ...?
PEOPLE ONLINE ARE SAYING THAT THE M.O. IS THE SAME AS THESE CASES.
...
HUH?

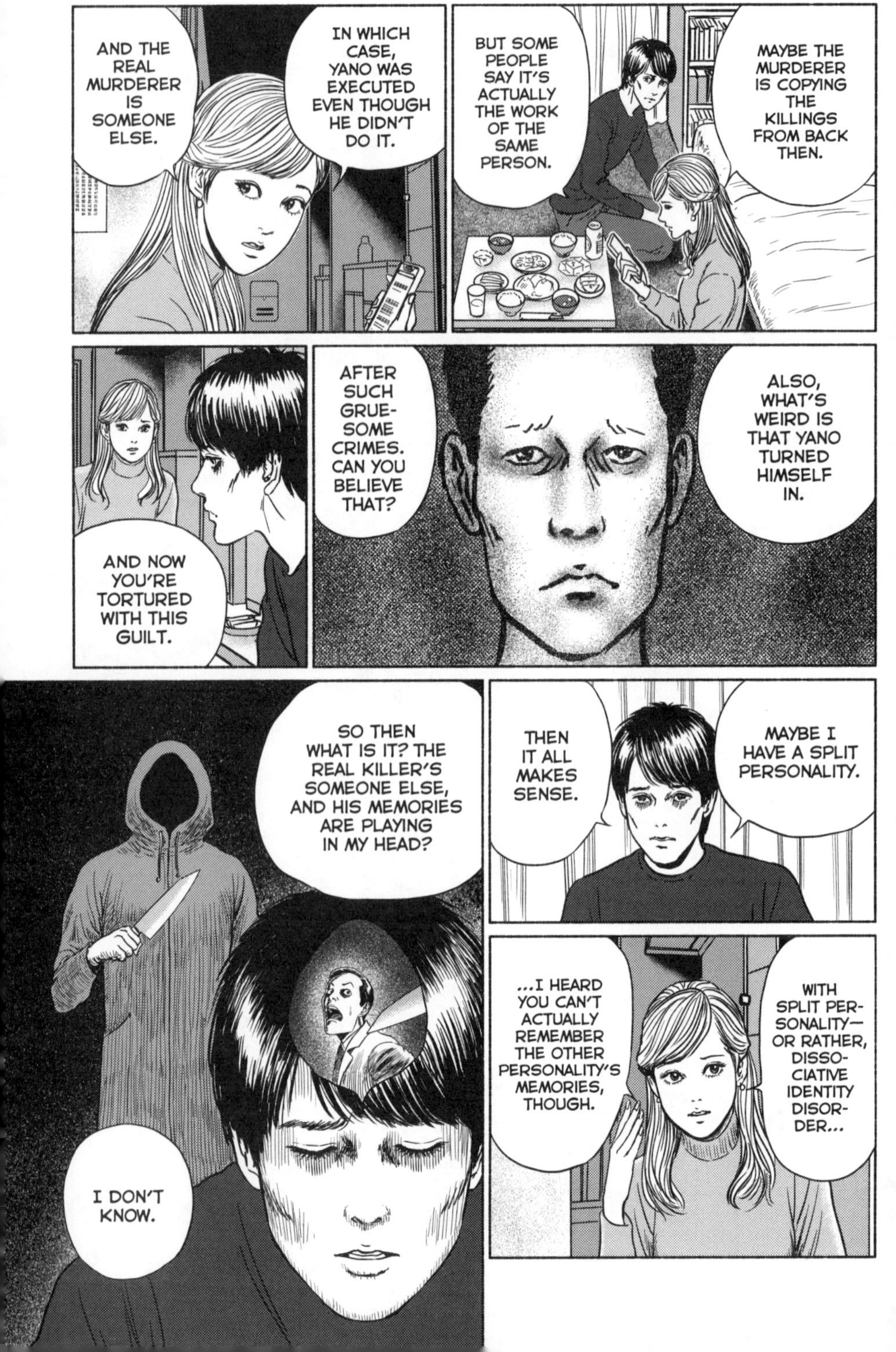
MAYBE THE MURDERER IS COPYING THE KILLINGS FROM BACK THEN.
BUT SOME PEOPLE SAY IT'S ACTUALLY THE WORK OF THE SAME PERSON.
IN WHICH CASE, YANO WAS EXECUTED EVEN THOUGH HE DIDN'T DO IT.
AND THE REAL MURDERER IS SOMEONE ELSE.
ALSO, WHAT'S WEIRD IS THAT YANO TURNED HIMSELF IN.
AFTER SUCH GRUESOME CRIMES. CAN YOU BELIEVE THAT?
AND NOW YOU'RE TORTURED WITH THIS GUILT.
MAYBE I HAVE A SPLIT PERSONALITY.
THEN IT ALL MAKES SENSE.
WITH SPLIT PERSONALITY— OR RATHER, DISSOCIATIVE IDENTITY DISORDER...
...I HEARD YOU CAN'T ACTUALLY REMEMBER THE OTHER PERSONALITY'S MEMORIES, THOUGH.
SO THEN WHAT IS IT? THE REAL KILLER'S SOMEONE ELSE, AND HIS MEMORIES ARE PLAYING IN MY HEAD?
I DON'T KNOW.

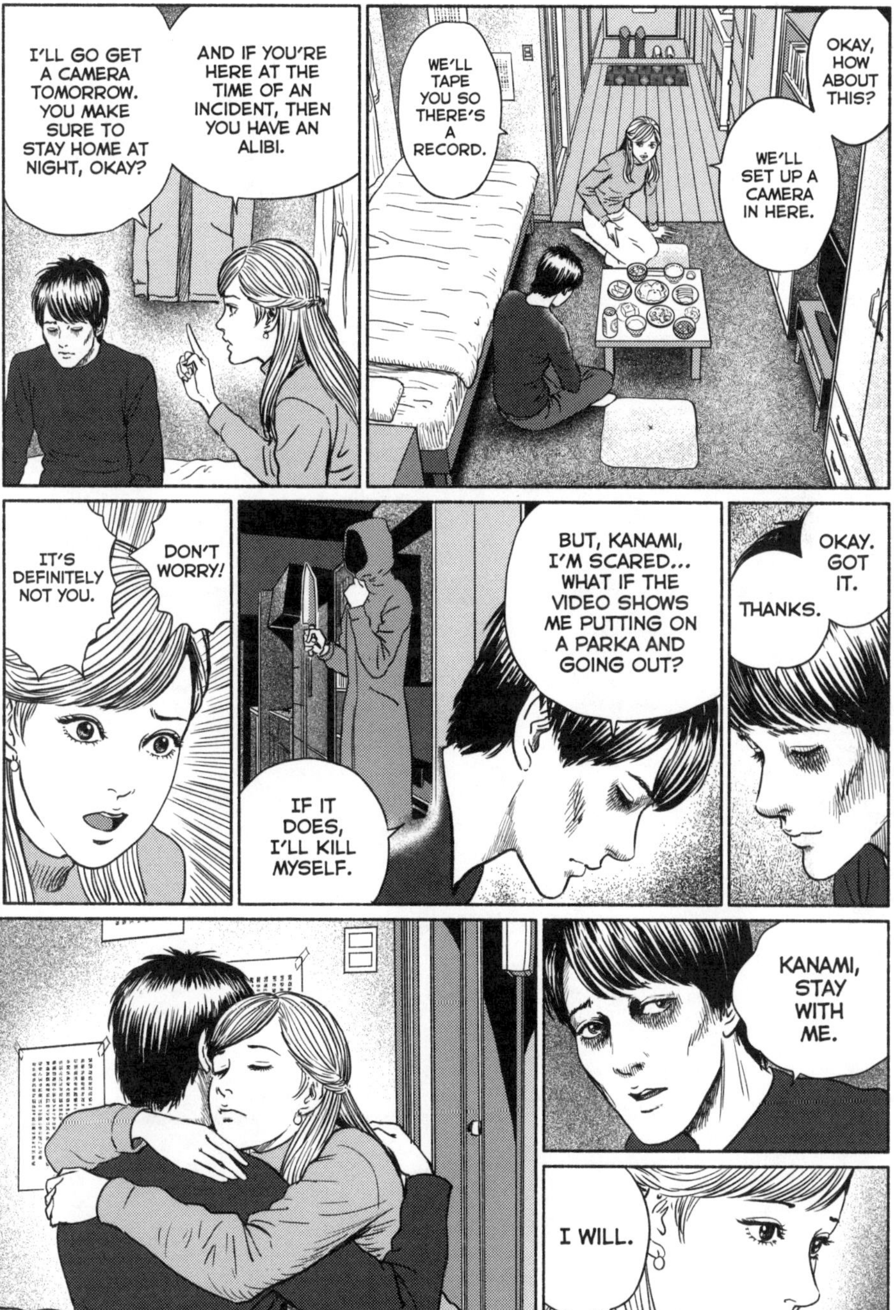
OKAY, HOW ABOUT THIS?
WE'LL SET UP A CAMERA IN HERE.
WE'LL TAPE YOU SO THERE'S A RECORD.
I'LL GO GET A CAMERA TOMORROW. YOU MAKE SURE TO STAY HOME AT NIGHT, OKAY?
AND IF YOU'RE HERE AT THE TIME OF AN INCIDENT, THEN YOU HAVE AN ALIBI.
OKAY. GOT IT.
THANKS.
BUT, KANAMI, I'M SCARED... WHAT IF THE VIDEO SHOWS ME PUTTING ON A PARKA AND GOING OUT?
IF IT DOES, I'LL KILL MYSELF.
DON'T WORRY!
IT'S DEFINITELY NOT YOU.
KANAMI, STAY WITH ME.
I WILL.

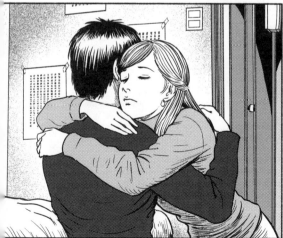

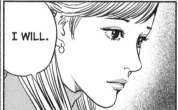

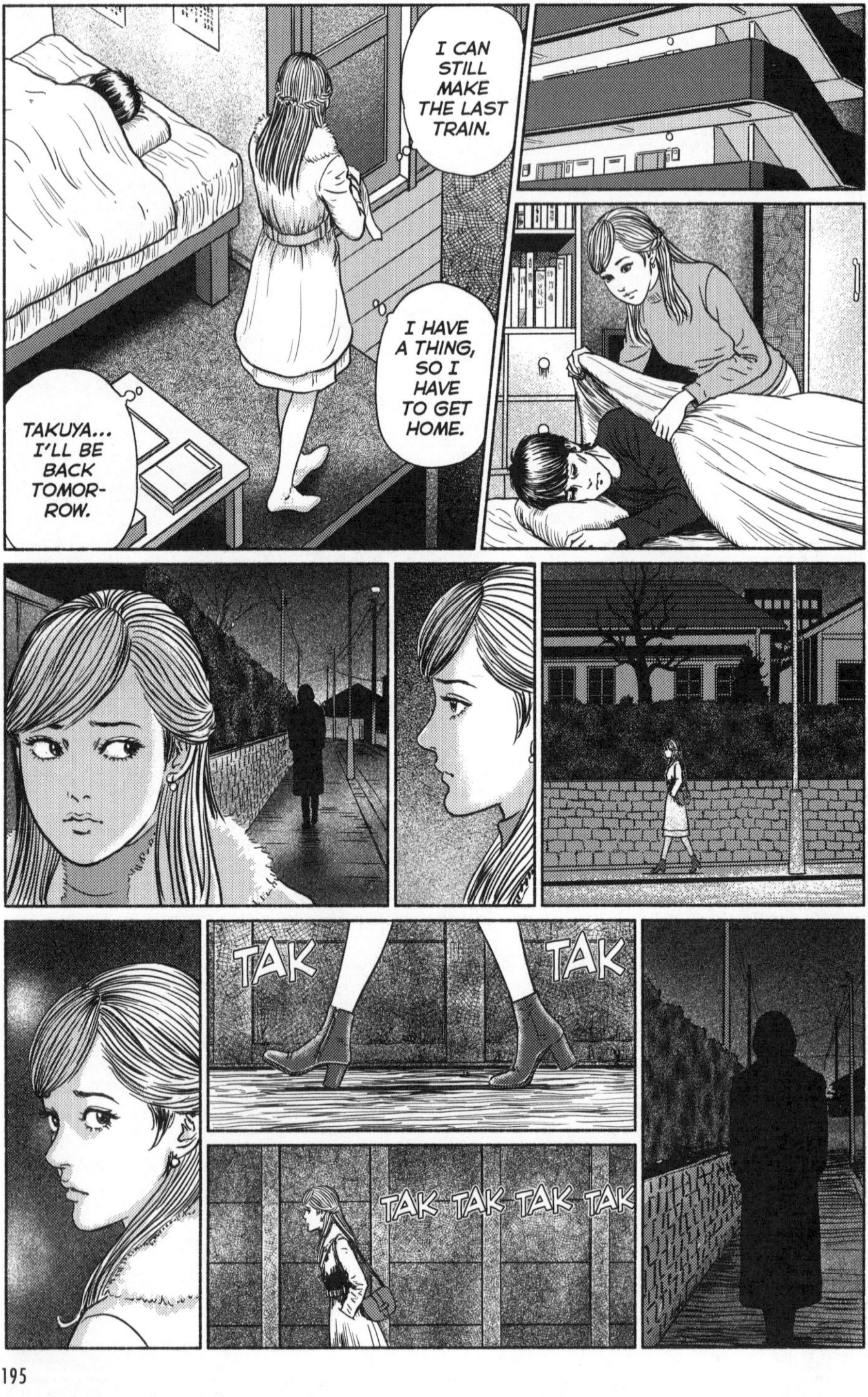
I CAN STILL MAKE THE LAST TRAIN.
I HAVE A THING, SO I HAVE TO GET HOME.
TAKUYA... I'LL BE BACK TOMOR-ROW.
TAK
TAK
TAK TAK TAK TAK

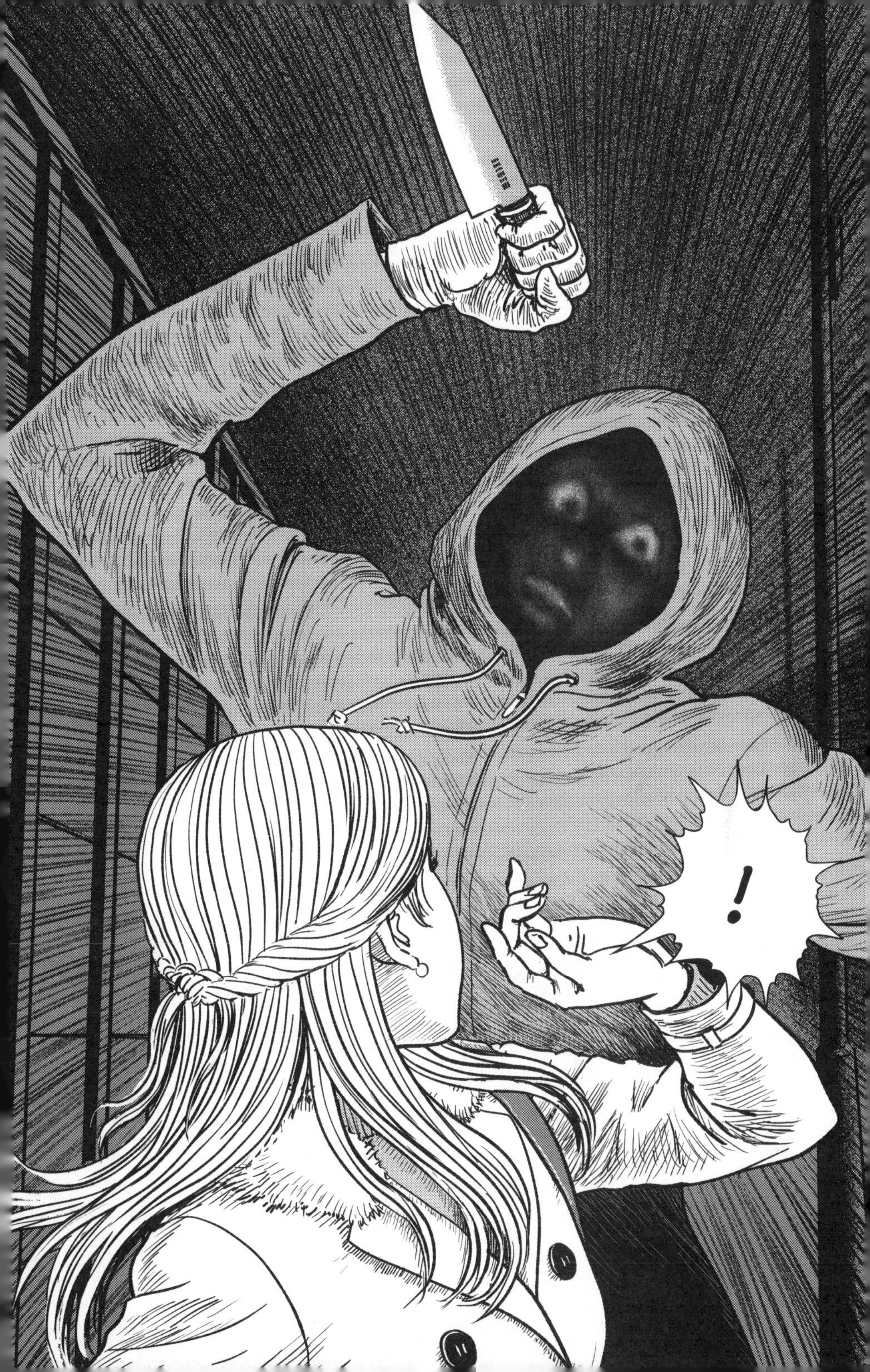
!

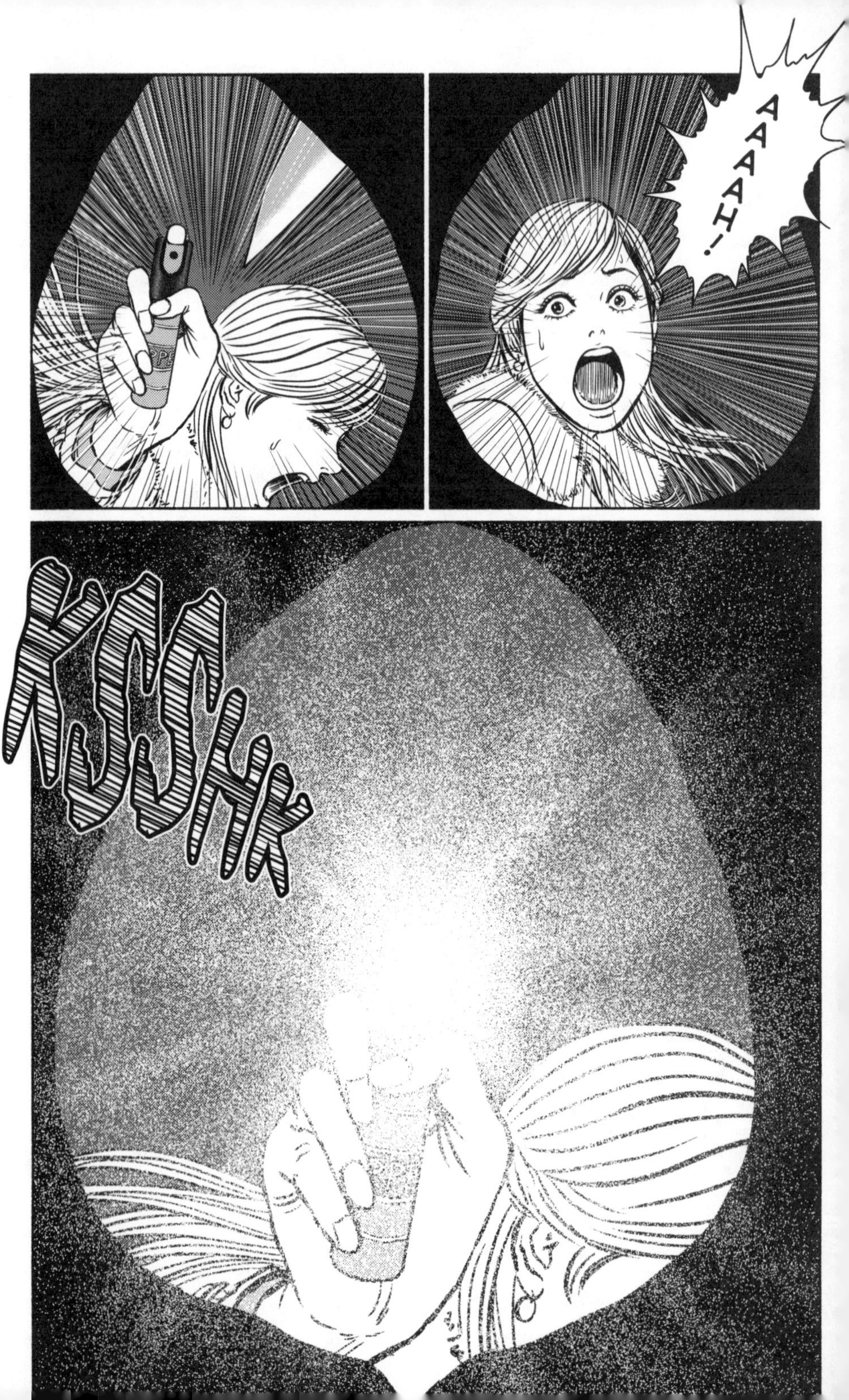
AAAAH!
KSSHK

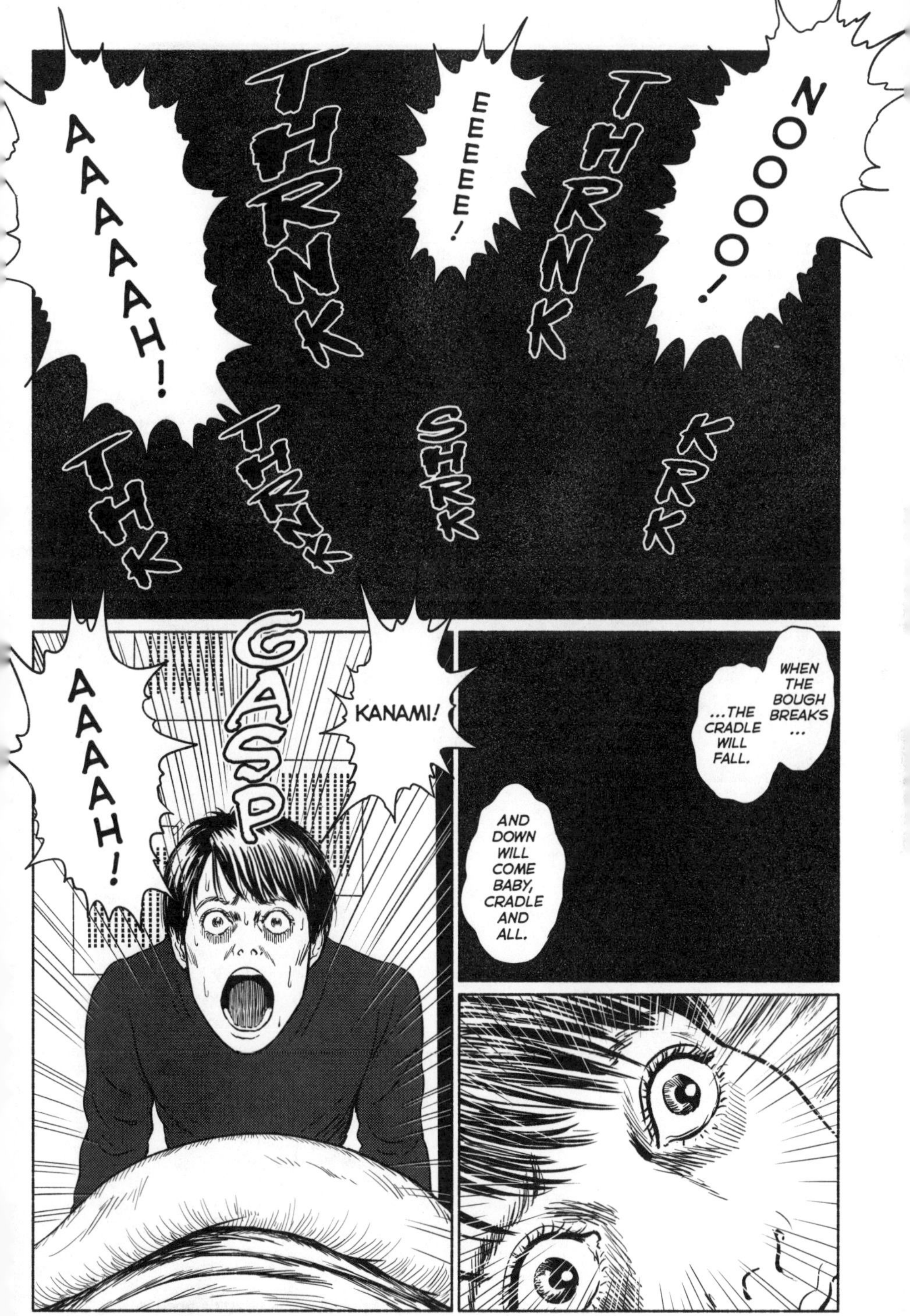
NOOOOO!
THRNK
EEEEE!
THRNK
AAAAAAH!
KRK
SHRK
THRNK
THK
WHEN THE BOUGH BREAKS...
...THE CRADLE WILL FALL.
AND DOWN WILL COME BABY, CRADLE AND ALL.
KANAMI!
GASP
AAAAAH!

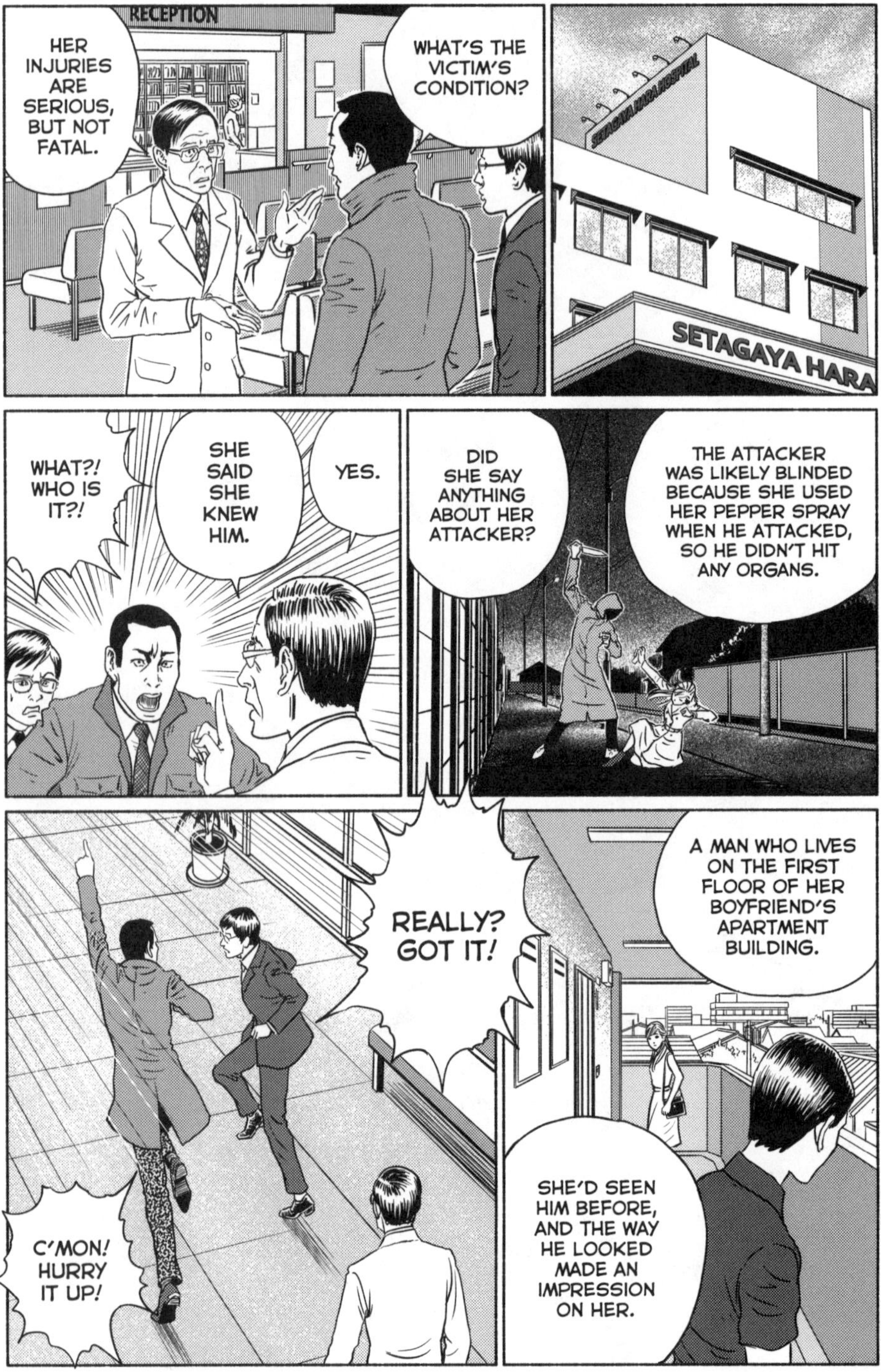
SETAGAYA HARA HOSPITAL
SETAGAYA HARA
RECEPTION
WHAT'S THE VICTIM'S CONDITION?
HER INJURIES ARE SERIOUS, BUT NOT FATAL.
THE ATTACKER WAS LIKELY BLINDED BECAUSE SHE USED HER PEPPER SPRAY WHEN HE ATTACKED, SO HE DIDN'T HIT ANY ORGANS.
DID SHE SAY ANYTHING ABOUT HER ATTACKER?
YES.
SHE SAID SHE KNEW HIM.
WHAT?! WHO IS IT?!
A MAN WHO LIVES ON THE FIRST FLOOR OF HER BOYFRIEND'S APARTMENT BUILDING.
SHE'D SEEN HIM BEFORE, AND THE WAY HE LOOKED MADE AN IMPRESSION ON HER.
REALLY? GOT IT!
C'MON! HURRY IT UP!

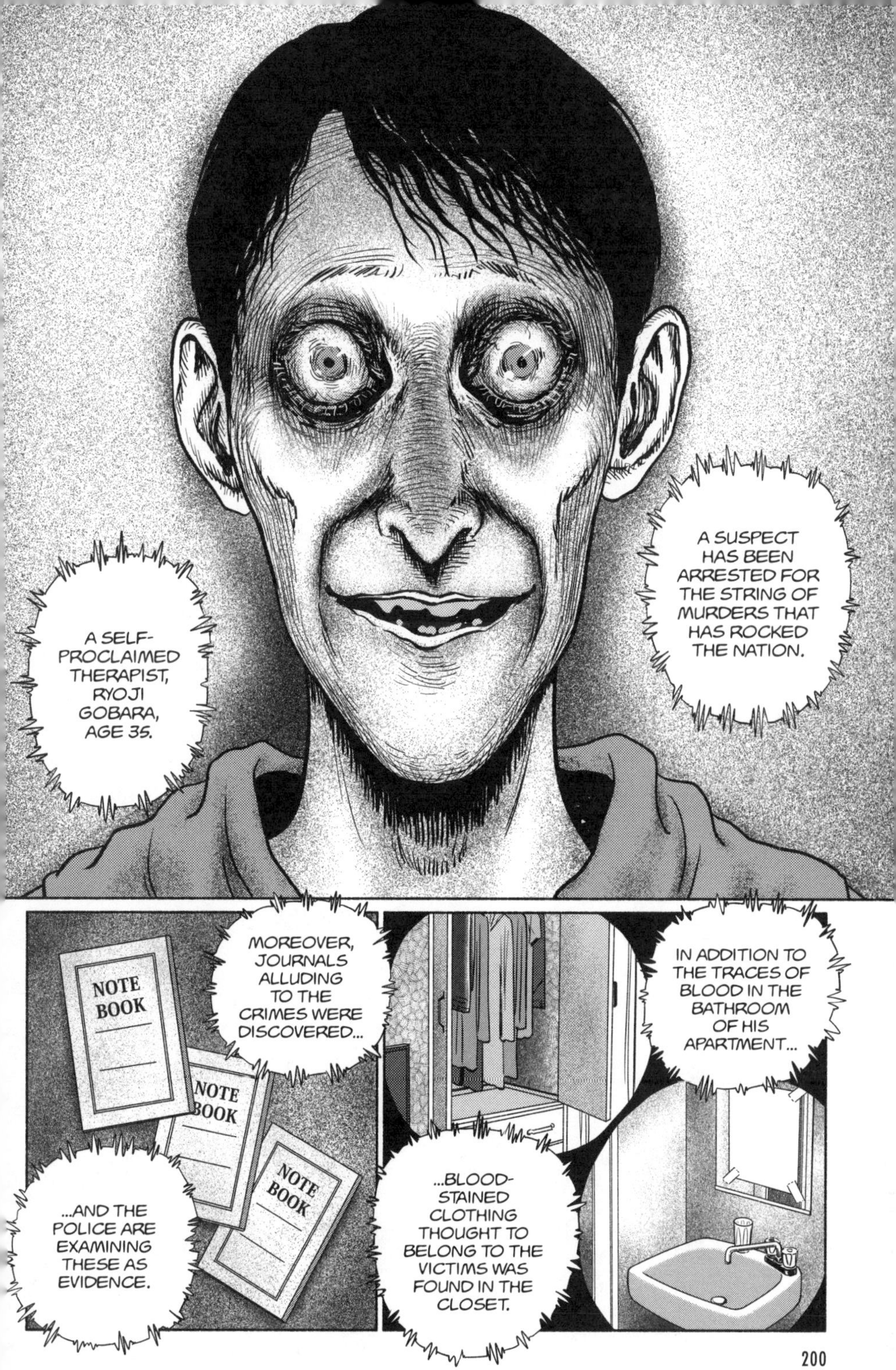
A SUSPECT HAS BEEN ARRESTED FOR THE STRING OF MURDERS THAT HAS ROCKED THE NATION.
A SELF-PROCLAIMED THERAPIST, RYOJI GOBARA, AGE 35.
IN ADDITION TO THE TRACES OF BLOOD IN THE BATHROOM OF HIS APARTMENT...
...BLOOD-STAINED CLOTHING THOUGHT TO BELONG TO THE VICTIMS WAS FOUND IN THE CLOSET.
MOREOVER, JOURNALS ALLUDING TO THE CRIMES WERE DISCOVERED...
NOTE BOOK
NOTE BOOK
NOTE BOOK
...AND THE POLICE ARE EXAMINING THESE AS EVIDENCE.

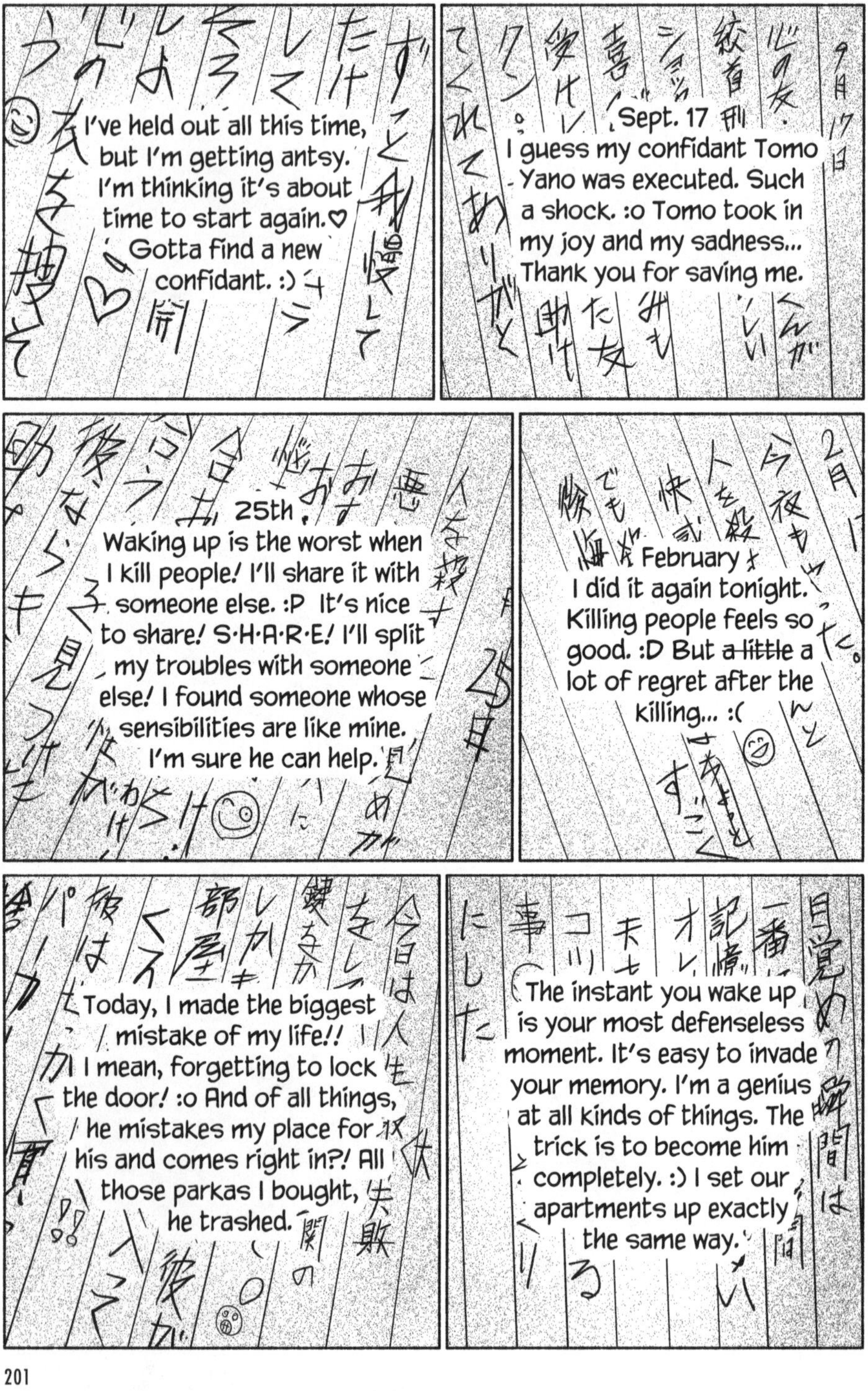
Sept. 17
I guess my confidant Tomo Yano was executed. Such a shock. :o Tomo took in my joy and my sadness... Thank you for saving me.
I've held out all this time, but I'm getting antsy. I'm thinking it's about time to start again.♡ Gotta find a new confidant. :)
February
I did it again tonight. Killing people feels so good. :D But ~~a little~~ a lot of regret after the killing... :(
25th
Waking up is the worst when I kill people! I'll share it with someone else. :P It's nice to share! S·H·A·R·E! I'll split my troubles with someone else! I found someone whose sensibilities are like mine. I'm sure he can help.
The instant you wake up is your most defenseless moment. It's easy to invade your memory. I'm a genius at all kinds of things. The trick is to become him completely. :) I set our apartments up exactly the same way.
Today, I made the biggest mistake of my life!! I mean, forgetting to lock the door! :o And of all things, he mistakes my place for his and comes right in?! All those parkas I bought, he trashed.

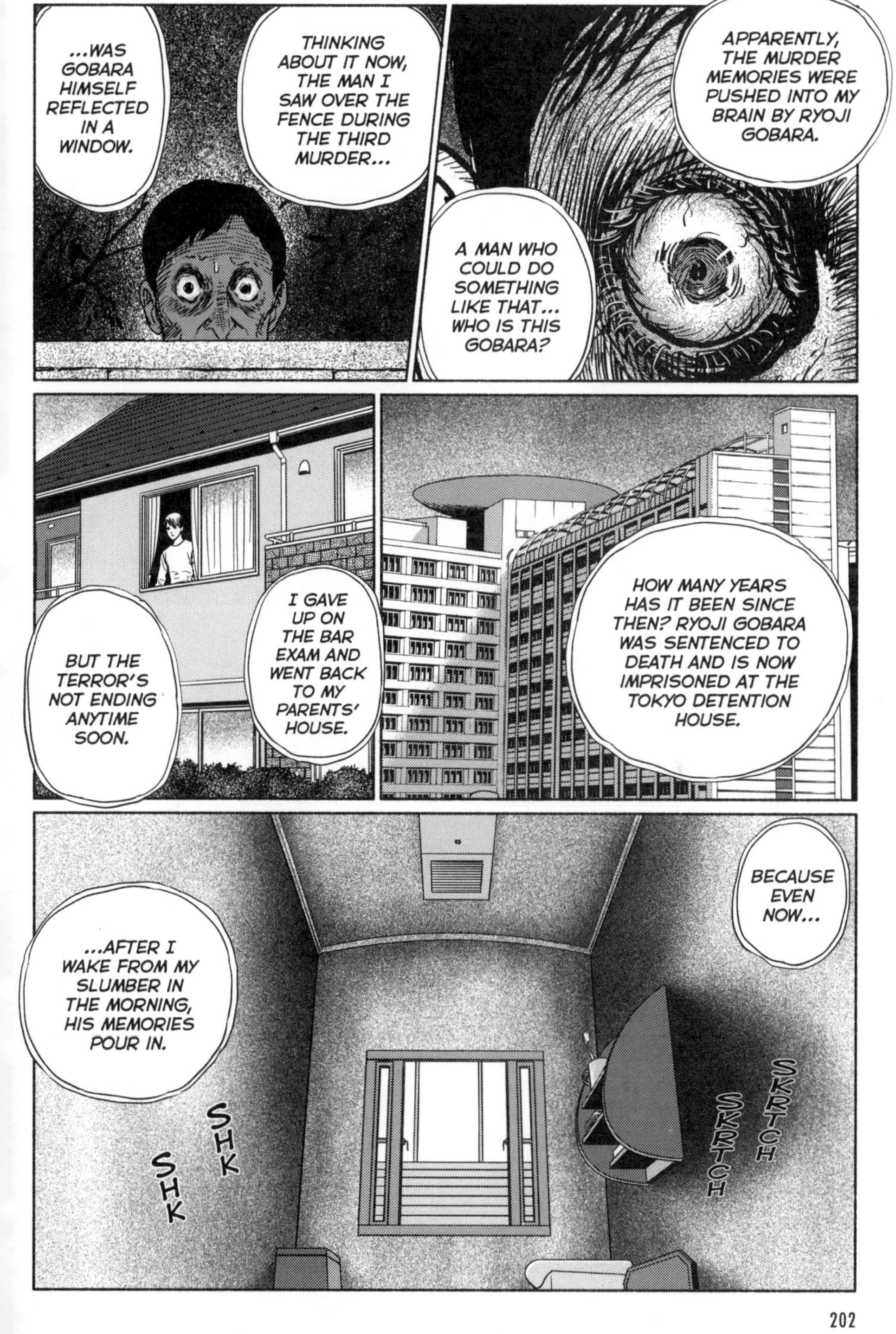
APPARENTLY, THE MURDER MEMORIES WERE PUSHED INTO MY BRAIN BY RYOJI GOBARA.
A MAN WHO COULD DO SOMETHING LIKE THAT... WHO IS THIS GOBARA?
THINKING ABOUT IT NOW, THE MAN I SAW OVER THE FENCE DURING THE THIRD MURDER...
...WAS GOBARA HIMSELF REFLECTED IN A WINDOW.
HOW MANY YEARS HAS IT BEEN SINCE THEN? RYOJI GOBARA WAS SENTENCED TO DEATH AND IS NOW IMPRISONED AT THE TOKYO DETENTION HOUSE.
I GAVE UP ON THE BAR EXAM AND WENT BACK TO MY PARENTS' HOUSE.
BUT THE TERROR'S NOT ENDING ANYTIME SOON.
BECAUSE EVEN NOW...
...AFTER I WAKE FROM MY SLUMBER IN THE MORNING, HIS MEMORIES POUR IN.
SKRTCH
SKRTCH
SHK
SHK

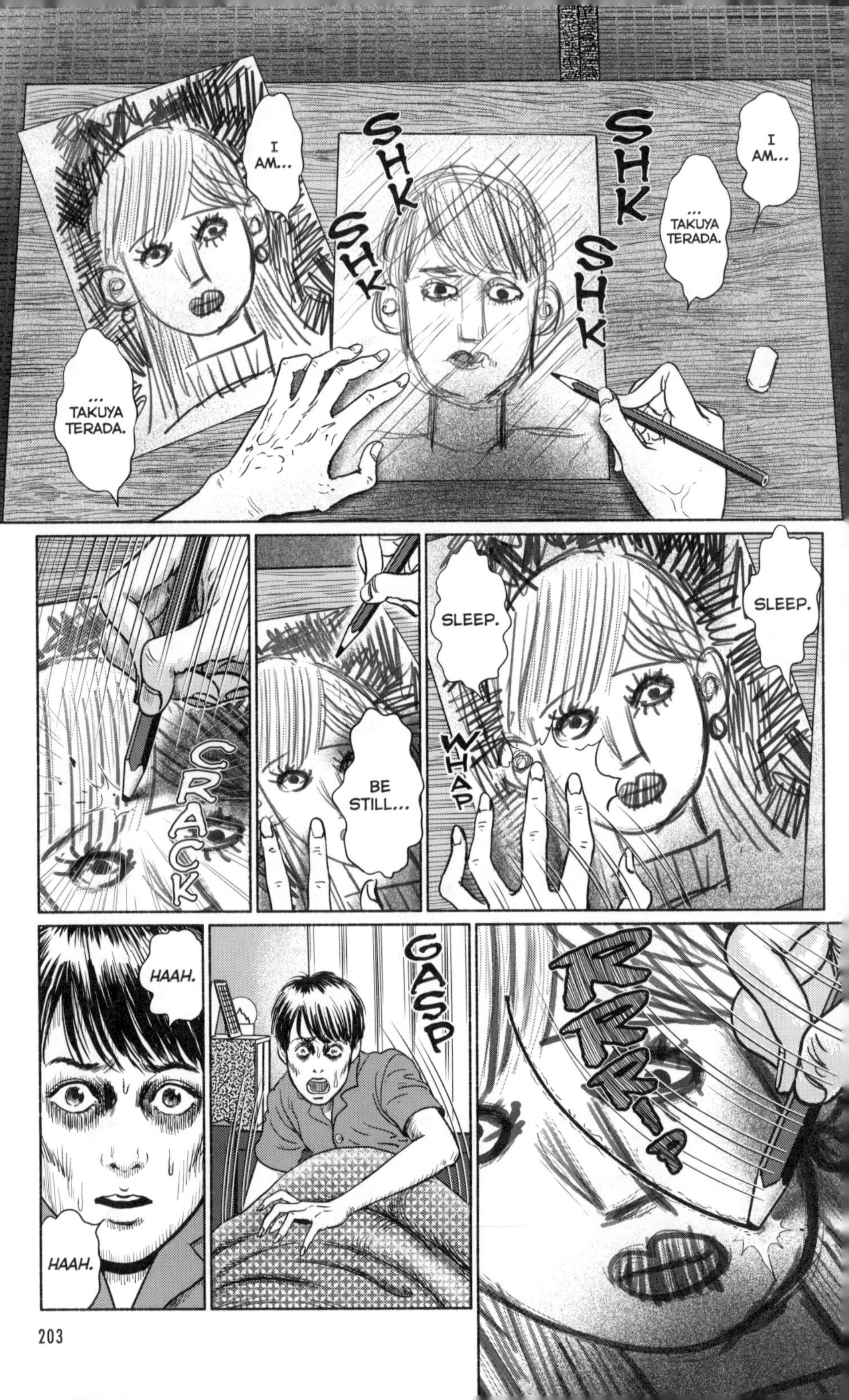
I AM...
...TAKUYA TERADA.
SHK
SHK
SHK
SHK
I AM...
...TAKUYA TERADA.
SLEEP.
SLEEP.
WHAP
BE STILL...
CRACK
KRRIA
GASP
HAAH.
HAAH.

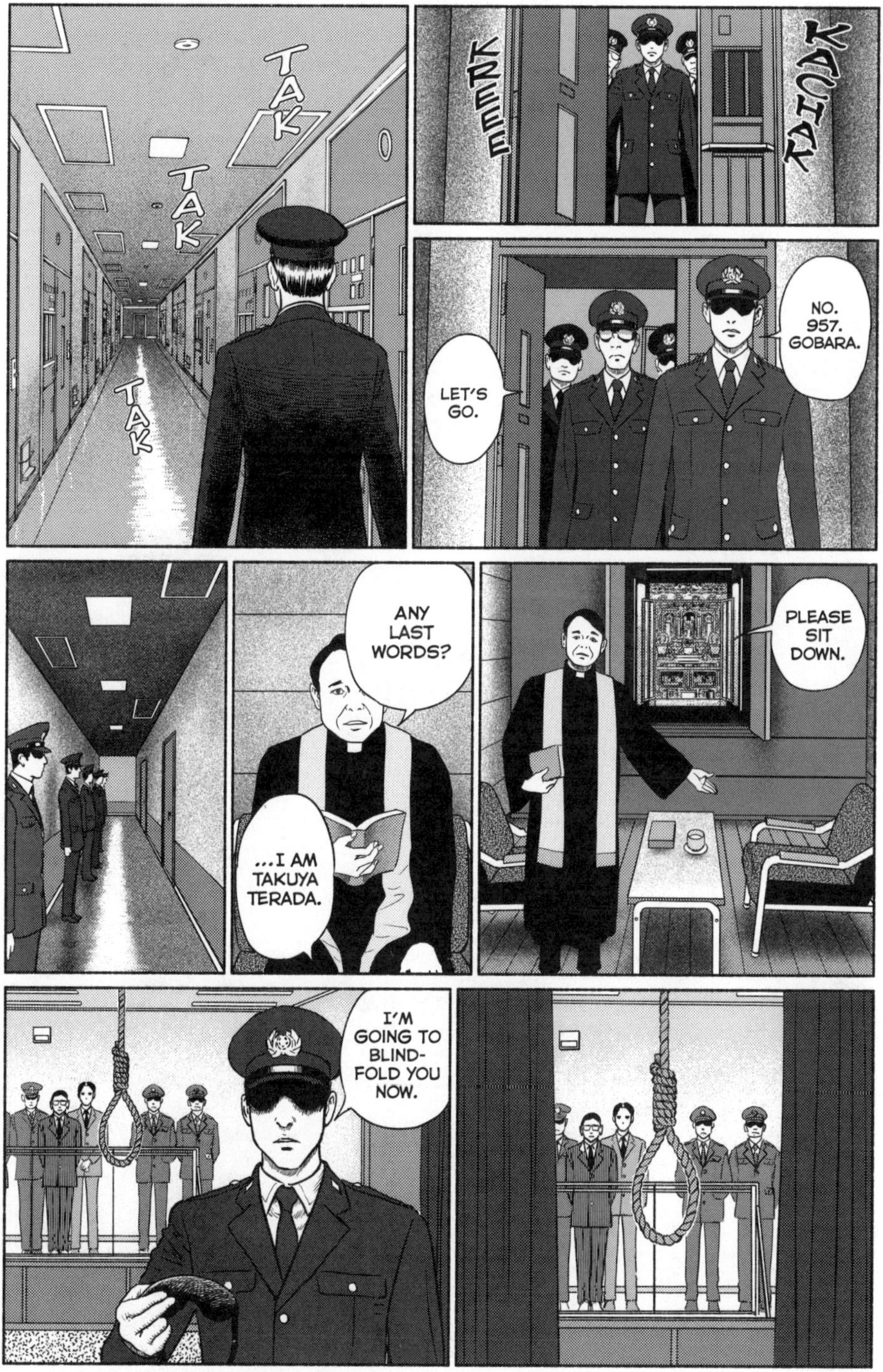
KACHAK
KREEE
NO. 957. GOBARA.
LET'S GO.
TAK
TAK
TAK
TAK
PLEASE SIT DOWN.
ANY LAST WORDS?
...I AM TAKUYA TERADA.
I'M GOING TO BLIND-FOLD YOU NOW.

AND DOWN WILL COME BABY...
THNK
THNK
...CRADLE AND ALL.
THNK
KREE
KATAK
CRRRACK
WHRR
WHRR
WHRR
WHRR
WHRR
WHRR

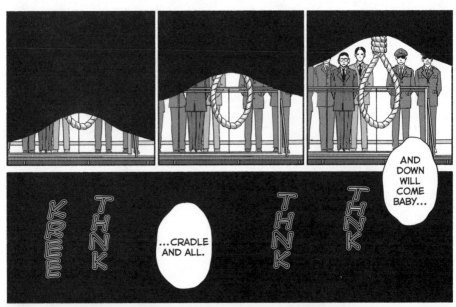

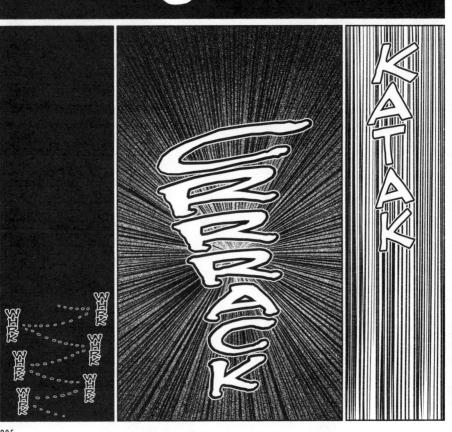

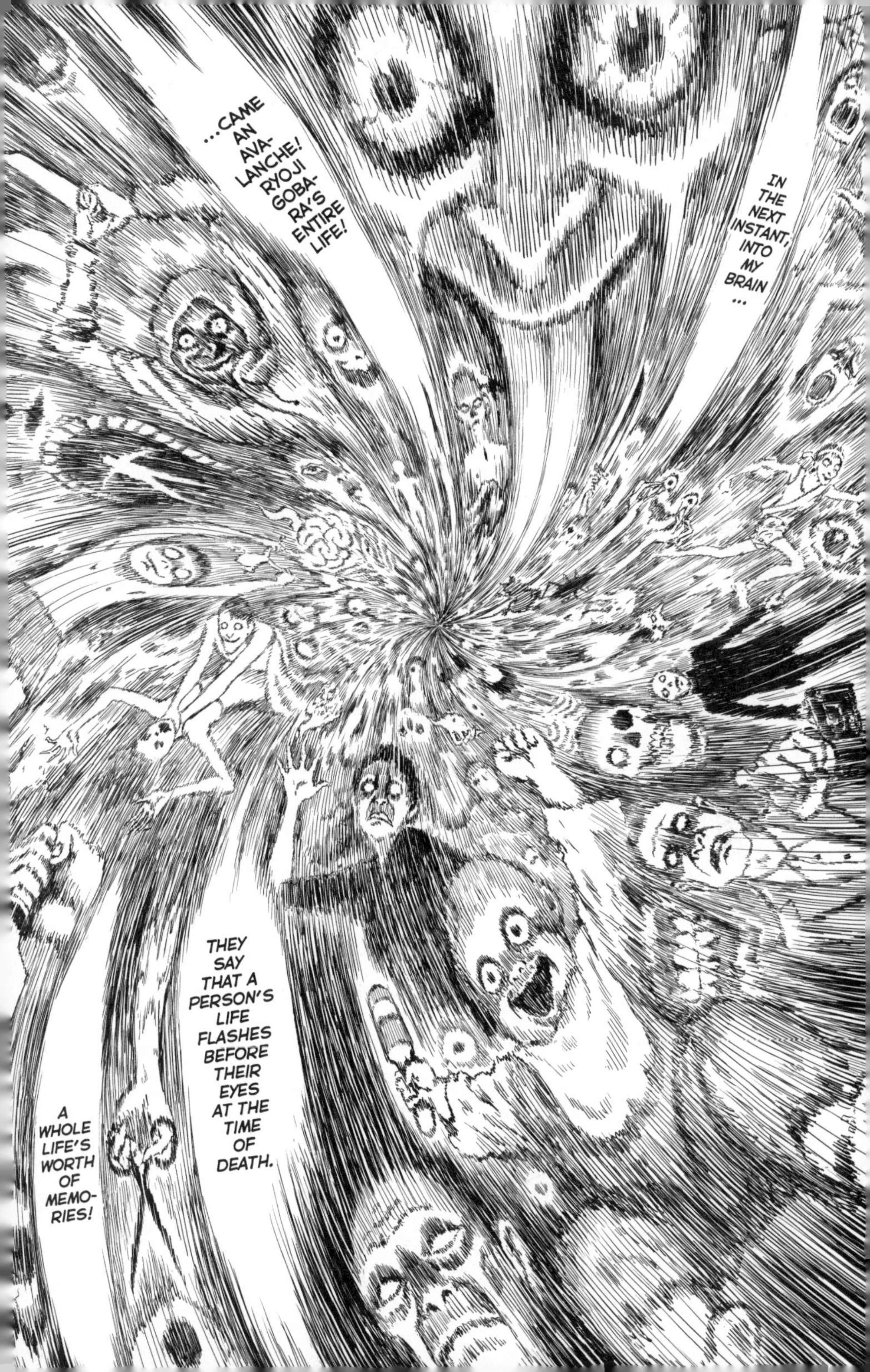
IN THE NEXT INSTANT, INTO MY BRAIN...
...CAME AN AVALANCHE! RYOJI GOBARA'S ENTIRE LIFE!
THEY SAY THAT A PERSON'S LIFE FLASHES BEFORE THEIR EYES AT THE TIME OF DEATH.
A WHOLE LIFE'S WORTH OF MEMORIES!

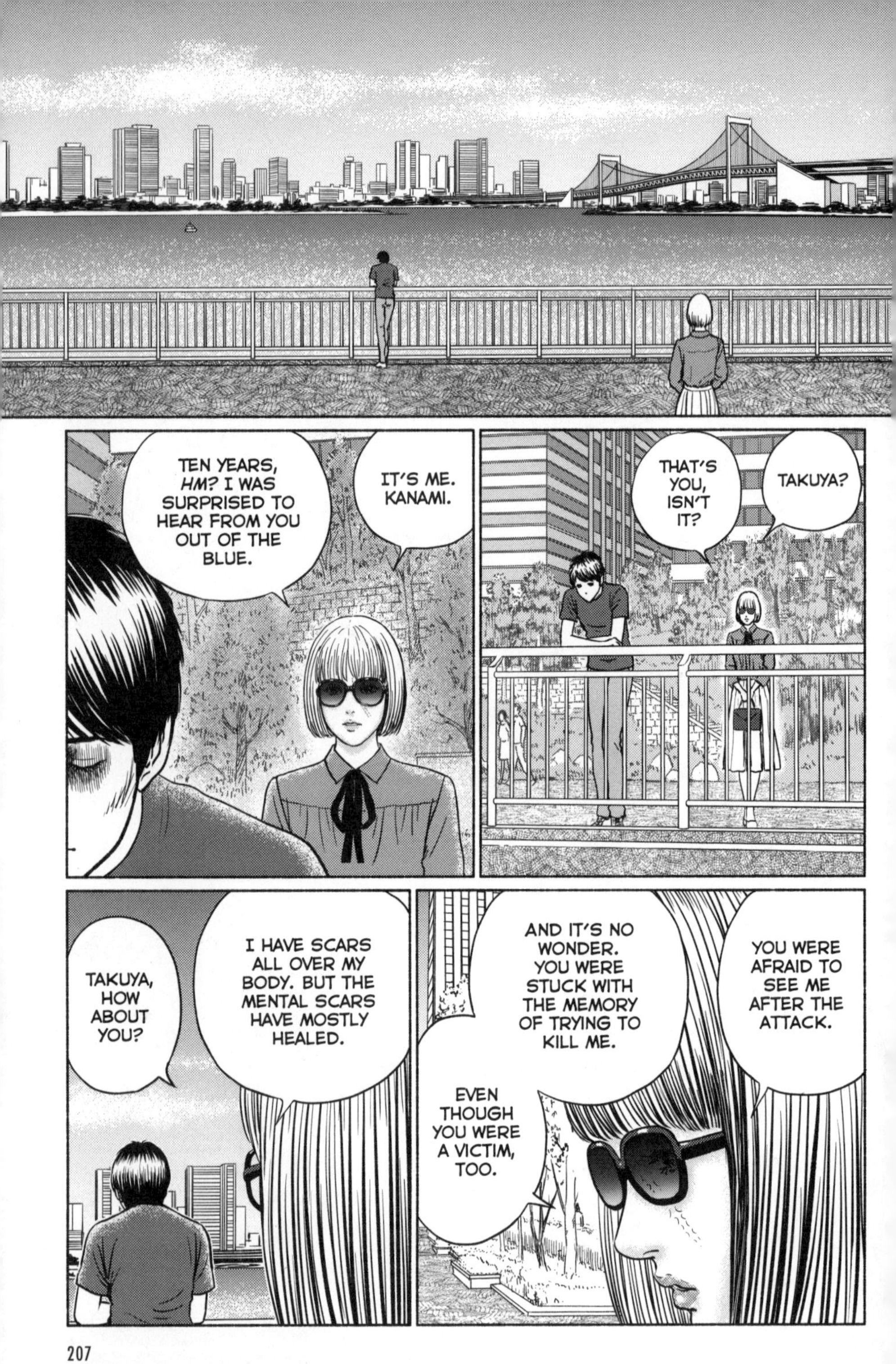
TAKUYA?
THAT'S YOU, ISN'T IT?
IT'S ME. KANAMI.
TEN YEARS, *HM*? I WAS SURPRISED TO HEAR FROM YOU OUT OF THE BLUE.
YOU WERE AFRAID TO SEE ME AFTER THE ATTACK.
AND IT'S NO WONDER. YOU WERE STUCK WITH THE MEMORY OF TRYING TO KILL ME.
EVEN THOUGH YOU WERE A VICTIM, TOO.
I HAVE SCARS ALL OVER MY BODY. BUT THE MENTAL SCARS HAVE MOSTLY HEALED.
TAKUYA, HOW ABOUT YOU?

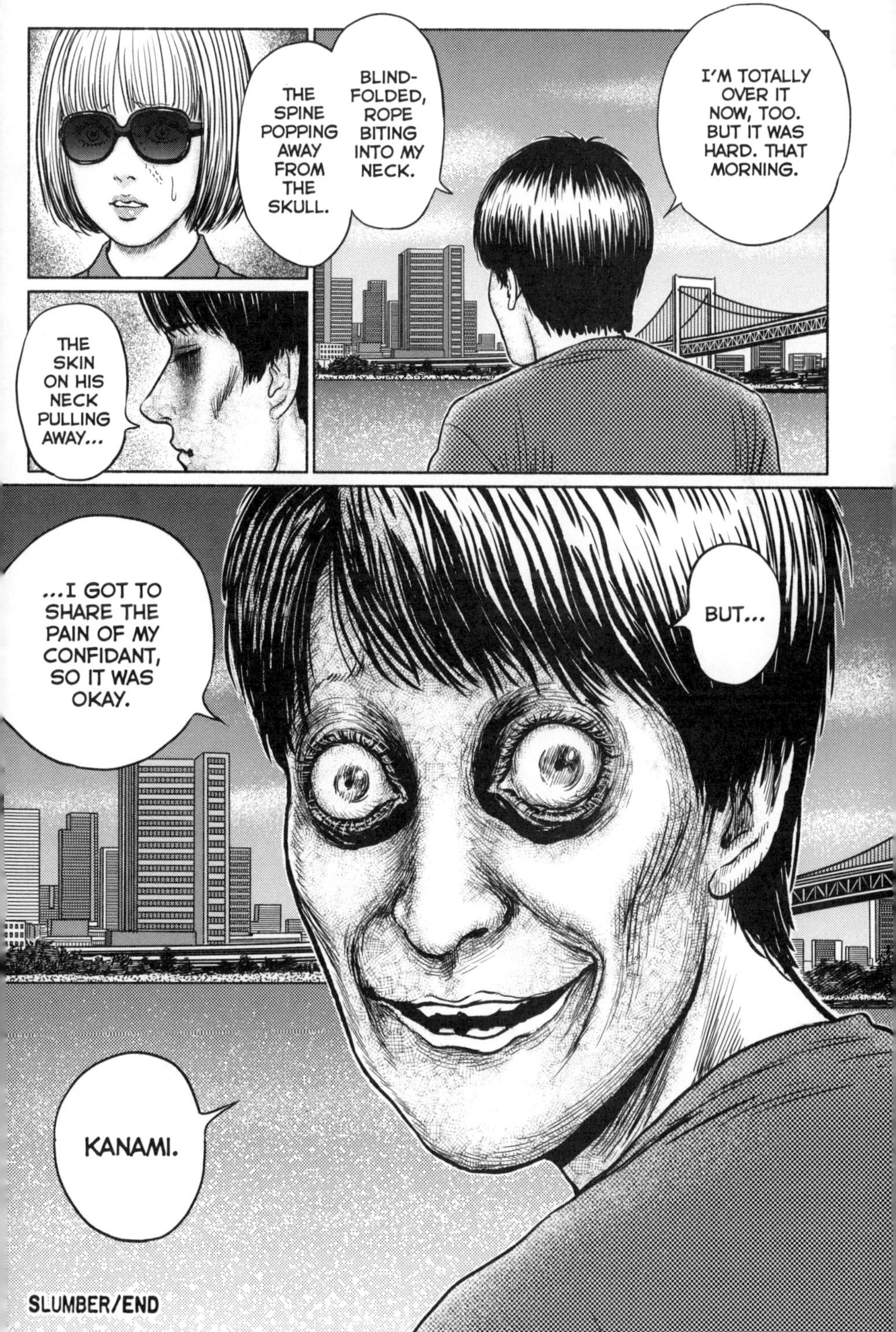
I'M TOTALLY OVER IT NOW, TOO. BUT IT WAS HARD. THAT MORNING.
BLIND-FOLDED, ROPE BITING INTO MY NECK.
THE SPINE POPPING AWAY FROM THE SKULL.
THE SKIN ON HIS NECK PULLING AWAY...
BUT...
...I GOT TO SHARE THE PAIN OF MY CONFIDANT, SO IT WAS OKAY.
KANAMI.
SLUMBER/END

roads." I didn't really make much use of that keyword "sobbing roads," though. (Incidentally, the sobbing road was inspired by Fujiko A. Fujio's "manga road.")

The entire foundation for "Madonna" was the silly idea of "write characters for 'angry witch woman,' read it as 'Madonna.'" Below that in my notebook, there is a scribble added of unclear meaning "witch husband (madanna—a play on "danna," the word for husband and Madonna)" and that was the end of it.

With "The Spirit Flow of Aokigahara," I originally was going to make it a story of the evolution of the bodies of a new species of humanity into a streamlined shape. The idea was "eventually, humanity evolves to avoid a powerful solar wind or something that assaults the Earth with streamlined bodies." But I dismissed it as being too absurdly science fiction, and once the supernatural element was added in, it became a deeply bizarre story.

"Slumber" is an idea I asked to wake up after I let it sleep for a very long time. (So only the idea gets to sleep. Of course.) "The moment you wake up in the morning, you forget all of the unpleasant things of everyday life and are immersed in a feeling a pure bliss, but memories of harsh reality quickly come back to you"—I think a lot of people have likely experienced this moment, and I decided to make a horror story about it, but I couldn't quite pull it together into a narrative.

And so *The Liminal Zone* ended up being a collection of four longish stories.

I'd like to take the opportunity here to express my gratitude to LINE Manga for giving me a new challenge in drawing these works, my editor Makiko Hara and everyone in the Asahi Shimbun Publications comic editorial division for helping me craft these stories, the designer Kazuhiro Fukami for yet another wonderful cover, and everyone else involved in the production of the book.

—JUNJI ITO
January 26, 2021

AFTERWORD

COVID-19 has been running rampant globally and shows no signs of slowing down now, at the beginning of 2021. I feel like I spent most of my time during this coronavirus storm locked up in my studio drawing *The Liminal Zone*.

The Liminal Zone is a collection of short stories serialized on the LINE manga app.

This was the first time I've been serialized on a manga app, and I was so excited by how different it was from serialization in a magazine. There were no strict page limits. In a magazine, you have to make sure you draw the specified number of pages. For a long-form series, this isn't too much of an issue, but for a one-shot—if, for instance, you have thirty-two pages—you must finish the story in those thirty-two pages. A professional manga artist can neatly pack their story into the set number of pages, but for some reason, I'm not very good at this. When I draw storyboards—the blueprint for the manga—I generally go over the page limit. Then I have to whittle away the excess to fit it in, but when I still can't get it down to size even after that, I will go so far as to change the ending. It's embarrassing—or rather, it's unbecoming of a professional.

But with this series, I had the flexibility to increase the number of pages, and I happily went over the page limit to draw exactly what I wanted. I won't be able to judge whether or not that's good for the work itself, though, until a little time has passed and I go back over the stories. While I was doing the revisions for "Weeping Woman Way," I started to wonder if it wasn't a bit too long.

Still, perhaps I'm tired after drawing manga for years on end. I'm out of good ideas. The stories in this book were created drawing on ideas that I'd left unused in an old notebook of possible topics.

I drew "Weeping Woman Way" with the (Japanese ballad) *enka*-style topic of "a woman who cries too much and gutters form on her cheeks where the tears roll down. Those gutters are called sobbing

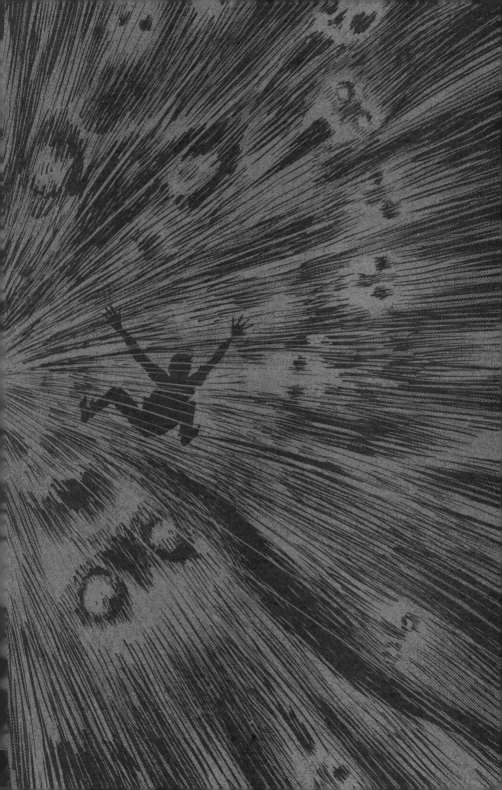

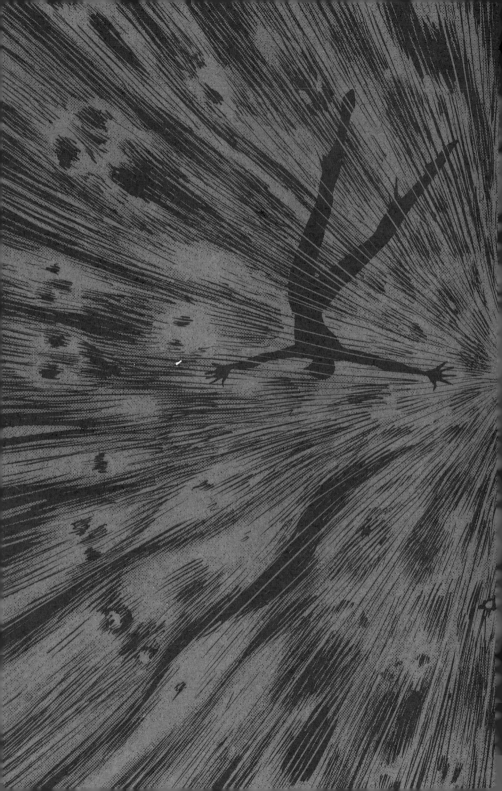

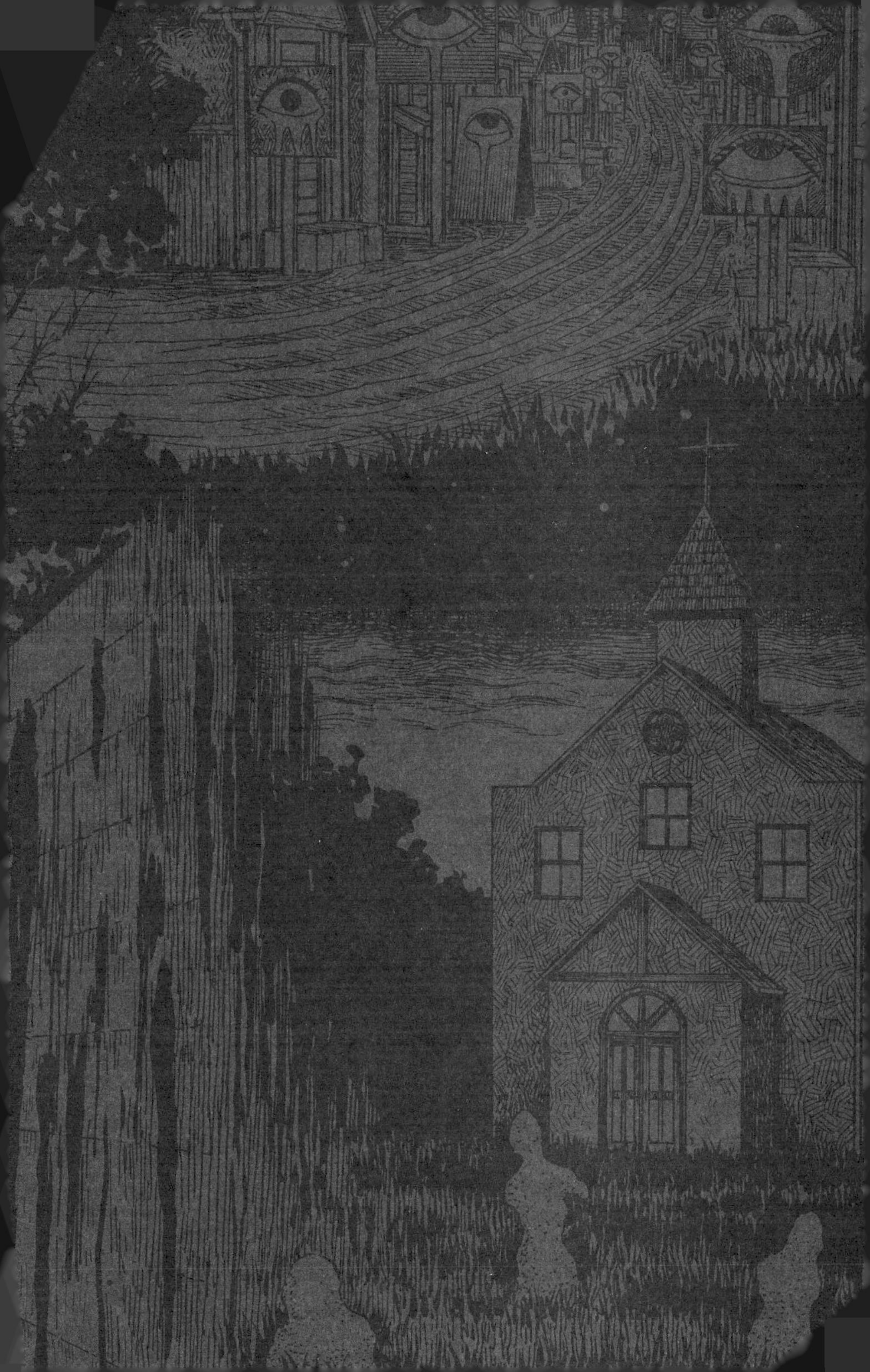

THE LIMINAL ZONE

STORY & ART BY JUNJI ITO

Translation & Adaptation: **Jocelyne Allen**
Touch-Up Art & Lettering: **Eric Erbes**
Cover & Graphic Design: **Adam Grano**
Editor: **Masumi Washington**

The Liminal Zone
© JI Inc. 2021
Originally published in Japan in 2021 by Asahi Shimbun
Publications Inc., Tokyo. English translation rights arranged
with Asahi Shimbun Publications Inc., Tokyo through
TOHAN CORPORATION, Tokyo.

Printed in the U.S.A.

Published by VIZ Media, LLC
P.O. Box 77010
San Francisco, CA 94107

10 9 8 7 6 5 4 3 2 1
First printing, July 2022

VIZ MEDIA   **VIZ SIGNATURE**
viz.com   vizsignature.com

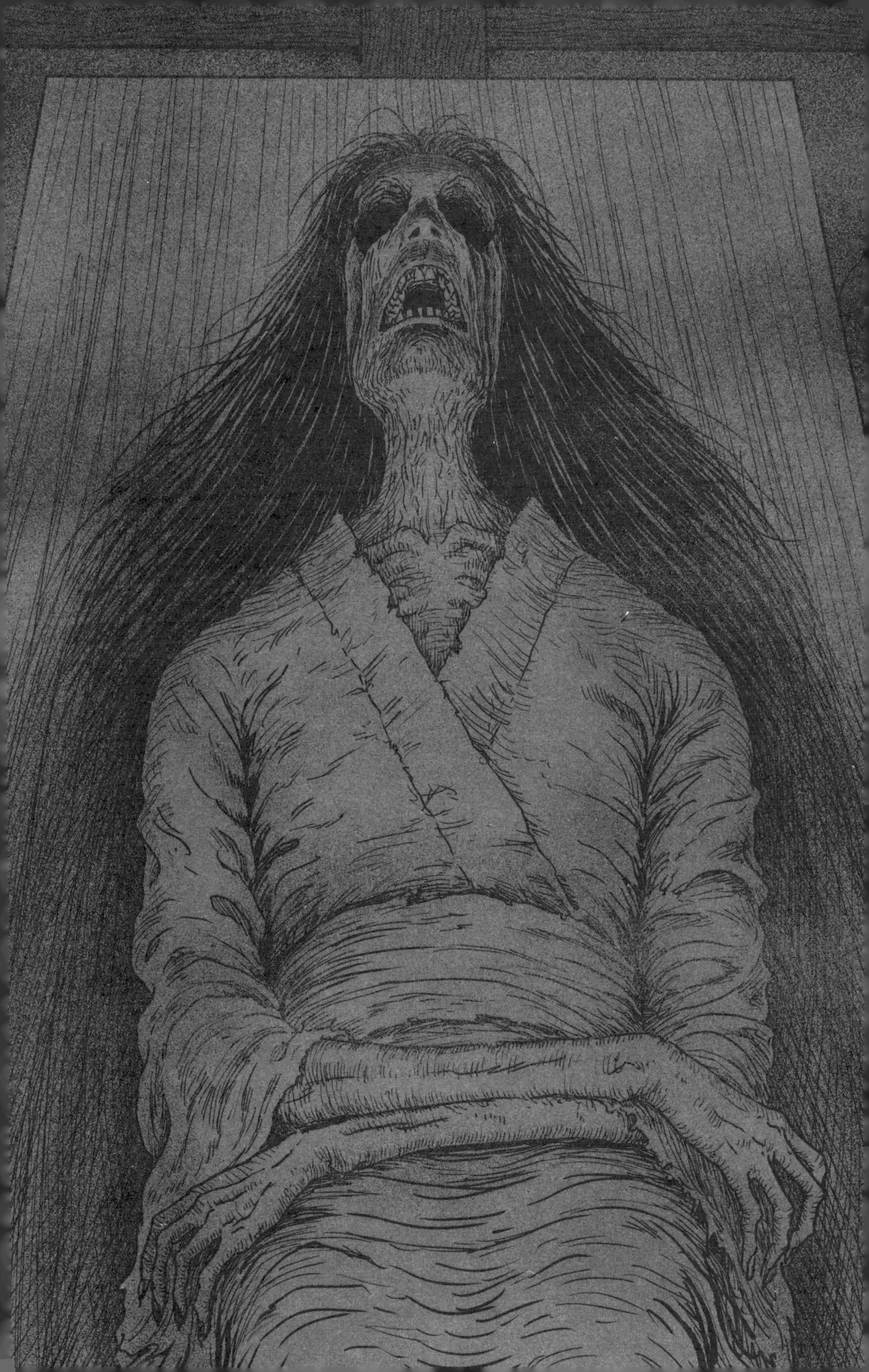

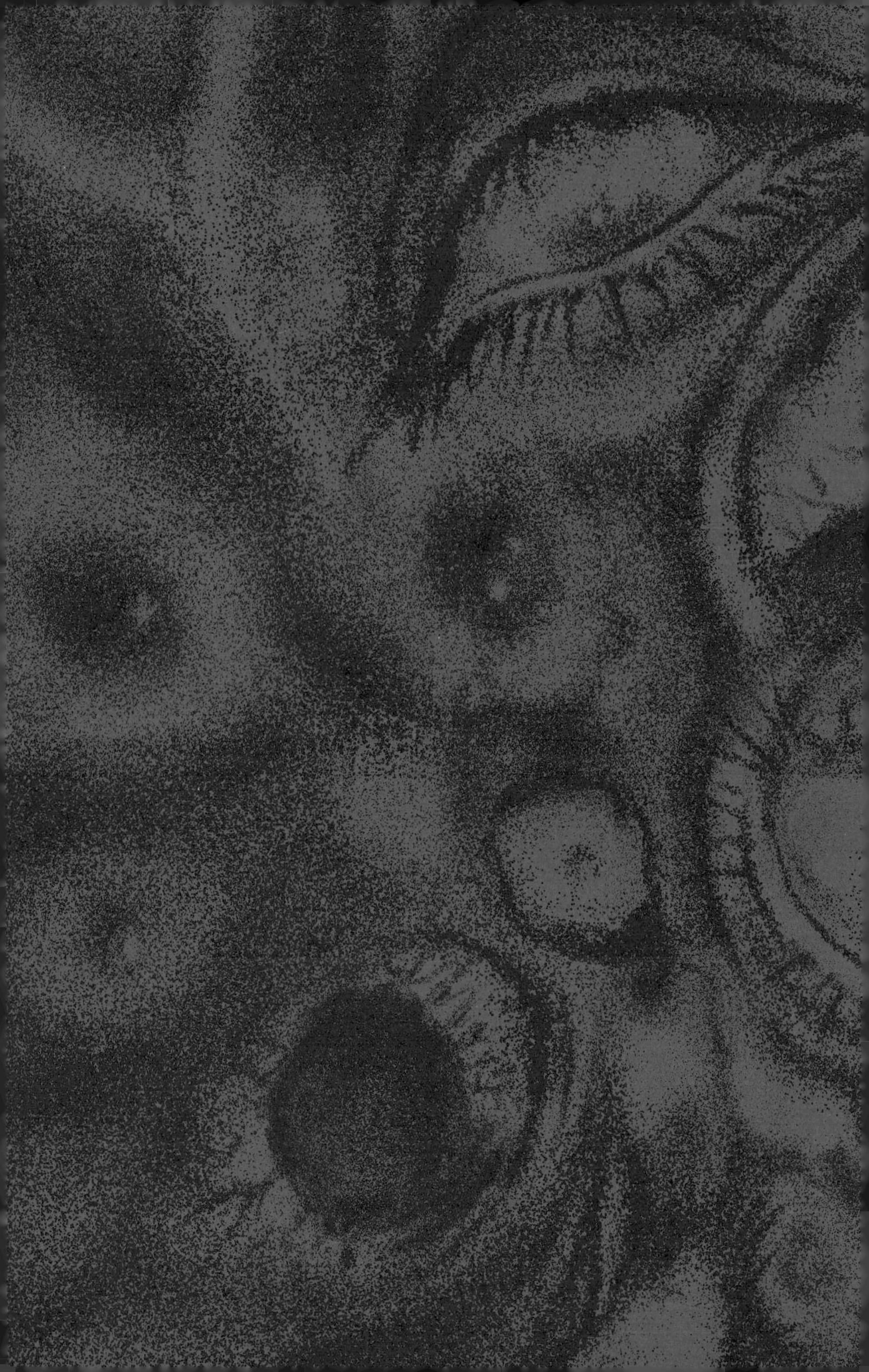

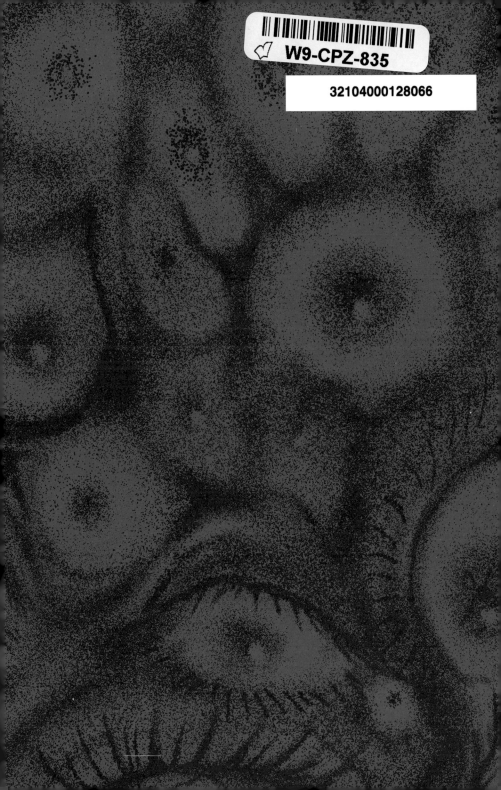